D0712884

THOMAS JEFFERSON

Jeffersonian America

Jan Ellen Lewis, Peter S. Onuf, and Andrew O'Shaughnessy, Editors

THOMAS JEFFERSON

REPUTATION AND LEGACY

• • •

FRANCIS D. COGLIANO

University of Virginia Press
Charlottesville

To my father
and the memory
of my mother

University of Virginia Press

First published in the UK in 2006 by
Edinburgh University Press

© 2006 by Francis D. Cogliano

Printed and bound in Great Britain by
The Cromwell Press, Trowbridge, Wilts

First published 2006

9 8 7 6 5 4 3 2 1

U.S. Library of Congress Cataloging-in-Publication Data

Cogliano, Francis D.
  Thomas Jefferson : reputation and legacy / Francis D. Cogliano.
    p. cm. – (Jeffersonian America)
  Includes bibliographical references and index.
  ISBN-13: 978-0-8139-2619-3 (cloth : alk. paper)
  1. Jefferson, Thomas, 1743–1826—Influence. 2. Jefferson, Thomas,
1743–1826—Philosophy. 3. Presidents—United
States—Biography—History and criticism. 4. United
States—History—Revolution, 1775–1783—Historiography. 5. United
States—History—1783–1865—Historiography. 6. United
States—History—Philosophy. 7. Slavery—Political aspects—United
States—History. 8. Hemings, Sally. I. Title. II. Series.
  E332.2.C64 2006
  973.4'6092–dc22
  [B]
                                                                2006012445

CONTENTS

ACKNOWLEDGMENTS

When he became secretary of state in 1790, Jefferson wrote, 'I have but one system of ethics for men & for nations – to be grateful, to be faithful to all engagements and under all circumstances, to be open & generous, promotes in the long run even the interests of both; and I am sure it promotes their happiness.' What Jefferson wrote of relations between humans and states can also be applied to scholarship. I am very grateful to have been the beneficiary of extraordinary openness and generosity of many people in the course of researching and writing this book.

In the world of Jefferson scholarship all roads lead to Monticello and the Thomas Jefferson Foundation. While writing this book, I benefited greatly from two research fellowships at Monticello's Robert H. Smith International Center for Jefferson Studies – one at the beginning of this project and another during my final, writing-up, period. While at the ICJS I enjoyed a warm welcome from its directors, Andrew O'Shaughnessy and his predecessor, Jim Horn. Among the many friendly and helpful people at Monticello I am grateful to (present and previous) staff at the ICJS including: Betsy Altheimer, Anna Berkes, Bryan Craig, Sanders Goodrich, Jack Robertson, Mary Scott-Fleming, Eleanor Sparagana and Gaye Wilson. John Rudder assisted me with a series of queries regarding the history of the public tours at Monticello. Cinder Stanton patiently and cheerfully responded to numerous questions about Sally Hemings and the history of slavery at Jefferson's home. Jeff Looney and Sue Perdue of the *Retirement Papers* helped me to understand the evolution of the various editions of Jefferson's papers and Jefferson's last years. Among the benefits of Monticello's fellowship program is the opportunity to interact with the other scholars. This book benefited from the discussions I enjoyed with George Boudreau, Tony Iaccarino, Martha King, Catherine Kerrison, Jim Walvin, and Henry Wiencek, who made my visits to Monticello fellowships in every sense of the word. During Jefferson's lifetime Monticello was renowned as a center of hospitality and intellectual conviviality. It remains so today.

In January 2004 I was fortunate to hold a Mellon Fellowship at the Virginia Historical Society. Nelson Lankford, Frances Pollard, E. Lee

Shepard and Greg Stoner insured that my visit to Richmond was both productive and enjoyable. In addition to the staff of the Virginia Historical Society I would thank the librarians and archivists at the University of Virginia's Alderman Library, the Boston Public Library, the New York Public Library, the Edinburgh University Library and the Special Collections Department at Tufts University's Tisch Library.

While finishing this book I enjoyed a year's worth of funded leave provided by the Arts and Humanities Research Council and the University of Edinburgh's College of Humanities and Social Science. I am grateful to both institutions for providing the funding that allowed me the time to complete this book. Many Edinburgh colleagues assisted me in the completion of this project through their advice, support, and friendship. Among these are Donald Bloxham, Colin Coates, Alan Day, Harry Dickinson, Rhodri Jeffreys-Jones, Richard Mackenney, Jim McMillan, Robert Mason, Susan Manning and Jill Stephenson. Noteworthy too are the fourth-year students who took my Monday morning seminar on 'the Age of Jefferson' with whom I profitably discussed several chapters. Further, I have benefited from the advice and support of many other friends and colleagues with whom I discussed this project at various times, including: Lance Banning, Joanne Freeman, Paul Gilje, Colin Kidd and Alan Taylor. Simon Newman read portions of the manuscript and provided timely advice with several conceptual problems.

I am especially grateful to four individuals – Richard Bernstein, Andrew Burstein, Peter Onuf and Hannah Spahn – who generously read the entire manuscript of this book. Richard, Andy and Hannah turned the manuscript around on very short notice and improved it greatly by their comments and advice. My greatest intellectual debt is to Peter Onuf. He shaped this book through his criticism, insightful questions and constant encouragement. Peter's generosity to fellow scholars is legendary. I am profoundly grateful to have been the beneficiary of his kindness.

I made frequent trips to the United States while writing this book. During those journeys I enjoyed the hospitality of many people, including Chuck and Andrea Katter as well as Alan Swartz, who allowed me to stay in their homes. My parents, Ann and Frank Cogliano, to whom this book is dedicated, always made me feel welcome during extended visits to their home where I wrote several sections of this book. They provided an environment conducive to writing as well as lively and distracting conversation when the writing wasn't going well. We often enjoyed what the British call a 'full and frank exchange of views' on various historical matters relating to Jefferson and his world. My mother did not live to see the publication of this book but I hope she would have liked it and recognized some of its arguments. In my adopted home of Scotland, my own family – Mimi, Edward and Sofia – know all too well that writing is a collaborative (and sometimes painful) process. I owe them a debt that I cannot properly express, let alone repay.

Needless to say, while all of the people named above have made this a better book for my contact with them, any faults or errors that remain are mine alone.

ABBREVIATIONS

LoC: Library of Congress

Malone, *Jefferson and His Time*:   Dumas Malone, *Jefferson and His Time*, 6 vols. (Boston: Little, Brown, 1948–81)

PTJ: Julian P. Boyd et al. eds., *The Papers of Thomas Jefferson*, 32 vols. to date (Princeton: Princeton University Press, 1950–)

Peterson, *Jefferson Image*:   Merrill D. Peterson, *The Jefferson Image in the American Mind* (New York: Oxford University Press, 1960; repr. Charlottesville: University Press of Virginia, 1998)

TJ: Thomas Jefferson

TJF: Thomas Jefferson Foundation

TJMF: Thomas Jefferson Memorial Foundation

TJP: 'The Thomas Jefferson Papers at the Library of Congress', online at:
            http://memory.loc.gov/ammem/mtjhtml/mtjhome.html

TJW: Merrill D. Peterson, ed., *Thomas Jefferson: Writings* (New York: Library of America, 1984)

WMQ: *The William and Mary Quarterly*, 3rd Series

INTRODUCTION:
THE ESTIMATION OF THE WORLD

I

In March of 1807 Thomas Jefferson wrote to the comte de Diodati-Tronchin, an old friend from his days among the diplomats at Versailles. Reminiscing about 'the many happy hours' he had spent with the comte and Madame Diodati on the banks of the Seine, Jefferson recalled, 'those were indeed days of tranquility & happiness'. Jefferson then shifted his focus from personal matters to the geopolitical situation. Writing from the comfort of his home at Monticello, he drew an unfavorable contrast between the tumult to be seen in Napoleonic Europe and the supposed tranquility of Jeffersonian America.

> Were I in Europe *pax et panis* would certainly be my motto. Wars & contentions indeed fill the pages of history with more matter, but more blest is the nation whose silent course of happiness furnishes nothing for history to say. That is my ambition for my own country, and what it has fortunately now upwards of 24 years while Europe has been in constant volcanic eruption.[1]

Jefferson boasted of the peace enjoyed by the United States when he was halfway through his difficult second presidential term. As he wrote to Diodati his former vice president, Aaron Burr, was awaiting trial in Richmond, Virginia on charges of treason for allegedly attempting to detach the western states from the American union. American commerce was beset by trade restrictions imposed by France and Britain. Within two months the British warship *Leopard* would fire on the USS *Chesapeake*, threatening to start a war between Britain and the United States. Given such turmoil, how could Jefferson justify his optimistic view of recent American history?

Jefferson believed that if the American republic succeeded, the result would be a republican millennium that would witness the triumph of liberty over tyranny across the globe. As a consequence there would be no more 'wars and contentions' and history itself would end. He believed, as his letter to Diodati suggests, that such a transformation had begun in the United States. Jefferson made the realization of the republican millennium his life's work.[2] Early in his career, as a revolutionary ideologue who drafted the Declaration of Independence and redrafted his state's laws, Jefferson sought to articulate and implement the principles of republican government. As a partisan political leader during the 1790s he sought to protect those principles from internal enemies: Federalist counter-revolutionaries and hidden monarchists. During his presidency he sought to expand the boundaries of the republican 'empire for liberty' while defending the nation's interests – and hence its republican mission – in a dangerous world characterized by strife and war among powerful nations. Indeed, Jefferson believed that only through geographic expansion could the American republic thrive, thus bringing about the triumph of republicanism and the end of history that he predicted in his letter to Diodati. Compared with the widespread bloodshed and turmoil in Napoleonic Europe, the disturbances that threatened the United States, such as the Burr conspiracy or disputes over Atlantic trade seemed minor. Jefferson recognized, nonetheless, that the ultimate triumph of republicanism would not occur during his lifetime. As a consequence, he sought, through the preservation and careful organization of his papers, to influence how future historians would write the history of his life and times. In so doing he intended, with the assistance of future historians, to safeguard America's globally important republican experiment in the years after his death.

For Jefferson, the consequences of historical writing extended to the present and the future. History that accurately presented the right lessons about the past served a positive end and promoted liberty. Good histories could even end the apparently endless cyclical struggle between liberty and tyranny chronicled by whig historians – as they would help insure the ultimate triumph of republican government. A nation so truly blessed as to be without history would then be free of the cumbersome burdens imposed by the past. In an 1824 letter in which he traced the lineage of modern rights in Britain and America to the Saxon past, Jefferson asked, 'Can one generation bind another, and all others, in succession forever?' He answered:

> I think not. The Creator has made the earth for the living, not the dead. Rights and powers can only belong to persons, not to things, not to mere matter, unendowed with will. The dead are not even things. The particles of matter which composed their bodies, make part now of the bodies of other animals, vegetables, or minerals, of a thousand forms. To what then are attached the rights and powers they held while in the form of men? A generation may bind itself as long as its majority continues in life; when

that has disappeared, another majority is in place, holds all the rights and powers their predecessors once held, and may change their laws and institutions to suit themselves. Nothing then is unchangeable but the inherent and unalienable rights of man.[3]

For Jefferson it was necessary to study the past in order to define and preserve 'the inherent and unalienable rights of man'. If this goal could be achieved, then in the future humanity, its rights secure, would no longer generate the war, bloodshed and tumult that filled the pages of history.

Good history would be so successful that it would render history itself redundant. Jefferson recognized that the job would not be completed during his lifetime, and so he bequeathed to posterity his version of the republic's early history so that we, his successors, would be guided to a bright republican future, a future of peace, harmony and liberty. The history of the American Revolution was, in Jefferson's mind, closely linked to his own image. Reputation was important to Thomas Jefferson. In 1601 Francis Bacon, whom Jefferson considered one of the three greatest men who ever lived, argued that the highest category of honor and reputation was reserved for 'founders of states and commonwealths'. Four years later, in his *Advancement of Learning*, Bacon argued that the supreme honor, the greatest fame and reputation, was reserved for those philosophers who used their reason to improve mankind. Men who achieved such 'sovereign honour' achieved a kind of immortality and would be remembered forever. For Jefferson, who had dedicated his life to founding a new state and improving humanity through republican government, personal achievements and the public good were one and the same thing. Jefferson was a thin-skinned man who shrank from conflict, yet he engaged in the dirty business of politics with ruthlessness and sometimes duplicity. Perhaps because of his occasional recourse to less-than-honorable methods, Jefferson worried about his reputation. Bacon had written, 'The winning of honour, is but the revealing a man's virtue and worth, without disadvantage. For some in their actions, do woo and effect honor and reputation, which sort of men, are commonly much talked of, but inwardly little admired.'[4] If Jefferson were seen to promote his own reputation or his methods were exposed as less than virtuous, his reputation would suffer. In his first inaugural address in 1801 Jefferson frankly (and accurately) confessed that few men retired from the presidency 'with the reputation and favor which bring [them] into it.'[5]

As his career in public office drew to a close, Jefferson wrote a letter to his favorite grandson, fifteen-year-old Thomas Jefferson Randolph, who was about to leave home to study. The older man counseled his grandson that he would be confronted by dangers and temptations as he went out into the world. The best way to avoid these would be to take heed of the opinions of others. 'A determination never to do what is wrong, prudence and good humor', advised Jefferson, 'will go far towards securing to you the estimation of the world.' Jefferson reflected on his own youth and the approval that he had sought from his mentors. 'Under temptations and difficulties, I could ask myself what would Dr. [William] Small, Mr. [George] Wythe, Peyton Randolph do in this situation? What course will ensure their approbation? I am certain that this mode of deciding on my conduct tended more to it's correctness than any reasoning powers I possessed.' Remembering the temptations of student life such as gambling, foxhunting and debating, Jefferson recalled 'many a time I have asked myself, in the enthusiastic moment of the death of a fox, the victory of a favorite horse, the issue of a question eloquently argued at the bar or in the great Council of the nation, well which of these kinds of reputation should I prefer? That of a horse jockey? A foxhunter? An Orator? Or the honest advocate of my country's rights?' Jefferson did not need to respond to his own question because the answer was obvious. He wanted to be remembered as a statesman. During his life he had sought the approval of his peers as well as his mentors. In retirement and death he sought the approbation of posterity.[6]

Jefferson believed that his reputation and the success of the American republic were closely linked. If his achievements were properly understood and remembered then it was likely that the American republic would be on a sound footing. The success of the republic was, in Jefferson's mind, a project of world historical proportions. For Jefferson, the success of his reputation was ultimately tied to the success of the global republican movement. If he failed in his posthumous campaign to safeguard his reputation, then the republican cause to which he had dedicated his life would suffer.

II

There are four stages in the history of Jefferson's reputation. The first, extending from Jefferson's death in 1826 until the end of the Civil War in 1865, saw Jefferson's image and legacy contested by the proponents and opponents of slavery, nullification, states' rights and secession. Jefferson's shadow loomed large over American life during these years and adversaries in the great sectional crisis vied for his posthumous imprimatur. The second stage extended from the end of the Civil War until the 1920s. During this period Jefferson's reputation steadily declined. In the aftermath of the Civil War enthusiasm for Jefferson diminished; many Americans increasingly saw him as an early advocate of nullification, secession and slavery. Indirectly, Jefferson was blamed for the Civil War. Moreover, in an age of industrialization and centralized government,

Jefferson's beliefs in the virtues of small government and rural agriculture seemed increasingly inappropriate. Rather, Jefferson's great adversary Alexander Hamilton, as an advocate of concentrated national political and economic power, seemed a more appropriate historical figure from whom Americans should draw inspiration in the early twentieth century. The excesses of the 1920s followed by the onset of the Great Depression spurred an improvement in Jefferson's image that marked the beginning of the third stage in the history of his reputation. For most of its history American political life had been divided along the lines set down by Jefferson and Hamilton in the 1790s. Only with the Roosevelt revolution of the 1930s was the schism ended as the government sought to reach Jeffersonian ends by Hamiltonian means. With the commencement of World War II Jefferson was fully rehabilitated as a national hero. No longer a divisive figure, he came to be seen as a symbol of the nation and the embodiment of its founding principles.[7]

On 13 April 1943, the two-hundredth anniversary of Jefferson's birth, his successor, Franklin D. Roosevelt, paid homage to Jefferson's outlook when he dedicated the Jefferson Memorial by the Tidal Basin in Washington. Standing before the gleaming white marble monument, Roosevelt addressed a crowd of more than 5,000 spectators and millions more throughout the country via a live radio broadcast. Conscious that Jefferson had received his monument in the nation's capital long after Washington and Lincoln had been so honored, Roosevelt asserted, 'To Thomas Jefferson, Apostle of Freedom we are paying a debt long overdue.' Yet if the payment was belated it was timely. 'Today in the midst of a great war for freedom', Roosevelt declared, 'we dedicate this shrine to freedom.' Invoking World War II, Roosevelt reminded his listeners 'that men who will not fight for freedom will lose it; that conscience and mind were battles constantly to be rewon.' Jefferson epitomized the ideals for which Americans fought in 1943. 'His cause', Roosevelt intoned, 'was a cause to which we are committed, not by our words alone but by our sacrifice.' Roosevelt invoked his predecessor's language, carved around the inside of the memorial, to close his address: 'I have sworn upon the altar of God eternal hostility against every form of tyranny over the mind of man.' Panels inside the monument were inscribed with selections from Jefferson's writings that emphasized his devotion to democracy and freedom.[8]

Merrill D. Peterson, the leading student of Jefferson's reputation, declared that the building and dedication of the Jefferson Memorial was 'the most important thing to happen to Jefferson since July Fourth 1826' – the day Jefferson died. No longer a figure of political controversy, Jefferson emerged as the symbol of the principles for which the nation fought. Peterson writes:

On the two hundredth anniversary of his birth the nation was locked in a
desperate world struggle for the rights he had declared inalienable. The
nation, the world, were so distressingly different from anything Jefferson
had envisioned; yet, fundamentally, his faith was the American faith,
reaching out now to the world from which he had reluctantly withdrawn.
And so during the Bicentennial nearly every celebrant saluted Jefferson's
livingness . . . What was living was, in general, the idea of the rights of
man. The world might still need instruction in this idea; but among
Americans it was generally accepted as the definition of national character
and purpose. Largely framed by this idea, Jefferson was a patriotic
symbol. The old rage of controversy receded from the image. Viewed
as a patriotic rite, the Bicentennial marks Jefferson's passage into the
American pantheon.

No longer an object of partisan squabbling, by 1943 Jefferson had come
to embody America itself. Peterson concluded his study by speculating
that Jefferson 'may yet go on vindicating his power in the national life as
the heroic voice of imperishable freedoms. It is this Jefferson who stands
at the radiant center of his own history, and who makes for the present a
symbol that unites the nation's birth with its inexorable ideal.'[9]
   The image of Jefferson as the Apostle of Freedom was very powerful
during the 1940s. Indeed, the era we can see as the age of Jefferson
monuments. In 1938 the United States mint introduced a new nickel coin
with Jefferson's profile on the obverse and Monticello on the reverse
side. In 1941 the massive sculptured monument to Jefferson (as well as
Washington, Lincoln and Theodore Roosevelt) was completed on Mount
Rushmore, South Dakota. After the completion and dedication of the
Jefferson Memorial in 1943, the memorializing of Jefferson continued. In
1948 Dumas Malone published the first volume of what would become a
six-volume biography, *Jefferson and His Time*. Malone presented Jefferson in a very sympathetic light and emphasized his myriad contributions
to advancing the cause of freedom in America and the world. This was
followed by the appearance of the first volume of the Princeton edition of
The Papers of Thomas Jefferson in 1950, an enormous undertaking, still
ongoing, likely to total more than sixty volumes when completed. Julian
P. Boyd, who launched the project and edited its first volumes, conceived
of it as a tribute to Jefferson's life and ideals during the 1943 bicentennial.
Taken together, these various efforts, popular and scholarly – graven in
stone, metal and print – presented an image of Jefferson as the champion
of democracy and freedom in the United States, and the embodiment of
the nation's principles to the wider world. This was an image of Jefferson
fit for World War II and the Cold War.[10]
   Not until the early 1960s did the revisionist fourth stage in the history

of Jefferson's reputation commence with the publication of Leonard W. Levy's *Jefferson and Civil Liberties: The Darker Side* in 1963. Levy, a constitutional historian, attacked Jefferson's supposed devotion to civil liberties as hypocritical and inconsistent. He portrayed Jefferson as a ruthless political ideologue with scant regard for the rights of his political opponents, whom he persecuted with tactics that were sometimes illegal.[11] Although Jefferson continued to have many scholarly and popular admirers, *Jefferson and Civil Liberties* marked the beginning of a more critical trend in Jefferson historiography. In the aftermath of World War II the United States underwent a rapid economic, social and political transformation. More people attended colleges and universities as the provision of higher education expanded to include those beyond the traditional social and cultural elite who had attended such institutions before the war. The new students, especially as they proceeded through the system and became academics themselves, asked new and different questions of the past. The 'New Social History' of the 1960s (which built on the pioneering social history of the Progressive school earlier in the century), focused on groups – racial, ethnic and religious minorities, women, the poor – whom historians had previously marginalized or ignored. Against the backdrop of the Civil Rights movement, the war in Vietnam and the Watergate scandal, American historians, like Americans generally, became more critical of their nation's rulers and institutions. For many historians, increasingly concerned with questions of class, gender and (especially where Jefferson was concerned) race, Jefferson's limitations seemed more important than his achievements. Whereas the Jefferson of the 1940s and 1950s was seen as the embodiment of American freedom, the Apostle of Liberty, for many historians since the 1960s he has come to represent the limits of the American Revolution and has emerged as the patron saint of American hypocrisy.[12]

The downward trend in Jefferson's reputation since the 1960s was an inevitable corrective to the hagiographic excesses of the 1940s and 1950s. Despite the increasing scholarly criticism of many aspects of Jefferson's life and achievements, other writers continued to produce works that were generally sympathetic to Jefferson. The final four volumes of Dumas Malone's admiring biography were published between 1962 and 1981. Merrill Peterson's generally favorable portrait, *Thomas Jefferson and the New Nation*, was published in 1970 and Noble Cunningham's sympathetic study, *In Pursuit of Reason: The Life of Thomas Jefferson*, appeared in 1987. The proponents of the Apostle-of-Freedom interpretation continued to write in the face of a burgeoning literature that was much more critical of their subject. To a large extent the third and fourth stages in the history of Jefferson's reputation overlapped for several decades. By the 1990s two schools had emerged in the study of Jefferson – one that was sympathetic to Jefferson and defended him against the charge of hypocrisy leveled by the other school, whose numbers were much more critical of Jefferson and his legacy.[13]

In the past decade, some scholars have attempted to move beyond the defense/attack paradigm. Numerous studies have sought to situate Jefferson in his time and place. These works, which presage a fifth stage in the history of Jefferson's reputation, aim to recover the context in which Jefferson lived, thought and wrote without using it as an excuse to exonerate him for his supposed crimes before the bar of history.[14] The effort to contextualize Jefferson has coincided with a popular and scholarly boom in the study of the American revolutionary era, particularly the 'Founding Fathers'. Indeed, the past decade has produced such a volume of material – including numerous best-selling biographies as well as television documentaries – on different aspects and figures related to the founding period that some scholars have complained that the United States is suffering from 'Founders' Chic' – an excessive fascination with the thoughts and actions of a small group of elite men at the expense of other political actors and social groups. Critics claim that scholars and authors who continue to supply the public with such works do a disservice to the complexity of the American founding and serve a conservative political agenda.[15] Despite the increased interest, Founders' Chic has done little to help Thomas Jefferson's image, which, already in relative decline, has not been burnished by the 'War on Terror'. Jefferson's tendency to resort to economic coercion to solve international disagreements, and his disastrous stint as governor of Virginia when the state was invaded by the British in 1781, make him an unsympathetic leader during times of war. It is no surprise that in a period of intense patriotism and military action Ron Chernow's biography of Alexander Hamilton, a successful soldier and the architect of the American fiscal-military state, made the best-seller lists in the United States during the summer of 2004. 'Alexander Hamilton is the clear winner in the most recent round of "Founders' Chic",' writes Stanford University's Jack Rakove. 'Hamilton's soberly realistic views of national security seem more suited to our age of holy terror than Thomas Jefferson's touching faith that our coasts could best be protected by gunboats.' The contrast between Jefferson's treatment during the War on Terror and during World War II suggests that the ideological forces at play in both conflicts are quite different. During World War II and the Cold War the United States confronted formidable and coherent ideologies that made Jefferson attractive as the embodiment of American ideals appealing. Such has not been the case in the aftermath of September 11th.[16]

Despite his current loss of stature, Jefferson remains a towering historical and historiographical figure. He is, as Joseph J. Ellis wrote in the aftermath of the DNA testing that confirmed Jefferson's paternity of one of Sally Hemings's children, 'the dead-white-male who matters most'.[17] Although George Washington, John Adams, Alexander Hamilton and Benjamin Franklin have recently garnered significant scholarly and popular attention, Jefferson remains the most compelling, popular and controversial of the major figures who helped to establish the American republic.[18] Books, popular and scholarly, on various aspects of Jefferson's life continue to appear and sell in the thousands and seem likely to do so for the foreseeable future. Ellis concludes, 'If the American past were a gambling casino, everyone who has bet against Jefferson has eventually lost.' While not disputing Ellis's point, this study seeks to go beyond it – arguing that, in Ellis's metaphysical casino of America's past, Jefferson sought to stack the deck in his favor.[19]

III

Merrill Peterson ended his *Jefferson Image in the American Mind* with the 1943 dedication of the Jefferson Memorial. Writing during the third, Apostle-of-Freedom, stage of Jefferson's reputation, Peterson concluded that Jefferson was safely ensconced in the American pantheon. Peterson published his book in 1960 just as the more critical fourth stage in the Jefferson image was beginning. This study begins where Peterson's magisterial study ends, considering Jefferson's treatment by historians since the mid-1940s, and may thus be read as a sequel to *The Jefferson Image in the American Mind*. It differs from Peterson's study, however, in two important respects. First, this book focuses on Jefferson's treatment at the hands of scholars, where Peterson sought to situate the Jefferson image in the broader culture of nineteenth- and early twentieth-century America. The mass of published scholarship on Jefferson since 1945 is much greater than it was for the period from Jefferson's death until 1945.[20] This increase is owing to a number of factors: the development of history as a professional discipline; the printing and dissemination of Jefferson's papers; increased institutional support for the study of Jefferson and his time; and breakthroughs in research that have encouraged still further research. In many respects we know more about Jefferson and his time than our predecessors did a century ago. This development has led to an exponential increase in the number of studies on (seemingly) all aspects of his life.

In this book I aim to survey the major trends in this literature as a means to trace the history of Jefferson's reputation in the latter twentieth and early twenty-first centuries. From time to time I also reflect on Jefferson's place in modern American culture more broadly. Indeed, I assume that the scholarly Jefferson image and the popular image are

closely linked. As this study shows, scholarship reflects the times in which
it was written just as it helps to shape those times. Nonetheless this is not a
history of Jefferson's modern popular image and there remains a need for
such a volume.

This work differs from *The Jefferson Image in the American Mind*
in another, more significant, way. In *The Jefferson Image*, Peterson
declared, 'This is not a book on the history Thomas Jefferson made
but a book on what history made of Thomas Jefferson.'[21] This study
takes Peterson's statement as a point of departure. However, rather than
assuming that history was something that Jefferson made or was subjected to, it recognizes and argues that Jefferson consciously sought to
shape his historical legacy. Long after his death, Jefferson has continued
to be an active participant in the efforts to research and write about his
life. All research about Jefferson is, to some extent, a conversation with
Jefferson. This is as Jefferson intended. He was acutely aware that his
actions and writings would face the judgment of posterity. In anticipation
of such judgment he took steps – especially the preservation and organization of his papers – to protect his reputation at the hands of future
historians. In light of these facts, this book considers how Jefferson
intended historians to portray him and how they have presented Jefferson's life, thought and actions. It is, therefore, a three-way conversation
among Jefferson, his third- and fourth-stage scholarly interpreters and
myself as a student of Jefferson and his scholarly admirers and critics.

The first half of this study considers Jefferson's ideas about history –
traced through the books he read and the letters he wrote – in the context
of the development of history as a discipline during the eighteenth
century. Chapter 1 examines Jefferson's philosophy of history and his
attempts to promote its study. It shows that for Jefferson history must
serve a political and moral purpose and that there was a tension in
Jefferson's conception of history between the demand that one write
history that promoted the correct moral and political lessons and the
need to tell the 'truth' based on primary sources. Chapter 2 examines
Jefferson's own attempts at writing history and his efforts – through his
autobiography and Anas – to shape the history of his life and times,
especially the history of the Revolution. For Jefferson, history writing was
a form of political combat. He believed that his historical legacy and the
meaning of the American Revolution were one and the same, and that
they were threatened by common enemies. To combat the forces of
counter-revolution in the future, Jefferson took deliberate steps to influence his treatment at the hands of historians.

Although Jefferson sought to shape his historical legacy, he was
reluctant to go into print himself and engage in controversy during his
lifetime. As a student of the Enlightenment, Jefferson was aware of the

importance of primary sources as the basis of historical writing. He believed that credible and valuable histories must be based on primary sources carefully interpreted by historians. For these reasons Jefferson carefully edited and preserved his massive collection of personal papers in order to safeguard his vision of the past for the future. Chapter 3 traces the history of Jefferson's papers – from the publication of the first edition of his *Memoirs* in 1829 to the online version offered by the Library of Congress today. The history of Jefferson's papers reveals the central paradox at the heart of this study: the more we come to know Jefferson, the further we depart from his vision of how the history of his life and times should be written. The better we think we know Jefferson, the further we get from his conception of the past. Yet Jefferson, himself, has provided us with the means, through his documentary legacy, to ignore his conception of history. The modern scholarly edition of Jefferson's papers, when completed, will provide students of Jefferson with one of the most complete possible records of an individual's life. Scholars use this material to ask new and different questions that enrich our understanding of Jefferson's life and times. As they do, they lose sight of the political significance of history writing for Jefferson. We do not use his papers as he intended that we should.

This paradox also applies to other aspects of Jefferson's legacy. Perhaps the most important bequest that Jefferson left, after his papers, was his home at Monticello. Approximately half a million people visit Jefferson's home annually, and it probably does more to shape Jefferson's reputation than his copious writings. During his lifetime Jefferson intended that his home should be a statement of his political principles. For decades after his death it largely, if not completely, ceased to be so. After briefly considering its history during the nineteenth century, Chapter 4 considers the development of Monticello as a tourist destination and educational center under the auspices of the Thomas Jefferson Memorial Foundation (now the Thomas Jefferson Foundation) that owns and runs the house and grounds. Monticello – both the home as presented to visitors, and the Foundation that owns it and promotes the study of Jefferson – presents an image of Jefferson unlike that which he intended.

The latter half of this book considers the extent to which Jefferson was successful in safeguarding his reputation by considering his treatment at the hands of modern historians. On his gravestone Jefferson highlighted three achievements by which he most wanted to be remembered: his authorship of the Declaration of Independence and of the Virginia Statute for Religious Freedom and his role in founding the University of Virginia. Jefferson saw these achievements – mainly concerned with defining and advancing human freedom – as illustrating his life's work. Chapter 5 reviews the treatment of these achievements by historians and shows that

Jefferson was largely successful in being remembered for them in the manner that he wished.

Posterity's treatment of Jefferson was not limited, however, to the achievements highlighted on his gravestone. Perhaps the most notable development in Jefferson studies in recent years has been confirmation that Jefferson had a sexual relationship with one of his slaves, Sally Hemings. Chapter 6 traces the long controversy over the Hemings relationship while considering the implications of the relationship (and of its confirmation) for our understanding of Jefferson with respect to the vexing questions of gender and race. It shows that the definitive biography of Jefferson has yet to be written. Further, it shows that Jefferson's conception of history, with its emphasis on history as a political contest between liberty and tyranny, did not consider the most intimate aspects of an individual's life a suitable subject for historical examination. Jefferson's more sympathetic biographers and historians adhered to this view and were blinkered by assumptions not only about race but also about ideology in considering the Hemings matter. Jefferson's relationship with Sally Hemings underscores not only the complexity of Jefferson's relationship with slavery but also the limits of the whig approach to history embraced by Jefferson (and some of his scholarly admirers).

Jefferson was both the foremost expositor of human freedom and equality in eighteenth-century America and the owner of approximately six hundred African slaves over the course of his lifetime. This apparent contradiction, more than anything, has contributed to the decline of Jefferson's reputation. The years since World War II have seen an explosion in the historiography on American slavery. As a result, as we have learned more about slavery, we have come to learn more about Jefferson. Chapter 7 traces the rich, and richly critical, literature on Jefferson and slavery. It shows that Jefferson was aware that he would be judged by posterity for his slaveholding. It examines the steps he took, largely successful until the 1960s, to protect himself from criticism on the issue. Jefferson saw slavery as a threat not only to his personal legacy but to the American republic. He sought, with partial success, to limit the damage done by slavery to his reputation and to the future of the republic.

Jefferson believed that if his vision of global republicanism – his end of history – was to be realized then the United States must grow geographically. It must also be able to project its power and defend its interests in a world of rapacious illiberal empires. He spoke of creating an 'Empire for Liberty' in North America. Chapter 8 considers the statecraft and foreign policy of Jefferson while he was president. It traces Jefferson's efforts to protect and promote American interests during the Napoleonic wars while advocating the continued westward expansion of the United

States. It considers the consequences of Jefferson's statecraft for Native Americans who were displaced by his vision of a republican empire.

As a study of the dialogue between Jefferson and historians this book neglects large portions of the immense literature on Thomas Jefferson. Since it focuses on the major historical themes – politics, religion, education and geographic expansion – that Jefferson deemed the most important aspects of his historical legacy, it neglects other significant aspects of Jefferson historiography – such as the history of science and architecture. Slavery and the Sally Hemings relationship are considered because the study of race has been among the most important themes in American historiography over the past sixty years. The study of race has, more than any other factor, contributed to the transformation of Jefferson's reputation over the past half-century. Even with regard to the topics included in this study it has been impossible to consider all of the thousands of relevant titles. What I have sought to do is to examine the major themes in Jefferson historiography through representative works. My experience in researching and writing this book has suggested to me that, like Peterson's earlier work, it should be seen as part of an ongoing discussion of Jefferson's meaning. It certainly is not, and cannot be, the last word on the subject.

Historians have long studied the political, ideological, diplomatic and geographic aspects of Jefferson's republican conception of the world. By and large, they have, ignored the temporal dimension to Jefferson's republicanism. This omission is ironic because Jefferson expected that future historians would have an important role to play in the struggle over republicanism in America after his death. A crucial component of this future struggle would concern how the history of Jefferson's life and times would be written. Historians, guided by Jefferson, would not only reinterpret the past, but if they did so correctly they might help to bring about a republican millennium and transform the world. Twentieth- and twenty-first-century historians have not been concerned with the whig interpretation of history as Jefferson expected. Our concerns, rightly, are not Jefferson's. Jefferson, who believed that the earth was for the living, could not bind the hands – or direct the minds – of future historians from beyond the grave. Our concern with questions of race, class and gender over the past fifty years has called Jefferson's reputation into question in ways that he could not foresee – and that he probably would not understand. As a result we know more about Jefferson and his world than ever before. In acquiring this knowledge we have focused on Jefferson at the expense of what he held to be the wider significance of his life and ideas. Jefferson hoped that future historians would focus on this broader, indeed global, significance because he believed we might thus bring about a triumph of republicanism that would initiate international peace and an end to history. We have not done so. We have not yet reached Jefferson's bright republican future, his future without history. Wars and contentions continue to fill the pages of our history. In consequence the study of history, and the study of Jefferson, continues.

NOTES

1. TJ to Count Diadati, 29 March 1807, TJP.
2. For a discussion of Jefferson and 'the end of history' see Peter S. Onuf and Nicholas G. Onuf, *Nations, Markets and War: Modern History and the American Civil War* (Charlottesville: University of Virginia Press, 2006), ch. 7. I am grateful to the Onufs for allowing me to read this while it was in production. The most recent exponent of the 'end of history' is Francis Fukuyama. In an influential 1989 article in *The National Interest*, Fukuyama anticipated the global triumph of liberal capitalism in the wake of the collapse of communism and the end of the Cold War. His conception of the world is not dissimilar to Jefferson's. See Francis Fukuyama, *The End of History and the Last Man* (New York: Free Press, 1992).
3. TJ to Major John Cartwright, 5 June 1824, *TJW*, 1493–4.
4. Francis Bacon, 'Of Honour and Reputation', in *Essays or Counsels, Civil and Moral* (1625) and *The Advancement and Proficiencie of Learning* (1605), repr. in Francis Bacon, *Major Works*, Brian Vickers, ed. (Oxford: Oxford University Press, 2002), quotation, 445. Jefferson owned both the *Essays* and the *Advancement of Learning*. See E. Millicent Sowerby, *Catalogue of the Library of Thomas Jefferson*, 5 vols. (Washington, DC: 1952–9), 5:166–8. Jefferson considered Bacon, Locke and Newton to be the greatest men who ever lived. For Jefferson's opinion of Bacon see TJ to Benjamin Rush, 16 Jan. 1811, *TJW*, 1236.
5. First Inaugural Address, 4 March 1801, *TJW*, 495. After he lost the presidential election of 1796, Jefferson wrote, 'I protest before my god that I shall from the bottom of my heart, rejoice at escaping [the presidency]. I know well that no man will ever bring out of that office the reputation which carries him into it.' TJ to Edward Rutledge, 27 Dec. 1796, *PTJ*, 29:232.
6. TJ to Thomas Jefferson Randolph, 24 Nov. 1808, in Edwin M. Betts and James A. Bear, Jr., eds., *The Family Letters of Thomas Jefferson* (Charlottesville: University Press of Virginia, 1966), 362–3.
7. Richard B. Bernstein, one of Jefferson's most able recent biographers, discusses the four stages in the history of Jefferson's reputation. R. B. Bernstein, *Thomas Jefferson* (New York: Oxford University Press, 1993), 191–3. Peterson, *Jefferson Image* is the pre-eminent study of

Jefferson's image. While Bernstein acknowledges his debt to Peterson's analysis, his concise four-part conception is original and elegant.

8. Franklin D. Roosevelt, Address at the Dedication of the Thomas Jefferson Memorial, Washington, DC, 13 April 1943, in Samuel I. Rosenman and William D. Hassett, eds., *The Public Papers and Addresses of Franklin D. Roosevelt*, 13 vols. (New York: Random House, 1938–1950), 12:162–4. Jefferson quotation, TJ to Benjamin Rush, 23 Sept. 1800, *TJW*, 1082. For the building and dedication of the Jefferson Memorial see Peterson, *Jefferson Image*, 377–8, 420–32 and Merrill D. Peterson, *Jefferson Memorial: An Essay* (Washington, DC: National Park Service, 1998).

9. Peterson, *Jefferson Image*, 379, 457.

10. The various Jefferson monuments are discussed in Bernstein, *Thomas Jefferson*, 193. For examples of third-stage, Apostle-of-Freedom portrayals of Jefferson see Marie Kimball, *Jefferson: The Road to Glory* (New York: Coward-McCann, 1943); Marie Kimball, *Jefferson: War and Peace, 1776 to 1784* (New York: Coward-McCann, 1947); Marie Kimball, *Jefferson: The Scene of Europe, 1784 to 1789* (New York: Coward-McCann, 1950); Karl Lehman, *Thomas Jefferson: American Humanist* (New York: MacMillan, 1947); Daniel J. Boorstin, *The Lost World of Thomas Jefferson* (New York: Henry Holt, 1948); Nathan Schachner, *Thomas Jefferson: A Biography*, 2 vols. (New York: Appleton-Century-Crofts, 1951); Marguerite Eyer Wilbur, *Thomas Jefferson: Apostle of Liberty* (New York: Liveright Publishing, 1962); Leonard Wibberley, *Man of Liberty: A Life of Thomas Jefferson* (New York: Farrar, Straus and Giroux, 1963).

11. Leonard W. Levy, *Jefferson and Civil Liberties: The Darker Side* (Cambridge, MA: Harvard University Press, 1963).

12. For reviews of Jefferson historiography from the early 1960s until the early 1990s see Gordon S. Wood, 'The Trials and Tribulations of Thomas Jefferson', and Scot A. French and Edward L. Ayers, 'The Strange Career of Thomas Jefferson: Race and Slavery in American Memory, 1943–1993', both of which appeared in Peter S. Onuf, ed., *Jeffersonian Legacies* (Charlottesville: University Press of Virginia, 1993), 395–417; 418–56. Also see Peter S. Onuf, 'The Scholars' Jefferson', *WMQ*, 50 (1993), 671–99.

13. Dumas Malone, *Jefferson and the Ordeal of Liberty* (Boston: Little Brown, 1962); *Jefferson the President: First Term, 1801–1805* (Boston: Little Brown, 1970); *Jefferson the President: Second Term, 1805–1809* (Boston: Little Brown, 1974); *The Sage of Monticello* (Boston: Little Brown, 1981); Merrill D. Peterson, *Thomas Jefferson and the New Nation* (New York: Oxford University Press, 1970); Noble Cunningham, Jr., *In Pursuit of Reason: The Life of Thomas Jefferson* (Baton Rouge: Louisiana State University Press, 1987).

14. See Norman K. Risjord, *Thomas Jefferson* (Madison, WI: Madison House, 1994); Andrew Burstein, *The Inner Jefferson: Portrait of a Grieving Optimist* (Charlottesville: University Press of Virginia, 1995); Andrew Burstein, *Jefferson's Secrets: Death and Desire at Monticello* (New York: Basic Books, 2005); Bernstein, *Thomas Jefferson*. Bernstein also published a young-adult version of his biography; see R. B. Bernstein, *Thomas Jefferson: The Revolution of Ideas* (New York: Oxford University Press, 2004).

15. The term 'Founders' Chic' first appeared in *Newsweek* magazine in July 2001. See Evan Thomas, 'Founders Chic: Live from Philadelphia', *Newsweek*, 9 July 2001, 48. For a thoughtful critique of the scholarly attention which the Founding Fathers have received recently see the introduction to Jeffrey L. Pasley, Andrew W. Robertson and David Waldstreicher, eds., *Beyond the Founders: New Approaches to the Political History of the Early American Republic* (Chapel Hill: University of North Carolina Press, 2004). Also see David Waldstreicher, 'Founders Chic as Culture War', *Radical History Review*, 84 (2002), 185–94; and H. W. Brands, 'Founders Chic: Our Reverence for the Founding Fathers has Gotten Out of Hand', *The Atlantic Monthly*, 292:2 (Sept. 2003), 101–10. See also Jan Ellen Lewis, 'Is There a New Political History? Review of Jeffrey L. Pasley, Andrew W. Robertson and David Waldstreicher, eds, *Beyond the Founders: New Approaches to the Political History of the Early American Republic*', H-SHEAR, H-Net Reviews, July, 2005. http://www.hnet.org/reviews/showrev.cgi?-path=266671128697568.

16. Jack Rakove, 'Hamilton, Presidents' Friend, Co-author of the Federalist Papers Defined Executive Power Perhaps too Expansively', *San Francisco Chronicle*, 18 July 2004, E-3. Historically, when Hamilton's reputation is in the ascent, Jefferson's is in decline. For Alexander Hamilton's reputation see Stephen F. Knott, *Alexander Hamilton and the Persistence of Myth* (Lawrence: University Press of Kansas, 2002). These paragraphs on Founders Chic are derived from my review essay on the subject. See Francis D. Cogliano, 'Founders Chic', *History*, 89 (2005), 411–19. Recently some writers and historians have tried to portray Jefferson as an effective war leader during the conflict with Tripoli during his first administration. See A. B. C. Whipple, *To the Shores of Tripoli: The Birth of the U.S. Navy and Marines* (Annapolis: Naval Institute, 2001); Joseph Wheelan, *Jefferson's War: America's First War on Terror, 1801–1805* (New York: Carroll and Graf, 2003); Frank Lambert, *The Barbary Wars: American Independence in the Atlantic World* (New York: Hill and Wang, 2005); and Richard Zacks, *The Pirate Coast: Thomas Jefferson, the First Marines, and the Secret Mission of 1805* (New York: Hyperion, 2005). It remains to be seen whether this usable-past view of a more bellicose Jefferson, fit for the War on Terror, will take hold.

17. Joseph J. Ellis, 'Jefferson: Post DNA', WMQ, 57 (2000), 125–38, quotation 136.
18. For example, in the summer of 2004 Jefferson appeared on the cover of *Time* magazine. Approximately 500,000 people visit Jefferson's home, Monticello, near Charlottesville, Virginia, each year.
19. Ellis, 'Jefferson: Post-DNA', 128–9.
20. Frank Shuffleton's indispensable bibliographies of Jeffersoniana list more than 4,800 titles on Jefferson published between 1826 and 2000. Of these the vast majority of scholarly articles and books were published since 1945. Indeed approximately 30 percent of the titles have been published since 1980. See Frank Shuffleton, ed., *Thomas Jefferson: A Comprehensive, Annotated Bibliography of Writings About Him (1826–1980)* (New York: Garland, 1983); and Frank Shuffleton, ed., *Thomas Jefferson, 1981–1990: An Annotated Bibliography* (New York: Garland, 1992). These bibliographies are available online (updated through 2000) as Frank Shuffleton, ed., *Thomas Jefferson: A Comprehensive, Annotated Bibliography of Writings about Him, 1826–1997*, http://etext.virginia.edu/jefferson/bibliog/.
21. Peterson, *Jefferson Image*, xiii.

CHAPTER 1

HISTORY

I

Throughout his adult life Thomas Jefferson dispensed academic and educational advice to younger relatives, friends and protégés. For fifty years he based his ideas on a 'course of reading' that he had developed during the 1760s after he completed his own studies at William and Mary. Jefferson recommended that students should read across a range of subjects because 'Variety relieves the mind, as well as the eye, palled with too long attention to a single object.' According to Jefferson's plan, the period from sunrise until eight o'clock in the morning should be devoted to the study of the natural sciences, ethics and religion. From eight o'clock until noon, students should read law. The hour from noon to one in the afternoon should be given over to politics. 'In the Afternoon', Jefferson counseled, 'Read History'. From sunset until bedtime the followers of this ambitious program could relax with *belles-lettres*, criticism, rhetoric and oratory.[1] Students who followed Jefferson's program would devote most of their time to two subjects – the law and history.

Jefferson read widely in history throughout his life, believing that it was an essential subject. In his retirement he professed to be disgusted with current affairs and claimed a preference for history.

> I turn from the contemplation [of politics] with loathing, and take refuge in the histories of other times, where if they also furnished their Tarquins, their Catilines & Caligulas, their stories are handed to us under the brand of a Livy, a Sallust, and a Tacitus, and we are comforted with the reflection that the condemnation of all succeeding generations has confirmed the censures of the historians, and consigned their memories to everlasting infamy, a solace we cannot have with the Georges & Napoleons, but by anticipation.[2]

For Jefferson, history did not simply offer diversion; it offered a guide to the present and provided moral and political lessons for the future. Further, it was a subject in which he had a personal stake. As a figure

of considerable historical importance himself, Jefferson worried about the
'censures of the historians' and sought to shape the way he would be
treated by posterity. In order to comprehend his efforts to safeguard his
reputation we must first consider Jefferson's approach to history and the
actions he took to promote its study and production.

II

During his lifetime Thomas Jefferson acquired three personal libraries.
The first, consisting of between and three and four hundred volumes, was
destroyed by fire in 1770. The second, which he began building immediately after the fire, was probably the most substantial private library
in eighteenth-century America, consisting of more than 4,900 titles and
6,700 volumes. He offered this library for sale to the United States in
1814 to replace the Congressional library burned by the British during
their occupation of Washington DC. This collection formed the core of
the Library of Congress. Finally, between the 1815 sale and his death in
1826, Jefferson acquired a third library.

An inveterate record-keeper, Jefferson compiled a detailed catalog of
his second library. This gives us an insight into his approach to knowledge and the place of history in his thinking and reading.[3] Taking his cue
from Francis Bacon's division of knowledge into three categories –
memory, reason and imagination – Jefferson arranged his books under
three headings: History, Philosophy and Fine Arts. His 'history' category
included all the known facts of the universe. This consisted of information
about human activity through time, which he designated 'Civil History',
and information discovered about plants, animals and minerals, or
'Natural History'. Civil history was divided into two categories: civil
history proper and ecclesiastical history. Civil history proper was then
further divided into ancient and modern history, which in turn was
subdivided into foreign, British and American history. According to the
catalogue of the second library Jefferson owned 132 titles in ancient
history, 189 titles under the heading 'modern history foreign', 118 titles
under the heading 'modern history British' and 90 titles relating to
American history. Titles with substantial historical content can be found
under other headings. For example, the forty-seven titles under the
heading 'Law of Nations' are mainly concerned with European diplomatic history and treaty-making. Jefferson's politics category also contained titles relating to ancient, modern European, British and American
history; his geography catalog included 173 titles on the Americas
including accounts of the exploration of North and South America
and European encounters with Native Americans; and his 'Common
Law' heading contained a number of titles relating to English history.[4]

During his lifetime Jefferson read widely in ancient, medieval and modern history. He did so, when possible, in original languages. He owned and read historical works in English, French, Spanish and Italian as well as classical Greek and Latin. Jefferson's efforts to organize the books in his vast library, dividing and subdividing titles according to their content, reflects a concern with systematizing knowledge that was a characteristic of the Enlightenment. Jefferson began reading and studying history at a time when the discipline was changing. Enlightenment historians, whom Roy Porter calls 'philosophic historians', placed an increasing emphasis on the use of primary sources and accuracy. They rejected providential explanations for historical development in favor of those that stressed human agency and social evolution. Perhaps most crucially, the philosophic historians assumed that human nature was universal across time and space, and that lessons could therefore be drawn from across history. The true value of history lay in the universal truths about humanity and society that it revealed. Henry St John, Viscount Bolingbroke, summed up the major questions of Enlightenment historiography: 'What then is the true use of history? [I]n what respects may it serve to make us better and wiser? [A]nd what method is to be pursued in the study of it, for attaining these great ends?' He answered these questions with an aphorism he attributed to Dionysius of Halicarnassus, 'history is philosophy teaching by examples'.[5]

Just what were the lessons that history should teach? Like most students of history in eighteenth-century America, Jefferson's historical thinking derived from the whig interpretation of English and American history. During the seventeenth and eighteenth centuries English whig politicians, writers and ideologues championed the claims of Parliament against royal prerogative. Whigs and historians sympathetic to their outlook delved into the English past to justify their position. The whigs interpreted history as an ongoing struggle between liberty and tyranny. They claimed that traditional English liberties, protected by Parliament, had a long lineage, originating with the ancient Saxons and undermined by the Norman Conquest. The more recent history of Britain under the Tudors and Stuarts demonstrated that the battle between liberty and tyranny was ongoing as numerous monarchs sought to increase their power at the expense of popular liberty. According to the whigs, Parliament was the bulwark of British liberty. It was not clear by the latter part of the eighteenth century that the forces of liberty would prevail in England, however. Indeed, by 1776 many Americans felt that the effort to preserve liberty in Britain had failed and America had become the final refuge for freedom-loving Britons. The history of British America demonstrated that Parliament, in league with the monarchy, could also threaten liberty. When liberty was thus endangered, resistance was justified. Even violent resistance could be defended as a last resort. The chief lesson that history taught, according to the whig historians, was that liberty was always in danger and that it could only be protected by a virtuous, informed and vigilant citizenry. Knowledge of history was essential if citizens were to recognize the dangers which tyranny and its allies, luxury, vice and corruption, posed to freedom. The histories of ancient Greece and Rome, modern Europe and especially England provided many examples of the perilous fate of liberty.[6] While the whig interpretation was not the only approach to the past in the English-speaking world during the eighteenth century, it predominated in British North America.[7] Jefferson was well versed in it. At the age of fourteen he inherited Paul Rapin's whiggish *History of England* from his father.[8] Jefferson's writings reveal that he also inherited a whig historical sensibility. Jefferson's whiggish approach to history found particular expression in his enthusiasm for Saxon history and his antipathy for David Hume's *History of England*.

In February 1814 a young Bostonian, Francis Calley Gray, visited Jefferson at Monticello. The former president invited the New Englander to spend the night. The next morning after breakfast Gray enjoyed a singular experience as Jefferson gave him a tour of the Monticello library. Gray spent the morning discussing the collection – the large second library prior to its sale to Congress – and examining its contents with Jefferson. Among the various works Gray noticed that:

> Mr. Jefferson also has a fine collection of Saxon and Moeso Gothic books, among them Alfred's translations of Orosius and Boethius, and shewed us some attempts he had made at facilitating the study of this language. He thought the singularity of the letters one of the greatest difficulties and proposed publishing the Saxon books in four columns, the first to contain the Saxon, the second the same in Roman characters, the third a strictly verbal translation and the fourth a free one.[9]

Nothing came of Jefferson's plan to publish Saxon texts, but his interest in Saxon culture and history was longstanding. Nearly fifty years before Gray discussed the subject with him, Jefferson began transcribing passages of Saxon history into a notebook, while he was a law student in Williamsburg during the 1760s.[10] According to Jefferson's reading of early English history the Saxons had enjoyed liberty and representative government before the Norman conquest. The advent of the Normans introduced feudal tyranny and also launched the ongoing struggle between liberty and tyranny in English history. Such an interpretation was common to whig historiography during the eighteenth century.[11]

For Jefferson the history of early medieval England was directly relevant to the American Revolution. In his first publication on the colonial crisis, *A Summary View of the Rights of British America* (1774), Jefferson invoked the Saxons to defend colonial resistance to British taxation. He asserted that Parliament had no right to tax the colonies because the settlement of America by Britons was similar to that of Britain by the Saxons; therefore British Americans, like their Saxon predecessors should be free from outside interference.[12] Two years later he appealed to Saxon precedent to justify the abolition of primogeniture and entail in Virginia:

> Are we not the better for what we have hitherto abolished of the feudal system? Has not every restitution of the Antient Saxon laws had happy effects? Is it not better now that we return at once into that happy system of our ancestors, the wisest & most perfect ever yet devised by the wit of man, as it stood before the 8th century.[13]

Little more than a month after Congress had adopted his Declaration of Independence, Jefferson – usually depicted as a forward-looking optimist – justified the revolution as a return to a glorious moment a thousand years earlier when the English enjoyed the liberty that Americans were seeking to revive.

Jefferson's interest in Saxon history was not simply a passing fancy. Fifty years after he drew on Saxon precedents to justify resistance to British taxation in the *Summary View* he declared, 'It has ever appeared to me, that the difference between the whig and tory of England is, that the whig deduces his rights from the Anglo-Saxon source, and the tory from the Norman.'[14] Jefferson devoted himself to serious study of Saxon history for more than five decades, collecting records and reading primary and secondary sources. He found in Saxon history lessons and justifications in contemporary disputes. Although he adopted a scholarly approach to the study of the past, he did so selectively, for history was a weapon in a perpetual struggle between liberty and tyranny. This view explains Jefferson's antipathy toward David Hume's *History of England*.

Nearly sixty years after he inherited a copy of Rapin's history of England from his father, Jefferson still valued the work. During his 1814 tour of the library at Monticello, Francis Gray noted, 'Rapin was here in French, though very rare in that language.' Gray continued, 'Mr. Jefferson said that after all it was still the best history of England, for Hume's tory principles are to him unsupportable.'[15] Jefferson subjected Gray to a disquisition on the faults in David Hume's *History of England*. This was a subject dear to Jefferson's heart. Counteracting the deleterious effects of Hume's *History* was one of the preoccupations of Jefferson's years of retirement.[16]

Jefferson felt that knowledge of English history was essential for

Americans. He wrote in 1810, 'Our laws, language, religion, politics, & manners are so deeply laid in English foundations, that we shall never cease to consider their history as a part of ours, and to study ours in that as it's origin.' Unfortunately, in Jefferson's view, there was no adequate history of England available for American readers. The most popular and influential English history at the time was Hume's *History of England*. '[E]very one knows that judicious matter & charms of stile have rendered Hume's history the Manual of every student', lamented Jefferson. 'I remember well the enthusiasm with which I devoured it when young, and', he continued, 'the length of time, the research & reflection which were necessary to eradicate the poison it had instilled into my mind.'[17] The problem with Hume's history was not its style but its content. Jefferson explained:

> he gave his history the aspect of an apology, or rather a justification of his countrymen the Stuarts. their good deeds were displayed their bad ones disguised or explained away, or altogether suppressed where they admitted no palliation, and a constant vein of fine ridicule was employed to disparage the patriots who opposed their usurpations, and vindicated the freedom and rights of their country. the success of this work induced him to go back to the history of the Tudors, and having now taken his side as the apologist of arbitrary power in England, the new work was to be made a support for the old. accordingly all the arbitrary acts of the Tudor sovereigns were industriously selected and displayed, as regular exercises of constitutional authority, and the resistance to them assumes the hue of factious opposition. he then went back the last step, and undertook to fill up the chasm from the Roman invasion to the accession of the Tudors, making this, as the second work, still a justification for the first; and of the whole, a continued advocation of the heresy that, by the English constitution, the powers of the monarch were every thing, and the rights of the people nothing.[18]

The consequences of such a misreading of the past could be drastic. The combination of Hume's misinterpretation of history with his engaging style was fraught with political danger. In 1818, Jefferson accused Hume of destroying liberty in England:

> as the elementary & standard book of English history, the whig spirit of that country has been compleatly sapped by it, has nearly disappeared, and toryism become the general weed of the nation. what the patriots of the last age dreaded & deprecated from a standing army, and what could not have been atchieved for the crown by any standing army, but with torrents of blood, one man, by the magic of his pen, has effected covertly,

insensibly, peaceably; and has made voluntary converts of the best men of the present age to the parricide opinions of the worst of the last.

This danger was not limited to Britain. Jefferson feared that Hume's book might have the same impact in the United States, where it was popular. The American who read Hume as a student would eventually grow up to become a statesman and, wrote Jefferson, 'he will become also the tory of our constitution, disposed to monarchise the government, by strengthening the Executive, and weakening the popular branch, and by drawing the municipal administration of the states into the vortex of the general authority.'[19] History was of such importance, according to Jefferson, that 'bad' history such as Hume's could endanger liberty and security in the United States.

What was the antidote to Hume's poisonous history? Jefferson suggested two alternatives. The first would be to publish Hume's text with corrections and amendments drawn from primary and other secondary sources presented in footnotes or a separate column paralleling Hume's text. The second would be to present an abridged or corrected version of Hume. Jefferson had such a text in mind. In 1796 a British radical, John Baxter, published *A New Impartial History of England* that presented an edited version of Hume's history (without acknowledging Hume). Jefferson greatly admired the book, writing, 'Baxter has performed a good operation on it. He has taken the text of Hume as his ground work, abridging it by the omission of some details of little interest, and wherever he has found him endeavoring to mislead, by either the suppression of a truth or by giving it a false coloring, he has changed the text to what it should be, so that we may properly call it Hume's history republicanised.' During his last years, Jefferson endeavored unsuccessfully to convince a publisher to bring out an American edition of Baxter's *Impartial History* which he hoped would replace Hume's work as the standard English history read by Americans.[20]

Jefferson's attack on Hume epitomized his attitude toward history. He admired Hume's history for its style but condemned its interpretations. There was more at stake in this dispute than narrow questions of historiography. Hume's style was so appealing that the unsuspecting reader would be seduced by his interpretations. Hume's history should be the last work that a student read. Armed with a broad knowledge, and an edited and corrected version of English history such as Baxter's, the student could enjoy Hume's stylistic achievement without falling prey to his misinterpretations. Without such protection, Hume's book was dangerous indeed. '[I]f first read Hume makes an English tory', Jefferson warned in 1825, 'from whence it is an easy step to American toryism.'[21] Inaccurate history, such as Hume's, distracted readers and students from history's true objectives – liberty and virtue – and threatened America's experiment with republican government. Such history had to be countered and corrected. If it was not, then humanity was destined to endlessly repeat the bloody contest between liberty and tyranny that had characterized history since ancient times.

III

Jefferson read the major philosophic historians of the seventeenth and eighteenth centuries – including Gibbon, Hume, Robertson, Bolingbroke, Montesquieu and Voltaire – and he endorsed their views on the utilitarian value of the study of history. In his 1785 *Notes on the State of Virginia* Jefferson outlined a plan for universal education in his native state. He recommended that all children in the state receive free education for three years – with the brightest students proceeding to more advanced study. Jefferson explained: 'The first stage of this education being the schools of the hundreds, wherein the great mass of the people will receive their instruction, the principal foundations of future order will be laid here.' This would be achieved by instruction not in religion but in history. 'Instead', wrote Jefferson, 'of putting the Bible and Testament into the hands of children, at an age when their judgments are not sufficiently matured for religious enquiries, their memories may here be stored with the most useful facts from Grecian, Roman, European, and American history.' Thomas Jefferson believed in the power of history. As he wrote of the people of Virginia:

> History by apprising them of the past will enable them to judge of the future; it will avail them of the experience of other times and other nations; it will qualify them as judges of the actions and designs of men; it will enable them to know ambition under every disguise it may assume; and knowing it, to defeat its views. In every government on earth is some trace of human weakness, some germ of corruption and degeneracy, which cunning will discover, and wickedness insensibly open, cultivate, and improve. Every government degenerates when trusted to the rulers of the people alone. The people themselves therefore are its only safe depositories. And to render even them safe their minds must be improved to a certain degree.

In Jefferson's view knowledge of history was necessary for the people of Virginia if they were to protect their liberty. It was a political necessity in a republic.[22]

There was a tension, never entirely resolved in Enlightenment historiography or Jefferson's thinking, between the demands of accuracy and those of style. The eighteenth century witnessed important methodological advances in the writing of history. Historians increasingly based their findings on research into primary sources – the preservation and publication of which had been increasing since the Renaissance. Eighteenth-century historians also wanted to entertain and teach rather than merely chronicle. They emphasized style as well as 'the most useful facts' when they wrote. As David Hume wrote in 1742, 'The advantages found in history seem to be of three kinds, as it amuses the fancy, as it improves the understanding, and as it strengthens virtue.'[23] It was not always possible to reconcile the requirement to base history on the accurate use of primary sources and the desire to entertain and to teach. Jefferson was aware of this difficulty. In 1771 he wrote:

> We never reflect whether the story we read be truth or fiction . . . I appeal to every reader of feeling and sentiment whether the fictitious murther of Duncan by Macbeth in Shakespeare does not excite him as great horror of villainy, as the real one of Henry IV by Ravaillac as related by Davila? . . . Considering history as a moral exercise, her lessons would be too unfrequent if confined to real life. Of those recorded by historians few incidents have been attended with such circumstances as to excite in any high degree this sympathetic emotion of virtue. We are therefore wisely framed to be as warmly interested for a fictitious as for a real personage.[24]

In other words there was more to historical truth than the recitation of simple facts to be gleaned from the records. The moral lessons of history were not to be derived solely from the documentary record.

These were not Jefferson's last words on the subject. As we shall see, he was a devoted collector of primary sources and believed that documents should be published accurately and disseminated widely for the benefit of historians and the public. He often stressed that history should be based on primary sources. For example, in 1819 he criticized Carlo Giuseppe Gugliemo Botta's Italian-language history of the American Revolution because Botta made up the speeches delivered in the Continental Congress when that body debated American independence in 1776. Jefferson, who felt that aspects of Botta's analysis had merit, faulted the Italian for 'giving fiction as a specimen of fact'. Jefferson explained the mistake: 'Botta was seduced into this error by the example of the Greek and Roman historians, who composed speeches which they supposed adapted to the circumstances and put them into the mouths of persons named by themselves.' Jefferson felt that Botta should have followed David Hume's stylistic example in his *History of England*: 'he says on such occasions that it was argued so on one side, and so and so on the other, summing up the propriate reasonings on each side without ascribing them to particular

persons by name'.[25] It was not that Jefferson was repudiating his earlier
assertion that the moral lessons of history should be paramount. Rather
he felt that historians needed to weigh their evidence carefully when
presenting historical 'truths'. Botta's error was not in describing the
different positions in the debate over independence, but the manner in
which he did so.[26]

Jefferson felt that historians had an obligation to tell the truth, and to
delineate the moral lessons of the past. He believed that history should be
based on primary sources carefully interpreted by historians. Throughout
his life Jefferson sought to preserve and disseminate primary sources as
well as to promote historical writing. All three activities – the preservation
and dissemination of historical documents, and writing histories based on
those documents – were necessary if the full political, social and moral
benefits of history were to be realized.

IV

During the American Revolution Thomas Jefferson played a leading role
in rewriting the constitution and laws of his native Virginia. Twenty years
later he recalled that one of the most severe problems he faced was in
locating copies of the former colony's laws:

> Very early in the course of my researches into the laws of Virginia, I
> observed that many of them were already lost, and many more on the
> point of being lost, as existing in single copies in the hands of careful or
> curious individuals, on whose death they would probably be used for
> waste paper. I set myself therefore to work, to collect all which were then
> existing, in order that, when the day should come in which the public
> should advert to the magnitude of their loss in these precious monuments
> of our property, and our history, a part of their regret might be spared by
> information that a portion has been saved from the wreck, which is
> worthy of their attention and preservation.[27]

Near the end of his life Jefferson declared, 'it is the duty of every good
citizen to use all the opportunities which occur to him for preserving
documents relating to the history of our country'.[28] For most of his adult
life, Jefferson collected such sources. As a result he amassed one of the
most important manuscript collections in eighteenth-century America.
His collecting and preservation of such documents, which required a
substantial investment of time, effort and money, is testimony to the
importance of primary sources in Jefferson's thinking about history.

Jefferson had a particular interest in collecting manuscripts and printed
sources relating to his native Virginia. The Thomas Jefferson Papers in the

Library of Congress contain most of the manuscript records on Virginia that Jefferson acquired during his lifetime. These consist of twenty-one large folio volumes, mainly contemporaneous handwritten copies of seventeenth- and eighteenth-century originals, most of which have not survived. The collection ranges widely and is particularly strong with respect to the earliest English settlement and the legal history of Virginia.[29] Among the valuable works that he acquired and preserved were a manuscript account of Bacon's Rebellion and the original manuscript of William Byrd's *Secret History of the Line*.[30] He also acquired a substantial collection of books, pamphlets and newspapers published in Virginia.[31]

Among the valuable documents to be found in Jefferson's collection of Virginia records are two volumes of documents relating to the Virginia Company of London, which established the first permanent British settlement in North America.[32] Jefferson's account of how he came to possess the volumes suggests the uncertainty and difficulties of documentary collection and preservation in eighteenth-century America. In 1823 Jefferson wrote:

> The only manuscripts I now possess are some folio volumes. Two of these are proceedings of the Virginia company in England . . . They contain the records of the Virginia co. copied from the Originals, under the eye, if I recollect rightly of the Earl of Southampton, a member of the company, bought at the sale of his library by Dr. [William] Byrd of Westover, and sold with that library to Isaac Zane. These volumes happened at the time of the sale to have been borrowed by Colo. R[ichard] Bland, whose library I bought, and with this they were sent to me. I gave notice of it to Mr. Zane but he never reclaimed them. I shall deposit them in the library of the University of Virginia, where they will be most likely to be preserved with care.[33]

The records, copied from lost originals in the seventeenth century, had changed hands several times over the course of the eighteenth century. They had been purchased and borrowed by men interested in the history of the company and Virginia. Serendipity, and the fact that Richard Bland had borrowed the documents without returning them, had brought them to Jefferson's hands at Monticello. The story of these documents, crucial to the history of early Virginia – first copied by the Earl of the Southampton, purchased by William Byrd and Isaac Zane, borrowed by Richard Bland and finally (and inadvertently) purchased by Jefferson – was a clear example of documents 'existing in single copies in the hands of careful or curious individuals, on whose death they would probably be used for waste paper'.

Many of the documents that Jefferson obtained were extremely fragile. In 1796 Jefferson wrote with respect to his manuscript copies of early Virginia laws, 'some of them will not bear removal, being so rotten, that in turning over a leaf it sometimes falls into powder. These I preserve by wrapping & sewing them up in oiled cloth so that neither air nor moisture can have access to them.' These efforts at documentary preservation did not address the larger issue posed by manuscripts. 'Our experience', Jefferson lamented, 'has proved to us that a single copy, or a few, deposited in MS. in the public offices, cannot be relied on for any great length of time. The ravages of fire and ferocious enemies have had but too much part in producing the very loss we now deplore.' Preserving manuscripts in archives, while a necessary step, was not sufficient. 'How many of the precious works of antiquity were lost, while they existed only in manuscript?' asked Jefferson. He answered his question with another question: 'Has there ever been one lost, since the art of printing has rendered it practicable to multiply and disperse copies?'[34] The best way to preserve and protect valuable historical documents was to publish and circulate them as widely as possible. Jefferson himself acted on this principle when he transcribed, edited and arranged for the publication of Thomas Mathew's manuscript account of Bacon's Rebellion. Throughout his life Jefferson supported such efforts to preserve historical records through publication.[35]

Jefferson's first such encounter with documentary publishing occurred on the eve of the American Revolution. On 23 August 1774, a New York printer, Ebenezer Hazard, sent Jefferson a prospectus for a proposed five-volume collection of documents relating to the history of the American colonies from the voyages of John Cabot down to 1774. These would include royal grants and charters, acts of Parliament and the proceedings of the various colonial assemblies in America, as well as local records and 'such political Pamphlets and other fugitive Pieces as are properly connected with the general Design, and are worthy of Preservation'. Hazard intended that the work should have a lengthy historical introduction 'containing an Account of the Constitution of the different British American Colonies and a very copious Index'. Hazard requested Jefferson's assistance in locating relevant documents in Virginia as well as subscribers for the work.[36] Jefferson was enthusiastic about Hazard's proposal. He compiled a list of nearly sixty documents – ranging from the early Virginia charters to the Stamp Act resolutions – that he recommended for inclusion in Hazard's collection.[37] Further, he offered to assist Hazard in locating and copying documents and to find subscribers for the work in Virginia. Ultimately he found eighteen subscribers among his Virginia friends and neighbors and subscribed to the work itself.[38]

Ebenezer Hazard's effort at archival publishing, the first in American history, got off to a slow start. His work was disrupted by the War of Independence and by the need to support a young and growing family. During the war Hazard's publishing and bookselling business failed and he served as postmaster for New York and later as surveyor of the post roads. After the war he served as postmaster-general of the United States from 1782 until 1789. He was a diligent and effective administrator of the nation's nascent, and somewhat chaotic, postal services. The demands of Hazard's job enabled him to travel the country all the while spending his own time, money and effort to collect and copy documents for his proposed collection. In February 1791, having been discharged as post-master-general by President George Washington in the mistaken belief that he had opposed ratification of the Constitution, Hazard sent two unbound manuscript volumes, comprising his copy of the Records of the United Colonies of New England, to Jefferson, who was then secretary of state. Hazard shared a sample of his forthcoming work with Jefferson in the hope that he would secure an endorsement from the Virginian that he could use in promoting his long-awaited work.[39]

Jefferson's response to Hazard reveals his attitude to the importance of preserving and publishing primary sources. Jefferson promptly returned Hazard's manuscript with an enthusiastic endorsement:

> I learn with great satisfaction that you are about committing to the press the valuable historical and state-papers you have been so long collecting. Time and accident are committing daily havoc on the originals deposited in our public offices. The late war has done the work of centuries in this business. The lost cannot be recovered; but let us save what remains: not by vaults and locks which fence them from the public eye and use, in consigning them to the waste of time, but by such a multiplication of copies, as shall place them beyond the reach of accident.[40]

Jefferson had written not only an endorsement that Hazard could use when advertising his work, but a mission statement for all documentary publishing projects, from the early initiatives of the nineteenth century, through the letter-press editions of the twentieth century (including, of course, *The Papers of Thomas Jefferson*), through the digital editions of the twenty-first century.[41]

Jefferson's exchange with Hazard reveals that he appreciated the value of primary sources. Fifteen years earlier, when Hazard had first approached him about his publishing venture, Jefferson immediately grasped the value of such a collection, 'as it will not only contribute to the information of all those concerned in the administration of government, but will furnish to any historical genius which may happen to arise those materials which he would otherwise acquire with great

difficulty and perhaps not acquire at all'.[42] To be sure, access to published
primary sources would assist contemporary political leaders in their
deliberations in the short term, but their long-term historiographical
significance was greater still. Jefferson believed that historians must base
their writings upon such sources. He welcomed the appearance of
Hazard's first volume in 1792 and hailed it as an important step in
the history and historiography of the United States.[43]

Hazard's was not the only documentary collection to which Jefferson
gave his support. He played a much greater role in another project that
combined his interests in history, the law and Virginia. In late 1806
William Waller Hening, clerk of the Virginia chancery court in Richmond, wrote to President Thomas Jefferson. Hening, an active legal
scholar, had been encouraged by members of the Virginia legislature to
publish a comprehensive collection of Virginia laws from the first settlement of the colony until the present. Hening was aware of Jefferson's
extensive collection of printed and manuscript Virginia legislative records, and wrote to request the president's assistance before undertaking
the project.[44] Jefferson enthusiastically encouraged Hening, and offered
him the use of both his printed and manuscript laws. The former were
'well bound' and could be transported to Richmond for Hening to copy.
The manuscript laws were so fragile that 'the leaf can never be opened but
once without falling into powder. These can never bear removal further
than from their shelf to a table.' Jefferson stipulated that these should be
copied, under his supervision, at the library at Monticello.[45]

Jefferson and Hening corresponded about hiring a scribe to copy the
manuscripts at Monticello while awaiting the legislature's approval for
Hening's project. In February 1808, more than a year after his first
approach to Jefferson, Hening wrote to confirm that the assembly had
approved the project. In response, Jefferson confirmed his offer of 'free
use of his collection' to assist Hening. The two men met at Monticello in
May 1808 to discuss the project. Hening must have made a good
impression because Jefferson allowed the legal scholar to borrow bound
volumes in both print and manuscript from the Monticello library.[46]
After Jefferson left the presidency in March 1809 he took a more
particular interest in Hening's project. The two men corresponded
regularly about the provenance, location and editing of the documents.[47]

In September 1809, Hening informed Jefferson that the first volume of
The Statutes at Large would soon be published. Hening, like Jefferson,
appreciated that the work would be of use to historians as well as
legislators and jurists. 'It comes down to the termination of the commonwealth of England and gives an entirely different view of our history,
especially during the four years immediately preceding the restoration of
Charles II from any thing represented by English historians. Indeed,'

Hening wrote, 'every important public transaction during the existence of the commonwealth, has been grossly *misrepresented*.'[48] Hening reiterated the point when he presented Jefferson with the first volume, noting, 'The views which all our historians have taken of the early history of Virginia, (even Marshall & Burk) have been so grossly inaccurate, that I have felt it a duty incumbent upon me to intersperse the volume with various notes, pointing those errors out.'[49]

When Ebenezer Hazard had approached him for support in publishing his collection of historical documents thirty-five years earlier, Jefferson had immediately grasped that such a collection would be useful to contemporary politicians and future historians. From the appearance of its first volume, William Waller Hening intended his *Statutes at Large* to fulfill similar functions. Jefferson appreciated that the work should serve multiple purposes. After receiving the first volume, he provided the editor with an endorsement that Hening could use to promote the book. He wrote, 'the opinion I entertain of the importance of the work may be justly inferred from the trouble & expence I incurred during the early parts of my life, to save such remains of our antient laws as were then still in existence. The compilation appears to be correctly & judiciously made, and gives us exactly what I had so long considered as a desideratum for our country. It sheds a new light on our early history, and furnishes additional security to the tenure of our rights & property.'[50] In praising Hening's work Jefferson gave priority to its value as an historical rather than a legal resource, suggesting that, to him, this is where its greatest value lay.

Jefferson's collaboration with William Waller Hening was one of the notable intellectual achievements of his life. According to Jefferson's foremost biographer, 'He seems to have taken greater pride in the help he gave to Hening than in anything he did for any other writers and collectors who sought his aid. And the contributions to the history of his native region that he made indirectly in the *Statutes at Large* may be regarded as his greatest after the publication of his *Notes on Virginia*.'[51] The publication of Hening's *Statutes at Large* was the culmination of a long process. Throughout his adult life Jefferson carefully collected and preserved the documentary history of Virginia. He did so not simply for his own edification or to gratify his vanity but also to transmit the records to posterity. 'The only object I had in making my collection of the laws of Virginia,' he wrote in response to Hening's original approach, 'was to save all those for the public which were not already lost, in the hope that at some future day they might be republished. Whether this be by public or private enterprise, my end will be equally answered.'[52] That Hening completed his *Statutes at Large* in 1823, several years before Jefferson's death, must have been gratifying indeed to both men.

The encouragement and support that Jefferson gave to Ebenezer Hazard and William Waller Hening suggests the importance that he ascribed to primary sources in writing history. Such sources were the essential matter upon which the moral lessons of the past must be based. Nonetheless, he was aware of the limits of historical records, important though they might be. Records could be lost, damaged and incomplete. Writing history, therefore presented a dilemma. Where possible, historians should base their findings on documentary evidence. Documents, however, did not always convey the whole truth. They were often incomplete and biased and could be misleading. To counter these effects, the historian needed to exercise careful judgment about his or her subject when writing. The judgments of the historian were a corrective to the inherent flaws in primary sources. The historian was a crucial interlocutor between the past and the present. Thus, just as he sought to preserve and assist in the publication of primary sources, Jefferson also assisted some historians in their craft.

V

Almost four years before William Waller Hening approached Jefferson about his *Statutes at Large*, an aspiring historian contacted the president for assistance with an intended history of Virginia. John Daly Burk wrote confidently, 'I am employed in writing an history of Virginia. My contract is made; the Subscription fills beyond my expectations and I shall doubtless receive the stipulated sum, whether the work be excellent or otherwise: but my pride and principles instruct me that something more is expected from me; that it is my duty to make my book, as far as my opportunities will admit, correct and interesting.' Burk averred that he wrote to Jefferson to ask 'the aid of your experience & Information & solicit your permission to send you a copy of the work previous to its publication'.[53]

John Daly Burk was known to Jefferson. Born in Dublin in 1772, Burk entered Trinity College in his native city in 1792. He deviated from the curriculum and pursued his own course of reading which led him to embrace rational religion and political radicalism. In 1794 he was expelled from Trinity for his heterodox views and became active in the United Irish movement. By 1797 he fled Ireland and sought refuge in America. *En route* to America he wrote a play, *Bunker-Hill, or the Death of General Warren: An Historic Tragedy in Five Acts*, which premièred at Boston's Haymarket Theatre in February 1797 to popular, though not critical, acclaim. Burk unsuccessfully tried his hand at editing a radical newspaper in Boston, the *Polar Star*. He eventually moved to New York to pursue his interests in playwriting, newspaper editing and radical politics. He became one of the editors of the *Time-Piece*, a Jeffersonian newspaper. In July 1798 Burk was arrested for violating the Sedition Act. With the assistance of leading New York Republicans, including Aaron Burr, Burk struck a bargain with the government under the terms of which the charges against him would be dropped if he left the country. Rather than return to Ireland, Burk went to Virginia, where he married and established himself as a lawyer in Petersburg. He campaigned for Jefferson's election in 1800.[54]

In June 1801 Burk wrote to Jefferson requesting an appointment to a government position that would allow him a salary to continue his writing. Jefferson politely declined Burk's patronage request.[55] Despite this earlier rebuff, Burk's confidence about Jefferson's support for his projected history was well placed. Nearly three weeks after he received Burk's letter, Jefferson responded, asking to be added to the list of subscribers to Burk's history. Further, Jefferson offered Burk the use of his printed and manuscript collections. He called Burk's attention particularly to his collections of Virginia state papers and printed and manuscript laws, and his file of Virginia newspapers from 1733 to 1775, the free use of all of which he offered to Burk.[56]

Burk did not immediately take up Jefferson's offer of assistance. Indeed, he did not contact Jefferson again until after his first volume had appeared and his second volume was on the eve of publication. In late May 1805 Burk requested the use of Jefferson's newspaper collection and printed laws. 'My second volume is already written: but the use of those papers, if I am fortunate enough to have the opportunity of seeing them in season,' wrote Burk, 'will enable me to mingle their contents either in my notes or narrative.' Jefferson agreed and instructed Thomas Mann Randolph to send the volumes of laws and a portion of his newspaper collection covering the period from 1741 to 1752 (requested by Burk) to Burk via Jefferson's old friend John Page, who was then serving as governor of Virginia. The legal documents were to remain with Page but Burk was allowed to take the newspapers to Petersburg.[57]

Jefferson took a considerable risk in sending his newspapers to Burk, as he was well aware. He wrote of them 'being the only collection probably in existence'.[58] Unfortunately, Jefferson's trust in Burk was not rewarded. Burk had finished his first three volumes by 1805. Progress on his final volume went more slowly and Burk had not completed the task in April 1808 when he was overheard excoriating the French in a Virginia tavern. A Frenchman overheard Burk and killed him in a duel. Burk died with his history unfinished and Jefferson's newspapers were lost in the disposition of Burk's estate.[59]

Why had Jefferson entrusted an invaluable historical resource to a man whom he would not appoint to a government post? Jefferson had not acquired his collection of newspapers and other historical documents to satisfy his own curiosity or vanity. As he wrote to Burk before sending the collection, 'I purchased & cherish it with a view to the public utility. It is answering one of it's principal objects when I put it into your hands.'[60] Part of the value of the collection was derived from its unique nature. However, it would only be truly valuable if, in appropriate hands, its 'public utility' was realized. Just as Jefferson had made his collection of legal documents available to William Waller Hening so that he could edit and publish them, thus preserving them for posterity, he made other documents available to Burk to interpret in his history of Virginia. Although Jefferson did not know Burk well, he trusted the Irishman with the documents because he trusted his politics. Burk had been forced to flee Ireland owing to his political radicalism. In the United States he had been persecuted by the Federalists and proved himself a loyal Jeffersonian. This background qualified Burk to be trusted with precious and unique historical records. For Jefferson, writing history was a political act. Historians had a crucial political role to play by interpreting the documentary record and delineating the lessons of the past for future generations. It was essential in a healthy republic that the appropriate lessons were learned and disseminated. This was the all-important role of the historian. Unsurprisingly these beliefs informed Jefferson's attitudes, actions and writing with regard to the history of the American Revolution and its aftermath – history in which Jefferson felt he had a political, moral and personal stake.

NOTES

1. TJ to John Minor, 30 Aug. 1814, with a copy of a reading list to Bernard Moore, TJP.
2. TJ to William Duane, 4 April 1813, TJP.
3. For a concise study of Jefferson's various libraries, see Douglas L. Wilson, *Jefferson's Books* (Charlottesville: Thomas Jefferson Memorial Foundation, 1996). During his lifetime Jefferson created catalogs of his library collections. Although no such catalog exists for his first library there are several for his second, and largest, library. These are: 1783 Catalog of Books [c. 1775–1812] by Thomas Jefferson [electronic edition]. *Thomas Jefferson Papers: An Electronic Archive*. Boston, MA: MHS, 2003. http://www.thomasjefffersonpapers.org/ and 1789 Catalog of Books [c. 1789] by Thomas Jefferson [electronic edition]. *Thomas Jefferson Papers: An Electronic Archive*. Boston, MA: MHS, 2003. http://www.thomasjefffersonpapers.org/. Around 1812 Jefferson created another library catalog which reflected the collection he sold

to the Library of Congress. An amended version of this, which altered the order in which Jefferson had arranged his books, was published in 1815 by George Watterston, the Librarian of Congress, as *Catalogue of the Library of the United States: To Which is Annexed, a Copious Index, Alphabetically Arranged* (Washington, DC: Jonathan Elliott, 1815). In the mid-twentieth century E. Millicent Sowerby made an invaluable contribution to Jefferson studies when she recreated Jefferson's original catalog order, with annotations on most of the titles in the *Catalogue of the Library of Thomas Jefferson*, 5 vols. (Washington, DC, 1952–9). This catalog is not without problems, see Douglas L. Wilson, 'Sowerby Revisited: The Unfinished Catalogue of Thomas Jefferson's Library', *WMQ*, 41 (1984), 615–28. A more recent catalog of the second library based on a manuscript reconstruction of the original catalog made in 1823 by Nicholas Trist, in consultation with Jefferson, is also available. See James A. Gilreath and Douglas L. Wilson, eds., *Thomas Jefferson's Library: A Catalog with Entries in his Own Order* (Washington, DC: Library of Congress, 1989). Finally there are manuscript and published catalogs of Jefferson's third library. The manuscript, Thomas Jefferson, no date, Second Library; Offered for Sale at Public Auction, 27 Feb. 1829, is in the Thomas Jefferson Papers in the Library of Congress, http://memory.loc.gov/ammem/mtjhtml/ mtjhome.html. A published version appeared in 1829 to accompany the auction of the books: Nathaniel P. Poor, ed., *Catalogue of President Jefferson's Library* (Washington, DC: Gales and Seaton, 1829). For a concise summary of history titles in Jefferson's various libraries see H. Trevor Colbourn, *The Lamp of Experience: Whig History and the Intellectual Origins of the American Revolution* (Chapel Hill: University of North Carolina Press, 1965), 217–21.

4. The information in this paragraph is derived from Gilreath and Wilson, eds., *Thomas Jefferson's Library* and Sowerby, *Catalogue*, vol. 1. Also see H. Trevor Colbourn, 'Thomas Jefferson's Use of the Past', *WMQ*, 15 (1958), 56–70, esp. 58.

5. Henry St. John, Viscount Bolingbroke, *Letters on the Study and Use of History* (London, 1752), Letter 2, p. 14. Jefferson owned this book, Sowerby, *Catalogue*, 3:132. Also see Isaac Kramnick, ed., *Lord Bolingbroke: Historical Writings* (Chicago: University of Chicago Press, 1972). For the development of history as a discipline during the eighteenth century see J. G. A. Pocock, *Barbarism and Religion: Volume 2, Narratives of Civil Government* (Cambridge: Cambridge University Press, 1999); Roy Porter, *Enlightenment: Britain and the Creation of the Modern World* (London: Penguin Books, 2000), ch. 10; Hugh Trevor-Roper, 'The Historical Philosophy of the Enlightenment', *Studies on Voltaire and the Eighteenth Century*, 27 (1963), 1667–87; R. G. Collingwood, *The Idea of History* (1946, repr. 1993) and R. N.

Stromberg, 'History in the Eighteenth Century', *Journal of the History of Ideas*, 12 (1951), 295–304.

6. The classic examination of the whig ideology is Bernard Bailyn, *The Ideological Origins of the American Revolution* (Cambridge, MA: Harvard University Press, 1967), esp. ch. 3. For whig historiography see Colbourn, *Lamp of Experience*, chs. 2–3. See also John Phillip Reid, *Constitutional History of the American Revolution*, 4 vols. (Madison: University of Winsconsin Press, 1986–93; one-vol. abridged edn., 1995).

7. Bailyn, *Ideological Origins*, ch. 1.

8. Colbourn, 'Thomas Jefferson's Use of the Past', 60. For the books inherited by Jefferson see 'Books in Colonial Virginia', *Virginian Magazine of History and Biography*, 10 (1903), 391. Paul de Rapin-Thoyras, *History of England*, 2 vols. Trans. N. Tindal (London, 1732–3). In addition to Rapin's history Jefferson owned many other standard whig works including the histories of James Tyrell, Bishop Burnet, Catherine Macaulay and William Belsham. James Tyrell, *The General History of England, both Ecclesiastical and Civil from the Earliest accounts of the Time to the Reign of his present Majesty, King William III*, 3 vols. (London: Rogers, Taylor, Knaplock, Bell and Cockerill, 1700–4), Sowerby, *Catalogue*, 1:148; Gilbert Burnet, *Bishop Burnet's History of His Own Time, 1643–1715*, 2 vols., vol. 1 (London: Thomas Ward, 1724), vol. 2 (London: Downing and Woodfall, 1734), Sowerby, *Catalogue*, 1:161; Catherine Macaulay, *History of England*, 9 vols. (London, 1763–83), Sowerby, *Catalogue*, 1:164; William Belsham, *History of Great Britain from the Revolution to the Accession of the House of Hanover*, 2 vols. (London: C. G. and J. Robinson, 1798), Sowerby, *Catalogue*, 1:166.

9. Francis Calley Gray, *Thomas Jefferson in 1814*: Being an Account of a Visit to Monticello, Virginia (Boston: The Club of Odd Volumes, 1924), 72.

10. Wilbur Samuel Howell, ed., *Jefferson's Parliamentary Writings: The Papers of Thomas Jefferson, Second Series* (Princeton: Princeton University Press, 1988), pp. 47–9.

11. Colbourn, *Lamp of Experience*, ch. 2.

12. [Thomas Jefferson] *Summary View of the Rights of British America* (Williamsburg: n.p., 1774), repr. in *PTJ*, 1:121–37.

13. TJ to Edmund Pendleton, 13 Aug. 1776, *PTJ*, 1:492.

14. TJ to Major John Cartwright, 5 June 1824, *TJW*, 1491.

15. Gray, *Thomas Jefferson in 1814*, 71–2.

16. The most complete treatment of this subject is Douglas L. Wilson, 'Jefferson vs. Hume', *WMQ*, 46 (1989), 49–70. Also see Craig Walton, 'Hume and Jefferson on the Uses of History', in Donald W. Livingston and James T. King, eds., *Hume: A Re-Evaluation* (New York: Fordham University Press, 1976), 389–403.

17. TJ to William Duane, 12 Aug. 1810, *TJW*, 1227.
18. TJ to Matthew Carey, 22 Nov. 1818, TJP.
19. TJ to Matthew Carey, 22 Nov. 1818, TJP.
20. TJ to John Norvell, 14 June 1807, TJP. John Baxter, *A New Impartial History of England* (London: Symonds, 1796). For various comments on Hume and Baxter by Jefferson, as well as his efforts to publish an American edition of Baxter, see: TJ to William Duane, 12 Aug. 1810, *TJW*, 1227–31; TJ to Matthew Carey, 22 Nov. 1818, TJP; TJ to George Washington Lewis, 25 Oct. 1825, TJP and Wilson, 'Jefferson vs. Hume'.
21. TJ to George Washington Lewis, 25 Oct. 1825, TJP.
22. Thomas Jefferson, *Notes on the State of Virginia* (London: John Stockdale, 1787), repr. in *TJW*, 123–325, quotations, 273, 274. In 1779 Jefferson outlined a similar plan in his unsuccessful Bill for the More General Diffusion of Knowledge, *PTJ*, 2:526–7.
23. David Hume, 'Of the Study of History', in *The Philosophical Works of David Hume*, 4 vols. (Edinburgh: Black and Tait, 1826), 4:510. This essay originally appeared in David Hume, *Essays Moral, Political and Literary*, 2 vols. (Edinburgh: Kincaid, 1741–2), although it was omitted from later editions of the book. Jefferson owned an edition of Hume's *Essays* (Sowerby, *Catalogue*, 2:14) but it is unclear which one. For a thorough discussion of the various editions of the *Essays* see Eugene F. Miller's introduction to the *Essays Moral, Political and Literary* (Indianapolis: Liberty Fund, 1985).
24. TJ to Robert Skipwith, 3 Aug. 1771, *PTJ*, 1:77.
25. TJ to Louis Girardin, 16 March 1819, TJP, Sowerby, *Catalogue*, 1:251–2. The work in question is Carlo Giuseppe Gugliemo Botta, *Storia della Guerra dell'Independenza degli Stati Uniti d'America* (Paris: D. Colas, 1809).
26. My understanding of Jefferson's approach to the past and the use of sources has benefited from Hannah Spahn's, '"Beyond Example in the History of Man": The Problem of Enlightenment History in Jefferson's Retirement', presented at the Thomas Jefferson and the Founding Fathers in Retirement Conference at Monticello on 4 March 2005. I am grateful to Ms. Spahn for allowing me to cite her, as yet, unpublished paper.
27. TJ to George Wythe, 16 Jan. 1796, *PTJ*, 28:583.
28. TJ to Hugh P. Taylor, 4 Oct. 1823, TJP.
29. See TJP, Series 8, Virginia Records. These have been published as Susan M. Kingsbury, ed., *Records of the Virginia Company*, 4 vols. (Washington, DC: Government Printing Office, 1906–35). See Statement of the Laws of Virginia, *PTJ*, 28:585–91, for a list of the legal records – in print and manuscript – which Jefferson had collected by January 1796.
30. For Jefferson's acquisition of Thomas Mathew's account of Bacon's

Rebellion, *The Beginning, Progress, and Conclusion of Bacon's Rebellion in Virginia in the Years 1675 & 1676*, 13 July 1705, now in the Library of Congress, see TJ to Rufus King, 17 Feb. 1804, TJP, and Sowerby, *Catalogue*, 1:265. The story of Jefferson's acquisition of William Byrd's *Secret History of the Line*, now in the American Philosophical Society (APS), is complex. It is likely that Jefferson was given the manuscript in 1808. See John Davis to TJ, 28 Nov. 1808, TJP. Jefferson eventually gave the manuscript to the American Philosophical Society and assisted in early, unsuccessful efforts to publish Byrd's account. See the Letterbook of the APS's Historical Committee for correspondence between Peter S. Du Ponceau and Jefferson regarding the manuscript between 1815 and 1818. I am grateful to Kirsten Phimister for tracking down these documents at the American Philosophical Society. There are typescript copies of many of these documents in the file, 'American Philosophical Society, Historical and Literary Committee, Records, 1815–1818', in the Virginia Historical Society. For a concise summary, Kathleen L. Leonard, 'Notes on the Text and Provenance of the Byrd Manuscripts', in Louis B. Wright, ed., *The Prose Works of William Byrd of Westover: Narratives of a Colonial Virginian* (Cambridge, MA: Harvard University Press, 1966), 417–23.

31. Richard Beale Davis, 'Jefferson as Collector of Virginiana', *Studies in Bibliography*, 14 (1961), 117–44.

32. Charters of the Virginia Company of London; Laws; Abstracts of the Rolls in the Offices of State, 1606–92; and Virginia Company of London and the Colony. Miscellaneous Papers, 1606–92; vols. 6 and 13 respectively of TJP, Series 8: Virginia Records, 1606–1737.

33. TJ to Hugh P. Taylor, 4 Oct. 1823, TJP. The volumes were sold to the Library of Congress in 1829 by Thomas Jefferson Randolph as part of the settlement of Jefferson's estate.

34. TJ to George Wythe, 16 Jan. 1796, *PTJ*, 28:583–4.

35. *Richmond Examiner*, 1, 5, 8 Sept. 1804; Sowerby, *Catalogue*, 1:265–6. Mathew's account was republished as *The Beginning, Progress, and Conclusion of Bacon's Rebellion in Virginia in the years 1675 & 1676* (Washington, DC: Peter Force, 1835).

36. Ebenezer Hazard to TJ, 23 Aug. 1774, *PTJ*, 1:144–6. At that time Jefferson was thirty-one years old and was little known outside of Virginia. He had been elected to the Virginia Convention in July 1774. Illness prevented him from attending the convention, but his draft resolutions were printed anonymously and without his consent in August, as *A Summary View of the Rights of British America*. The leading student of the subject has suggested that this pamphlet brought Jefferson to the attention of Hazard, and prompted Hazard's letter of 23 August. Fred Shelley, 'Ebenezer Hazard: America's First Historical Editor', *WMQ*, 12 (1955), 50. This is possible, since Hazard was

involved in the printing business in New York and may have learned the identity of the then-anonymous author of the pamphlet, but it is not probable, since Hazard's letter appeared so quickly after the appearance of *A Summary View*. It is more likely that Hazard wrote to Jefferson as part of a broader effort to promote his proposed book in Virginia. For the publication of *A Summary View* see *PTJ*, 1:121–37 and Malone, *Jefferson and His Time*, 1:181–90.

37. List of Papers for Hazard's Proposed Collection, *PTJ*, 1:146–9. In the *Notes on the State of Virginia*, Jefferson broadened the list of 'American state-papers' chronologically and geographically to include nearly 240 documents encompassing most of British North America from the fifteenth to the mid-eighteenth centuries. He noted, 'An extensive collection of papers of this description has been for some time in a course of preparation by a gentleman [Hazard] fully equal to the task, and from whom, therefore, we may hope ere long to receive it.' *TJW*, 304–25, quotation, 304.

38. TJ to Ebenezer Hazard, 30 April 1775, *PTJ*, 1:164. On subscriptions for Hazard's work, see Shelley, 'Ebenezer Hazard', p. 50. Nearly thirty years later, Jefferson claimed that he had given Hazard assistance in locating and copying documents from the list he had compiled, though he did not specify which ones. TJ to John Daly Burk, 21 Feb. 1803, TJP.

39. Ebenezer Hazard to TJ, 17 Feb. 1791, *PTJ*, 19:284. For Hazard's wartime experiences see Shelley, 'Ebenezer Hazard', 51–8.

40. TJ to Ebenezer Hazard, 18 Feb. 1791, *PTJ* 19:287.

41. Jefferson's letter of 18 Feb. 1791 letter to Ebenezer Hazard *does* suggest that he would have favored efforts such as that of the Library of Congress to make available its complete collection of Jefferson's papers (among others) on the World Wide Web. The Jefferson papers will be discussed more fully in Chapter 3.

42. TJ to Ebenezer Hazard, 30 April 1775, *PTJ*, 1:164.

43. Ultimately Hazard published two volumes. The work, while a landmark in the history of American publishing, did not enjoy the financial success that Hazard had anticipated. Ebenezer Hazard, *Historical Collections; Consisting of the State-Papers . . . Intended as Materials for an History of the United States*, 2 vols. (Philadelphia, 1792–94).

44. William Waller Hening to TJ, 26 Dec. 1806, TJP. George Wythe had published Jefferson's 1796 'Statement of the Laws of Virginia', *PTJ*, 28:585–91 for members of the Virginia assembly and it is likely that Hening had seen this detailed list of Jefferson's collection of printed and manuscript legal documents.

45. TJ to William Waller Hening, 14 Jan. 1807, TJP.

46. 'Manuscripts of the laws sent to Mr Hening, June 1808', in Sowerby, *Catalogue*, 2:258.

47. See William Waller Hening to TJ, 4 Feb. 1807; TJ to William Waller

Hening, 28 Feb. 1807; William Waller Hening to TJ, 7 Feb. 1808; TJ to William Waller Hening, 26 Feb. 1808; William Waller Hening to TJ, 17 May 1808; William Waller Hening to TJ, 24 May 1808; William Waller Hening to TJ, 23 April 1809; William Waller Hening to TJ, 8 July 1809; TJ to William Waller Hening, 25 July 1809; William Waller Hening to TJ, 31 July 1809; TJ to William Waller Hening, 28 Aug. 1809, TJP. Extracts of these letters can be found in Sowerby, *Catalogue*, 2:256–9. For a concise discussion of Jefferson's assistance to Hening see Malone, *Jefferson and His Time*, 6:215–17.

48. William Waller Hening to TJ, 4 Sept. 1809, TJP, emphasis in original.
49. William Waller Hening to TJ, 22 Oct. 1809, TJP. For an example of Hening's corrections to the historical record see William Waller Hening, ed., *The Statutes at Large: Being a Collection of the All of the Laws of Virginia from the First Session on the Legislature in the Year 1619*, 13 vols. (Richmond and Philadelphia: various printers, 1809–23), 1:xii–xiii.
50. TJ to William Waller Hening, 1 Dec. 1809, TJP.
51. Malone, *Jefferson and His Time*, 6:217.
52. TJ to William Waller Hening, 14 Jan. 1807, TJP.
53. John Daly Burk to TJ, 2 Feb. 1803, TJP.
54. For Burk's background see Joseph I. Shulim, 'John Daly Burk, Irish Revolutionist and American Patriot', American Philosophical Society, *Transactions*, New Series, 54 (1964), 3–60; Charles Campbell, ed., *Some Materials to Serve for a Brief Memoir of John Daly Burk* (Albany, NY, 1868); Michael Durey, *Transatlantic Radicals and the Early American Republic* (Lawrence, KS: University Press of Kansas, 1997) and David Wilson, *United Irishmen, United States: Immigrant Radicals in the Early Republic* (Ithaca, NY: Cornell University Press, 1998). For Burk's published writings see his *The Trial of John Burk, of Trinity College, for Heresy and Blasphemy* (Dublin: n.p., 1794); *Bunker-Hill, or The Death of General Warren: An Historic Tragedy in Five Acts* (New York: T. Greenleaf, 1797); *Female Patriotism, or The Death of Joan d'Arc: An Historic Play in V Acts* (New York: Robert M. Hurtin, 1798); *History of the Late War in Ireland: With an Account of the United Irish Association* (Philadelphia: Francis and Robert Bailey, 1798); *An Oration, Delivered on the 4 of March 1803 at the Courthouse in Petersburg* (Petersburg, VA, 1803).
55. John Daly Burk to TJ, 19 June 1801; TJ to John Daly Burk, 21 June 1801, TJP.
56. TJ to John Daly Burk, 21 Feb. 1803, TJP.
57. John Daly Burk to TJ, 26 May 1805; TJ to John Daly Burk, 1 June 1805; TJ to John Page, 2 June 1805; TJ to Thomas Mann Randolph, 2 June 1805, TJP.
58. TJ to John Daly Burk, 1 June 1805, TJP.

59. The fourth and final volume of the history was published in 1816 by
L. H. Girardin. Another man, Skelton Jones, had continued Burk's
history but he, like Burk, was killed in a duel in 1812 before he could
complete the history. John Daly Burk, Skelton Jones and L. H. Girardin,
The History of Virginia from its First Settlement to the Present Day, 4
vols. (Petersburg: Dickson & Pescud, 1804–16); see Chapter 2 below.
Jefferson wrote to Jones in an attempt to recover his newspapers. Jones
reported that they had been returned to John Page and could be
recovered from Page's widow. The newspapers were never found. TJ
to Skelton Jones, 28 July 1809; Skelton Jones to TJ, 17 April 1811, TJP.
During the Civil War Union soldiers plundering the Page family home
discovered a bound volume of the *Virginia Gazette* which may have
been one of Jefferson's lost volumes. See Seth Eyland, *The Evolution of a
Life* (New York: S.W. Green's, 1884), 206.
60. TJ to John Daly Burk, 1 June 1805, TJP.

CHAPTER 2

THE REVOLUTION

I

During his retirement Thomas Jefferson was increasingly preoccupied with the history of the American Revolution and its aftermath. As the years passed and the number of men and women who had lived through the struggle for independence dwindled, Jefferson despaired of preserving the history of the Revolution. In 1815 he wrote to John Adams, 'On the subject of the history of the American Revolution, you ask who shall write it? Who can write it? And who will ever be able to write it? Nobody; except merely its external facts.' This was because 'all it's councils, designs and discussions, having been conducted by Congress with closed doors, and no member, as far as I know, having made notes of them, these which are the soul and life of history must forever be unknown'.[1] A true history of the Revolution would have to be written by a participant or someone with a close knowledge of the major events and people.

For Jefferson, the question of who would write the history of the American Revolution was of more than academic interest. In his mind the fate of the American experiment with republican government was closely linked with the history of its birth. The whiggish interpretation of British history to which Jefferson subscribed taught him that the forces of tyranny constantly sought to subvert liberty. If, as Jefferson believed, David Hume's Tory *History of England* threatened liberty in Britain, what might happen if the Federalists, whom Jefferson often derided as American Tories, wrote the history of the American Revolution? They would appropriate and pervert its legacy and threaten its achievements. Throughout his retirement Jefferson worried that this was occurring. 'We have been too careless of our future reputation,' he lamented in 1823, 'while our tories will omit nothing to place us in the wrong.'[2] To combat this threat Jefferson undertook to promote his version of revolutionary history in a variety of ways. Beginning in the 1780s he encouraged and promoted writers whom he felt would write sound histories of the Revolution. As time passed and he became aware of the danger posed by Federalist historians, he supplied some authors with source materials and information. Ultimately he took up his pen himself and prepared an incendiary history of the early republic to be published after his death in order to set the record straight. In so doing Jefferson sought to safeguard his own posthumous reputation and the legacy of the Revolution from the false and perverted histories promulgated by his Federalist adversaries and personal enemies. For Jefferson the battle over the history of the Revolution was an ongoing political struggle. In many respects it was the most important political battle of his life for, he believed, the future of the United States and, ultimately, the world would be determined by its outcome.

II

Jefferson first demonstrated an interest in promoting the writing of the history of the American Revolution while serving as American minister in Paris during the mid-1780s. As an acknowledged expert on America after the publication of *Notes on the State of Virginia*, he was consulted by some French intellectuals when they wrote about the United States. Jefferson sought to influence the way the French viewed his country and its revolution through the information and advice he provided to writers who sought the benefit of his expertise. These efforts met with mixed success.

During the first half of 1786 Jefferson collaborated with Jean Nicolas DéMeunier, the compiler of the *Encyclopédie méthodique*. Jefferson provided DéMeunier with extensive information relating to the constitutional, political, economic and social development of the United States since independence and may have commented on DéMeunier's draft entries on the United States and Virginia for the section of the *Encyclopédie* entitled *Economie politique et diplomatique*.[3] Jefferson sought to counter the misinformation, inaccuracy and bias that he felt marred earlier entries relating to America in the *Encyclopédie*. William Short, Jefferson's private secretary, wrote of DéMeunier, 'after putting this article under Mr. Jefferson's inspection, he readily struck out and altered the most flagrant errors. It remains at present as different from what he had written it, as to matters of fact, as virtue from vice, and as to reflexions it is changed from censure to eulogy.'[4]

Perhaps inspired by his apparent success in influencing DéMeunier, Jefferson soon undertook to shape the views of another French scholar writing on America. In 1785 François Soulés published a two-volume history of the American Revolution.[5] Jefferson acquired the book, possibly during his visit to London during the spring of 1786. During the summer of 1786, after his successful collaboration with DéMeunier, Jefferson began to compile a list of comments on and corrections to

Soulés' *Histoire*. Sometime during the summer Jefferson met Soulés and learned that the author was planning to bring out a revised and expanded edition of his history. In response Jefferson provided Soulés with notes and comments on the first edition of the *Histoire* in August and September. Jefferson also supplied Soulés with information regarding his efforts to reform the laws of Virginia during the Revolution – including his Bill for Proportioning Crimes and Punishments and his Act for Establishing Religious Freedom – which Soulés incorporated into the fourth volume of the 1787 edition of his work published in Paris. Although Jefferson was able to transform DéMeunier's censure of the United States into a eulogy, he did not enjoy the same success with Soulés, who remained critical of the American experiment with republican government. Soulés focused on the military history of the War of Independence; when he considered post-war American society he concluded that ambition and corruption had undermined the ideals of the Revolution.

Jefferson's experiences with DéMeunier and Soulés suggested that influencing history-writing by dispensing expert advice was an uncertain undertaking. Jefferson could provide such writers with information but he could not guarantee the uses to which they would put his knowledge and opinions.[6] Jefferson always felt that the most successful historians were those who had a personal connection with the people and events about which they wrote. In August 1786, at the time that he was dealing with Soulés, he wrote, 'An author who writes of his own times, or of times near his own, presents in his own ideas and manner the best picture of the moment of which he writes.'[7]

At the same time that he was sharing his expertise on America with Soulés and DéMeunier, Jefferson sought also to promote the works of American writers who had lived through the Revolution. One of the earliest beneficiaries of Jefferson's assistance was the South Carolina physician-turned-historian David Ramsay. During the summer of 1785 Ramsay, who had met Jefferson briefly several years earlier, wrote to the Virginian in Paris and sent him page proofs of his first major historical work, *The History of the Revolution of South-Carolina, from a British Province to an Independent State*, which was soon to be published in Trenton, New Jersey. Ramsay requested Jefferson's assistance in securing the translation and publication of the work in France. Jefferson responded favorably to Ramsay's request. He was pleased with Ramsay's state-centered history, as he welcomed 'special histories of the late revolution which must be written first before a good general one can be expected', and agreed to attempt to find a French publisher to translate, publish and sell the work in Europe. The process took longer than either man expected and the French edition of Ramsay's book, which was a commercial disappointment, did not appear until 1787.[8]

Soon after he arranged for the publication of Ramsay's *History of the Revolution of South-Carolina*, another aspiring historian approached Jefferson for assistance. William Gordon was an English-born dissenting minister who emigrated to Massachusetts in 1770. Soon after arriving in New England, Gordon became pastor of the Third Church in Roxbury and took an active interest in public affairs. He was sympathetic to the whig cause in the run-up to the Revolution and served for a time as chaplain to the Massachusetts Provincial Congress during the War of Independence. Gordon was well acquainted with the leading revolutionary figures in Massachusetts. He returned to England in 1786 and began writing a history of the Revolution. In February, on the suggestion of John Adams, Gordon wrote to Jefferson to request his patronage for his forthcoming history.[9]

Jefferson's response to Gordon was delayed by his trip to southern France and northern Italy during the spring of 1787. However, when he replied in July, he expressed doubts that an English edition of Gordon's history would sell in France, but offered to help to arrange for a French translation of Gordon's history as he had for Ramsay. Although he had not seen any of Gordon's history, Jefferson was optimistic about the project, as he wrote to the minister: 'From the opportunities you have had of coming at facts known as yet to no other historian, from your disposition to relate them fairly, and from your known talents, I have sanguine expectations that your work will be a valuable addition to historical science: and the more so, as we have little yet on the subject of our war which merits respect.' Unfortunately Jefferson's optimism was misplaced. A year later he reported to Gordon that the poor sales of Ramsay's history made it impossible for him to arrange for a French translation of Gordon's work, the first volumes of which had begun to appear. Jefferson cushioned the blow by subscribing to buy six copies of the history and providing Gordon with an account of the 1781 British raid on Monticello that the minister incorporated into his fourth volume.[10]

Thomas Jefferson acted as literary agent for David Ramsay and William Gordon because he believed that they had the skills he sought in historians of the revolution. Both men were sound politically – they had been unwavering supporters of American independence – each was a skilled writer,[11] and, most important, they were well placed to observe the people and events which were central to the Revolution in their locales. As chaplain to the Massachusetts Provincial Congress, Gordon was well connected to the whig elite in Massachusetts, a state that rivaled Jefferson's Virginia in importance in the history of the Revolution. During the war David Ramsay had served in the Continental Army and the South Carolina Assembly. In the early 1780s, while he was preparing his history, Ramsay represented South Carolina in the Confederation

Congress. Jefferson admired the histories of Ramsay and Gordon. He protested on Ramsay's behalf when British publishers proposed editing his history 'in order to accommodate it to the English palate and pride' and praised Gordon's more general account as 'replete with good matter, news, and exact as far as I can judge'.[12]

While Jefferson recognized the importance of historians like Ramsay and Gordon who could bring personal experience and knowledge to their work, he also retained his conviction that the publication and dissemination of primary sources was essential to the historian's enterprise. In consequence he sought to preserve and publish sources relating to the history of the Revolution – as his early support for Ebenezer Hazard's *Historical Collections* indicates. In June 1792 Jefferson received a letter from John Carey, a radical Irish émigré writer. Carey wrote to request permission from Jefferson, then secretary of state, to copy records in Jefferson's office for a proposed edition of the journals of the Continental Congress. Jefferson responded positively, while noting the challenges posed by those papers that, owing to their sensitive nature, could not yet be made public. Jefferson felt that he could not give Carey access to all of the records of the State Department and suggested that Carey provide him with a list of the documents he would like to consult and publish.[13]

By the autumn of 1792 Carey was consulting and copying State Department records with Jefferson's blessing. For example, he copied wartime correspondence between Washington and his generals.[14] Throughout the first half of 1793 Carey and Jefferson corresponded as Carey prepared his documentary collection – and prepared to move to Britain, where he later established himself as a writer and teacher. Jefferson provided the editor with documents and advice. When Carey left for Britain Jefferson sent his documentary copies ('about 12 or 13 packets') under diplomatic cover to the American ambassador in London, Thomas Pinckney. Carey's project evolved from a published edition of the journals of the Continental Congress to a collection of letters between George Washington and the Congress. It was published in two volumes in London in 1795.[15]

Carey's collection was one of the earliest collections of published American state papers. As official documents, the letters often related to wartime diplomacy and other confidential matters. Jefferson and Carey developed a system for dealing with sensitive material. Carey submitted his copies to Jefferson, who examined them for passages that he judged should be kept secret. Jefferson identified questionable passages and sent them to President Washington for his opinion. Carey and Jefferson seem to have differed somewhat as to the criteria they employed to exclude material from the collection. According to Carey, Jefferson advocated omitting 'everything which might at the present day, have an unpleasing tendency', that is any matter that might be controversial. Jefferson claimed to be more inclusive. He wrote: 'tho' there were passages which might on publication create uneasiness in the minds of some, & were therefore referred by me to the President, yet I concurred fully in the opinion he pronounced that as these things were true they ought to be known.' Undoubtedly there was a tension between the editor and Jefferson as the source of the documents that Carey sought to publish.

Jefferson claimed to be guided by a principle of openness. 'To render history what it ought to be,' he wrote, 'the whole truth should be known. I am no friend to mystery & state secrets. They serve generally only to conceal the errors & rogueries of those who govern.'[16] During his retirement Jefferson developed a strategy to expose the 'errors & rogueries' of his political enemies that involved the judicious publication of secret material.

III

Despite Jefferson's 1815 lament to Adams, by the early nineteenth century there were numerous histories of the American Revolution available in several languages, such as those by Ramsay and Gordon, Mercy Otis Warren's *History of the Rise, Progress, and Termination of the American Revolution* (1805) and notable histories of individual states. Jefferson was reasonably satisfied with historical accounts of the War of Independence. A year before complaining to Adams about the difficulties the Revolution posed to historians he recommended David Ramsay's *History of the American Revolution* despite the moderate federalism that imbued it. Ramsay argued that the primary lesson to be derived from the War of Independence was the need for a strong national government. This was an interpretation that Jefferson did not take exception to. Almost twenty years earlier Jefferson included Ramsay in a list of scholars he deemed 'respectable characters worthy of confidence as to any facts they may state, and rendered, by their good sense, good judges of them'.[17]

Jefferson was not satisfied, however, with the historical accounts of the period after the ratification of the Constitution. This was a politically contentious era which witnessed the rise of intense political partisanship and in which he played a crucial role as secretary of state and leader of the nascent Republican party. Historical accounts of this period had implications for the future of the republic as they would influence how the public and posterity viewed the parties. Jefferson believed that the fate of the republic itself depended on the historiographical battle between those writers who were sympathetic to the Federalists and those who sympathized with Jefferson's Republicans. He worried that, despite their apparent political decline during the early nineteenth century, the Federalists were winning the intellectual war over the history of the early republic. As a consequence Jefferson sought to promote a republican history as a matter of political necessity.

In May 1802 President Jefferson attempted to recruit the writer Joel Barlow to write a history of the early republic. 'Mr. Madison and myself have cut out a piece of work for you,' wrote Jefferson, 'which is to write the history of the United States, from the close of the War downwards. We are rich ourselves in materials, and can open all the public archives to you; but your residence here is essential, because a great deal of the knowledge of things is not on paper, but only within ourselves for verbal communication.' Barlow would have access to the president, to his closest ally and to their papers. Time was of the essence, Jefferson warned, because Federalist Supreme Court Justice 'John Marshall is writing the life of Gen. Washington from his papers. It is intended to come out just in time to influence the next presidential election. It is written therefore principally with a view to electioneering purposes; but it will consequently be out in time to aid you with information as well as to point out the perversions of truth necessary to be rectified.'[18] Barlow, who was *en route* to Europe, declined Jefferson's invitation.

Jefferson's fear that Marshall's book might influence the 1804 election was unfounded. The first of Marshall's five-volume *Life of George Washington* appeared in the election year but did not have any discernible impact on the presidential contest, which Jefferson won handily. More than a biography of Washington, Marshall's book offered a panoramic view of American history from the advent of European settlement until the end of the eighteenth century. Marshall's first volume presented a history of colonial British America from the voyages of John Cabot down to the Seven Years' War. His second, third and fourth volumes, published in 1804 and 1805, dealt with the War of Independence. The fifth volume, which appeared in 1807, considered the history of the United States from the end of the revolutionary war until Washington's death in 1799.[19]

The first four volumes of Marshall's history were relatively uncontroversial. Like David Ramsay, Marshall stressed the importance of public virtue, national unity and the need for a strong government as the major lessons to be derived from the history of colonial and revolutionary America. For Jefferson, Marshall's fifth volume, which dealt with Washington's presidency and the contentious politics of the 1790s, was problematic. At the outset of the volume Marshall explained the partisan differences between the Federalists and Republicans that beset Washington's administration:

The continent was divided into two great political parties, the one which contemplated America as a nation, and laboured incessantly to invest the federal head with powers competent to the preservation of the union. The other attached itself to the state authorities, viewed all the powers of congress with jealousy; and assented reluctantly to measures which would enable the head to act, in any respect, independently of the members. Men of enlarged and liberal minds . . . arranged themselves generally in the first party.[20]

According to Marshall's interpretation, the Federalists were enlightened and reasonable nationalists who sought to create a competent, credible and stable government in the face of the petty parochialism of the Republicans, who would have preferred anarchy to good government.

Later in his fifth volume, Marshall drew an unfavorable contrast between Jefferson as the leader of the Republicans and the Federalist leader Alexander Hamilton. Marshall argued that Hamilton's experiences as a soldier and congressman taught him that the 'imbecility of the government' under the Articles of Confederation imperiled the United States. 'Mr. Hamilton', wrote Marshall, 'was the friend of a government which should possess in itself sufficient powers and resources to maintain the character and defend the integrity of the nation.'[21] According to Marshall, Hamilton intended his fiscal programs during the 1790s to foster a strong government that would guarantee the prosperity and stability of the United States. According to this view Hamilton's policies would safeguard the American republic and the legacy of the Revolution.

Thomas Jefferson, by contrast, did not fare so well at Marshall's hands. According to Marshall, Jefferson had had little experience of the weakness of the national government during the War of Independence. Although Jefferson had served in Congress, he had done so early in the war before financial problems had threatened the success of the American rebellion. After that his experiences were confined to state government. During the Confederation era Jefferson was abroad representing the United States:

while the people of France were taking the primary steps of that immense revolution which has astonished and agitated two-quarters of the world. In common with all his countrymen, he took a strong interest in favour of the reformers; residing at that court, and associating with those who meditated some of the great events which have since taken place, his mind might be warmed with the abuses of the monarchy which were perpetually in his view, and he might be led to the opinion that liberty could sustain no danger but from the executive power. Mr. Jefferson therefore seems to have entertained no apprehensions from the debility of the government; no

jealousy of the state sovereignties; and no suspicion of their encroach-
ments. His fears took a different direction, and all the precautions were
used to check and limit the exercise of the authorities claimed by the
government of the United States. Neither could he perceive danger to
liberty except from the constituted authorities, and especially from the
executive.

Marshall's Jefferson, infected by his sympathy for the French Revolution,
was a lukewarm supporter of the Constitution: 'He did not feel so
sensibly as those who had continued in the United States the necessity
of adopting the constitution' and, by implication, the Revolution to which
he had contributed so much. Jefferson's fear of executive power (according to Marshall he opposed the eligibility of the president for re-election)
can be seen as criticism of the all-popular George Washington.[22]

Although Marshall's history did not prevent Jefferson's own re-election
as president, Jefferson's apprehension about the long-term influence of
Marshall's biography was justified. Marshall's *Life of George Washington* received critical acclaim and a wide readership. The first American
edition sold more than 7,000 copies and was followed by a British
edition, as well as translations into French, German and Dutch.[23] As
we have seen, for Jefferson all history had political implications. This was
particularly true of the history of post-revolutionary America. Jefferson
believed that Hume's history had the power to corrupt British politics and
threaten the stability of the American republic. Similarly, Marshall's
history could undermine the American experiment with republican
government. It could not go unchallenged: the stakes in the battle over
history were too high. As Joanne Freeman has written, 'To Jefferson, it
was a critical fight, for Marshall's false history threatened to corrupt the
future by misinterpreting the past.'[24]

For Jefferson one of the problems posed by *The Life of George
Washington* was its quasi-official nature. John Marshall cooperated
closely with Washington's heir, Bushrod Washington, who allowed
the jurist access to Washington's papers in preparing his biography.
According to Jefferson, Marshall used the papers selectively, giving
greater emphasis to letters sent *to* Washington than to those written
by him. *The Life of George Washington* epitomized the difficulties posed
by primary sources. Although Jefferson recognized that such sources must
be the basis of history, in the wrong hands (such as Marshall's) primary
sources could be manipulated to distort history in a dangerous fashion.
Marshall's use of the documents with the blessing of Bushrod Washington, whose name appeared on the title page of Marshall's book, seemed
to give Washington's posthumous imprimatur to *The Life of George
Washington* and its interpretations.[25]

There was no equivalent of John Baxter's corrected version of Hume to act as an antidote to the poison of Marshall's history. Jefferson undertook to provide one. He attempted to make page-by-page corrections to Marshall's fifth volume but gave up after three extensive corrections because of the impracticality of such an approach and the magnitude of the project.[26] In April 1811 Jefferson again wrote to Joel Barlow inviting him to write a history to counter Marshall. 'What is to become of our Post-revolutionary history?' Jefferson enquired, 'of the antidotes of truth to the misrepresentations of Marshall?'[27] Barlow, whom James Madison had appointed to represent the United States in Paris in 1811, again declined Jefferson's request. Frustrated but undeterred, Jefferson concluded that a more substantial work was necessary to counter Marshall's account.

Between 1809 and 1818 Jefferson decided to prepare a documentary collection of his papers as secretary of state. While public papers and official documents would make up the majority of items in the collection, these would be supplemented by Jefferson's private notes and memoranda containing critical information on events and people. During the period when he was compiling his documentary collection Jefferson wrote to William Wirt, a Virginia lawyer who was preparing a biography of Patrick Henry and had sought Jefferson's advice:

> It is truly unfortunate that those engaged in public affairs so rarely make notes of transactions passing within their knowledge. Hence history becomes fable instead of fact. The great outlines may be true, but the incidents and coloring are according to the faith or fancy of the writer. Had Judge Marshall taken half your pains in sifting and scrutinizing facts, he would not have given to the world, as true history, a false copy of a record under his eye.[28]

Jefferson had kept such notes and he would preserve them for posterity in order to challenge Judge Marshall's 'fable'. By February 1818 Jefferson had edited and arranged the selections of his public and private papers in three large manuscript volumes which he had bound in marbled paper. These are usually referred to as 'The Anas' although this is not a title Jefferson used. He wrote an introduction in which he explained his method in compiling the collection:

> In these volumes will be found copies of the official opinions given in writing by me to General Washington while I was Secretary of State, with sometimes the documents belonging to the case. Some of these are the rough draughts, some press copies, some fair ones. In the earlier part of my acting in that office, I took no other note of the passing transactions; but

after awhile I saw the importance of doing it in the aid of my memory. Very often, therefore, I made memorandums on loose scraps of paper, taken out of my pocket in the moment and laid by to be copied fair at leisure, which, however, they hardly ever were. These scraps, therefore, ragged, rubbed, and scribbled as they were, I had bound with the others by a binder who came into my cabinet, doing it under my own eye, and without the opportunity of reading a single paper. At this day, after a lapse of twenty five years or more, from their dates, I have given the whole a calm revisal, when the passions of the time are passed away, and the reasons of the transactions act alone on the judgment. Some of the informations I had recorded are now cut out from the rest, because I have seen that they were incorrect or doubtful, or merely personal or private, with which we have nothing to do. I should perhaps have thought the rest not worth preserving, but for their testimony, against the only history of that period which pretends to have been compiled from authentic and unpublished documents.[29]

Jefferson believed that history must be based on primary sources. Moreover, given that, as he had written to John Adams in 1815, private notes were the 'soul and life' of history, Jefferson supplemented the official documents and state papers with his own personal memoranda. Just as he believed that John Baxter could 'republicanize' Hume's *History of England* and mitigate against its negative influence, Jefferson's Anas would answer the unfair and dangerous interpretations advanced by Marshall.

Jefferson's efforts at history-writing did not cease with the compilation of his papers as secretary of state. Between January and July 1821 he wrote a memoir usually referred to as his autobiography. Jefferson stated at the outset that he wrote the autobiography 'for my own more ready reference & for the information of my family'.[30] Nonetheless, the work is more concerned with Jefferson's public life and times than with his experiences as private figure and family man. For example, early in the autobiography Jefferson challenged the view that Massachusetts played a leading role in the establishment of committees of correspondence.

The origination of these commees of correspondence between the colonies has been since claimed for Massachusetts and Marshall II. 151 has given into this error, altho' the very note of his appendix to which he refers, shows that their establmt was confined to their own towns. This matter will be seen clearly stated in the letter of Samuel Adams Wells to me of Apr. 2, 1819, and my answer of May 12. I was corrected by the letter Mr. Wells in the information I had given Mr. Wirt, as stated in his note, pa. 87, that the messengers of Massach. & Virga crossed each other on the way bearing similar propositions, for Mr. Wells shows that Mass. did not adopt the measure but on the receipt of our proposn delivered at their next session.[31]

Jefferson's handling of the relatively small matter of whether credit for the creation of the committees of correspondence belonged to Virginia or Massachusetts is instructive both as to his historical method and the purpose behind his autobiography. Jefferson addressed an error in the historiography – the crediting of Massachusetts authorities with the creation of the committees of correspondence – that appeared in the works of Marshall and William Wirt by resorting to the primary sources. He refers to Samuel Adams Wells's 1819 letter to claim pride of place for Virginia. The passage, with its references to the secondary and primary literature, suggests that Jefferson intended the autobiography to reach an audience far wider than his family.

Jefferson's autobiography is usually read as an incomplete fragment as it takes his life down to 1790, when he returned from France and took up his post as secretary of state. Rather than as a separate work, the autobiography should be seen as an extended introduction to the Anas.[32] As such, the autobiography and the documentary history should be read in conjunction. Together they provide a coherent, didactic history of the Revolution and early republic that advances a republican interpretation of events. The autobiography and the manuscript volumes presented a counter-narrative to Marshall's false history.

In the autobiography Jefferson clearly asserted his revolutionary credentials. He provided a detailed account of his authorship of the *Summary View of the Rights of British America* as well as his experiences in the Virginia Assembly and the Continental Congress. He paid particular attention to the debate over the Declaration of Independence as well as his role in drafting the Declaration. He supplemented his account with his own contemporaneous notes of the debates and his draft of the Declaration, 'as originally reported. The parts struck out by Congress shall be distinguished by a black line drawn under them; & those inserted by them shall be placed in the margin or in a concurrent column.'[33] By claiming authorship of the Declaration in his autobiography Jefferson asserted a central place in the history of the American Revolution. Such a claim refuted the jibes of Marshall and other critics that Jefferson's contribution to the Revolution had been marginal.[34]

Congress having declared, in Jefferson's words, that all men were created equal, legal and constitutional reform was necessary to make this so. Soon after Congress adopted the Declaration of Independence, Jefferson returned to Virginia to assist in rewriting the state's constitution

and legal code. He continued his autobiography with a lengthy account
of his own contributions to legal reform in his home state. This was a
laborious undertaking in which Jefferson took justifiable pride. He
sought to rewrite the laws in order to eliminate inherited privilege and
was especially satisfied with the bills to abolish entail and primogeniture
as the basis of inheritance, as well as the bill to establish religious freedom
which disestablished the Anglican Church. In his autobiography he wrote
of the bill to abolish entail:

> To annul this privilege, instead of an aristocracy of wealth, of more harm
> and danger, than benefit, to society, to make an opening for the aris-
> tocracy of virtue and talent, which nature has wisely provided for the
> direction of the interests of society & scattered with equal hand through all
> it's conditions, was deemed essential to a well-ordered republic. To effect it
> no violence was necessary, no deprivation of natural right, but rather an
> enlargement of it by a repeal of the law. For this would authorize the
> present holder to divide the property among his children equally, as his
> affections were divided; and would place them, by natural generation on
> the level of their fellow citizens.[35]

Having provided Congress with the language to declare Americans free
and equal, Jefferson sought to remove the legal barriers that prevented an
'aristocracy of virtue and talent' from rising in revolutionary America.

The bulk of Jefferson's autobiography concerns his years in Europe as a
diplomat representing the new American republic during the 1780s.
Owing to his service as a diplomat, Jefferson did not attend the Constitutional Convention during the summer of 1787. According to his
autobiography, Jefferson supported the Constitution as a necessary reform, but was anxious about its lack of a Bill of Rights to safeguard
individual liberty. It was for this reason that he originally concluded that
nine states should ratify the document and four should reject it – a
position that Marshall criticized. Jefferson further explained that,
although he feared the perpetual re-election of the president and preferred
one seven-year term, he was satisfied with the precedent set by 1821 that
presidents retired after two terms in office.[36]

During his tenure abroad Jefferson witnessed the early stages of the
French Revolution. According to Marshall's history Jefferson's experience of the last days of *ancien régime* had taught him of the dangers posed
by absolute monarchy, but not of the consequences of a weak central
government, such as had beset the United States prior to the adoption
of the Constitution, while Jefferson was abroad. In his autobiography,
Jefferson countered this claim by arguing that the two revolutions
were related. Whereas Marshall, like other Federalists, saw the French

Revolution as a dangerous deviation from the principles of the American Revolution, Jefferson viewed the two revolutions as distinct, but related, aspects in a global republican movement to expand human liberty. Jefferson saw his efforts at promoting and writing the history of the American Revolution as a crucial contribution to that movement.

If read as an account of Thomas Jefferson's life, the autobiography appears to be an incomplete fragment as it focuses on its subject's public career down to 1790, neglecting his contributions as secretary of state, vice president, president and leader of the Republican party. However, as previously noted, the autobiography is best read as an extended introduction to the Anas.[37] Jefferson takes the story to 1790 because his documentary history begins with his assuming the office of secretary of state. As such the 'autobiography' actually presents a coherent introduction to the documentary history. It shows Jefferson to have been a prime mover of the revolution – an early advocate of independence who articulated the core principles of republican revolution before seeking to enshrine those principals in law. Jefferson then went abroad to represent the interests of the new republic and was able to witness, and understand, the beginning of the revolution in France as the next step in a global movement to expand human liberty. As an introduction to Jefferson's documentary history of the Washington administration, the autobiography presents a world divided between those who supported the irresistible movement for republican government and expanded human liberty and those who opposed it. The autobiography showed that Jefferson was an early and fervent supporter of republicanism. The Anas would show that some of the most prominent leaders of the United States were not.

According to Jefferson's documentary history of the Washington administration as presented in the Anas, the Federalists, especially Alexander Hamilton, were incipient monarchists intent on subverting America's republican experiment for their own benefit. Jefferson contended that Hamilton sought through his financial policies to foster corruption and dependence within the government and allow the secretary of the treasury to control the government and promote monarchism. Jefferson described how the system worked in his introduction to the Anas:

> I know well, and so must be understood, that nothing like a majority in Congress had yielded to this corruption. Far from it. But a division, not very unequal, had already taken place in the honest part of that body, between the parties styled republican and federal. The latter being monarchists in principle, adhered to Hamilton of course, as their leader in that principle, and this mercenary phalanx added to them, insured him always a majority in both Houses: so that the whole action of the legislature was now under the direction of the Treasury.[38]

As evidence Jefferson related an anecdote from a dinner he had had with Hamilton and John Adams in 1791. Adams, according to Jefferson, said of the British constitution, 'purge that constitution of its corruption and give to its popular branch equality of representation, and it would be the most perfect constitution ever devised by the wit of man'. Hamilton declared such changes would make Britain ungovernable and that, complete with its corruption and undemocratic features, the British constitution was 'the most perfect government which ever existed'. Jefferson concluded that Hamilton's preferred system of government was 'an hereditary King, with a House of Lords and Commons corrupted to his will, and standing between him and the people'.[39]

According to Jefferson the republican opposition that coalesced in opposition to Hamilton's fiscal policies were the true heirs to the Revolution and the avatars of liberty in the United States. He wrote:

> Here then was the real ground of the opposition which was made to the course of the administration. Its object was to preserve the legislature pure and independent of the executive, to restrain the administration to republican forms and principles, and not permit the constitution to be construed into a monarchy, and to be warped, in practice, into all the principles and pollutions of their favorite English model.[40]

According to this interpretation, the Republicans, led by Jefferson within the administration and James Madison in Congress, sought to defend and uphold the Constitution in the face of Hamilton's attempts to subvert the law and impose monarchical rule on the United States. For the Republicans, the struggle to maintain liberty continued during Jefferson's presidency and beyond so it was crucial to write a correct account of their origins.

Jefferson was careful to distinguish between the monarchical designs of Hamilton and the extreme Federalists, on the one hand, and the views of President Washington, probably the most popular and influential man in America during his lifetime and the nominal leader of the Federalists as well as the leader of the country, on the other hand. Jefferson asserted that the Republicans were opposed to the political, economic and social objectives of Hamilton, not to President Washington. He wrote:

> Nor was this an opposition to General Washington. He was true to the republican charge confided to him; and has solemnly and repeatedly protested to me, in our conversations, that he would lose the last drop of his blood in support of it; and he did this the oftener and with the more earnestness, because he knew my suspicions of Hamilton's designs against it, and wished to quiet them. For he was not aware of the drift, or of the

effect of Hamilton's schemes. Unversed in financial projects and calculations and budgets, his approbation of them was bottomed on his confidence in the man.[41]

For Jefferson, Washington was loyal to the principles of republican government. His only fault was in trusting Hamilton and failing to appreciate the political implications of his fiscal program. In challenging Hamilton, Jefferson, a member of Washington's cabinet of course, endeavored to show that he was not being disloyal to Washington.

Jefferson's relationship with Washington is a central theme of the Anas. Jefferson was careful to present himself as a loyal servant and friend of the president who steadfastly attempted to convince Washington of the threat posed by Hamilton. In a typical passage he records a conversation with the president that took place on 1 October 1792 at Washington's home at Mount Vernon. According to Jefferson, Washington sought to convince Jefferson, who wanted to resign as secretary of state, to stay in his administration: 'he thought it important to preserve the check of my opinions in the Administration in order to keep things in their proper channel and prevent them from going too far'. Washington then expressed regret at the deteriorating relationship between Jefferson and Hamilton. The president sought to reassure Jefferson, 'That as to the idea of transforming this Government into a monarchy, he did not believe there were ten men in the United States whose opinions were worth attention, who entertained such a thought'. Jefferson dissented and told the president that there were more monarchists than he suspected, including Hamilton, and he reported that Hamilton had told him that the Constitution 'was a shilly shally thing, of mere milk and water, which could not last, and was only a step to something better'. Washington attempted to point out the benefits of Hamilton's fiscal system and enjoined Jefferson not to resign. Before they could resolve their difference of opinion, the two men were called to breakfast.[42]

This conversation, recorded by Jefferson on his way back to Philadelphia that afternoon, is typical of the private memoranda Jefferson inserted into the Anas. It advanced the overall theme of the work – that Jefferson fought to maintain republican values in the face of the monarchical threat posed by Hamilton and the arch-Federalists. It made a distinction between Washington and Hamilton. Although it suggested that Washington was misguided in trusting Hamilton, the implication of the conversation was that Washington in no way sympathized with the object of transforming the United States into a monarchy. Finally it demonstrated that Jefferson was a trusted confidant of the president. This was crucial since Marshall's distorted and inaccurate history purported to be based on Washington's papers and showed Jefferson to be out of step with the president.

Taken together, the documents now known as Jefferson's autobiography and the Anas – the complete version of the latter, that is the personal memoranda interspersed among Jefferson's public papers and letters as secretary of state – constitute a major work of history by Jefferson. Although its main themes are political, Jefferson's history is not a simple work of political propaganda. Jefferson was a serious student of history. While he felt that history must teach the appropriate lessons – and his history sought to promote republicanism to counter the incipient monarchism of the Federalists – he also believed that it must be based on the appropriate primary sources. These linked concerns explain the care with which Jefferson compiled his history. It is not a scholarly history such as David Ramsay's, but rather a didactic rough draft intended to advance Jefferson's version of events and lead future scholars to reach the correct (Jefferson's) conclusions when writing a history of the early republic. In so doing it would serve to promote Jeffersonian republicanism in the future by safeguarding its place in the nation's past.

Jefferson did not publish his carefully crafted history. In April 1796 he had written a private letter to a friend and former neighbor, Philip Mazzei, who was then living in Pisa. The letter contained comments critical of George Washington and the Federalists. Mazzei allowed for the controversial passages to be translated and published in a French newspaper, the *Gazette nationale ou Le Moniteur universel*, in January 1797. American newspapers, especially Federalist newspapers, retranslated and published the letter beginning in May 1797. Jefferson, who had written the letter after his resignation as secretary of state and thus as a private citizen, was serving as vice president when the letter appeared in the American press. The ensuing controversy contributed to the estrangement of Washington and Jefferson, and fueled intensely partisan attacks against Jefferson and the Republicans.[43] Jefferson, who had always been reluctant to appear in print, was badly bruised by this affair. The letter was used by Jefferson's personal and political enemies throughout his life and beyond to question Jefferson's loyalty to Washington, the Constitution and the Revolution. Merrill Peterson wrote of the 'Mazzei Letter' that 'No single writing from Jefferson's pen pursued him so remorselessly beyond the grave'.[44] In light of this experience Jefferson did not intend to publish his incendiary secret history of the Washington administration. Rather he put aside his autobiography and the documents for posthumous publication.

In his will Jefferson left all of his papers to his grandson, Thomas Jefferson Randolph. In 1829 Randolph brought out a four-volume selection which he had selected and arranged, entitled *Memoirs, Correspondence and Private Papers of Thomas Jefferson*.[45] Randolph disrupted Jefferson's carefully crafted history when he edited his grandfather's papers. As a result the autobiography and the Anas were separated. The autobiography, identified as Jefferson's memoir, was published at the beginning of the first volume. Randolph also unbound Jefferson's collection of manuscripts that comprised his documentary history of the Washington administration. He excluded the public documents and extracted the private memoranda which he published as an appendix to his fourth volume under the title of 'Anas', Latin for table-talk or gossip – the name by which they are still generally known. Randolph edited the Anas so as to remove the most stinging criticism of John Marshall – who in 1829 was still serving as chief justice of the United States. Despite these efforts, the publication of the Anas stirred immediate controversy. Jefferson's posthumous attack on some of the leading Federalists – among the foremost of the Founding Fathers – was shocking and controversial. Although Jefferson's reputation suffered somewhat as a result of the publication, his history served its purpose. The Federalists, a spent political force by 1829, were discredited and Jefferson's interpretation of the origins of the republic gained primacy during the Jacksonian era and persisted throughout the nineteenth century and well into the twentieth. Politicians and historians for many years were drawn to Jefferson's *Memoirs*, even though they presented a garbled version of his original documentary history, as an important source for the history of the early republic.[46] They were not the only source, however. Eight editions of John Marshall's *Life of George Washington* were published in the United States during the nineteenth and twentieth centuries. These included a popular two-volume abridgement for schools first published in 1838 and republished in 2000. The contest between Jefferson and Marshall before the bar of history continued long after both men died. Prior to his death, Jefferson fought a much more personal battle to protect his reputation. This too was with another Virginian – Henry Lee – and it also concerned Jefferson's place in history.[47]

IV

On 26 August 1824 Henry Lee, the son of the revolutionary war general of the same name ('Light Horse Harry' Lee) wrote to Thomas Jefferson. The younger Lee informed Jefferson that he had 'a desire to affect immortality as a writer, & feel inclined to direct my pen into the spending work of biography'. As subjects Lee proposed to write biographies of leading Virginians including James Madison, John Marshall, James Monroe and Thomas Jefferson. He wrote to request Jefferson's support for the project and to seek access to any relevant papers Jefferson might possess. Jefferson responded immediately. He declared on 6 September 'I possess no such materials. I have gone thro' life acting as well as I could, without taking account of what I did. The fact is that men fully engaged in business have no time to take notes of it; and it is a circumstance which prevents history from being written by those who know it's details.' Nothing could be further from the truth. As we have seen, Jefferson had kept extensive private notes that he had recently organized for future publication. Further, Jefferson kept meticulous track of the letters he wrote and received. Moreover, as we have seen, Jefferson had long been in the habit of assisting writers and scholars. Why, then, did he deceive Lee? Jefferson feared the treatment he would receive at Lee's hands. His concern proved to be well founded.[48]

In 1812 Light Horse Harry Lee published a book, *Memoirs of the War in the Southern Department*, which recounted his experiences during the War of Independence. The elder Lee was a successful soldier who had fought in the campaigns in New York, New Jersey and Pennsylvania in 1776. He spent the latter part of the war in the southern theater, serving with distinction under Nathanael Greene in the Carolinas. After the war Lee became a staunch Federalist. He had a poor head for business and was jailed for debt in Virginia in 1808–9. While in the Orange County jail he wrote his memoirs. The decline in Lee's fortunes coincided with the decline in the Federalist Party. Charles Royster has shown that Lee blamed the Republicans – especially Jefferson – for his struggles in the post-war world. He expressed his antipathy in his memoirs, castigating Jefferson's leadership as governor of Virginia in 1780 and 1781 when the British invaded the state.[49]

The British sent two expeditionary forces to invade Virginia while Jefferson was serving as governor: in December and January of 1780–1 and in May–June 1781. The first raid, commanded by Benedict Arnold, captured the new state capital, Richmond, forcing Jefferson and the legislature to flee. The following summer the infamous Banastre Tarleton led a raid on Charlottesville. Tarleton dispatched a force to Monticello to capture Jefferson, who fled a few minutes before the British arrived. Dumas Malone, Jefferson's most sympathetic and thorough biographer, concedes that the British attacks on Virginia were the lowest point in Jefferson's public life.[50]

Henry Lee sharply criticized Jefferson's leadership during the War of Independence. According to Lee, despite the substantial resources at his command, Jefferson failed to prepare the state's defenses adequately. Lee suggested that Jefferson was responsible for the British capture of Richmond and implied that he was guilty of cowardice when he fled from Monticello. In the manuscript version of the memoir, when Lee described the 'disgraces and distresses' that resulted from Jefferson's failure to defend the state, he scribbled a note to his copyist in the margin: 'Take care how you copy here'. Lee intended that his criticism should harm Jefferson's reputation. In so doing he sought to undermine Jefferson's political legacy as well. As Charles Royster has written, 'For Jefferson as for Lee, American history's central question was, Which Americans had won the Revolutionary War? Implicit in the question lay the assumption that the answer would determine who had the best claim to preserve and govern the republic.' By discrediting Jefferson personally as an incompetent coward, Lee could discredit the Republicans politically, thereby leading to a revival of the Federalists.[51]

Jefferson could not allow Lee's criticism to go unanswered. He would not, however, engage with Lee directly. Rather, he recruited surrogates to put his case before the public. This strategy served several purposes. In the first place, as noted above, Jefferson was very reluctant under any circumstances to appear in print engaging in public disputes. As a rule, he did not respond publicly to attacks and criticism. Second, if, as a former president and a notable figure (with a far greater public profile than Henry Lee), he publicly answered Lee's criticisms he would do much to amplify Lee's charges against him. Finally, both he and Lee appreciated that they were addressing an audience far broader than the American public in 1812. They were contesting before posterity. With this in view, works written by apparently objective third party authors would carry more weight than personal, *ad hominem* attacks of the kind produced by Lee.

In response to Lee's charges, Jefferson recruited a French émigré, Louis H. Girardin, to complete John Daly Burk's unfinished history of Virginia. At the time of Burk's death the Irishman had taken the story down to 1775. By recruiting Girardin, Jefferson could see to it that a work to which he had previously given extensive support was completed. In so doing he would not appear to be promoting the writing of a work specifically intended to answer Lee's criticisms – though it was intended to serve just such a purpose. Girardin lived near Monticello while he researched and wrote his history. In his preface Girardin acknowledged his debt: 'During my residence in the vicinity of Monticello, I enjoyed the incalculable benefit of a free access to Mr. Jefferson's Library; and as his historical collection was no less valuable than extensive, that happy circumstance proved of infinite service to my undertaking.'[52] Girardin's account of Jefferson's actions as governor during the British invasions was all that Jefferson could have wished. According to Girardin's account, Jefferson had done all that could be reasonably expected to defend Virginia, especially Richmond, from attack, but the Continental Congress had not provided him with enough resources to do so successfully. In his telling of the attack on Charlottesville and Monticello, Girardin noted that Jefferson's priority had been to safeguard his family, which he did by sending them to a neighboring plantation. Jefferson himself escaped only ten minutes before the British arrived. Girardin provided a lengthy appendix reviewing Jefferson's career as a war governor which included extracts from Jefferson's diary suggesting that he responded to the British invasion conscientiously and vigorously. He noted that Jefferson's conduct was subsequently investigated by the Virginia Assembly which vindicated the governor's actions. Jefferson was satisfied with Girardin's account. He did not discuss the controversy over his governorship in his autobiography except to say that Girardin 'had free access to all my papers while composing it, and has given as faithful an account as I could myself. For this portion therefore of my own life, I refer altogether to his history.'[53]

Jefferson was not content to have Girardin answer Henry Lee's charges against him. He also sought to discredit Lee. To that end he recruited a political ally, Supreme Court Justice William Johnson of South Carolina (whom Jefferson had named to the court), to write a history of the southern theater in the War of Independence. Johnson's book, *Sketches of the Life and Correspondence of Nathanael Greene*, appeared in 1822. It gave the lion's share of the credit for the rebel victory in the South to Nathanael Greene and downplayed the contributions of Henry Lee. Jefferson was satisfied with the work and encouraged Johnson to pursue further historical research and to write a history of the development of the political parties in the United States that would show that the Republicans had been loyal supporters of the Constitution in the face of the monarchical tendencies of the Federalists. Jefferson offered Johnson access to all of his papers – including his documentary history – should he wish to undertake the project.[54]

Jefferson effectively countered the charges made by Henry Lee through his use of surrogates. Girardin first addressed the charges made by Lee concerning Jefferson's performance as a war governor. Subsequently William Johnson undermined Lee's own war record and, consequently, his credibility as Jefferson's critic. Jefferson's indirect counter-attacks did not go unanswered. General Henry Lee died in 1818. His son, however, took up the challenge posed to his father's reputation by Jefferson. In 1824 he published a lengthy critique of William Johnson's book. In defending his father, Lee largely ignored Jefferson and concentrated his attack on Johnson. Lee focused on the factual and interpretive errors he felt marred Johnson's analysis. In so doing he did not need to consider Jefferson – who did not really figure in Johnson's book – because his objective was to undermine Johnson's credibility and so discredit his analysis.[55]

The younger Henry Lee sent a copy of his critique of Johnson's book to Thomas Jefferson. This initiated a remarkable series of letters between the two men that focused on the history of the American Revolution, including Lee's request to use Jefferson's papers to write a biography of his father's adversary. In May 1826, two months before Jefferson's death, Lee informed the former president that he intended to publish a new edition of his father's memoirs. Jefferson responded by suggesting that Lee edit the portions of the memoirs relating to the invasions of Virginia since General Lee was in South Carolina at the time and had no first-hand knowledge of the situation in Virginia in 1780–1. Jefferson provided a detailed account of the invasion, which he must have hoped that Lee would include in the second edition, and he recommended that Lee consult Girardin's history. A few weeks before Jefferson's death Lee came to Monticello, at Jefferson's invitation, and the two men discussed the events of 1781 in detail.[56]

Light Horse Harry Lee and Thomas Jefferson died in 1818 and 1826 respectively. Their historiographical duel continued after their deaths. Although Jefferson had hoped that he could convince the younger Lee to excise the unflattering references to his governorship in the second edition of General Lee's memoirs, he was unsuccessful. The younger Lee published the second edition of his father's memoirs in 1827 complete with the passages that Jefferson found objectionable.[57] Two years later Thomas Mann Randolph published Jefferson's *Memoirs, Correspondence and Private Papers*, which contained unflattering references to General Lee including an 1815 letter from Jefferson to James Monroe referring to Lee's memoirs as 'the romances of his historical novel, for the amusement of credulous and uninquisitive readers'.[58] In response the younger Lee published an extensive, vituperative critique of Jefferson's *Memoirs* which presented Jefferson as an unprincipled, dishonorable coward.[59]

V

The image of the dying Jefferson vainly trying to charm the younger Henry Lee in the weeks before his death is poignant testimony to Jefferson's faith in the importance of history. Jefferson believed in the power of history to shape the political and social development of the United States; that is why he devoted so much energy and effort to shaping and writing the history of the Revolution and early republic. It was vital, in his mind, that the lies and distortions of Federalist historians such as John Marshall and Henry Lee be countered and corrected so that a true history could be written to teach future generations that the Republicans had preserved liberty and republican government in the United States from the monarchical ambitions of the Federalists.

Thomas Jefferson's reputation was closely linked to the history wars of the early republic. It depended on the success and survival of Jeffersonian republicanism, which in turn traced its lineage to Jefferson's activities as a revolutionary and party leader. The embittered Federalist Henry Lee recognized the connections linking Jefferson's reputation, history and politics when he sought to discredit Jeffersonianism and revive federalism by demonstrating that Jefferson had been an incompetent and cowardly governor during the War of Independence. Jefferson, in turn, sought to defend his political program when he defended his reputation against criticism through the use of political allies as surrogates to answer charges such as Lee's.

The historiographical battle over the Revolution and early republic was a continuation of the partisan political struggles of the 1790s. Rather than appeal to a relatively narrow electorate for support, the protagonists sought to convince succeeding generations that they presented a true picture of the origins of the republic. They believed that the future of the United States and the world was at stake in their struggle. As an expert politician with a deep understanding of history, Jefferson was exceptionally well qualified to participate in such a contest. He created what might be termed an historical patronage network through his use of influence on behalf of aspiring writers and by sharing his library and manuscript collections with those he deemed worthy of his support. As a consequence, when he needed to, Jefferson could call on suitably qualified allies such as Louis Girardin or William Johnson to represent his interests and defend his reputation. Most importantly, Jefferson had the skills and resources to engage in historiographical debate himself, as he did when he compiled his massive documentary history (the autobiography and Anas) to counter John Marshall's 'five volume libel'. Recognizing the controversial nature of the material he had compiled, and appreciating that he created his history for posterity, Jefferson left his work unpublished at his death.

Unfortunately his grandson, in publishing a selection of Jefferson's papers, failed to retain the structure and content of the collection as Jefferson intended. This lessened, but did not entirely negate, the intended impact of the work. In consequence historians have not fully appreciated the magnitude, significance, coherence and purpose of Jefferson's documentary history. In compiling the Anas Jefferson demonstrated an appreciation for the importance of the documentary record in shaping his posthumous reputation. He preserved a massive collection of personal and state papers that, as he intended, have formed the basis of all studies of Jefferson's life and times. However, just as he could not have foreseen that his grandson would break up his documentary history, Jefferson could not foresee the use future historians would make of his papers. Nonetheless, in preserving his papers Jefferson sought to shape his legacy from beyond the grave. Before considering the use to which historians have put the papers, we must first consider their history.

NOTES

1. TJ to John Adams, 10 [11] Aug. 1815, in Lester J. Cappon, ed., *The Adams–Jefferson Letters*, 2 vols. (Chapel Hill: University of North Carolina Press, 1959), 2:452.
2. TJ to William Johnson, 4 March 1823, TJP.
3. For the most thorough account of the cooperation between Démeunier and Jefferson see 'The Article on the United States in the *Encyclopédie Méthodique*', PTJ, 10:3–65.
4. William Short to William Nelson, 25 Oct. 1786, Short Papers, LoC, as quoted in PTJ, 10:3.
5. François Soulés, *Histoire des troubles de l'Amérique anglaise*, 2 vols. (London: n.p., 1785). This history was published as a revised four-volume work by Buisson in Paris in 1787. The most complete treatment of Jefferson's involvement with Soulés can be found in 'Jefferson's Comments on François Soulés' *Histoire*', PTJ, 10:364–83.
6. Soulés, *Histoire*, 4:263–6.
7. TJ to Thomas Mann Randolph, Jr., 27 Aug. 1786, PTJ, 10:305–9, quotations 306–7.
8. TJ to David Ramsay, 31 Aug. 1785, PTJ, 8:457. For the complete exchange between Ramsay and Jefferson on this matter see: David Ramsay to TJ, 15 June 1785, PTJ, 8:210–11; David Ramsay to TJ, 13 July 1785, 8:293–4; David Ramsay to TJ, 8 Aug. 1785, 8:359–60; TJ to David Ramsay, 12 Oct. 1785, PTJ, 8:629; David Ramsay to TJ, 10 Dec. 1785, PTJ, 9:89–90; TJ to David Ramsay, 26 Jan. 1786, PTJ, 9:228; TJ to David Ramsay, 10 July 1786, PTJ, 10:122; TJ to David Ramsay, 27 Oct. 1786, PTJ, 10:490–1; David Ramsay to TJ, 8 Nov. 1786, PTJ, 10:513–14; David Ramsay to TJ, 7 Apr. 1787, PTJ, 11:279–80; TJ to David Ramsay, 4 Aug. 1787, PTJ, 11:686–7; David Ramsay to TJ, 7 March 1788, PTJ, 12:654–5; TJ to David Ramsay, 7 May 1788, PTJ, 13:138–40. The work in question was David Ramsay, *The History of the Revolution of South-Carolina, from a British Province to an Independent State*, 2 vols. (Trenton, NJ: n.p., 1785). The French edition which Jefferson arranged to publish appeared as *Histoire de la Révolution d'Amérique, par rapport à Caroline Méridionale*, 2 vols. (London and Paris: Foullé, 1787).
9. John Adams to TJ, 20 Feb. 1787, PTJ, 11:170; William Gordon to TJ, 20 Feb. 1787, PTJ, 11:172.
10. TJ to William Gordon, 2 July 1787, PTJ, 11:525; TJ to William Gordon, 16 July 1788, PTJ, 13:362–5. Gordon's history, *The History of the Rise, Progress, and Establishment of the Independence of the United States of America*, 4 vols., was published in London by Charles Dilly and James Buckland. The account of the raid on Monticello, which closely follows Jefferson's version in his letter of 16 July 1788, appears in 4:402–3.

11. Both Ramsay and Gordon had published minor works prior to writing their histories. See [David Ramsay], *A Sermon on Tea* (Lancaster, PA: n.p., 1774); David Ramsay, *An Oration on the Advantages of American Independence* (Charleston, SC: John Wells, 1778); William Gordon, *Plan of a Society for Making Provision for Widows by Life Annuities* (Boston: J. Edwards and J. Fleming, 1772); William Gordon, *A Discourse Preached December 5, 1774: Being the Day Recommended by the Provincial Congress* (Boston: T. Leverett, 1775); William Gordon, *A Sermon Preached before the Honorable House of Representatives* (Watertown: Benjamin Edes, 1775); William Gordon, *The Separation of the Jewish Tribes . . . First Anniversary Sermon After the Declaration of Independence* (Boston: J. Gill, 1777); William Gordon, *The Doctrine of Final Universal Salvation* (Boston: T. & J. Fleet, 1783). David Ramsay would achieve subsequent renown as an historian writing histories of the United States and South Carolina. His most famous work was his *History of the American Revolution*, 2 vols. (Philadelphia: R. Aitken & Son, 1789), which was the first work to be copyrighted in the United States.

12. TJ to William Stephens Smith, 9 July 1786, *PTJ*, 10:115–17; TJ to David Ramsay, 10 July 1786, *PTJ*, 10:122; TJ to William Gordon, 18 March 1789, *PTJ*, 14:674–5.

13. John Carey to TJ, 30 June 1792, *PTJ*, 24:140; TJ to John Carey, 3 July 1792, *PTJ*, 24:151. Carey was one of a large family of Irish radicals that included his brothers, James and Matthew, both of whom emigrated to the United States and became active in radical politics and publishing. See Michael Durey, *Transatlantic Radicals and the Early American Republic* (Lawrence: University Press of Kansas, 1997), 91–2.

14. George Washington to TJ, with Jefferson's Comment, 19 Nov. 1792, *PTJ*, 24:642. On 6 October Carey wrote to Jefferson to apply for a job as a translator in the State Department. He included with his letter a packet of papers that he had copied for Jefferson's approval. John Carey to TJ, 6 Oct. 1792, *PTJ*, 24:443–4.

15. John Carey, ed., *Official Letters to the Honorable American Congress, Written during the War between the United Colonies and Great Britain, by his Excellency George Washington, Commander in Chief of the Continental Forces, now President of the United States*, 2 vols. (London: Cadell, Davies and Robinson, 1795). For the relevant correspondence see John Carey to TJ, 31 Jan. 1793, *PTJ*, 25:105–6; John Carey to TJ, 20 Feb. 1793, *PTJ*, 25:236; John Carey to TJ, 23 Apr. 1793, *PTJ*, 25:581–2; TJ to Thomas Pinckney, 27 Apr. 1793, *PTJ*, 25:595–6; John Carey to TJ, 1 May 1793, *PTJ*, 25:630.

16. George Washington to TJ, with Jefferson's Comment, 19 Nov. 1792, *PTJ*, 24:642; John Carey to TJ, 6 Apr. 1795, *PTJ*, 28:324–5; John Carey to TJ, 1 Sept. 1796, *PTJ*, 29:180–2; TJ to John Carey, 10 Nov. 1796, *PTJ*, 29:205.

17. TJ to John Minor, 30 Aug. 1814, TJP; 'Notes on the Letter of Christoph Daniel Ebeling', *PTJ*, 28:506. For the development of revolutionary historiography see, Arthur H. Shaffer, *The Politics of History: Writing the History of the American Revolution, 1783–1815* (Chicago: Precedent Publishing, 1975); William Raymond Smith, *History as Argument: Three Patriot Histories of the American Revolution* (The Hague: Mouton, 1966); Lester H. Cohen, *The Revolutionary Histories: Contemporary Narratives of the American Revolution* (Ithaca: Cornell University Press, 1980) and Lester H. Cohen, 'Creating a Usable Future: The Revolutionary Historians and the National Past', in Jack P. Greene, ed., *The American Revolution: Its Character and Limits* (New York: New York University Press, 1987), 309–30.

18. TJ to Joel Barlow, 3 May 1802, TJP.

19. John Marshall, *The Life of George Washington*, 5 vols. (Philadelphia: C. P. Wayne, 1804–7). For a concise account of Marshall's writing of the biography see Jean Edward Smith, *John Marshall: Definer of a Nation* (New York: Owl Books, 1996), 327–34. For a critical study of Marshall's work see William A. Foran, 'John Marshall as a Historian', *American Historical Review*, 43 (1937), 51–64.

20. Marshall, *Life of Washington*, 5:33.

21. Marshall, *Life of Washington*, 5:353.

22. Marshall, *Life of Washington*, 5:354–5.

23. Smith, *John Marshall: Definer of a Nation*, 330.

24. Joanne B. Freeman, *Affairs of Honor: National Politics in the New Republic* (New Haven: Yale University Press, 2001), 63.

25. John Marshall, 1807, Life of G. Washington with Thomas Jefferson Notes, TJP. The corrections can also be found in Franklin B. Sawvel, ed., *The Complete Anas of Thomas Jefferson* (New York: Round Table Press, 1903), 41–3.

26. John Marshall, 1807, Life of G. Washington with Thomas Jefferson Notes.

27. TJ to Joel Barlow, 16 Apr. 1811, TJP.

28. TJ to William Wirt, 14 Aug. 1814, TJP. Also see TJ to William Wirt, 12 May 1815. In each of these letters Jefferson provided extensive recollections of events in pre-revolutionary and revolutionary Virginia for Wirt's biography of Patrick Henry. See William Wirt, *Sketches of the Life and Character of Patrick Henry* (Philadelphia: William Brown, 1818). Wirt sought advice and information about Henry from Jefferson, who also read proofs of Wirt's biography. Although Jefferson praised Wirt in his letter, he was not satisfied with his biography of Henry. In 1824 Jefferson told Daniel Webster, '[Wirt] sent the sheets of his work to me, as they were printed, & at the end asked my opinion. I told him it would be a question hereafter, whether his work should be placed on the shelf of *history*, or of *panegyric*. It is a poor book, written in bad taste, &

gives so imperfect an idea of Patrick Henry, that it seems intended to show off the *writer*, more than the subject of the work.' Notes of Mr. Jefferson's Conversations 1824 at Monticello, Charles M. Wiltse, ed., *The Papers of Daniel Webster: Correspondence*, 14 vols. (Hanover, NH: University Press of New England, 1974–89), 1:373. Jefferson seems to have objected to Wirt's biography because the author was not as critical of Henry as Jefferson was.

29. Introduction to the Anas, 4 Feb. 1818, TJP, 1, also in Sawvel, *Complete Anas of Thomas Jefferson*, 23–4. Jefferson's documentary notes are usually referred to as the Anas, though Jefferson himself never referred to them as such. This name was given to the collection after Jefferson's death (see below). For a discussion of their provenance and compilation see *PTJ*, 22:33–8. The most thorough analysis of the Anas to date is in Freeman, *Affairs of Honor*, ch. 2, an earlier version of which appeared as Joanne B. Freeman, 'Slander, Whispers, and Fame: Jefferson's "Anas" and Political Gossip in the Early Republic', *Journal of the Early Republic*, 15 (1995), 25–58. Also see Andrew Burstein, *Jefferson's Secrets: Death and Desire at Monticello* (New York: Basic Books, 2005), chs. 7–8. Although Sawvel's is the best of several published editions of the Anas, it is a problematic work, partly because, despite its title, Sawvel's it is not complete. It does not include the documents that Jefferson compiled to accompany his personal memoranda, and it includes material from after 1793 that Jefferson did not intend to include in his documentary history. Where possible I have relied on the manuscript introduction in Jefferson's own hand in the Library of Congress (cited above) and the individual memoranda known to have been included in the Anas but published in chronological order in the Princeton edition of *The Papers of Thomas Jefferson*.

30. For a published version of Jefferson's autobiography see, *TJW*, 1–101, quotation 3. The manuscript is: Thomas Jefferson, 27 July 1821, Autobiography, Draft Fragment, TJP.

31. Autobiography, *TJW*, 7.

32. The autobiography has been somewhat neglected by historians. The best study, on which my analysis is based, is Herbert Sloan, 'Presidents as Historians', in Richard A. Ryerson, ed., *John Adams and the Founding of the Republic* (Boston: The Massachusetts Historical Society and Northeastern University Press, 2001), 266–83. Sloan argues that Jefferson's autobiography should be read as an introduction to the Anas. Sloan discussed the autobiography at length in a paper delivered at Monticello in 1993, 'The Search for a Useable Past: Jefferson as Autobiographer', an unpublished paper in the ICJS library. I am grateful to Professor Sloan for permission to cite this work. This view is echoed in Robert M.S. McDonald, 'Thomas Jefferson's Changing Reputation as Author of the Declaration of Independence: The First Fifty Years',

Journal of the Early Republic, 19 (1999), 169–95, p. 189. Also see James M. Cox, 'Jefferson's *Autobiography*: Recovering Literature's Lost Ground', *Southern Review*, 14 (1978), 633–52.
33. Autobiography, *TJW*, 18.
34. Marshall, *Life of Washington*, 2:377n. McDonald, 'Thomas Jefferson's Changing Reputation as Author of the Declaration of Independence'. McDonald argues that the anonymity of the Declaration's author was originally an advantage as the document purported to represent the views of all Americans. With the appearance of intense political partisanship in the 1790s, Jefferson's authorship of the Declaration became known and celebrated. Also see Philip F. Detwiler, 'The Changing Reputation of the Declaration of Independence: The First Fifty Years', *WMQ*, 19 (1962), 557–74.
35. Autobiography, *TJW*, 32–3.
36. Autobiography, *TJW*, 71–2.
37. Some of the confusion arises from the use of the term 'Autobiography' to describe the document. Jefferson referred to the document as 'Memoranda', which is consistent with his documentary history. When the document was first published in 1830 (discussed below) it appeared under the title *Memoir*. Only in modern editions has the document in question come to be called the *Autobiography of Thomas Jefferson*. See James M. Cox, 'Jefferson's *Autobiography*', 633–4, for a discussion of the confusion arising from this question of nomenclature.
38. Introduction to the Anas, 4 Feb. 1818 TJP.
39. Introduction to the Anas, 4 Feb. 1818 TJP, 13–14.
40. Introduction to the Anas, 4 Feb. 1818 TJP, 14.
41. Introduction to the Anas, 4 Feb. 1818 TJP, 14.
42. Notes of a Conversation with George Washington, 1 Oct. 1792, *PTJ*, 24:433–6.
43. TJ to Philip Mazzei, 24 Apr. 1796, *PTJ*, 29:81–3. Also see the lengthy editorial note on the affair and the various newspaper versions of the letter in the *PTJ*, 29:73–8; and Malone, *Jefferson and His Time*, 3:302–7.
44. Peterson, *Jefferson Image*, 118.
45. Thomas Jefferson Randolph, ed., *Memoirs, Correspondence and Private Papers of Thomas Jefferson*, 4 vols. (Charlottesville, VA and London: Colburn and Bentley, 1829).
46. Merrill D. Peterson, 'The Jefferson Image, 1829', *American Quarterly*, 3 (1951), 204–20.
47. The most recent edition of Marshall's history is Robert K. Faulkner and Paul Caresse, eds., *Life of George Washington*, 2 vols. (Indianapolis: Liberty Fund, 2000), which is reprint of the 1838 edition for schools.
48. Henry Lee, Jr. to TJ, 26 Aug. 1824, TJP; TJ to Henry Lee, 6 Sept. 1824, TJP. Lee is usually referred to as 'Henry Lee, Jr.'. He was actually Henry

Lee, IV. This was not the first time that Jefferson discouraged an historian whom he did not trust. In 1807 he refused to give the moderate Federalist senator William Plumer access to his papers for a proposed history. See Everett Somerville Brown, ed., *William Plumer's Memorandum of Proceedings in the United States Senate, 1803–1807* (New York, Macmillan, 1923), 600–2 as quoted in Freeman, *Affairs of Honor*, 273. In her book's epilogue Freeman presents an elegant and concise analysis of Plumer's efforts as an historian, placing them in the context of early national politics. She argues, persuasively in my view, that for the founding generation history-writing was a political contest. I have taken her analysis as a point of departure.

49. Henry Lee, *Memoirs of the War in the Southern Department of the United States*, 2 vols. (Philadelphia: Bradford and Inskeep, 1812). There is a modern edition of Lee's memoirs (a reprint of the 1869 edition edited by Lee's son, Robert E. Lee). See Robert E. Lee, *Memoirs of the War in the Southern Department of the United States* (New York: University Publishing, 1869), repr. as *Revolutionary War Memoirs of General Henry Lee* (New York: Da Capo, 1998). Also see Charles Royster, *Light-Horse Harry Lee and the Legacy of the American Revolution* (New York: Alfred A. Knopf, 1981), ch. 6.

50. For Jefferson's tenure as governor during the British invasions see Malone, *Jefferson and His Time*, 1:314–69.

51. Lee, *Revolutionary War Memoirs of General Henry Lee*, pp. 297–9; Henry Lee, Manuscript Memoirs, Virginia Historical Society. Royster, *Light-Horse Harry Lee*, 217.

52. Louis Hue Girardin and Skelton Jones, *The History of Virginia Commenced by John Burk*, vol. 4 (Petersburg: M.W. Dunnavant, 1816), vi.

53. Girardin, *History of Virginia*, 4:453–60; 498–503; Appendix xi–xii. Autobiography, *TJW*, 45.

54. William Johnson, *Sketches of the Life and Correspondence of Nathanael Greene*, 2 vols. (Charleston: A. E. Miller, 1822). Also see TJ to William Johnson, 27 Oct. 1822, TJP; TJ to William Johnson, 4 March 1823, TJP; TJ to William Johnson, 12 June 1823, TJP.

55. Henry Lee, *The Campaign of 1781 in the Carolinas: With Remarks Historical and Critical on Johnson's Life of Greene to Which is Added an Appendix of Original Documents Relating to the History of the Revolution* (Philadelphia: E. Littell, 1824).

56. TJ to Henry Lee, Jr., 16 May 1824; Henry Lee, Jr. to TJ, 14 July 1824; TJ to Henry Lee, Jr., 10 Aug. 1824; Henry Lee, Jr. to TJ, 26 Aug. 1824; TJ to Henry Lee, Jr. 6 Sept. 1824; Henry Lee, Jr. to TJ, 29 Apr. 1825; TJ to Henry Lee, Jr., 8 May 1825; Henry Lee, Jr. to TJ, 9 May 1826; TJ to Henry Lee, Jr., 15 May 1826; Henry Lee, Jr. to TJ, 25 May 1826; TJ to Henry Lee, Jr., 27 May 1826; TJ to Henry Lee, Jr., 30 May 1826; TJP.

57. Henry Lee, *Memoirs of the War in the Southern Department of the United States* (Washington, DC: Peter Force, 1827).

58. TJ to James Monroe, 1 Jan. 1815, TJP.

59. Henry Lee, *Observations on the Writings of Thomas Jefferson with Particular Reference to the Attack they Contain on the Memory of the Late Gen. Henry Lee* (New York: Charles De Behr, 1832).

CHAPTER 3

JEFFERSON'S PAPERS

I

During the summer of 1809, several months after Thomas Jefferson had left the presidency and retired permanently to Monticello, John W. Campbell, a bookseller and printer from Petersburg, Virginia, wrote to him proposing to publish 'a complete edition of your different writings, as far as they may be designed for the public; including the "Notes on Virginia"'. Jefferson was not especially encouraging in his reply to Campbell. He wrote that he intended to revise and enlarge his *Notes on Virginia* before it could be republished. With regard to the large body of official papers he had generated as a congressman, governor, diplomat, secretary of state, vice president and president, he dismissed interest in these, noting, 'Many of these would be like old newspapers, materials for future historians, but no longer interesting to the readers of the day.' He concluded:

> So that on a review of these various materials, I see nothing encouraging a printer to a re-publication of them. They would probably be bought by those only who are in the habit of preserving State papers, and who are not many . . . I have presented this general view of the subjects which might have been within the scope of your contemplation, that they might be correctly estimated before any final decision. They belong mostly to a class of papers not calculated for popular reading, and not likely to offer profit, or even indemnification to the re-publisher.[1]

Jefferson convinced his would-be editor that there would be little or no profit in publishing his writings and the matter died.

John Campbell's approach represents the first attempt to publish Jefferson's papers. It was not to be the last. It seems likely that Jefferson discouraged Campbell for several reasons not mentioned in his dissuading letter. As noted in Chapter 2, Jefferson was reluctant to appear in print during his lifetime and he may have wished that his papers – some of which would be controversial – should be published posthumously.

Campbell, moreover, approached Jefferson when he was several months into what would be a long – seventeen-year – and active retirement. Jefferson spent a good deal of time during these years organizing, amending and adding to his papers – as evidenced by his compiling his secret history of the first Washington administration and writing his autobiography. These efforts strongly suggest that Jefferson intended at least a portion of his papers to be published. They also suggest that Jefferson felt that his papers were not yet properly organized when Campbell approached him with his proposition. Despite discouraging Campbell, there is every reason to conclude that Jefferson hoped his papers would be published in the future.

Upon his death in 1826, Thomas Jefferson left a massive documentary legacy. Over the course of his long life Jefferson wrote around eighteen thousand letters and received twenty-five thousand more. He also wrote or compiled hundreds of other documents such as memoranda, state papers, legal papers, architectural drawings, account books, commonplace books, his life of Jesus redacted from the New Testament, and meteorological observations, to name a few. This documentary legacy, unprecedented in American history for its size and breadth, has been the key to the evolution of Jefferson's reputation. From it, all subsequent Jefferson scholarship has developed. This is as Jefferson intended, and it accounts for his careful preservation of his papers. We have seen in previous chapters that Jefferson believed strongly in the potency and importance of history – and that history, to retain its power and significance, must be based on primary sources. In transmitting to posterity such a substantial documentary legacy Jefferson sought to shape his posthumous reputation. He made an error, however, in not publishing his papers during his own lifetime, or leaving detailed instructions for how they should be handled. In so doing Jefferson lost control over his documentary legacy and, by extension, his reputation. This chapter considers the history of Jefferson's papers both during and after his lifetime, which is the key to evaluating his changing place in history.

II

'The letters of a person,' Jefferson wrote late in life, 'especially of one whose business has been chiefly transacted by letters, form the only full and genuine journal of his life.'[2] Throughout his life Jefferson devoted significant time and effort not only to writing many thousands of letters, the 'journal of his life', but to preserving and organizing them, as well as the many other documents that he created and collected. As one of his later editors wrote, 'No other President except the second Roosevelt has possessed so strong an archival instinct; and however badly his papers have been manhandled since, Jefferson himself left them in beautiful order.'[3] This archival instinct manifested itself in compulsive record-keeping, as well as in his preservation and organization of his papers.

Beginning in June of 1779, with his election as governor of Virginia, Jefferson began to keep a register of his outgoing letters. This was an incomplete effort that continued until May 1781, although most of his letter-books as governor were lost during Benedict Arnold's raid on Richmond in December 1780. In order to reconstruct his records from this confusing – and controversial – period of his life, Jefferson later borrowed and copied his gubernatorial letters to George Washington. In 1793 he borrowed General Horatio Gates's letterbook and copied nearly 187 letters he had written during the period from 21 June 1780 to October 1781 to replace lost originals.[4] In November 1783 Jefferson undertook a more comprehensive record of his letters, listing incoming and outgoing letters in sequence, usually providing brief summaries of outgoing letters. This record, which Jefferson kept for nearly forty-three years, became increasingly sophisticated, and is known today as Jefferson's epistolary record or, as it is referred to in *The Papers of Thomas Jefferson*, the Summary Journal of Letters (SJL).[5]

Technology transformed Jefferson's efforts to keep track of his records. In March of 1785, while serving as a diplomat in Paris, Jefferson obtained a copy press, a device invented by James Watt in 1780. This allowed a writer to make a copy of a letter or document through the use of a letterpress which made an impression of a letter by pressing a thin sheet of moist paper against the original. In late June of 1785 Jefferson had become proficient at using the copy press and ceased summarizing his outgoing letters because he retained copies of them. In September he boasted to James Madison about the virtues of the press. 'Have you a copying press? If you have not', he advised, 'you should get one. Mine (exclusive of paper which costs a guinea a ream) has cost me about 14 guineas. I would give ten times that sum that I had it from the date of the stamp act.'[6] By September Jefferson had become so adept at using the press that he adopted a more sophisticated method for recording information in the SJL, using parallel columns to note the date and recipient of outgoing letters and recording the authors and dates (sent and received) of incoming correspondence. In this form, Jefferson maintained the SJL for the next forty-one years, making his last entry on 25 June 1826. Jefferson used versions of the copy press for two decades, switching to a polygraph – a device that produced an exact copy through the use of parallel pens linked by a mechanical apparatus – in 1804. In retaining copies of his outgoing and incoming correspondence, as well as register-ing – and occasionally indexing – his letters, Jefferson created a vast personal archive that was supplemented by his other writings, the many historical and legal manuscripts he had acquired and his substantial library.[7]

In his will Jefferson bequeathed his papers to his favorite grandson, Thomas Jefferson Randolph. Jefferson stated: 'My papers of business going of course to him as my executor, all others of a literary or other character I give to him as of his own property.'[8] Twenty-four years after he inherited them, Randolph provided a description of the state of Jefferson's papers that is testimony to the care Jefferson took to preserve and organize his documentary legacy:

> The letters written by Mr. Jefferson are all arranged together in chron-ological order. The papers, documents, official correspondence, notes of transactions while Secretary of State to Gen Washington, are bound in three volumes of marbled paper [the Anas], marked A. B. C.: The letters received are in three series alphabetically arranged – The first, received during his residence in Paris; the second, during his residence in Phila-delphia as Secretary of State, Vice President and President at Washington; the third after his return home.
>
> These are contained in paper boxes, open at top and back, the width and breadth of letter paper folded lengthwise; the name of the writer and date endorsed across the end, added to these are packages with the contents endorsed on the wrapper. There is also an index containing some 40,000 entries of letters written and received, partly in a bound volume and continued on loose sheets stitched together. The arrangements [*sic*] for reference is very convenient and it would be desirable to preserve it.[9]

Jefferson had arranged and preserved his papers so carefully with poster-ity in mind. He intended, as in the case of the Anas, that they should be published after his death, enabling him to reach from beyond the grave and win the battle over history and his place within it against his Federalist foes. Unfortunately for Jefferson, as the history of the pub-lication of the Anas shows, he could not control what his heir did with his papers. Prior to writing his description of the wonderful organization of Jefferson's papers, Thomas Jefferson Randolph had taken a step that led to the breakup of the collection.

III

Despite the care with which Jefferson organized his papers, and the best efforts of his literary heir, Thomas Jefferson Randolph, it proved very difficult to keep Jefferson's papers intact during the nineteenth century. In 1829, when the Library of Congress purchased Jefferson's third library (which he had acquired between his 1815 sale to the Library of Congress

and his death in 1826), it also acquired some of his manuscript collections
– including his sizeable collection of materials on the early history of
Virginia. Nonetheless Randolph was at first able to maintain the integrity,
coherence and relative completeness of the Jefferson papers. In 1829
Randolph published a four-volume selection of the papers (discussed
more fully below). Randolph allowed Jefferson's first biographer, George
Tucker, to examine Jefferson's letters while preparing an 1837 biography
that was a defense of Jefferson in response to the harsh partisan criticism
that the *Memoir* had provoked.[10] Apart from Tucker, Randolph declined
all requests to examine the papers. He intended to sell the collection as a
unit in order to clear the substantial debt his family had inherited from
Jefferson along with the papers, and he did not want to devalue the
collection by making parts of it too widely available before its sale.[11]

Randolph did not succeed in selling his grandfather's papers *en masse*.
In 1848 he agreed to sell his grandfather's 'public' papers to the United
States government for $20,000. The secretary of state, James Buchanan,
insisted that Randolph send the entire collection to the State Department,
where it would be examined. Jefferson's 'personal' papers would be
separated from those manuscripts deemed to be 'public' in nature and
the private papers would be returned to Randolph. The task of sorting,
selecting and indexing the papers fell to Henry A. Washington, a
professor of history, political economy and international law at the
College of William and Mary (Jefferson's alma mater), who was also
charged with editing a selection of the documents for publication by the
government. Washington was allowed to take the papers to Williamsburg, where he hastily sorted them into five series, disrupting the carefully
ordered system designed by Jefferson and described by Randolph.
Washington's edited collection was inadequate and his handling of the
documents shoddy. In addition to mixing up the documents from their
original order, Washington damaged some and likely did not return all of
the papers he borrowed.[12] If Randolph's 1848 description is correct, then
it was Washington who unbound the 'three volumes of marbled paper'
and thereby destroyed Jefferson's carefully crafted secret documentary
history that had been published in an incomplete form by Randolph as
the Anas in 1829.

By 1854 Washington sorted the papers into two general categories –
manuscripts 'worthy of preservation', approximately 134 volumes which
he had indexed and advised should be bound and held in the State
Department; and 'The refuse matter, constituting a mass considerably
larger than the selected matter, [which] has already been deposited in the
State Department in the same condition in which it was received by me'.[13]
There was another category that Washington did not describe – more
than 2,500 letters from the papers that he apparently retained and that

were sold by one of his descendants in 1912. Thus between 1848, when Thomas Jefferson Randolph sold the collection intact to the government, and 1854 serious damage had already been done to the archival integrity of the Jefferson papers – actively by Henry A. Washington and passively by the State Department, whose administrators lost track of some of the manuscripts which Washington had deemed 'refuse matter'.

It was not until the turn of the twentieth century that most of the manuscripts sold to the United States government in 1848 were finally gathered together in one place. On 25 February 1903 Congress required all government agencies to turn over 'books, maps, or other material' that they no longer required. On 25 July 1904 the Library of Congress received most of the Jefferson papers, with the exception of diplomatic correspondence retained by the State Department. Over the next several decades additions were made to the collection, including a transfer of the outstanding documents held by the State Department in January 1922, amongst which was Jefferson's annotated draft of the Declaration of Independence.[14]

The government's relative neglect of Jefferson's 'public' papers during the latter nineteenth century appears to be careful stewardship by comparison with the scattering of the 'private' papers during the same period. In 1869 Thomas Jefferson Randolph contacted the department to point out that Jefferson's personal papers had never been returned to him. As anyone who has read Jefferson's correspondence knows, the division between the public and the private in his manuscripts is difficult to discern. Paul G. Sifton has written, 'If there is such a thing as an average Jefferson letter, it might touch upon such disparate subjects as crops, politics, violins, astronomy, diplomacy, and wines.'[15] Nonetheless, three boxes – containing thousands of letters and documents deemed private – were finally returned to the Randolph family in 1871, twenty-three years after they were sent to the State Department.

Thomas Jefferson Randolph died in October 1875 and the private papers passed to his daughter Sarah Randolph. Sarah Randolph proposed to Congress that she edit the papers and produce a collection which corrected the deficiencies and inaccuracies that marred Henry A. Washington's earlier edition of Jefferson's writings. Nothing came of the proposal except that it prompted congressional debate about whether to appropriate the money to acquire the private papers from the Randolph family and reunite the Jefferson papers (with the exception of the documents purloined by Henry Washington). Congress decided against making the purchase. Sarah Randolph died in April 1892 and she left the papers to her sister, Caroline Ramsey Randolph. In 1898 Caroline Randolph sold more than seven thousand items from the collection to her kinsman, Thomas Jefferson Coolidge of Massachusetts, a great-grandson of Thomas Jefferson. Coolidge gave the papers, including thousands of letters, account books, almanacs, legal documents and manuscript volumes of Jefferson's farm and garden books, as well as his library catalogs, to the Massachusetts Historical Society.[16] When Caroline Randolph died in 1902 the remaining papers in her possession were divided among her three nieces. Some of these were lost in a subsequent fire. Others were dispersed among other descendants and some were eventually deposited in the library of the University of Virginia. In 1912 a St. Louis collector named William K. Bixby acquired 2,500 Jefferson letters from George Coleman of Virginia. Coleman's mother had been married to Henry A. Washington before marrying Coleman's father (after Washington's death). It seems likely that Coleman, who was descended from George Tucker, Jefferson's first biographer, obtained the letters from his mother after she had inherited them from Washington, who had failed to return them to the State Department. Bixby had some of the letters printed and donated the largest share of this cache of documents, approximately 1,100 items, to the Missouri Historical Society. Others he donated and distributed to more than forty other repositories and individuals.[17]

By the early twentieth century the carefully organized and complete collection of papers that Thomas Jefferson Randolph had inherited from his grandfather in 1826 had been severely disrupted. Although the Library of Congress held the largest portion of the papers, they were not in the order in which they had been transmitted to the government in 1848, having been sifted and reorganized by Henry A. Washington. Perhaps more significantly, portions of the collection had been broken up and dispersed. Although the Massachusetts Historical Society held a large cache of Jefferson papers, others were scattered among several other archives as well as among private collectors. The story of Jefferson's account books is telling. Throughout his life Jefferson kept records in meticulous detail of his income and spending. Although these records, preserved in a series of account books, did not prevent Jefferson from falling into debt, they do present an invaluable insight into Jefferson's lifestyle and values. Unfortunately the account books themselves, which cover the years from 1767 to 1826, carefully preserved by Jefferson, have been scattered around the United States and can be found in the Library of Congress, the Massachusetts Historical Society, the Huntington Library in San Marino, California, the New York Public Library and the New-York Historical Society. Only the development of photocopying and microfilm in the mid-twentieth century made it possible to view copies of the complete series of Jefferson's account books. Although the debt chronicled in the account books partially helps to explain why Jefferson's papers were dispersed after his death, the resort to technology in order to bring the set together again – at least in facsimile – suggests one means by which Jefferson's larger documentary legacy could be reunited and transmitted to posterity as a coherent whole.[18]

IV

After inheriting Jefferson's papers, Thomas Jefferson Randolph initially intended to publish Jefferson's autobiography in order to generate funds to relieve the massive debts that were another of Jefferson's legacies. Upon examining the papers, Randolph decided to publish a more significant collection. He selected and edited four volumes of documents which he published in 1829 as *Memoir, Correspondence, and Miscellanies from the Papers of Thomas Jefferson.*[19] The collection consisted of letters, the autobiography, the Anas and miscellaneous state papers. In making his selections for the collection, Randolph focused on his grandfather's public life, giving particular emphasis to official letters and documents. He did so, however, in a deliberately uneven manner. Almost half of the letters concerned Jefferson's five-year tenure as a diplomat in France. By contrast Randolph omitted all but official and semi-official letters from the crucial period during the early 1790s when Jefferson served as secretary of state, and as a leader of the opposition to the Federalists. Randolph omitted critical references to George Washington, John Adams and Jefferson's *bête noire*, John Marshall, who was still alive when the *Memoir* was published. He also excluded all references to James Callender, the incendiary newspaper editor who was Jefferson's one-time ally but later spread rumors about his relationship with Sally Hemings. In short, Randolph attempted to portray his grandfather as a steadfast, largely uncontroversial public figure who made a substantial contribution to the founding of the American republic. Through the autobiography and the Anas, Randolph helped to advance Jefferson's claim as the author of the Declaration of the Causes of Taking Up Arms and the primary author of the Declaration of Independence. The documents, even the truncated version of the Anas, presented Jefferson as a consistent supporter of republican liberty, while softening the rough edges of Jefferson's character and conduct by omitting the strongest criticisms of his rivals.[20]

Although Thomas Jefferson Randolph was the nominal editor of his grandfather's papers, he relied on the labors of his extended family, particularly his mother and his sisters, to complete the task. The Randolph family faced several difficulties as editors of Jefferson's papers. The fragile condition of the documents, especially copies of Jefferson's letters produced by his letterpress, posed a particular challenge. Martha Jefferson Randolph described the process whereby she and her daughters transcribed the documents:

[T]he originals themselves are in many places so faded as to be almost entirely obliterated. [F]or pages together the girls have to take advantage of the broad light of the noon day sun, frequently unable to read them but with the assistance of a looking glass applied to the back, where alone the impression shews; a few lines will sometimes cost as many days. This is not the state of the *whole* but a *very considerable* portion.

Martha Jefferson Randolph reported that she and the Randolph women spent between five and eight hours per day transcribing and checking the letters before handing them over to her son, 'the editor, whose trouble is much lessened by our *pioneering* the way before him'. Inevitably mistakes were made in transcribing the documents. Some of these errors were replicated in subsequent editions of Jefferson's writings.[21]

Jefferson's *Memoir*, as edited by his grandson, was a limited work. It contained a small fraction of Jefferson's correspondence, carefully edited and marred by errors. Since Randolph had focused on Jefferson's public career, the *Memoir* had an especially significant political and constitutional impact, which was as Jefferson intended. As an anonymous reviewer commented in the *Edinburgh Review*, Jefferson 'will be a necessary witness whenever we survey the successive constitutional questions which have so furiously divided parties in America'. The *Memoir* also assisted antebellum historians and biographers seeking guidance on the origins of the republic. According to Merrill D. Peterson, the *Memoir* had a profound impact on Jefferson's historical legacy, and provided the basis for all the major studies of Jefferson undertaken during the mid-nineteenth century.[22]

The *Memoir, Correspondence, and Miscellanies from the Papers of Thomas Jefferson* was the first published edition of Jefferson's papers. The first print run of six thousand copies, published in Charlottesville, was sold within a year. Other editions appeared in Boston, London and Paris within a few years.[23] It remained the only available edition of Jefferson's writings for a generation. After Congress purchased Jefferson's public papers from Thomas Jefferson Randolph in 1848, it commissioned the publication of a new edition of Jefferson's papers. In 1850 the congressional Joint Committee on the Library contracted Henry A. Washington to edit and publish a selection of the newly acquired collection of papers. Washington's edition of Jefferson's papers, *The Writings of Thomas Jefferson* (usually referred to as the 'Congress Edition'), appeared in nine volumes in 1853 and 1854. The first volume contained the autobiography and some correspondence. Volumes 2 through 6 consisted of correspondence exclusively. The seventh, eighth and ninth volumes contained some correspondence as well as a selection of Jefferson's public papers as secretary of state, vice president and president, the *Notes on Virginia* and the Anas. Henry Washington did a poor job editing the papers. As we have seen, his handling of the documents left much to be desired. As an editor, too, he was deficient: his transcription and proofreading of the documents were faulty and numerous errors appeared in *The Writings*. In part these faults can be ascribed to the speed at which Washington worked. Washington produced his nine-volume edition over the course of 480 days' work between 1850 and 1854, all the while fulfilling his teaching responsibilities at William and Mary.[24]

The deficiencies of the Congress Edition were not simply the result of Henry A. Washington's limitations as a documentary editor or the haste with which he produced the collection. Washington was particularly ill suited for the task owing to his hostility towards Jefferson. Representative James Murray Mason of the Joint Committee of the Library, a Virginian, insisted that 'it is of great importance to Virginia that this duty should be performed by one of her own citizens whose integrity & capacity may be relied on, that no injustice shall be done to the fame of Mr. Jefferson'.[25] Mason seems to have chosen the wrong Virginian for the task of editing Jefferson's papers. Washington was a conservative who claimed that the character of Virginia's people shaped its constitution and prevented the theoretical excesses and political radicalism of the likes of Jefferson. Moreover, Washington was an ardent defender of slavery who bridled at Jefferson's occasional criticisms of the institution in his writings. Further, he was offended by Jefferson's political methods, especially as reflected in the Anas, which he agreed to print reluctantly. Owing to his philosophical, political and moral antipathy to Jefferson, Washington altered or suppressed portions of Jefferson's writings pertaining to slavery, as well as other materials, such as critical references to George Washington, which he felt were objectionable. When coupled with his slipshod transcriptions and proofreading, Washington's silent but profound editorial interventions rendered *The Writings of Thomas Jefferson* a flawed and inadequate work.[26]

The pioneering editions of Jefferson's writings by Thomas Jefferson Randolph and Henry A. Washington epitomize the limits of documentary editing and publication during the early and mid-nineteenth century. During this period the editing and publication of historical documents was haphazard and inconsistent. Descendants – such as Randolph – often acted as editors, adopting a filiopietistic stance to protect the reputations of their forebears and suppressing or amending the records accordingly. Others, like Henry Washington, selected, and occasionally altered, documents with an eye to contemporary political questions. In any event most nineteenth-century editors, including Randolph and Washington, made little effort to transcribe original documents precisely, silently correcting spelling errors and standardizing punctuation and usage. In 1883 Charles Francis Adams, Jr., the great-grandson of John Adams (whose father had edited John Adams's papers for publication), complained that some editors carried fidelity to original manuscripts to the point of 'fanaticism'. It was not until the late nineteenth century, with the emergence of history as a professional academic discipline, that standardized practices for the handling, editing and publication of historical documents developed in the United States. These standards, which continued to evolve throughout the twentieth century, placed increased emphasis on publishing documents as transcriptions of the original sources, supported by explanatory footnotes and commentary as necessary.[27]

The beginnings of the twentieth-century revolution in documentary editing were foreshadowed in the next major edition of Jefferson's papers, a ten-volume set edited by Paul Leicester Ford that was published during the 1890s. Ford was not a professional historian but a novelist and book collector from a prominent New York family. His father, Gordon L. Ford, owned a world-renowned library of some 100,000 books and 60,000 manuscripts, mostly relating to colonial and revolutionary American history. The younger Ford availed himself of these resources and compiled bibliographies on Alexander Hamilton and the drafting and ratification of the Constitution. He became involved in documentary editing, publishing a fifteen-volume collection of American historical documents, *Winnowings in American History*, as well as two collections of pamphlets and essays on the Constitution and the writings of Christopher Columbus before he took on the task of editing Jefferson's papers for the publishing house of G. P. Putnam at the tender age of twenty-five.[28] According to Merrill Peterson, writing in 1960, Ford 'was the first editor of Jefferson, one of the first editors of any American's papers, to be guided by procedures that would now be taken for granted'. Ford sought documents beyond the main collection of Jefferson papers in the Library of Congress, drawing on the hitherto neglected 'personal' papers as well as tracking down far-flung items held by collectors. In his treatment of the documents themselves, Ford was more discriminating than his predecessors. In addition to Jefferson's correspondence, Ford included many of the important documents that Jefferson drafted, often collating and comparing multiple drafts. These included Jefferson's Revisal of the Laws of Virginia, the Kentucky Resolutions, and a variorum edition of the *Notes on Virginia*, all of which previous editors had neglected. Unlike Henry Washington, Ford went to great lengths to check his transcriptions and page proofs against the original documents. In so doing, Ford insured that his was the most accurate and scholarly edition of Jefferson's writings yet published.[29]

Ford's *Writings of Thomas Jefferson* was not a flawless work. Owing to the editorial rigor that he brought to the documents, especially the various state papers, Ford was not able to include as many papers as Henry Washington had. Like his predecessors, Ford focused mainly on Jefferson's contributions as a statesman and politician, neglecting his manifold interests outside of public life. Further, although not as hostile to Jefferson as Henry A. Washington had been, Ford was critical of his subject and occasionally went to lengths to present Jefferson in an unflattering light. Nonetheless Ford's *Writings of Thomas Jefferson* was a dramatic improvement over previous editions.[30]

Paul L. Ford's edition of Jefferson's writings appeared four decades after the Congress Edition of Henry A. Washington. Despite Ford's editorial rigor and the sophistication of his collection, it was soon followed by another, larger, collection of published Jefferson papers. In April 1903 a new organization, the Thomas Jefferson Memorial Association, was launched. The Association was dedicated to raising money and support for the building of a monument to Jefferson in Washington. It failed to do so owing to a lack of funds. The Association did sponsor a new edition of Jefferson's writings, edited by Andrew A. Lipscomb and Albert E. Bergh, usually referred to as the 'Memorial Edition', which appeared in twenty volumes in 1903 and 1904. Lipscomb and Bergh largely reprinted the content of the Congress Edition of the 1850s. They supplemented Washington's original edition with some notable additions including a cache of documents relating to Jefferson's controversial wartime governorship of Virginia, some two hundred letters from the family papers that had recently been published by the Massachusetts Historical Society and a selection of miscellaneous writings and essays. In terms of its scope and coverage, the Memorial Edition was the most ambitious and comprehensive of the four major collections of Jefferson's writing published between 1829 and 1904. Unfortunately, the editing of the documents was uneven. In transcribing documents, Lipscomb and Bergh replicated Henry Washington's earlier errors while introducing new mistakes of their own. They added new materials without explanation or commentary in seemingly random order. The volumes, intended as a memorial to Jefferson, were disrupted by unnecessary illustrations, as well as glowing tributes to Jefferson by early twentieth-century politicians. Although widely circulated, the Memorial Edition was inadequate for serious study of Jefferson. While it was more inclusive than Ford's recent *Writings of Thomas Jefferson*, it lacked the editorial sophistication and scholarly reliability that characterized Ford's edition.[31]

By the early twentieth century four major editions of Jefferson's papers had been published. Regardless of their editorial limitations, which reflect the prevailing standards of the times in which they were published, each of these editions of Jefferson's papers focused narrowly on Jefferson's public life and achievements. This is as Jefferson wanted to be remembered. He believed that his political legacy would be contested by future politicians and historians, and he therefore preserved and carefully organized his papers so that his perspective on events would prevail. Unfortunately for Jefferson, only one of his subsequent editors, his grandson Thomas Jefferson Randolph, was sympathetic to his political agenda and presented Jefferson's actions and ideas in a sympathetic light. Randolph, of course, disrupted the coherence of Jefferson's history, while Jefferson's other editors were uninterested in advancing his views. As such, they present visions, often unsympathetic, of Jefferson as a politician and statesman.

During the twentieth century, documentary editors became increasingly interested in Jefferson's activities outside of politics and sought to convey the breadth, depth and coherence of Jefferson's massive documentary legacy – qualities that were lacking in the earlier editions of Jefferson's work. Individual scholars and editors published selections of Jefferson's papers that revealed aspects of his character or achievements which had been neglected or unknown. For example, in 1916 architectural historian Fiske Kimball published a selection of Jefferson's architectural drawings held by the Massachusetts Historical Society. In the 1920s and 1930s the French historian of ideas Gilbert Chinard shed light on Jefferson's intellectual development by editing and publishing his literary commonplace book as well as his correspondence with Du Pont de Nemours and Lafayette. In the middle of the century Edwin M. Betts provided a valuable insight into Jefferson as an agronomist, plantation manager and slaveholder when he edited the Jefferson's garden and farm books. Not only were these valuable additions to the corpus of printed Jefferson papers; they underscored the need for a more comprehensive edition than had previously appeared. Not until the bicentennial of Jefferson's birth in 1943, however, was another edition of the papers contemplated. This would be far more comprehensive than any previous edition of Jefferson's work.[32]

V

In 1940 the United States Congress created the Thomas Jefferson Bicentennial Commission to commemorate the two hundredth anniversary of Jefferson's birth. The commission took its cue from a similar body created in 1932 to mark the bicentennial of George Washington's birth. Under the auspices of that commission, Congress had authorized the publication of a modern edition of Washington's papers.[33] With this precedent in mind, Congress directed the Jefferson Commission 'to prepare as a congressional memorial to Thomas Jefferson a new edition of the writings of Thomas Jefferson, including additional material and unpublished manuscripts preserved in the Library of Congress and elsewhere, at a cost not to exceed, $15,000 for the preparation of the manuscript'.[34] In March 1943 the commission appointed Julian P. Boyd, the librarian at Princeton University, to undertake a feasibility study for a new edition of Jefferson's writings.

Boyd submitted his report on 25 September 1943. He surveyed the corpus of Jefferson papers comparing manuscripts to the four previous editions of Jefferson's published writings. He estimated that only around 30 percent of the letters that Jefferson wrote and only 7 percent of the letters that he received had been published. Boyd recommended the publication of a new edition of Jefferson's writings. He concluded that:

> [an] edition presenting this rich treasury of American history and thought should be so complete in its inclusiveness, so scholarly in its presentation, so carefully edited in its details, and so well presented in its format, as to constitute a worthy and enduring memorial to one of the greatest of Americans and a constant beacon for the American people in their understanding of the principles upon which the Republic is founded.

Boyd conceived of the project as a monument to Jefferson as the Apostle of Freedom spoken of by President Franklin D. Roosevelt. He estimated that a new, comprehensive, edition of Jefferson's writings would fill forty-four volumes and could be completed in ten years at a cost of $300,000.[35]

Cost proved to be the biggest obstacle to realizing Julian Boyd's vision of editing and publishing a new edition of Jefferson's writings. The government, which had funded the bicentennial edition of Washington's writings several years before, was an unlikely source given the financial demands of World War II. In 1943 Congress had authorized only $15,000 for a new edition, a mere 5 percent of Boyd's estimate of the cost. Although several universities and private foundations expressed interest in the project none could make a firm commitment of support. Boyd appealed to Arthur Hays Sulzberger, the publisher of the *New York Times*, which had subsidized the recent publication of the twenty-volume *Dictionary of American Biography*. Sulzberger agreed to provide $200,000 to support the project if Princeton University would undertake to provide the balance of the funding and if the published volumes were dedicated to Adolph S. Ochs, Sulzberger's father-in-law and the former owner and publisher of the *Times*. Negotiations between the Jefferson Bicentennial Commission, the *New York Times* and Princeton ensued in the autumn of 1943. Sulzberger's terms were accepted, Princeton agreed to provide the project with a home and Princeton University Press

committed to publish the volumes. The enterprise received the blessing of
the Bicentennial Commission and President Roosevelt. Appropriately,
Julian Boyd was appointed to direct the enterprise. In the spring of 1944
he returned to the Princeton library as the editor of *The Papers of Thomas
Jefferson*.

Julian P. Boyd took several decisions soon after his appointment as
editor of the Jefferson papers that fundamentally changed the nature of
the specific project in which he was engaged as well as of historical editing
more generally. First, he resolved that the project should embrace the
latest technology – microfilm cameras – in order to obtain duplicates,
photofacsimiles as Boyd termed them, 'of every known copy of every
Jefferson document'. Having acquired the copies from archives, libraries
and private collectors around the world, thereby recreating the contents
if not the order of Jefferson's original documentary collection, Boyd
decided that all of the documents, not a selection of them, should be
published. As Boyd wrote in his introduction to the first published volume
of the *Papers*, 'The purpose of this work is to present the writings and
recorded actions of Thomas Jefferson as accurately and completely as
possible.' After noting the deficiencies of the four previous editions of
Jefferson's writings Boyd asserted his intention that the Princeton edition
should be 'so comprehensive in scope and so accurate in presentation that
the work would never need to be done again'. In short he proposed to edit
the most comprehensive and ambitious edition of Jefferson's works ever
published.[36]

Although he intended his edition to be comprehensive, Boyd recognized
there were limits to what he could include in an edition he estimated
would fill fifty volumes. He accepted, for example, that it would be
impractical, if not counter-productive, to reprint the volumes of statutes
and manuscripts that Jefferson himself had transcribed. Rather, Boyd
wrote, 'The editors have aimed at the inclusion of everything legitimately
Jeffersonian by reason of authorship or of relationship, and at the
exclusion of great masses of materials that have only a technical claim
to being regarded as Jefferson documents.' By including documents that
were Jeffersonian by relationship, Boyd undertook to publish not only all
of Jefferson's letters and miscellaneous papers but all of the letters written
to Jefferson as well. The task of locating, editing and publishing more
than forty thousand letters as well as the many other papers that Jefferson
wrote or contributed to was a massive commitment unprecedented in the
history of documentary editing. To make the project manageable, Boyd
proposed that the papers should be published in two series. The first
would be a chronological series, which would mainly consist of all extant
correspondence to or from Jefferson as well as 'messages, speeches, reports,
legislative bills, state papers, memoranda, travel journals, resolutions,

petitions, advertisements, minutes of proceedings, and other non-episto-
lary documents which were written by Jefferson or have a direct relationship with Jefferson'. The second series would be topical and would
include Jefferson's autobiography, *Notes on the State of Virginia*, the
Manual of Parliamentary Practice, 'The Life and Morals of Jesus of
Nazareth', legal papers, architectural drawings, account books, the
garden and farm books, literary and linguistic papers, and the documents
relating to the founding of the University of Virginia, among others.[37]

Microfilming all the known Jefferson papers was the first step in Boyd's
ambitious program. Boyd and his assistant editors worked with the
Library of Congress, which had begun to microfilm its own collection
of Jefferson papers, to locate and microfilm Jeffersonian documents from
around the country and beyond. As Lyman H. Butterfield, one of Boyd's
editorial assistants (and an eminent documentary editor in his own right),
wrote in 1949:

> by the beginning of 1945 [we] had received and processed prints of some
> 31,000 Jefferson documents in the L.C., the Massachusetts Historical
> Society, and the Historical Society of Pennsylvania; during 1945 about
> 14,000 further documents were added from several large Virginia deposi-
> tories, the New-York Historical Society, the American Philosophical
> Society, the Huntington Library, the New York Public, and the Pierpoint
> Morgan Libraries. In 1946 and 1947 the large holdings of the Missouri
> State Historical Society, the Virginia State Library (a second crop), and
> several large private repositories were rounded up. A systematic search at
> the National Archives was begun before the end of 1947 but was
> interrupted and has not yet been completed. Soon after our operations
> started, the inflow of material from smaller repositories and private
> collections began. Though at times it has shrunk to a trickle, it has never
> dried up. Nearly eighty documents a month were accessioned during
> 1948.

Butterfield estimated that, as of 1949, over 50,000 documents had been
discovered and microfilmed from 423 different sources in forty states, the
District of Columbia, the territory of Hawaii and Puerto Rico as well
Canada, Australia and seven European countries.[38]

Having acquired tens of thousands of microfilm images of Jefferson
documents, the editors, Boyd and his assistants Butterfield and Mina R.
Bryan, set about the task of editing, transcribing and annotating the
documents for publication. One of the chief difficulties facing the editors,
as it had faced their predecessors, concerned how to transmit eighteenth-
century script into modern type. 'In general', Boyd wrote, 'the editorial
policy follows a middle course between those editors of historical

documents who believe, on the one hand, that nothing short of a facsimile reproduction can be faithful to the originals and those, who on the other hand, believe in complete modernization of the text.' Boyd explained that in the Princeton edition spelling and grammar would be maintained as they appeared in the original manuscripts but that contractions would be expanded and that punctuation would be preserved except where the clarity of the document required modern usage. The objective of the editorial policy was 'to present as accurate a text as possible and to preserve as many of Jefferson's distinctive mannerisms of writing as can be done'.[39]

Not only would the Princeton edition include all known Jefferson documents but it would also supply extensive editorial annotation of the documents. The four previous editions of Jefferson's writings had presented minimal annotations. By contrast, the Princeton edition would include several forms of annotation. Appended to each document would be a note that would normally consist of up to four parts: a descriptive note containing a physical description of the document, a record of all known copies and an indication of their locations; an explanatory note providing a brief commentary on the document's contents; and a textual note that would collate and explain textual differences between separate versions of the same document. Occasionally Boyd inserted a lengthy 'editorial note' to precede and explain groups of papers or especially significant or complex items. The first of these was a six-page analysis and explanation of Jefferson's authorship of the Declaration of the Causes and Necessity of Taking Up Arms adopted by the Continental Congress in 1775. Boyd described the process by which the declaration was written and adopted, and analyzed key textual changes in an introduction to a sequence of documents that included Jefferson's draft of the declaration, his fair copy presented to a congressional committee, John Dickinson's draft declaration and the declaration as finally adopted by Congress. Guided by Boyd's editorial note and the documents, the reader can follow the declaration through its drafting committee and sort out the competing claims to authorship of the document made by Jefferson and Dickinson after the Revolution. Boyd asserts that the differences between the versions of the declaration put forward by Jefferson and Dickinson were stylistic rather than political as previous historians had argued.[40]

The first volume of *The Papers of Thomas Jefferson*, covering the years from 1760 to 1776, was published in 1950. Beyond its contribution to the study of Jefferson's early life and career, the volume marked a significant milestone in the history and historiography of the United States. In the first place it significantly raised the standard of historical editing in the United States. By including all the letters written by and to Jefferson as well as all other documents that could be considered 'Jeffersonian', and by reproducing the documents as originally written, supported by extensive annotation, the *Papers* would be more detailed and comprehensive than any previous such project. Indeed, by comparison with the first volume of *The Papers of Thomas Jefferson*, the Fitzpatrick edition of Washington's writings completed in 1944 (which lacked editorial notes, was not comprehensive in the documents it included, and modernized spelling and punctuation) seemed archaic and inadequate. Inspired by the first volume of *The Papers of Thomas Jefferson* presented to him at the Library of Congress on 17 May 1950, President Harry S Truman revived the National Historic Publications Commission (NHPC, created in 1934 but largely inactive and ineffective since World War II). The revived commission submitted a report for a 'National Program for the Publication of Historical Documents' to President Eisenhower in 1954, calling for funding to assist the editing and publication of the papers of notable Americans beginning with John Adams and John Quincy Adams, James Madison, Benjamin Franklin and Alexander Hamilton. Over the next several decades the NHPC (later expanded to become the National Historical Publications and Records Commission, NHPRC) provided crucial funding to these and numerous other efforts at editorial publishing, including *The Papers of Thomas Jefferson*.[41]

After the publication of volume 1 of *The Papers of Thomas Jefferson* in 1950 subsequent volumes appeared regularly at the rate of approximately two volumes per year throughout the 1950s (see Table 3.1). This pace was impressive and in 1958 the fifteenth volume appeared. However, this was only approximately one-third of the forty-four volumes (since revised upwards to sixty-five volumes[42]) that Boyd had expected might be published in ten years. Volume 15 brought Jefferson's life down to the end of November 1789. Still in the future lay the document-rich periods of Jefferson's terms as secretary of state and president, as well as his lengthy retirement.

As impressive as the rate of publication of the first fifteen volumes had been, it was unlikely that Boyd and his various assistants could maintain such a pace. Indeed, having edited and published fifteen volumes between 1944 and 1958, Boyd would edit five more volumes over the next twenty-seven years, with his last, volume 20, appearing in 1982, two years after his death.

Over the course of four decades Julian P. Boyd emerged as one of the leading Jefferson scholars. The twenty volumes that he edited, taking Jefferson's life to August of 1791, reflect his editorial vision and expertise. To some extent, however, Boyd's vast knowledge of Jefferson proved to be an obstacle to the progress of the project. With each volume that he edited, Boyd's interventions through his editorial notes became longer and more frequent. The editorial notes in volume 1 totaled 55 out of 679 pages,

Table 3.1   *The Papers of Thomas Jefferson*

Volume	Year published	Editor
1	1950	Julian P. Boyd
2	1950	Julian P. Boyd
3	1951	Julian P. Boyd
4	1951	Julian P. Boyd
5	1952	Julian P. Boyd
6	1952	Julian P. Boyd
7	1953	Julian P. Boyd
8	1953	Julian P. Boyd
9	1954	Julian P. Boyd
10	1954	Julian P. Boyd
11	1955	Julian P. Boyd
12	1955	Julian P. Boyd
13	1956	Julian P. Boyd
14	1958	Julian P. Boyd
15	1958	Julian P. Boyd
16	1961	Julian P. Boyd
17	1965	Julian P. Boyd
18	1971	Julian P. Boyd
19	1974	Julian P. Boyd
20	1982	Julian P. Boyd
21	1983	Charles T. Cullen
Extracts from the Gospels (2nd Series)	1983	Dickinson W. Adams and Ruth W. Lester
22	1986	Charles T. Cullen
Parliamentary Writings (2nd Series)	1988	Wilbur Samuel Howell
Literary Commonplace Book (2nd Series)	1989	Douglas L. Wilson
23	1990	Charles T. Cullen
24	1990	John Catanzariti
25	1992	John Catanzariti
26	1995	John Catanzariti
27	1997	John Catanzariti
Memorandum Books, 2 vols. (2nd Series)	1997	James A. Bear, Jr. and Lucia C. Stanton
28	2000	John Catanzariti
29	2002	Barbara B. Oberg
30	2003	Barbara B. Oberg
31	2004	Barbara B. Oberg
Retirement Series, vol. 1	2005	J. Jefferson Looney

the longest note being ten pages long. In volume 20, Boyd's final volume, there were 246 pages of editorial notes (approximately one-third of the volume's 759 pages), the longest of which, 'Fixing the Seat of Government', was 70 pages long. As time passed, Boyd drew on his vast expertise to produce longer and longer notes – effectively scholarly essays and short monographs – on various, sometimes minor, aspects of Jefferson's life and career. This profusion of commentary inevitably slowed the production of new volumes, especially as Boyd increasingly attempted to do much of the editorial work on the project himself as his health declined. Despite the slow pace of publication of volumes 15 through 20 and Boyd's sometimes excessive editorial interventions in the later volumes, the twenty volumes of *The Papers of Thomas Jefferson* edited by Julian P. Boyd are perhaps the single greatest individual scholarly contribution to the study of Thomas Jefferson.[43]

Dr. Charles T. Cullen succeeded Julian Boyd as the editor of *The Papers of Thomas Jefferson*. After seeing Boyd's final volume to press, Cullen, who had three assistant editors to the single editor, Ruth W. Lester, who had assisted Boyd during his final two volumes, prepared a cumulative index to the first twenty volumes of the *Papers*. Boyd, originally intending that the project should be completed in ten years, envisioned a cumulative index for the whole collection and refused to include indexes for the individual volumes. Although occasional paperbound indexes were published for the first eighteen volumes, Cullen's index, published as volume 21 of the *Papers* in 1983, made Boyd's volumes fully accessible to scholars. In light of the slow progress of the project, Cullen undertook to include an index with every volume, beginning with volume 22, which appeared in 1986.

During the 1980s and 1990s funding was a persistent issue for successive editors of *The Papers of Thomas Jefferson*. After the initial contribution from the *New York Times* and Princeton the project received financial backing from the Ford Foundation, the National Historical Publications and Records Commission, the Time Corporation, the Dyson Foundation, the Andrew W. Mellon Foundation and the J. Howard Pew Freedom Trust, among others. In many cases the editors have made joint applications to foundations and government agencies in conjunction with the projects and bodies publishing the papers of Adams, Franklin, Madison, Hamilton and Washington via the Founding Fathers Corporation. Julian Boyd's successors, while they have been successful fundraisers, have not enjoyed the financial security that allowed Boyd the luxury of proceeding so slowly.[44]

Speed of publication remains the most pressing challenge for *The Papers of Thomas Jefferson*. There is an inherent tension between the exacting editorial standards established by Julian P. Boyd and the need to satisfy funding bodies, scholars and the public and to complete the project as soon as possible.[45] Boyd's successors, Charles T. Cullen (volumes 21–3, 1983–90), John Catanzariti (volumes 24–8, 1990–2000) and Barbara B. Oberg (volumes 29–31 [to date], 2000–), have together published ten volumes in twenty-four years in addition to overseeing the publication, under separate editors, of four titles in the topical second series during the 1980s. This is an impressive and consistent publication rate, but with thirty-one volumes published thus far (plus the volumes in the second series), the project has not yet reached its halfway point.

In an effort to complete publication of the *Papers* in a more timely manner, in 1998 the editors made a decision to split the chronological series. The office at Princeton, under the editorship of Barbara B. Oberg, would continue to publish the chronological volumes beginning with volume 29. A separate editorial project, under the auspices of the Thomas Jefferson Foundation at Monticello, would undertake to publish the papers from Jefferson's retirement. The Retirement Series, edited by J. Jefferson Looney, a former research associate and assistant editor of *The Papers of Thomas Jefferson* at Princeton, will appear concurrently with the volumes of the chronological series. The first volume of the Retirement Series was published in March 2005. It is hoped that by splitting the remaining volumes of *The Papers of Thomas Jefferson* between Princeton and Monticello and publishing them concurrently it will be possible to complete the project by the 250th anniversary of the Declaration of Independence in 2026, eighty-two years after Julian P. Boyd began the project.[46]

In 1950 the first volume of *The Papers of Thomas Jefferson* represented a major step forward in documentary editing. In the five decades since the appearance of the first volume, editorial standards have changed considerably. This is reflected in subsequent volumes. Under the editorial direction of Barbara Oberg and J. Jefferson Looney, respectively, recent volumes of the chronological and retirement series have been characterized by a more literal transcription style. The editors have also supplied translations of foreign-language documents. For example, with the publication of volume 30 of the *Papers* in 2004, Jefferson's idiosyncratic style of capitalization was retained and not modernized as in previous volumes. Although Boyd's three-part – descriptive, explanatory and textual – system of annotation has been retained, the long editorial notes which characterized Boyd's volumes have been dropped in recent volumes. When finally finished, *The Papers of Thomas Jefferson* will not only present a complete and definitive published version of Jefferson's papers but will constitute a sixty-volume testament to the evolution of documentary editing during the twentieth and twenty-first centuries.

VI

When Julian Boyd began to prepare the Jefferson papers for publication, microfilm cameras represented the cutting edge of technology in editorial publishing. The project approaches its halfway point at the dawn of the digital age. At the end of the twentieth century, the two institutions with the largest and most important collections of Jefferson manuscripts, the Library of Congress and the Massachusetts Historical Society, undertook to digitize their collections in order to make them available on the World Wide Web. Through his use of the letterpress and the polygraph, Jefferson embraced new technology in order to preserve his documentary legacy. Further, he believed that the best way to protect precious manuscripts was to print and distribute them in multiple copies. It is appropriate, therefore, that new technology is making Jefferson's documentary legacy more easily available and more widely dispersed than ever before.

In 1974 archivists at the Library of Congress microfilmed the Thomas Jefferson Papers held in the library's manuscript division. When filmed, the Library's collection of Jefferson papers – the largest in the world – filled sixty-five rolls of 35 millimeter microfilm. In 1998 and 1999 the Library arranged for Preservation Resources of Bethlehem, Pennsylvania to scan the millions of microfilm images to create digital images which could then be made available on the Internet via the Library of Congress's 'American Memory' website. The collection is accessible through 'search' and 'browse' pages that link to a database index of the papers. Readers can search the collection by the name of the author or recipient of a document, by its date and, for some documents, by text. For some documents brief explanatory notes as well as textual transcriptions are available. The digital Thomas Jefferson Papers allows anyone with access to the Internet to view manuscript images of almost the Library's entire Jefferson collection, thus providing unprecedented and unrestricted access for scholars. The site has had thousands of visitors since it was launched in 1999.[47]

In 1999 the second major holder of Jefferson documents, the Massachusetts Historical Society (MHS), also undertook to digitize its collections and make them available on the World Wide Web. Funded by the Save America's Treasures program and the Commonwealth of Massachusetts, the MHS launched the 'Thomas Jefferson Papers: An Electronic Archive', which presents digitized images of selected documents from the Coolidge Collection of the Thomas Jefferson Manuscripts held by the Society. The MHS website is not as comprehensive as the Library of Congress's 'Thomas Jefferson Papers', which presents *all* of its Jefferson manuscripts on the Web. The 'Thomas Jefferson Papers: An Electronic Archive' presents selected documents from the MHS including Jefferson's garden and farm books, book catalogs, architectural drawings, a hand-written copy of the Declaration of Independence to which will soon be added Jefferson's annotated draft of the *Notes on the State of Virginia*. The MHS 'Electronic Archive' allows readers access to some of the rarest and most significant documents in the corpus of Jefferson manuscripts. Like its counterpart at the Library of Congress, the 'Thomas Jefferson Papers: An Electronic Archive' is searchable and provides transcriptions and descriptive information about some documents.[48]

In 1796 Jefferson had noted that preserving documents in archives, while essential, was not enough. 'How many of the precious works of antiquity were lost, while they existed only in manuscript?' he asked. Jefferson was aware of the danger that manuscripts could be lost or destroyed, or could simply deteriorate due to the ravages of time. When William Waller Hening requested access to Jefferson's collection of Virginia laws, Jefferson feared that some of the volumes were so fragile that they would crumble to dust if handled. The best way to preserve manuscripts, he believed, was to publish them. 'Has there ever been one lost', he asked, 'since the art of printing has rendered it practicable to multiply and disperse copies?'[49] The digitization of manuscripts by the Library of Congress and the Massachusetts Historical Society provides for the reproduction and dispersal of original manuscript images, while allowing the widest access to Jefferson's papers without threatening the fragile originals. As such these projects represent the most important development in Jefferson studies since the publication of the first volume of *The Papers of Thomas Jefferson* in 1950.

The advent of digitized images of the Jefferson papers available free of charge on the World Wide Web raises a question whether it is necessary to continue publication of the volumes of *The Papers of Thomas Jefferson*, which are slow in coming, costly to produce and expensive to purchase. The cost of a complete set runs to thousands of dollars, beyond the reach of most readers. In consequence, most readers and researchers require access to a good research library in order to use a complete set of *The Papers of Thomas Jefferson*, whereas the digitized versions of the Jefferson papers are available to anyone with access to the Internet. Despite these limits and the intrinsic value of the digitized Jefferson papers, there is a clear need for *The Papers of Thomas Jefferson* in the digital age. This is owing to the weaknesses in the digital collections and the inherent strengths of the *Papers* as published.

While the digital versions of Jefferson's papers provide unprecedented and open access to the Jefferson papers, especially for those who live far from the archives in question, they are not without flaws. The most obvious challenge posed by the digitized documents is legibility. In most cases the digitized images were made from microfilm copies of the original documents. As such they are sometimes difficult to read and reproduce. Although notable (and largely successful) steps have been taken to produce true reproductions of the microfilmed documents, such as the use of compressed grayscale format, digitized documents, at least two steps from the originals themselves, can be difficult to read (although the online versions of the papers are often easier to read than the microfilm versions). This problem is exacerbated by the condition and legibility of the original manuscripts. A perfect reproduction of a somewhat blurry letterpress copy of a letter presents challenges notwithstanding the quality of the digitized image.

A second problem with the digital collections concerns their completeness. The Library of Congress's online Thomas Jefferson Papers presents nearly all of the Jefferson documents that the Library holds. The Massachusetts Historical Society's 'Thomas Jefferson Papers: Electronic Archive' presents an important but limited selection of its collection of Jefferson papers. Although these are the two most important archives possessing Jefferson manuscripts, their online collections, taken together, are not comprehensive. The online versions of the Jefferson papers provide greater accessibility, searchability and ease of use than the microfilm versions, but they are inferior, in important respects, to the printed versions available in *The Papers of Thomas Jefferson*.

The *Papers* provide the most complete and legible version of Jefferson's documentary legacy – in chronological order, including all extant documents written to as well as by Jefferson, accompanied by comprehensive indexes and now by translations of originals in foreign languages. Although Julian Boyd's introductory notes were occasionally excessive, the editorial notes still provide a useful guide for interpreting the documents. As important, useful and exciting as the digital collections of Jefferson documents are, they are not a replacement for *The Papers of Thomas Jefferson*, which remains the definitive source for Jefferson documents.

The advent of digital technology presents a challenge and opportunity to the editors of *The Papers of Thomas Jefferson*. The online versions of Jefferson's papers allow researchers to consult many of the original documents directly and thus complement the published versions found in *The Papers of Thomas Jefferson*. Further, the digitized collections are especially valuable in making the documents that have not yet appeared in the *Papers* more widely available to readers and researchers. As such they help rectify the problems arising from the relatively slow progress of the *Papers*. Digital technology may well transform the presentation of the *Papers*. It is possible to publish future (and past) volumes of the *Papers* in a digital as well as cloth-bound paper formats. Individual documents could have the definitive editorial apparatus that is the hallmark of the

Princeton edition while being completely searchable by subject, date, author, recipient, and so forth. The transcribed documents could then be linked directly to their manuscript originals in the Library of Congress, Massachusetts Historical Society and elsewhere. In 1950 Julian P. Boyd saw the advantage of such an arrangement when he noted that all of the transcriptions and microfilm images of Jefferson's papers would be deposited in the Library of Congress, '[t]hus it will be possible for future scholars to resort to one central depository to verify transcriptions or obtain full texts of summarized documents'. A digital version of the *Papers* allows for such verification. It could also provide affordable access, via online subscription for example, to the *Papers* for those who do not have access to a research library.[50]

VII

In 1960 Merrill Peterson prophesied that the publication of the Princeton edition would improve Jefferson's reputation.

> Primary documents are the beginning of historical understanding, but it was not until the end of the nineteenth century that American scholars made significant progress in the accumulation, verification, and analysis of the documentary record of the national life. The varied evidences of the movement in Jefferson historiography almost without exception, proved beneficial to his reputation. Jefferson's papers had been so badly managed – broken up, passed out as souvenirs, abandoned in private cabinets, or entirely lost, and botched in editing – that the recovery and purification of the record was one of the principal tasks of American scholarship.[51]

Thanks to the efforts of Julian P. Boyd and his successors, Charles T. Cullen, John Catanzariti, Barbara B. Oberg, J. Jefferson Looney and their assistants, 'the recovery and purification of the record' is well under way. Within a generation scholars and general readers will have access to as complete an edition of Jefferson's papers as it will be possible to reconstruct and reproduce since Jefferson's death in 1826. This will constitute one of the most significant achievements in the history of historical editing and American historiography. Despite Peterson's confidence, however, the publication of the definitive version of Jefferson's papers has not coincided with an improvement in Jefferson's treatment at the hands of historians. On the contrary, Jefferson's reputation has declined markedly over the past five decades.

Thomas Jefferson preserved his papers with an eye toward their eventual publication in the belief that he would be well served by future historians. They have told us much about Jefferson and his world –

ironically, perhaps more than he meant them to when he preserved them. Intended as a monument to Jeffersonian principles, the *Papers* have provided historians with a wealth of material on Jefferson that has allowed them to examine many different aspects of his life and legacy beyond the political concerns that Jefferson believed were at the center of historical inquiry. Their publication has coincided with the emergence of a more critical and comprehensive view of their subject. When Julian P. Boyd conceived of the project it was possible to represent Jefferson as he wished to be remembered, as *the* champion of America's republican values, which, in 1943, the United States sought to defend and export around the world. As the years have passed and successive volumes of the *Papers* have appeared, enriching our knowledge of Jefferson, such a view has become more difficult to sustain. Over the past sixty years historians have not, generally, viewed history as an ongoing struggle between liberty and tyranny as Jefferson did. As we shall see, they have brought different questions to the past – especially with regard to racial justice in the United States. This has prompted a more critical view of Jefferson, made possible, in part, by *The Papers of Thomas Jefferson*.

The Papers of Thomas Jefferson has emerged as one of the two most important institutions that have promoted the study of Jefferson over the past sixty years. The second institution is associated with his home, Monticello. Like the *Papers*, Monticello and the foundation that owns it were originally intended to memorialize Jefferson as the heroic Apostle of Freedom. Like the *Papers*, Monticello has come to epitomize a more complex view of Jefferson.

NOTES

1. John W. Campbell to TJ, 29 July 1809; TJ to John W. Campbell, 3 Sept. 1809, TJP.
2. TJ to Robert Walsh, 5 April 1823, TJP.
3. Lyman H. Butterfield, 'The Papers of Thomas Jefferson: Progress and Procedures in the Enterprise at Princeton', *American Archivist*, 12 (1949), 132.
4. *PTJ*, 3:497n. Jefferson wrote to Gates to request his assistance in recovering his lost records on 12 March 1793, *PTJ*, 25:363–4. Also see TJ to Horatio Gates, 21 March 1793, *PTJ*, 25:419–20; Horatio Gates to TJ, 15 April 1793, *PTJ*, 25:550; Horatio Gates to TJ, 19 April 1793, *PTJ*, 25:572. As a result of this transaction, transcripts of a significant body of Gates's letters from the southern campaign during the war are in the Jefferson papers in the Library of Congress. They are held as separate series, 'Series 2: Gates Letterbook Correspondence, 1780–81', in the TJP.

5. For a discussion of the SJL see *PTJ*, 6:vii–x. Also see John Catanzariti, ' "The Richest Treasure House of Information": The Papers of Thomas Jefferson', *Prologue: Quarterly of the National Archives*, 21 (1989), 42–3. Jefferson also kept a supplementary register of some correspondence and miscellaneous other papers not found in the SJL. This is known as the Summary Journal of Public Letters (SJPL) and is discussed in *PTJ*, 8:x.

6. TJ to James Madison, 1 Sept. 1785, *PTJ*, 8:462.

7. The information in this paragraph is based on Catanzariti, ' "Richest Treasure House of Information" ', 43, and Silvio A. Bedini, *Thomas Jefferson and His Copying Machines* (Charlottesville: University Press of Virginia, 1984). Jefferson made one exception when creating his personal archive. Although he preserved the letters he exchanged with his children and grandchildren, after the death of his wife, Martha Wayles Jefferson, at age 34 on 6 September 1782, he destroyed all the letters they had exchanged. As a consequence, historians know relatively little about Martha Wayles Jefferson or the nature of her relationship with Thomas Jefferson. See Malone, *Jefferson and His Time*, 1:396–7.

8. Original holograph will, Clerks Office, Albermarle County, Virginia, Photocopy TJP.

9. T. J. Randolph to H. A. Washington, 6 Aug. 1850, Tucker-Coleman Papers, College of William and Mary, microfilm copy Henry A. Washington Papers, LoC, as quoted in Paul G. Sifton, 'The Provenance of the Thomas Jefferson Papers', *American Archivist*, 40 (1977), 20–1. Sifton's article is the most complete account of the disposition of Jefferson's papers. A version of it can be found in the digital version of the Jefferson papers at the Library of Congress: 'Provenance and Publication History', http://lcweb2.loc.gov/ammem/collections/jefferson_papers/mtjprov.html.

10. George Tucker, *The Life of Thomas Jefferson*, 2 vols. (Philadelphia: Carey, Lea Blanchard, 1837).

11. T. J. Randolph to F. A. H. Muhlenberg, 27 Sept. 1846, Muhlenberg Family Papers, LoC, as quoted in Sifton, 'Provenance of the Thomas Jefferson Papers', 20.

12. These paragraphs are based on information in Sifton, 'Provenance of the Thomas Jefferson Papers', and Catanzariti, ' "Richest Treasure House of Information" ', 47–8.

13. H. A. Washington to James A. Pearce, 30 June 1854, Tucker-Coleman Papers, College of William and Mary, as quoted in Sifton, 'Provenance of the Thomas Jefferson Papers', 23.

14. Sifton, 'Provenance of the Thomas Jefferson Papers', 28–9.

15. Sifton, 'Provenance of the Thomas Jefferson Papers', 24.

16. Thomas Jefferson Coolidge, 'Remarks', Massachusetts Historical Society, *Proceedings*, 2nd series, 12 (1899), 264–73. During the twentieth

century, other members of the Coolidge family have made subsequent donations of Jefferson documents, mainly architectural drawings and personal correspondence to the Massachusetts Historical Society. The Society holds the second largest collection of Jefferson manuscripts after the Library of Congress. See 'The Coolidge Collection of Thomas Jefferson Manuscripts', http://www.thomasjeffersonpapers.org/about/.

17. *Thomas Jefferson Correspondence, Printed from the Originals in the Collections of William K. Bixby* (Boston: Private Printing, 1916). Twenty years later the Missouri Historical Society printed a selection of the letters that Bixby had given it. 'Correspondence of Thomas Jefferson in the Missouri Historical Society', *Glimpses of the Past*, 3 (1936), 77–133.

18. Helen Duprey Bullock, 'The Papers of Thomas Jefferson', in Constance E. Thurlow and Francis L. Berkeley, Jr., eds., *Jefferson Papers of the University of Virginia: A Calendar* (Charlottesville, VA, 1950), 279–91, 280n. Bullock's study originally appeared in *American Archivist*, 4 (1941), 238–49. The copies of complete sets of the account books are in the Library of Congress and the Alderman Library at the University of Virginia. Some of the account books are available online in Series 4, 'Account Books, 1767–1782' of the TJP.

19. Thomas Jefferson Randolph, ed., *Memoir, Correspondence, and Miscellanies from the Papers of Thomas Jefferson*, 4 vols. (Charlottesville, VA: F. Carr and Co., 1829).

20. For a discussion of the editing and publication of the *Memoir* see Peterson, *Jefferson Image*, 29–36.

21. Martha Jefferson Randolph to Joseph Coolidge, 12 May 1829, Jefferson Papers, MHS. Also see Martha Jefferson Randolph to Ellen Wayles Randolph Coolidge, 28 May 1829, Correspondence of Ellen Wayles Randolph Coolidge, Special Collections, University of Virginia. Both of these letters are available at the Family Letters Project: The Correspondence of Thomas Jefferson's Family Members: http://familyletters.data-format.com/default.aspx. I am grateful to Elizabeth Chew, the associate curator at Monticello, for sharing with me her unpublished paper, ' "Our Pioneering Way": Monticello, the Randolph Family and Jefferson's *Memoir* of 1829', presented at the 'Thomas Jefferson and the Founding Fathers in Retirement Conference' at Monticello on 4 March 2005. Chew's paper presents a detailed consideration of the editing of the papers and pays particular attention to the material circumstances in which the *Memoir* was edited.

22. 'Jefferson's *Memoirs and Correspondence*', *Edinburgh Review*, 1 (1830), 496–526; Peterson, *Jefferson Image*, 36.

23. After the original edition published in Charlottesville in 1829 by F. Carr and Company subsequent editions appeared in London in 1829 (published by H. Colburn and R. Bentley) and Boston in 1830 (published by

Gray and Bowen). An abridged French edition was published as *Mélanges politiques et philosophiques extraits des Mémoirs et de la correspondance de Thomas Jefferson*, 2 vols. (Paris: Paulin, 1833).

24. Henry A. Washington, ed., *The Writings of Thomas Jefferson*, 9 vols. (Washington, DC: Taylor and Maury, 1853–4). For details on Washington's appointment as editor and his working practices see Sifton, 'Provenance of the Thomas Jefferson Papers', 21–2.

25. J. M. Mason to H. A. Washington, 6 March 1850, as quoted in Sifton, 'Provenance of the Thomas Jefferson Papers', 21.

26. For Washington as a thinker see John Johns, *Memoir of Henry Augustine Washington, Late Professor of History, Political Economy and International Law, in William and Mary College, Virginia* (Baltimore: James Young, 1859) and Eugene Genovese, 'The President's Corner', *Historically Speaking*, 1:2 (March 2000), 1, available at www.bu.edu/historic.hs/sp00.html. For Washington's editorial bias see Peterson, *Jefferson Image*, 150n and L. H. Butterfield, 'Historical Editing in the United States I: The Recent Past', American Antiquarian Society, *Proceedings*, 72 (1963), 299.

27. Charles Francis Adams, Jr., 'The Printing of Old Manuscripts', Massachusetts Historical Society, *Proceedings*, 20 (1882–3), 182. Among the notable documentary publications of the mid-nineteenth century are Jared Sparks, *The Writings of George Washington*, 12 vols. (Boston: Ferdinand Andrews, Russell, Odiorne and Metcalfe, 1833–9); Peter Force, ed., *American Archives*, 4th Series, 6 vols. (Washington, DC: St. Clair and Force, 1837–46), 5th Series, 3 vols. (Washington, DC: St. Clair and Force, 1848–53); and Charles Francis Adams, *The Works of John Adams*, 10 vols. (Boston: Little Brown, 1850–6). Despite their limitations some of these collections – such as *American Archives* and *The Works of John Adams* – have stood the test of time rather well. The foremost twentieth-century editor of Jefferson's writings has cautioned against too much criticism of his nineteenth-century predecessors: 'Sparks and his contemporaries, as they proved over and over by the use of the words "life and correspondence" in their biographies made no nice professional distinction between editor, biographer, and historian. They were men of letters, using original sources and creating out of them books that had form, structure and, on the whole, integrity.' Julian P. Boyd, 'God's Altar Needs Not Our Pollishings', *New York History*, 39 (1958), 3–21, quotation pp. 10–11. For the development of historical editing and the emergence of professionalism among editors during the nineteenth century see: Butterfield, 'Historical Editing in the United States I: The Recent Past'; Boyd, 'God's Altar Needs Not Our Pollishings'; Lyman H. Butterfield, 'Editing American Historical Documents', Massachusetts Historical Society, *Proceedings*, 78 (1966), 81–104; Julian P. Boyd, 'Historical Editing in the United States II: The Next

Stage?', American Antiquarian Society, *Proceedings*, 72 (1963), 309–28. For commentary on the development of standardized practice in documentary editing at the turn of the twentieth century by two of its leading advocates see J. Franklin Jameson, 'Gaps in the Published Records of United States History', *American Historical Review*, 11 (1905–6), 817–31, and Worthington C. Ford, 'The Editorial Function in United States History', *American Historical Review*, 23 (1917–18), 273–86. Jameson, as director of the Carnegie Institution's Department of Historical Research, editor of the *American Historical Review* and director of the Manuscript Division of the Library of Congress, was a major proponent of documentary editing at the turn of the twentieth century.

28. For Ford's background see Allan Nevins, 'Paul Leicester Ford' in Allen Johnson and Dumas Malone, eds., *Dictionary of American Biography*, 20 vols. (New York: Charles Scribner's Sons, 1930–1), 6:518–20. Among the publications that Ford edited or compiled prior to taking on the Jefferson papers see: *Winnowings in American History*, 15 vols. (Brooklyn: Historical Printing Club, 1890–1); *Bibliotheca Hamiltoniana: A List of Books Written by, or Relating to Alexander Hamilton* (New York: Knickerbocker, 1886); *Bibliography and Reference List of the History and Literature relating to the Adoption of the Constitution of the United States, 1787–88* (Brooklyn: n. p., 1888); *Franklin Biography* (Brooklyn: n.p., 1889); *Writings of Christopher Columbus* (New York: C. L. Webster, 1892); and *The Federalist* (New York: Henry Holt and Company, 1898).

29. Paul L. Ford, ed., *The Writings of Thomas Jefferson*, 10 vols. (New York: G. P. Putnam and Sons, 1892–9). It also should be noted that Ford's edition appeared in two versions, one in ten volumes (1892–9) and another in twelve volumes – the Federal Edition appearing in a limited, numbered, signed edition of 1,000 sets (1904–5).

30. For Ford's editorial methods see Peterson, *Jefferson Image*, 294–5; Butterfield, 'Historical Editing in the United States I: The Recent Past', 300.

31. Andrew A. Lipscomb and Albert E. Bergh, eds., *The Writings of Thomas Jefferson*, 20 vols. (Washington, DC: Thomas Jefferson Memorial Association, 1903–4).

32. S. Fiske Kimball, ed., *Thomas Jefferson, Architect* (Boston: Riverside Press, 1916); Gilbert Chinard, ed., *The Commonplace Book of Thomas Jefferson* (Baltimore: The Johns Hopkins University Press, 1926); Gilbert Chinard, ed., *The Letters of Lafayette and Jefferson* (Baltimore: The Johns Hopkins University Press, 1929); Gilbert Chinard, ed., *The Correspondence of Jefferson and Du Pont de Nemours* (Baltimore: The Johns Hopkins University Press, 1931); Edwin M. Betts, ed., *Thomas Jefferson's Garden Book, 1766–1824* (Philadelphia: American

Philosophical Society, 1944); Edwin M. Betts, ed., *Thomas Jefferson's Farm Book* (Princeton: Princeton University Press, 1953).

33. John C. Fitzpatrick, ed., *The Writings of George Washington*, 39 vols. (Washington, DC: Government Printing Office, 1931–44).

34. *PTJ*, 1:xix. For the origins of the Princeton *Papers of Thomas Jefferson* see *PTJ*, 1:xviii–xx; Catanzariti, '"The Richest Treasure House of Information": The Papers of Thomas Jefferson', 49–51; and Lyman H. Butterfield, 'The Papers of Thomas Jefferson: Progress and Procedures in the Enterprise at Princeton', *American Archivist*, 12 (1949), 131–45; Peterson, *Jefferson Image*, 439–42.

35. Julian P. Boyd, 'Report to the Thomas Jefferson Bicentennial Commission on the Need, Scope, Proposed Method of Preparation, Probable Cost, and Possible Means of Publishing a Comprehensive Edition of the Writings of Thomas Jefferson', 25 Sept. 1943, as quoted in Catanzariti, '"The Richest Treasure House of Information: The Papers of Thomas Jefferson"', 51. The records of the Jefferson Bicentennial Commission are in the National Archives in Washington.

36. Julian P. Boyd, 'A General View of the Work', *PTJ*, 1:vii–xx, 'Editorial Method', *PTJ*, 1:xxv–xxxviii, quotations: xxvii, vii, xviii. Boyd proposed to publish a more comprehensive collection of papers than those assembled by Jefferson at his death since he would include Jeffersonian legislative, diplomatic and executive papers which were in public archives as well as those personal papers held by Jefferson at his death. See *PTJ*, 1:xiii–xiv for a discussion of the papers included (and excluded) from *The Papers of Thomas Jefferson*.

37. *PTJ*, 1:xiv, xv.

38. Butterfield, 'The Papers of Thomas Jefferson', 136, 138–9.

39. *PTJ*, 1:xxix.

40. For the different types of annotation included see *PTJ*, 1:xxxv–xxxvi. For the editorial note see 'Declaration of the Causes and Necessity for Taking Up Arms', *PTJ*, 1:187–92.

41. Catanzariti, '"The Richest Treasure House of Information: The Papers of Thomas Jefferson"', 39–41.

42. Catanzariti, '"The Richest Treasure House of Information: The Papers of Thomas Jefferson"', 52.

43. Noble E. Cunningham, Jr., 'The Legacy of Julian Boyd', *South Atlantic Quarterly*, 83 (1984), 340–4, esp. 343.

44. Catanzariti, '"The Richest Treasure House of Information: The Papers of Thomas Jefferson"', 52. As early as 1962 Julian Boyd was aware of the challenges funding posed to editorial publishing. See Boyd, 'Historical Editing in the United States II: The Next Stage?', 325–8.

45. In 1993 the *Princeton Alumni Weekly* estimated that the project might take 125 years to finish and thus would not be complete until the tricentennial of the Declaration of Independence in 2076. Tom

Krattenmaker, 'Reading Jefferson's Mail', *Princeton Alumni Weekly*, 10 Nov. 1993.

46. The information in this paragraph is based on a conversation between the author and J. Jefferson Looney at the International Center for Jefferson Studies at Monticello on 5 Aug. 2002. The process of concurrent publication has been employed by the University of Virginia Press in editing and publishing a modern edition of the *Papers of George Washington*. The Washington papers, currently totaling fifty volumes, have been published in five series over twenty-seven years.

47. Two portions of the Jefferson papers were not digitized: volume 10 of Series 7 (Miscellaneous Bound Volumes), which consists of newspaper clippings; and volume 3 of Series 8 (Virginia Records Manuscripts, 1606–1737), which could not be scanned owing to the poor quality of the original documents. See 'Building the Digital Collection', at: http://lcweb2.loc.gov/ammem/collections/jefferson_papers/mtjdigit.html.

48. See 'About this Website' at Thomas Jefferson [electronic edition]. *Thomas Jefferson Papers: An Electronic Archive*. Boston, MA: MHS, 2003. http://www.thomasjefffersonpapers.org/about/.

49. TJ to George Wythe, 16 Jan. 1796, *PTJ*, 28:583.

50. *PTJ*, 1:xxv. One model for how digital technology could be incorporated into *The Papers of Thomas Jefferson* is the new edition of the *Oxford Dictionary of National Biography* (H. C. G. Matthew and Brian Harrison, eds., Oxford University Press, 2004), which at sixty volumes and a cost of $13,000 is comparable to the projected final version of the *Papers*. In addition to the published version, Oxford University Press offers readers access to a searchable online version of the *Dictionary of National Biography*, which includes access to the complete text of the original 1884 edition for a subscription fee of $295 per year.

51. Peterson, *Jefferson Image*, 308–9.

CHAPTER 4

MONTICELLO

I

It is impossible to study the development of Thomas Jefferson's reputation since World War II without reference to the two institutions that have shaped and continue to dominate our understanding of Jefferson: *The Papers of Thomas Jefferson* and the Thomas Jefferson Foundation. Under the direction of Julian P. Boyd and his successors, the Princeton edition of *The Papers of Thomas Jefferson* has evolved into a sizeable, long-lived and immensely important entity. The *Papers*, along with the Thomas Jefferson Foundation, have been the driving forces behind the study of Jefferson since the mid-twentieth century. While the *Papers* have transformed Jefferson scholarship, presenting, albeit slowly, definitive texts of all Jefferson and Jefferson-related documents, the Thomas Jefferson Foundation, which owns Jefferson's home at Monticello, has been at the forefront of interpreting and presenting Jefferson to the public, while also engaging in and promoting the scholarly study of Jefferson. Either directly or indirectly these two institutions have contributed most to the burgeoning of Jefferson scholarship over the past half-century.

In 2004 and 2005 the United States Mint unveiled four new five-cent coins. Since 1938 the nickel featured a profile of Thomas Jefferson on its front and an image of his home, Monticello, on its reverse side. To mark the bicentenary of the Lewis and Clark expedition, Congress authorized the Mint to issue commemorative nickels. In March 2004 the Mint issued new coins that feature the traditional, left-facing profile of Jefferson on their obverse side. The reverse side of the new nickels for 2004 features either a facsimile of the 'Jefferson Peace Medal' that Lewis and Clark gave to Native American leaders on their westward journey, or an image of one of the keelboats that Lewis and Clark's Corps of Discovery used on its journey up the Missouri River. In September the Mint introduced new designs for 2005 nickels that feature a new image of Jefferson, facing right in a close-up three-quarters profile, accompanied by a reproduction of the word 'Liberty' in his handwriting. The reverse of the 2005 coins depicts either a bison or a view of the Pacific Ocean. Monticello was dropped from the new nickels in the 'Westward Journey Series'. In unveiling the new coins Becky Bailey, a spokeswoman for the Mint, stressed that while the new image of Jefferson would remain on the nickel in the future, Monticello would return to the reverse side of the coin in 2006. When Congress authorized the changes to the nickel to mark the Lewis and Clark expedition, Virginia's congressional delegation objected to the removal of Monticello and lobbied successfully to have Jefferson's home, one of their state's most popular tourist attractions, returned to the five-cent coin.[1] In 2006, a new five-cent coin will appear with a re-engraved depiction of Monticello on the reverse and a new, full-face Jefferson portrait on the obverse.

The numismatic negotiations between Virginia's congressional delegation and the Mint over Monticello give an indication of the close association in the public mind between Jefferson and his home. Along with his massive collection of papers, Monticello constitutes Jefferson's most tangible legacy. Unlike the papers, which, as they were originally published, focused on Jefferson's public career in a rather limited way, Monticello seems to reveal a more personal Jefferson to posterity. More than forty years ago Merrill D. Peterson wrote, 'Of Jefferson more than any other famed American it might be said that the history of the inner man was the history of his house.'[2] For scholars as well as the public at large this observation remains true. Approximately a half a million visitors a year trek up Jefferson's 'little mountain' to visit his home in an effort to learn about its owner and his times. Like Jefferson's papers, his home has informed and inspired successive generations as they seek to understand and interpret the meaning of Jefferson's life and times.

This chapter traces the history of the Thomas Jefferson Foundation and assesses its efforts to promote interest in Jefferson through his home. The history of the Foundation parallels that of *The Papers of Thomas Jefferson*. Both entities were created to celebrate Jefferson's achievements and his contributions to human liberty; they began as institutions devoted to perpetuating Jefferson's legacy as he wanted to be remembered. With the passage of time, both the *Papers* and the Foundation have contributed immeasurably to our knowledge of Jefferson and his time. In so doing they have moved well beyond celebrating Jefferson in their quest to better understand him. In consequence they have led students away from Jefferson's conception of the past and his place in history. Owing to the importance of Monticello in the history of the Foundation we must first consider briefly the history of Jefferson's home after his death in order to explain the origins and history of the Thomas Jefferson Foundation.

II

Thomas Jefferson spent more than forty years building and rebuilding Monticello on a mountaintop on the outskirts of Charlottesville. He began work on the original house in 1769. Over the next twenty-five years he constructed, but never quite completed, a Palladian mansion. In 1794, after retiring (temporarily) from public life, Jefferson returned to Monticello. Following his five-year sojourn in France during the 1780s, Jefferson had grandiose plans for his home. He began a remodelling project in 1796 that effectively meant tearing down and completely rebuilding Monticello. Although the workmen left in 1809 as Jefferson began his retirement, the final work on the porticoes of the second Monticello was not completed until 1823. It is the second Monticello, two and half stories high (though it appears to be only one story in height from the exterior through the use of trick windows), with its dome, east and west facing porticoes, and subterranean outbuildings extending in wings from the main house, that is a familiar image around the world and that has been visited by tens of millions of tourists over the past two centuries.[3]

When Jefferson lived there, Monticello was many things: a working plantation, a family home, an informal inn that provided hospitality to hundreds of visitors over the years – and not least a reflection of Jefferson's view of the world and how he wanted to be viewed by the world. The public rooms at Monticello conveyed Jefferson's interest in the past. He decorated Monticello's large entrance hall with art and relics that illustrated the natural, political and cultural history of America and Europe. These included Native American artifacts and evidence of North American natural history – including antlers, bows and arrows, lances, quivers, maps, buffalo skins, peace pipes and wampum belts – as well as classical sculptures and a copy of the Declaration of Independence, and busts of Voltaire and Turgot. On either side of the doors in the entrance hall were busts of Jefferson himself and of Alexander Hamilton. Monticello's parlor, the main social space in the building, was decorated with numerous religious and classical paintings along with portraits of historical figures including Columbus, Vespucci, Locke, Bacon, Washington, Franklin, Adams and Madison as well as Jefferson. The parlor also contained busts of Napoleon and Tsar Alexander I. The tea room was decorated with busts of revolutionary figures, Franklin, John Paul Jones, Lafayette and Washington.[4]

The décor of Monticello's public rooms reflected Jefferson's view of the past. The Native American artifacts were testimony to Jefferson's long-standing interest in the cultural history of America's indigenous peoples. They stand as tributes to cultures, the loss of which Jefferson mourned, but which were, in his conception of history, doomed to vanish before the progress of republican civilization. Many of the busts and portraits paid tribute to the thinkers and historical figures who had shaped modern history, the culmination of which would be the triumph of republicanism.

How does one explain the prominence given to Alexander Hamilton, Jefferson's great adversary or to such non-republicans as Napoleon and Tsar Alexander I? With regard to Hamilton Joanne Freeman writes:

> It was concern for his reputation that inspired him to put Hamilton's bust in the main entrance way to Monticello; there could be no nobler act than to acknowledge the greatness of one's enemies – and only the greatest of men could defeat such a foe. Positioned in Jefferson's American museum alongside Indian artifacts and moose antlers, Hamilton's bust is a political hunting trophy, evidence of the path not taken and the superiority of those who chose the right course.

The busts of Napoleon and Alexander in the parlor echoed the juxtaposition of Jefferson and Hamilton in the entrance hall. Although Jefferson expressed some optimism about the supposed scientific and philosophic interests of the tsar, Jefferson's admiration for Alexander derived from the Russian ruler's conquest of Napoleon. While the absolutism of the tsar was unfortunate, Alexander had played a crucial role in defeating the tyranny of Napoleon. Just as Jefferson had defeated Hamilton's anti-republican schemes, so too Alexander had thwarted Napoleon's ambitions for global dominance. If the bust of Hamilton represented a road not taken, so too did that of Napoleon. Jefferson intended that the busts of Alexander and Napoleon as well as the portraits and busts of leading figures from European history should underscore the global historical nature of the struggle between republicanism and tyranny. The men and women who visited Jefferson's parlor would be reminded just what was at stake in that struggle when they gazed upon the busts of Napoleon and his conqueror. Among its many purposes, Monticello stood as a physical monument to Jeffersonian principles.[5]

Sadly, when Thomas Jefferson died, Monticello also stood as a physical monument to his fiscal plight. On his death, Jefferson owed his creditors $107,273.63. He left Monticello to his daughter, Martha, and named her son, Thomas Jefferson Randolph, his executor. Six months after Jefferson's death, Randolph was compelled to sell much of Jefferson's property in an attempt to discharge the debt. On 9 January 1827 the *Richmond Enquirer* advertised that 'the whole residue of the personal property of Thomas Jefferson' would be auctioned at Monticello. The auction began on 15 January and lasted for five days. Among the 'residue' of Jefferson's property were 130 slaves, as well as Monticello's furnishings and farm equipment. The sale raised $47,840. Martha Jefferson Randolph retained the decaying Monticello, where she lived with her husband, Thomas Mann Randolph. In July 1828, after the death of Thomas Mann Randolph, Thomas Jefferson Randolph advertised the house for sale for $70,000 but found no buyers. Curious scavengers and souvenir hunters vandalized the empty, derelict house, which fell into a state of rapidly worsening disrepair.[6]

In 1831 Monticello passed out of the hands of Jefferson's descendants. A twenty-four-year-old Charlottesville apothecary named James Turner Barclay purchased the house for $4,500. Barclay, who had little regard for Jefferson, was not interested in the house, which he allowed to decay further. In 1832 a visitor wrote of Monticello, 'The first thing that strikes you is the utter ruin and desolation of everything.'[7] Rather, Barclay coveted the 550 acres of land around the house, upon which he intended to raise silkworms. The scheme failed and Barclay, frustrated by the steady stream of tourists and curiosity-seekers who constantly descended on the house, offered it and the grounds for sale. In 1834, Barclay sold Monticello to Uriah Levy, a lieutenant in the United States Navy, for $2,700. Levy was born in Philadelphia in 1792 and made a career in the navy and a fortune in New York real estate. Levy, who encountered constant anti-Semitism in the navy, was a great admirer of Jefferson, particularly his advocacy of freedom of conscience. In 1858 Levy wrote, 'Let every year add to our love and veneration for Thomas Jefferson. There is no fear of his being made an idol, his acts and example forbid that but the most grateful emotions of our hearts cannot inspire our lips to utter language which will more than express the just mode of our praise for him.' While Levy did not explain explicitly why he purchased Jefferson's home, one of the leading students of the subject suggests that the purchase was 'an act of homage to the author of the Declaration of the Independence and the [Virginia] Statute of Religious Freedom'.[8]

Uriah Levy was an infrequent visitor to Monticello, which he used mainly as a summer home. Nonetheless he cleaned up the house and grounds. He employed a caretaker, Joel Wheeler, to make repairs and to perform necessary maintenance on the building and grounds. During his ownership Uriah Levy reversed the decay of Monticello. When Levy died in 1862, shortly before his seventieth birthday, he left Monticello to the people of the United States. Of course the people of the United States were at war with one other in 1862 and the federal government rejected the bequest. Just before Uriah Levy's death the Confederate government seized Monticello as the property of an enemy alien. The Confederates briefly used the house as a military hospital. After the war different members of the Levy family were involved in a prolonged legal battle over the ownership of the house. The building continued to deteriorate owing to neglect and deliberate abuse at the hands of Wheeler (who had ably managed the house while employed by Uriah Levy) until 1879, when Jefferson Monroe Levy, Uriah Levy's nephew, gained legal ownership of Monticello by buying out the claims of his uncle's other heirs.

Jefferson M. Levy was a successful New York lawyer and businessman who, like his uncle, used the house as a vacation retreat. His efforts and substantial investment allowed the house to survive the ravages of time and neglect. While Jefferson Levy, a staunch Democrat and later a congressman from New York, admired Jefferson and honored his memory, he treated the house for what it was – a private home that he owned. Although Levy spent a considerable amount of money on restoring Monticello, he also made changes to the house; for example, he replaced skylights with dormer windows which altered the lines of Jefferson's original designs. While Levy tried to accommodate the thousands of visitors who flocked to Jefferson's home and grave annually, he also sought to maintain his privacy and occasionally imposed restrictions on the tourists.

Jefferson Levy's ownership had saved Monticello from ruin. Nonetheless his countrymen did not always appreciate his contribution to preserving one of the nation's most significant historic homes. At the turn of the twentieth century some campaigners called for Monticello to be made a public monument to Jefferson. Several factors lay behind this movement. The development of the automobile meant that more people could visit Monticello from afar. As the number of visitors increased to nearly 50,000 per year so too did reports that Jefferson Levy did not always provide a hospitable welcome for tourists to what remained his private home.[9] Further, by the turn of the twentieth century the historic homes movement had gained currency. In 1858 the Mount Vernon Ladies' Association had purchased the plantation of George Washington and restored and opened the home as a museum. The success of Mount Vernon suggested that other homes of the Founding Fathers might be similarly preserved for posterity, and Monticello seemed an appropriate candidate. Finally, the Levy family had never been popular as caretakers of Jefferson's home (and, by extension, his legacy) owing to their Judaism. The upsurge in nativism, xenophobia and anti-Semitism in response to the 'new immigration' of the early twentieth century reinforced, for some, the notion that the Jefferson M. Levy, as a Jew, was unworthy to own Jefferson's home.[10]

Early in the twentieth century, Maud Littleton, a Texan married to a New York congressman, began a campaign for the government to acquire Monticello. In 1909 she visited Monticello and was disappointed with the experience. She felt that Levy's ownership of the house diminished its connection to Jefferson. Several years later she recalled her visit:

Everything was disappointing. I had a heavy-hearted feeling. There was
nothing of Jefferson to me at Monticello. He had dropped out and the
Levys had come. One could hear and see only the Levys and the Levy
family, their deeds of valor, their accomplishments, their lives. And I
wished I could get them out of my mind, but when I left Monticello
Thomas Jefferson was but a disappearing memory, run out into and mixed
up with the Levys.[11]

Littleton was particularly aggrieved at what she felt was the poor state
of Jefferson's grave.[12] In 1911 she wrote a pamphlet, *One Wish*, that
presented an unfavorable picture of the history of Monticello while it was
owned by the Levy family and called for the United States to appropriate
the money to buy Monticello from Levy.[13] In 1912 Littleton founded a
group called the Jefferson-Monticello Memorial Association, which had
as its objective making Monticello a national shrine. In the summer and
autumn of 1912 Littleton testified on the issue before Congress, to which
Levy was elected as a representative from New York in October. In
December the House of Representatives rules committee voted against
purchasing Monticello by a margin of 141 to 110. Maud Littleton did not
give up. She continued to campaign for the public purchase of Monticello.
Although she won the support of prominent Democrats, including
Secretary of State William Jennings Bryan, she could not convince
Congress to appropriate the necessary funds. Unlike the Mount Vernon
Ladies Association, which successfully raised private money to purchase
Washington's home, the Jefferson-Monticello Memorial Association
failed in large part because it sought state funding exclusively for the
purchase of Jefferson's home. Maud Littleton did succeed in besmirching
the reputation of Jefferson M. Levy, who had done so much to preserve
Monticello from utter ruin in the aftermath of the Civil War.[14]

III

Jefferson M. Levy suffered financial and business setbacks as a result of
World War I. Soon after the conflict he was forced to put Monticello up
for sale for the price of $400,000. Two new women's organizations – the
Thomas Jefferson Memorial Association, based in Richmond, Virginia,
and the National Monticello Association, based in Washington, DC –
attempted unsuccessfully to raise the money to buy Monticello from Levy.
Early in 1923 two Virginia-born New York lawyers, Stuart Gibboney
and Henry Alan Johnston, hosted a private dinner at the Vanderbilt Hotel
in New York to discuss the possible purchase of Monticello with interested friends and acquaintances in New York's legal and financial
communities. The group nominated Gibboney and Moses H. Grossman,

another New York lawyer, to negotiate with Levy over the purchase of Monticello. Gibboney and Grossman met with Levy's lawyer and agreed on a price for Monticello and its grounds of $500,000. The buyers committed to making a down-payment of $100,000 by December 1923, with a payment of a further $100,000 upon taking title to the property and the balance of $300,000 paid off over a number of years by means of a mortgage. To borrow the money to purchase the home, a new foundation had to be created. On 13 April 1923, Thomas Jefferson's 180th birthday, the Thomas Jefferson Memorial Foundation (TJMF) was officially incorporated in Albany, New York, 'for the purpose of establishing Monticello as a memorial to the Author of the Declaration of Independence and for the purpose of inculcating through patriotic education a better understanding and appreciation of the life and service of Thomas Jefferson'. From its inception, the TJMF was dedicated to promoting the image of Jefferson as Apostle of Freedom. Its founders believed that the best manner of promoting such a view would be by presenting Jefferson's home to the public. Stuart Gibboney was elected president of the TJMF.[15]

Although the TJMF included Theodore Roosevelt, Jr. and University of Virginia president Edwin A. Alderman among its early incorporators, most of its early officers and governors were New York lawyers (many of whom had Virginia connections) with a strong allegiance to the Democratic Party. Among the original incorporators of the Foundation were once and future Democratic presidential aspirants, Alton Brooks Parker, William Gibbs McAdoo and the party's 1924 nominee John W. Davis. Patricia West, the leading student of the connection between the Foundation and politics, suggests that the links between the party and the TJMF during its early days were close. By appealing to Monticello and the Jefferson image, West argues, Democratic activists like Stuart Gibboney sought to bridge the rural/urban and wet/dry splits within the party. The Foundation's early involvement in politics occasionally aroused controversy. Gibboney, who had supported the McAdoo wing of the Democratic Party, invited the New York governor, Democrat Al Smith, to speak at Monticello on 4 July 1926. At the time Smith, a Catholic and a wet, was embarking on the campaign that secured him the Democratic nomination in 1928. His trip to Monticello would be his first public appearance in the South during the campaign. The Smith invitation ignited a firestorm of controversy around the TJMF. Angry prohibitionists, anti-Catholics and ordinary southern Democrats, as well as Ku Klux Klan members, objected to the proposed visit and besieged Gibboney and Smith with more than a million letters, some of which contained death threats. In May, Smith withdrew his acceptance of Gibboney's invitation. Eventually the political winds shifted in favor of the TJMF. The election in 1932 of Franklin D. Roosevelt, a governor of the TJMF and friend of Gibboney, meant that the Foundation had a friend in the White House. However, as the New Deal consolidated the Democratic coalition, the type of bridge-building among the party's different constituencies envisioned by Gibboney was no longer necessary. With the death of Stuart Gibboney in 1944 the TJMF shed its political allegiances.[16]

Despite their political sympathies, the officers and governors of the TJMF were far more concerned with paying for Monticello and promoting the Foundation's educational and patriotic mission during the 1920s and 1930s than playing politics. At the beginning of 1924 the TJMF owed its creditors and the Levy family $400,000. It also required hundreds of thousands of dollars in additional revenue to maintain, improve and restore the house, outbuildings, grounds and access to the site. On 13 April 1924 the Foundation launched a campaign to raise $1 million in order to clear the TJMF's debts and to pay for the running costs of Monticello. A variety of schemes were instituted to this end, including annual Jefferson's Birthday parties to be held in schools. In 1924 a 'Boys Pilgrimage Election Contest' was held in which boys received a vote for every 10 cents that they raised. Every boy who won 25,000 votes ($2,500) would be taken on a tour of Monticello, Washington and Philadelphia. Thirty-five boys were taken on the tour and, after the costs of the trip were taken into account, the TJMF raised more than $39,000 from the scheme. Building on the success of the boys' 'election' a grander event was held for girls in 1925. Each girl who received 50,000 votes ($5,000) would be taken on an educational trip to France. Fifty-eight girls were taken on the trip and the Foundation raised nearly $114,000. The TJMF also requested donations. Contributors who gave more than $1,000 were named 'Monticelleans' and given a lifetime pass to the site. Although there were some substantial donors during the early days – such as the financier Felix Warburg, who gave $35,000 to the TJMF – most of the funds raised by the Foundation came from small donors and from the entry fee, 50 cents, paid by Monticello's visitors (the number of whom increased from 20,000 in 1924 to more than 80,000 in 1937).[17]

At times during the Foundation's early years there seemed to be a tension between its need to raise money and its educational mission. In 1960 Merrill Peterson questioned the dignity and educational value of the early fundraising activities. His views were echoed in 1965 by Walter Muir Whitehill, who served on the TJMF board of governors from 1956 to 1976 and wrote:

> I doubt whether many of my fellow directors of the Thomas Jefferson Memorial Foundation know all of the complicated elements in the history of Monticello prior to its purchase in 1923 by the Foundation . . .

Certainly, if any of them remembered some of the corny antics that their predecessors had to indulge in to raise money for the purchase – senators disguised as railway conductors and popularity contests that sent pretty girls to Paris – they refrained from telling me when I joined the board.

Theodore Fred Kuper, the Foundation's national director during the early days, took exception to the characterization of the early fundraising activities as undignified diversions of little educational value. After Walter M. Whitehill's comments were published, Kuper wrote a lengthy letter to him explaining the severe financial challenges facing the Foundation that necessitated the 'corny antics' derided by Whitehill. In his manuscript notes on the early history of the Foundation, Kuper was more critical of Merrill Peterson (then holding the TJMF-endowed chair at the University of Virginia). He wrote:

> Unfortunately, Prof. Peterson got a warped, wrong view of the Foundation's work. Education is not a process limited to textbooks, college buildings, curricula, and seats and desks in school. Education is a lifetime process starting with the babe at its mother's breast and ends after the final illness. When children in schools all over the country learned about Jefferson, pronounced a pledge of faith, gave a penny – Even when thousands saw Jefferson's own gig on parade or in the Sesquicentennial World's Fair in Philadelphia. When the Foundation had a Freedom of Religion Day, a Freedom of the Press Day; a Future Farmers of America Day at Monticello, Everyone of the affairs or stunts (depending on whether one feels sweet or sour when he writes about it) all of these, in my mind, are educational . . . There never was one item in the work of the Foundation before I took hold or after I did that deserved any snicker or that violated the 'quiet dignity of Jefferson.' Absolute integrity, dignity, enlightenment and education were at all times our basic principles. We never broke them.

Several years later, James A. Bear, the Monticello curator (to whom Kuper had directed his comments), wrote more diplomatically of the TJMF's early fundraising efforts, 'It must be borne in mind that in seeking to raise money the Foundation always stressed its educational basis while making its appeal. This is one of the constants of its history.'[18]

In addition to its fundraising activities, the TJMF also sought to generate publicity for Monticello and Jefferson. It organized essay contests for schoolchildren; sponsored the placement of a bust of Jefferson in New York's Hall of Fame; lobbied Congress to establish a commission to commemorate the sesquicentennial of the Declaration of Independence as well as the hundredth anniversary of Jefferson's death on 4 July 1926;

shone a huge searchlight on Monticello, and arranged special days to celebrate freedom of religion and the press as Jeffersonian values.[19] According to Theodore Kuper the TJMF had several interrelated goals when it undertook such activities. On one level it was necessary to promote Monticello if the Foundation was to escape its debts.

> [I]f our aim was to assure self support for Monticello, it was necessary to carry out a nationwide selling job to publicize Monticello so thoroughly that the needed supporting visitors would come and continue to come in constantly growing numbers, notwithstanding the fact that Monticello was not close to a metropolitan city as Mt. Vernon is to Washington, notwithstanding that Charlottesville was off the main routes, and notwithstanding the early disinterest in Jefferson and continued disregard for him in some quarters. And all the time chasing the pennies and the dollars and struggling even through defaults in payment.[20]

Further, according to Kuper, it was necessary to resort to 'stunts' and 'events' to raise the profile of Jefferson, who was a 'forgotten man' in 1923 when the TJMF began its work. As Kuper remembered, 'when we started work there were no current books on Jefferson. Even old book shop[s] were surprised at our inquiries, and got rid of what old stuff they had at bargain prices. Three dollars bought the three volume set of Randalls and for $3, 4 or 5 I bought for myself and others the 20 volume set published in 1903.'[21] If the TJMF was to fulfill its mission to educate the public about Jefferson, it had to raise the money to retain and restore Monticello. In order to raise money it had to raise the profile of Jefferson and his home.

Despite the criticisms of later commentators and the occasional misstep, the TJMF's early efforts were remarkably successful. The fundraising program was so effective that in 1940 Stuart Gibboney was able to declare, 'the mortgage has been satisfied of record, Monticello is now entirely free of debt'.[22] Meanwhile the work of restoring Monticello remained a high priority. In 1924 Fiske Kimball, an expert on historic preservation and architecture, was named the chairman of the Foundation's restoration committee. Over the next thirty years – until his death in 1955 – Kimball oversaw the restoration of Monticello, including the house, dependencies and grounds. Those involved in the process intended to restore Monticello as much as possible to its condition in 1809 when Jefferson had 'completed' the construction of his home. By the early 1950s this had entailed removing the structural changes added by the Levys; rebuilding parts of the house and its dependencies which had deteriorated over time; replacing furniture, artifacts, and books with those owned by Jefferson or exact contemporary duplicates;

replanting the gardens according to Jefferson's records; and adding modern heating, air conditioning and fire protection systems. All of this required painstaking historical research as well as more than $500,000. Under Kimball's direction the house, grounds and furnishings of Monticello were returned to a state 'as close to Jefferson's conception as possible'.[23]

During the 1930s and 1940s, as the TJMF put its house in order (literally), and cleared its debts, Thomas Jefferson enjoyed a surge in popularity. As the bicentennial of his birth approached in 1943, Jefferson was no longer a 'forgotten man' as he had been in the 1920s. President Franklin D. Roosevelt was a professed admirer of his predecessor – he spoke at Monticello on 4 July 1936 – and a vigorous supporter of the proposed Jefferson memorial, which he dedicated in 1943. Numerous new publications and biographies of Jefferson appeared in the 1930s and 1940s, including the first volume of Dumas Malone's comprehensive *Jefferson and His Time* (1948), and Princeton University Press began the task of editing and publishing the definitive edition of Jefferson's papers. Through its efforts to publicize Jefferson and his home, and the participation of its officers and governors in various commemorative activities, the TJMF had contributed to the surge in enthusiasm for Jefferson. As Theodore Kuper had predicted, increased publicity for Jefferson led to an increase in the number of visitors to Monticello, which in turn fostered Jefferson's popularity. At the height of the Depression in 1937 Monticello attracted more than 80,000 visitors. After World War II Monticello attracted 100,000 visitors in 1946. That number doubled in 1951, the first year in which 200,000 tourists ascended Jefferson's 'little mountain'.[24]

In the latter half of the twentieth century the TJMF updated, shortened and subtly refocused its mission statement. By the late 1980s it was no longer necessary for the Foundation to generate publicity for Jefferson and to promote Monticello as a memorial to him. Rather than promoting Monticello as a monument to Jeffersonian ideals, the Foundation's new mission was 'Preservation and Education', defined as: 'Preservation – to conserve, protect, and maintain Monticello in a manner which leaves it enhanced and unimpaired for future generations – and Education – to interpret and present Thomas Jefferson to the widest possible audiences, including scholars and the general public.'[25] This represented a subtle transition in the Foundation's mission. The founders of the TJMF had intended that they should create a patriotic shrine to Jefferson at Monticello. Over the years the TJMF had moved away from simply promoting Jefferson as a patriotic symbol to adopting a more scholarly and critical view of Monticello's owner. Ironically, this refocusing was made possible by the accomplishments of the Foundation's founders.

In 1973 Theodore Kuper reflected with pride on the achievements of the founders of the TJMF:

> By 1954, the 'founding' administration has completed its task. All mortgages and debts were paid. The constantly growing attendance made Monticello, indeed, a self-supporting shrine the realization of the Founders, Gibboney's and Kuper's dream.
>
> Now not only the upkeep of the property, the handling of the visitors, the lectures by the guides, all could be and were improved. The established support provided funds for all of this.[26]

By the early 1950s the first generation of TJMF officers had given way to their successors. Having put Monticello on a sound footing financially and made great strides with regard to the restoration of the buildings and grounds, the TJMF could focus on its teaching mission. While the work of restoration and interpretation would continue over the subsequent fifty years, the Foundation would become more deeply involved in promoting the study of Jefferson. It would do so on a variety of levels, actively engaging in public and academic history. The shift is best represented in the Foundation's name. In 2000 the Thomas Jefferson Memorial Foundation dropped 'Memorial' from its name, becoming the Thomas Jefferson Foundation (TJF). Rather than simply promoting Jefferson's virtues, as the founders of the TJMF had, their successors would also take a more critical look at Monticello's owner. In so doing the TJMF/TJF has provided, along with *The Papers of Thomas Jefferson* at Princeton, much of the energy for the boom in the study of Jefferson since World War II.[27]

IV

Around 10:15 on the morning of 9 April 2004, Huaihai Wang, an interpreter at the United Nations, arrived at the Monticello ticket office with his wife, Grace, a real estate agent, and their eight-year-old son Matthew. The Wang family had travelled to Charlottesville from their home in Cresskill, New Jersey to visit Monticello for the first time. Upon their arrival, Daniel P. Jordan, the president of the Thomas Jefferson Foundation, greeted the Wangs because Huaihai Wang was the twenty-five millionth visitor to Monticello since the Foundation had acquired the house in 1923. Jordan presented the family with lifetime passes to Monticello as well as a basket of souvenirs, declaring, 'This is truly a historic milestone for Monticello and the Foundation's stewardship of this world treasure.' The Wangs were then taken on a special tour of the house.[28]

In the eighty years since the TJMF opened Monticello as a public attraction it has averaged 312,000 visitors per year. The number of visitors rose steadily from 20,091 in 1924 to nearly 463,000 in 2003. (See Table 4.1.) Monticello boomed during the 1970s, 1980s and 1990s. In 1976 a record number of visitors, 671,487, commemorated the bicentennial of the Declaration of Independence by visiting the home of its author; they also honoured the 150th anniversary of his death. In 1993 more than 620,000 people visited Monticello to mark Jefferson's 250th birthday. For twenty-one consecutive years Monticello attracted more than 500,000 visitors annually. However, in the aftermath of the attacks on the United States in September 2001 annual attendance dropped below 500,000 for the first time since 1980. In 2003, 463,000 tourists – slightly more than the figure for 1980 – went to Monticello, representing a decline of nearly 8 percent from the 2001 figure (and more than 17 percent from the number of visitors in 1996). It remains to be seen whether the recent decline in attendance signals a long-term trend or is merely an anomalous consequence of the disruption in travel and leisure that followed the attacks on 11 September 2001.[29]

Table 4.1   Annual Visitors to Monticello, 1923–2003

Year	Number of visitors	Adult admission price ($)
1924	20,091	.50
1927	49,446	.50
1937	80,513	.50
1948	136,751	.75
1958	237,020	1.00
1963	270,039	1.00
1969	383,692	1.25
1973	519,032	2.00
1976	671,487	2.00
1980	461,850	3.00
1984	507,174	4.00
1988	561,781	7.00
1993	622,137	8.00
1996	561,306	9.00
2003	463,733	11.00

Sources: Rebecca L. Bowman, 'A Chronology', in *Celebrating Seventy-five Years of Preservation and Education: The Thomas Jefferson Memorial Foundation, 1923–1998* (Charlottesville, VA: TJMF, 1998), 20–5; *Monticello Newsletter*, 15:1 (Spring, 2004).

For most of the more than eighty years during which the TJF has owned Monticello, guided tours have been the main means by which visitors have seen the house. During the earliest days of the Foundation's ownership, when there were relatively few visitors and the house was largely devoid of furnishings and decorations, tourists were allowed to wander through the house unescorted. Although this practice continued occasionally during quiet periods down to the early 1970s, the overwhelming majority of visitors to Monticello have seen the house on one of the guided tours provided by the Foundation.[30] By showing Monticello to more than twenty-five million visitors over more than eighty years, the TJF has probably done more to shape Jefferson's image than all of the scholars who have studied Jefferson during the same period. The number of readers of the thousands of scholarly articles and monographs written on Jefferson and aspects of his life is insignificant by comparison with the number of people who take the house tour at Monticello. Even more popular biographical studies aimed at a general audience cannot approach anything like such a large number of readers. For the majority of the hundreds of thousands of visitors who make the journey to Monticello annually, their most important source of information on Jefferson is their tour guide.

During the Foundation's early years a hostess greeted visitors in Monticello's entrance hall, and assigned them to one of six guides who escorted them through the house. Between 1923 and 1951 the guides were African American men who wore navy blue uniforms and red waistcoats with brass buttons. According to Mrs. Terry Tilman, who served as hostess in the early 1940s, 'Their tours were not difficult as the mansion was sparsely furnished . . . In each room a framed list of the contents hung on the wall. The guides pleased the guests. I feel they were more entertaining than factual and prone to delight in legends.' Although Theodore Kuper had lectured the early guides on Jefferson and 'frequently corrected fanciful additions' to the tour, according to Tilman, during the 1940s guides related popular legends such as 'Tarleton rode his horse in the entrance hall – a scar in the flooring gave evidence if not proof of this. [Body] Guards slept over Mr. Js bed – Portraits covered the oval openings but guards could peer through opening of eyes – And the bed could be pulled up to the ceiling. The most far out story was that Mr. J escaped from the British, by having his horse shoes reversed and riding out through the air or plumbing tunnel.'[31]

As the strenuous efforts of Fiske and Marie Kimball to restore Monticello and its décor met with success, there was more in the house for the guides to show to visitors. In the 1940s the Kimballs strove to improve the guides' presentation of the house by stressing 'Jefferson's recognized abilities and accomplishments' and excluding 'the numerous and exaggerated, but delightful tales' which had been a feature of the tours.[32] In 1951 the TJMF's board of trustees took a crucial decision to replace the African American men with middle-class white women as guides, who were now called 'hostesses'. Fiske Kimball, who had voted against the removal of the African American guides, and his wife collaborated with the new head hostess, Terry Tilman, to write a text of a new tour of the mansion, which presented descriptions of each room, its purpose and decorative elements. Tilman oversaw the training of the hostesses, which consisted of learning the text of the tour and reading Dumas Malone's biography of Jefferson as well as Sarah Jefferson Randolph's *Domestic Life of Thomas Jefferson*. For the next twenty-five years the format of the tour remained the same. Although Terry Tilman recalled that 'visitors resented our becoming more factual and less entertaining' the new format was largely successful as the number of visitors increased steadily over the next generation.[33]

Contemporary accounts suggest that race and gender bias were not explicit factors in the replacement of male African American guides with white female hostesses. Rather, those who recalled the decision stressed the improvement in the quality and accuracy of the tours as a result of the change. In 1973 Theodore F. Kuper contrasted the hostesses' performance with that of the earlier guides: '[The] Hostess system has proven much more successful, educational, inspirational, and results in much less vandalism than in most public places.' Kuper noted that on recent visits to Monticello he had been pleased by the performance of the hostesses: 'The excellence and inspiring manner of the service of the Monticello Hostesses delighted and thrilled me. Their service is a vital contribution to the effectiveness of the Life of Monticello and the work of the Foundation.'[34] Regardless of whether the replacement of the African American guides with white hostesses improved the quality of the house tour as intended, a crucial consequence of the decision was that the faces which greeted the swelling numbers of visitors to Jefferson's home over the next generation would be female, genteel, southern and white.[35]

At its meeting in the autumn of 1977, the TJMF board resolved to 'explore alternative options to the traditional tour of the house', which, according to member William Howard Adams, 'can become too rigid and stereotyped and frequently unsatisfying for more sophisticated or better informed visitors'.[36] The board of trustees created an Ad Hoc Committee on Interpretation to review the content and presentation of tours at Monticello, chaired by Adams. James A. Bear, who had succeeded Fiske Kimball as curator and then became research director at Monticello, prepared an internal report on the tour that he submitted to the Committee on Interpretation in June of 1978. The report noted that overall visitor reaction to the tour was excellent and strongly recommended retaining the tour as established in the 1950s – that is, presenting Jefferson to the public through a room-by-room examination of the ground floor of his home and its artifacts – while adapting the content as more items were added to the rooms in light of recent research, strengthening the training of the hostesses, and making a presentation to visitors outside of the house while they waited for their tours to begin. The report also urged that visitors be encouraged to examine the exterior of the house, particularly in light of the increased knowledge of Monticello's gardens and dependencies (thanks to the efforts of TJMF researchers). It urged visitors with specialized knowledge, who might be bored with the traditional tour, to phone ahead so that they could be shown around the house by a guide with particular expertise in their area of interest.[37]

During the 1980s the public presentation of the house and grounds at Monticello evolved significantly. In 1980 the hostesses became guides again as the first male docent since 1951 was employed to lead visitors around the house. Also in 1980 the National Endowment for the Humanities provided the first external funding for archaeological research at Monticello. This grant helped to fund excavations at Monticello, particularly relating to the dependencies of the main house – including the slave quarters on Mulberry Row – which began in 1982. In 1983 parking lots and the ticket office were removed from the mountaintop. In 1984 Dr. Daniel P. Jordan was appointed as director of the TJMF. Under Jordan's leadership the public presentation of the TJMF became more sophisticated. In 1985 a Monticello visitors' center was created on Route 20. Located near the main highway, the visitors' center presented an exhibit on Jefferson at Monticello while providing tourists with self-guided tours of the Monticello grounds as well as a gift shop. In the late 1980s the TJMF created departments of education, visitor services, restoration, development and public affairs, as well as centers for historic plants and research, all of which helped to incorporate the Foundation's research and restoration efforts with its presentation of Jefferson and his home to visitors. Nonetheless, the basic structure of the tour – presenting Jefferson to the public through a room-by-room examination of the ground floor of Monticello – remained largely unchanged.[38]

In one area – the treatment of slavery and race – change was relatively slow in coming to Monticello, but when it came, the pace of change was very rapid indeed. As late as 1989 James Oliver Horton and Spencer C. Crew lamented the treatment of slavery at Monticello:

> The innovation evident at some historic sites seems to have had little effect at Monticello . . . Docents continue to use the passive voice when referring to the activities of slaves, called servants on all but one occasion during our

visit in the spring of 1987. There is still the illusion that anything of importance at Monticello centered on Jefferson. Only if visitors toured, unescorted, the tunnels beneath the main house did they come upon a small photograph exhibit telling of an archaeological project to restore the slave quarters and study the social and cultural lives of the great plantation's residential majority. This was the only evidence of the influence of recent scholarship at this historic site.

Monticello visitors might never know that those referred to as cooks, farm workers, or even skilled craftsmen were in reality plantation slaves. Our informal visitor survey showed that tourists did not associate slaves with such titles and that although most of the adults understood that Jefferson held slaves (only two of the twelve children knew this), slave-holding was seen as incidental to his life and that of the plantation. Unfortunately, the tour encouraged such views and did more to glorify Jefferson than educate the public about life at Monticello.[39]

Whether the reluctance to discuss slavery reflects unease about discussing the more unpleasant aspects of Jefferson's life is impossible to determine. Regardless of the explanation, the omission of slavery from the Monticello tour was an egregious mistake. Since the 1950s the burgeoning scholarship on slavery in the United States was probably the most important development in American historiography. To neglect the subject at Jefferson's home – which had been a working plantation – left a huge gap in the coverage of Jefferson on the tour and in the view of Jefferson presented to the public.

The archaeological photographs of the Mulberry Row excavations that James Horton and Spencer Crew saw in 1987 were augurs of change, however. During the 1990s slavery assumed a much larger place in the work of the TJMF and on the Monticello tour. In 1989 the Foundation produced a brochure that enabled visitors to follow a self-guided tour of the slave quarters on Mulberry Row. Soon thereafter the Foundation created an African American advisory panel and in 1993 launched a themed tour devoted to Monticello as a plantation community which proved very popular. More significantly, slavery became a prominent feature of the main house tour. In a 1992 memo, all guides were instructed to 'make slavery a running theme on *every* tour; to do this pick up aspects of the theme on four or five of the nine stops'. The guides received advice on how to incorporate slavery by relating it to specific objects and rooms, were supplied with quotes by Jefferson relating to slavery, and were advised how to employ non-prejudicial language in discussing Jefferson's attitudes and practices with respect to slavery.[40] When, in 1998, DNA testing confirmed that Jefferson was the likely father of at least one child by one of his slaves, Sally Hemings, this development too was incorporated into the house tour. By the end of the 1990s slavery, for so long ignored on the Monticello tour, was one of its central features.[41]

In its treatment of race and slavery at Monticello, the TJF followed the general trend in Jefferson historiography over the past several generations. Having conceived Monticello as a patriotic shrine to Jefferson and the principles for which he stood, the Foundation neglected or ignored slavery during its early years. Eventually, in response to the growing literature on Jefferson's relationship to slavery – itself a product of broader study of slavery in the United States fuelled in part by the Civil Rights movement – the Foundation began to consider slavery as an aspect of Jefferson's legacy. As an inevitable consequence of such an approach, the heroic image of Jefferson as Apostle of Freedom that prevailed during the early years of the Foundation's history – the image that Jefferson sought to represent to posterity – was impossible to sustain. While the process was slower at Monticello than among Jefferson scholars more broadly, the Foundation's history of dealing with slavery and race as aspects of Jefferson's life illustrates why his legacy has become so complex.

By the end of the twentieth century the TJF began to undertake the most substantial changes to the house tour in fifty years. The goal of the $100 million *Jefferson Lives* fundraising campaign is to transform the presentation of Monticello to the public. The funding, raised ahead of schedule by June 2004, is being used to create three 'campuses' around Monticello – a scholarly center at nearby Kenwood which hosts the International Center for Jefferson Studies; an administrative center at the base of the mountain; and a 'Monticello Gateway and Jefferson History Center' on Route 20. The Gateway will be the first port of call for visitors, who will be able to view permanent and temporary exhibits on Jefferson and his time, and will include restaurant and shopping facilities. Tourists will then be able to approach the house itself, either on foot or by shuttlebus, via a parkway. Having first viewed the exhibits at the Gateway center, visitors to Monticello will be better informed before they undertake the guided tour of the house. The Monticello they see will be more like the home as it was in Jefferson's day. The restoration of the dependencies and gardens will continue and most modern changes to the mountaintop will be removed.[42]

In his 1978 report to the Committee on Interpretation, James A. Bear noted that among the 'soft areas' in the training of hostesses was that 'the unique Jefferson has been stressed'.[43] That the presentation of Jefferson as singular should be deemed a weakness seems an odd criticism. However, because the tour drew attention to Jefferson's home and possessions, particularly his various time-saving inventions, it tended to foster a view of Jefferson as a clever designer and architect, rather than as political theorist, revolutionary, party leader or president. Ten years earlier Bear had written:

[A]s more people came to Monticello, they and their hosts, realized what an attractive commodity the ingenious Jefferson had become. An immediate affinity sprang up between these hundreds of visitors and Mr. Jefferson. Visitors and the Foundation fathers soon rediscovered this other Jefferson, lost for so long in the limbo of public service. He must have come as a big surprise to those running Monticello who had spent the better part of fifteen years attempting to promulgate the Jefferson of the Declaration of Independence. After the 1930s they began to exhibit this other man while they went about restoring the house and grounds and trying to fill the latter with furnishings, many of which accentuated this utilitarian side. Like it or not, the American public was more interested in seeing and hearing about Jefferson, the gadgeteer, than Jefferson, the writer and disciple of human freedom.[44]

Although Bear originally wrote about Monticello during the 1930s, the problem persisted. When he reviewed the Monticello tour in 1978 he wrote, 'One important responsibility is the matter of presenting Jefferson and his remarkable dwelling with its automatic doors, folding ladder, seven day clock, the dumb waiters, and other characteristic contrivances without obscuring deeper truths.'[45]

The problem was not that Jefferson came across as unique. Rather, the nature of his uniqueness was the issue. Merrill Peterson writes, 'Monticello was meant to commemorate Jefferson's services to the nation, above all his political philosophy. It was meant to solemnize his place in history and to celebrate his ideas anew. It was meant to be a "mecca of democracy" or a symbol of "the American ideal of government", however that was understood.' By emphasizing his home and possessions, however, the 'deeper truths' of Jefferson's life and thought were hidden. Paradoxically, as the TJMF restored Monticello ever more accurately, Jefferson became a 'museum-piece . . . the general tendency was to feature Monticello rather than Jefferson, the relics of his domestic life and aesthetic vision rather than the political philosophy'.[46]

While by touring Monticello visitors can acquire a detailed understanding of Jefferson as a slaveholder, plantation manager, architect, natural historian and family man with a wide range of interests, the Jefferson who wrote the Declaration of Independence or compiled the Anas remains a distant figure. The political Jefferson, who sought through his actions and his documentary legacy to shape history's judgment of him, is all but absent. Hundreds of thousands of visitors tour Monticello annually. While they find much to admire and criticize about Jefferson they learn relatively little about Jefferson's politics or philosophy – the subjects upon which he expected to be judged and for which he wanted to be remembered. This problem reflects the nature of Monticello as an historic home and the difficulty of presenting intellectual history through artifacts on a relatively brief tour.[47]

V

The Thomas Jefferson Foundation's activities extend far beyond the house tour at Monticello, important though that may be in reaching the public at large. In addition to its active engagement in public history, it also funds and promotes research on all aspects of Jefferson's life and times. This scholarly engagement makes it among the most important institutions in shaping Jefferson's legacy.

By the mid-1950s, its financial status secure, the restoration of Monticello at an advanced stage, and the presentation of the house to the public through guided tours well established, the TJMF turned its attention to promoting the scholarly study of Jefferson. In the first instance the Foundation sought to collaborate with its near neighbor, the University of Virginia, the creation of Jefferson's retirement years. According to Theodore Kuper, 'From the beginning the Foundation properly regard[ed] the University as a living shrine of Jefferson.'[48] The university, for its part, had been a strong supporter of the Foundation and its goals throughout the years. Edwin Alderman, president of the university, had been one of the original incorporators of the TJMF in 1923 and had served on the Foundation's board of governors from 1923 until 1931. It was serendipitous that both the Foundation and the university underwent simultaneous, and mutually reinforcing, transformations during the 1950s that improved the quality of both institutions.

The university, historically all white and all male, had, since the Civil War, evolved into a comfortable regional university where members of the southern gentry and professional classes met to socialize and establish personal and business contacts that would serve them after graduation. In the wake of World War II the university was transformed by the demographic, social and educational changes that swept the United States. Between the 1950s and 1970s the university expanded its academic offerings, admitted African American and female students, and invested in faculty and resources, all of which enabled it to become one of the pre-eminent public universities in the United States. This occurred just as the TJMF, itself financially secure and seeking to complement its public history activities by promoting the academic study of Jefferson and his times, sought closer links with the university. In 1957 the Foundation made the first of a series of annual grants to the university's Alderman Library for the purchase of material – in print or manuscript – relating to Jefferson and his time. In 1958 the Foundation endowed a chair in history in its name at the university. Jefferson's biographer, Dumas Malone, was appointed as the first holder of the chair in 1959. Malone was succeeded by Merrill Peterson in 1962. Peterson held the chair until 1988 and was succeeded by Peter S. Onuf in 1993.

The Foundation's early collaboration with the University of Virginia benefited both parties. Reflecting on these activities, Theodore Kuper concluded, 'none of the Founders could have wished or dreamed for a better program of annual contribution by the Foundation to Jefferson's beloved university and the selection of Jefferson Professors'. The holders of the Jefferson Foundation chairs have each been major figures in their fields whose scholarship has made a significant contribution to our understanding of Jefferson and his time. Dumas Malone's six-volume *Jefferson and His Time* (1948–81) remains the definitive biography of Jefferson. Merrill Peterson wrote a superb study of Jefferson's reputation, *The Jefferson Image in the American Mind*, as well as an outstanding one-volume biography, *Thomas Jefferson and the New Nation* (1970). Peter Onuf's many publications have examined, among other themes, the intersection of American geographic expansion and Jeffersonian thinking. He has collaborated with many scholars as both an editor of essay collections and the supervisor of numerous Ph.D. theses. His essay collection, *Jefferson Legacies* (1993), is perhaps the most important such collection relating to Jefferson and should be read alongside the major works of Malone and Peterson. By endowing a chair in history at Virginia, the TJMF has made a major ongoing contribution to Jefferson studies.[49]

Since its inception the Foundation had always been involved in scholarship and research, with its employees actively engaging in research on the material culture, archaeology, architecture and history associated with Jefferson and Monticello. Beginning in the early 1990s the TJMF became more directly involved in promoting and disseminating research in Jefferson more widely. In 1993 the Foundation launched Monticello Monographs, a series of books – currently fourteen titles distributed by the University of North Carolina Press – written by leading scholars for a general audience on different aspects of Jefferson's life and career or the history of Monticello.[50] In the same year two of the Foundation's historians, Lucia C. Stanton and Diane Swann-Wright, undertook the *Getting Word* project in which they have collected and compiled oral histories of the descendants of Monticello's slaves. In 1994 the Foundation, in collaboration with the University of Virginia, established the International Center for Jefferson Studies (ICJS) at Kenwood, a tract of land adjoining Monticello. The ICJS, under successive directors Douglas L. Wilson, James Horn and Andrew Jackson O'Shaughnessy, has promoted Jefferson scholarship by sponsoring and hosting international conferences, seminars and lectures. It has awarded more than 150 research fellowships to pre- and post-doctoral scholars from around the world working on all aspects of Jefferson and his time. In 1999 the ICJS became home to the Retirement Series of *The Papers of Thomas Jefferson*, the purpose of which is to publish all of Jefferson's papers from 1809 to 1826 simultaneously with the ongoing project at Princeton. In 2002 the Jefferson Library, a 15,500 square foot research and study center, opened at the ICJS and has since become the hub of the ICJS's scholarly activities. In its decade of existence the ICJS has quickly emerged as the pre-eminent institution for the academic study of Jefferson, his time and his legacy.[51]

VI

In 1960, Merrill D. Peterson wrote: 'The knowledge of Jefferson possessed by some recent scholars surpasses that of his most intimate contemporaries (if there were any who were genuinely intimate with that reserved man). Their works have achieved a more richly textured and, as the candid observer must feel, a truer image of the man in his time.'[52] More than forty years later Peterson's words carry still more force. Thanks to the efforts of the Thomas Jefferson Foundation we know far more today about life at Jefferson's Monticello than we did forty or one hundred years ago. Similarly, owing to the labors of *The Papers of Thomas Jefferson* (which now collaborates closely with the TJF), we are privy to an increasing number of Jefferson's papers, which have opened up our understanding of Jefferson's intellect, his public life and his day-to-day experiences.

While anticipating that the future of Jefferson's reputation would still hold some surprises, Peterson concluded that Jefferson was safely ensconced in the pantheon as a national hero when the Jefferson Memorial was dedicated in 1943. As far as scholars are concerned this has not been the case. Herein lies the paradox at the heart of Jefferson's legacy. Jefferson provided historians with so much material that it has allowed them to study endlessly the many aspects of his life and times. In so doing he helped to ensure his own fame and to achieve a measure of immortality in the public and scholarly memory. However, as we have studied Jefferson based on his rich documentary and physical legacy we have moved steadily away from his conception of the past and of his place in it. Jefferson's belief that his life should be understood in the context of a global movement to advance republican values has been forgotten. Our knowledge of Jefferson has increased substantially over the past fifty years – thanks in large part to the efforts of the TJF and *The Papers of Thomas Jefferson*. This has led to a veritable explosion in publications on almost all aspects of Jefferson's life. Nonetheless, despite the best efforts of Jefferson himself to shape his posthumous reputation and the overtly patriotic motives of the founders of the TJF and the *Papers*, Jefferson's scholarly reputation has declined during the same period. One conclusion that can be drawn from this history is that Monticello is, among other things, a glorious monument to Jefferson's failure to win his battle with posterity.

NOTES

1. 'Westward Journey Series: First Changes for Nickel in 66 Years', United States Mint, Press Release, 4 March 2004; 'United States Mint Unveils Dramatic New Nickel Designs for 2005', Press Release, 16 Sept. 2004, both available at www.usmint.gov/pressroom. Also see Gordon T. Anderson, 'Another New Nickel on the Way', www.CNNMONEY.com, 13 Sept. 2004, 'House's Place on Nickel is Assured', *Monticello Newsletter*, 14:2 (Winter, 2003). On the new design for the 2006 nickel, see http://www.usmint.gov/mint_programs/nickel/index.cfm?action=returnToMonticello (viewed 5 March 2006).

2. Peterson, *Jefferson Image*, 380.

3. The most thorough study of Jefferson's building activities is Jack McLaughlin, *Jefferson and Monticello: The Biography of a Builder* (New York: Henry Holt, 1998). Also see William L. Beiswanger, *Monticello in Measured Drawings* (Charlottesville, VA: Thomas Jefferson Foundation, 1998); William L. Beiswanger et al., *Thomas Jefferson's Monticello* (Chapel Hill: University of North Carolina Press, 2002); and Susan R. Stein, *The Worlds of Thomas Jefferson at Monticello* (Harry N. Abrams: New York, 1993).

4. William Howard Adams, *Jefferson's Monticello* (New York: Abbeville Press, 1983); Beiswanger, *Thomas Jefferson's Monticello*; Stein, *The Worlds of Thomas Jefferson at Monticello*.

5. Joanne B. Freeman, *Affairs of Honor: National Politics in the New Republic* (New Haven: Yale University Press, 2001), 281–2. Jefferson wrote to John Adams on 5 July 1814, contrasting Napoleon and Alexander:

> Bonaparte was a lion in the field only. In civil life a cold-blooded, calculating unprincipled Usurper, without a virtue, no statesman, knowing nothing of commerce, political economy or civil government, and supplying ignorance by bold presumption . . . To the wonders of his rise and fall, we may add that of the Czar of Muscovy

> dictating, *in Paris*, the laws and limits to all the successors of the
> Caesars, and holding even the balance in which the fortunes of this
> new world are suspended.

TJ to John Adams, 5 July 1814, in Lester J. Cappon, ed., *The Adams–
Jefferson Letters*, 2 vols. (Chapel Hill: University of North Carolina
Press, 1959), 431.

6. For the sale of Jefferson's possessions and Randolph's attempt to sell
   Monticello itself, see 'Executor's Sale', *Richmond Enquirer*, 9 Jan. 1827;
   Niles' Weekly Register, 19 July 1828; 'Valuable Lands', Richmond
   Enquirer, 22 July 1828. Also see McLaughlin, *Jefferson and Monticello*,
   375–81.

7. John H. B. Latrobe, quoted in Merrill D. Peterson, ed., *Visitors to
   Monticello* (Charlottesville: University Press of Virginia, 1989), 120.

8. Quotations: [James A. Bear], Monticello since 1826: A Résumé Com-
   memorating the Fiftieth Anniversary of the Thomas Jefferson Memorial
   Foundation, 1973 (typescript), 3, TJF Archives; and Melvin I. Urofsky,
   The Levy Family and Monticello, 1834–1923 (Charlottesville: Thomas
   Jefferson Foundation, 2001), 68. Although the Levy family owned
   Monticello for longer than Jefferson and his descendants, their owner-
   ship received very little scholarly attention until recently. In addition
   to Urofsky's study see Marc Leepson, *Saving Monticello: The Levy
   Family's Epic Quest to Rescue the House that Jefferson Built* (New
   York: Free Press, 2001; repr. Charlottesville: University of Virginia
   Press, 2003). The next several paragraphs are based on these sources.

9. In 1902 Amos J. Cummings published in the *New York Sun* an account
   of a visit he made to Monticello in 1889: 'A National Humiliation'
   (which later appeared as a pamphlet). Cummings complained that he
   was charged by Levy's caretaker to see the house but forbidden from
   going inside because Levy was not in residence: 'Monticello is owned by
   a Levy, who charged patriotic Americans, Democrat and Republican,
   twenty-five cents admission to the grounds alone, and refuses admission
   to the house at any price during his absence.' He concluded that
   the federal government should appropriate the money to purchase
   Monticello. Amos J. Cummings, *A National Humiliation* (n.p.,
   1902); repr. in Peterson, ed., *Visitors to Monticello*, 174–82, quotation,
   181.

10. Peterson, *Jefferson Image*, 381–2. For the historic homes movement
    with particular regard to Monticello see Charles B. Hosmer, Jr., *Pre-
    sence of the Past: A History of the Preservation Movement in the United
    States before Williamsburg* (New York: G. P. Putnam's Sons, 1965), ch.
    viii; and Patricia West, *Domesticating History: The Political Origins of
    America's House Museums* (Washington, DC: Smithsonian Institution
    Press, 1999), ch. 3.

11. This quotation comes from Littleton's testimony before the House Rules

Committee in 1912 during hearings on whether Congress should appropriate the money to purchase Monticello. 'Statement of Mrs. Littleton before the House Rules Committee, July 24, 1912', *Congressional Record*, 62nd Congress, 2nd Session, Appendix, 859.

12. The descendants of Thomas Jefferson, *not* Jefferson M. Levy, owned the graveyard. During the nineteenth century Jefferson's gravestone had been vandalized over the years by souvenir-hunters who chipped fragments from the obelisk. In 1882 Congress appropriated $10,000 to replace the marker with a large facsimile. Some of the money was used to erect an iron fence around the cemetery and to build steps to it. Urofsky, *The Levy Family and Monticello*, 154. In response to public criticism about the poor state of Jefferson's grave, in 1913 his descendants – who, as owners of the graveyard, are entitled to burial there – established a formal group, the Monticello Graveyard Association, to maintain the site. At its first meeting on 14 April 1913 the group, whose membership was open to 'All lineal descendants of Thomas Jefferson', undertook to 'preserve, care for, and adorn the graves, grounds included in the Monticello Graveyard and to endeavor in every practicable way to protect and perpetuate the reputation and fame of Thomas Jefferson'. *Minutes of the First Meeting of the Monticello Graveyard Association* (Charlottesville, VA: Monticello Graveyard Association, 1913), 1, 2. The association changed its name to the Monticello Association in 1924. To this day the Monticello Association and not the owners of Monticello own and control the cemetery.

13. Peggy O'Brien [Maud Littleton], *One Wish* (Washington, DC: n.p., 1911).

14. Urofsky, *The Levy Family and Monticello*, ch. 5 and Leepson, *Saving Monticello*, ch. 4. Both Urofsky (155–61) and Leepson, (188–9) suggest that Maud Littleton employed anti-Semitic language in her attacks on Jefferson Levy.

15. Quotation, Stuart G. Gibboney, *Report of the President of the Thomas Jefferson Memorial Foundation* (25 Sept. 1926), 1. For the early history of the TJMF also see [Bear], Monticello since 1826. James A. Bear's original report was dated 1968; he revised it in 1973 and 1978. Also see 'The Record of the Purchase of Monticello (typescript, n.d.)', 73–18–35; James A. Bear, The History of Monticello and the Thomas Jefferson Memorial Foundation: Preparatory Notes and Manuscript, and [TJMF], *Celebrating Seventy-five Years of Preservation and Education: Thomas Jefferson Memorial Foundation, 1923–1998* (All of these documents are located in the TJF archives at the Robert H. Smith International Center for Jefferson Studies.) Additionally, see Hosmer, *Presence of the Past*, ch. 8; West, *Domesticating History*, ch. 3.

16. See West, *Domesticating History*, 108–21. For the furor over Gibboney's invitation to Al Smith see 113–14; 'Monticello since 1826', 19; and the *New York Times*, 15 and 16 June 1926. The officers of the

TJMF were sensitive to charges of partisanship. In his 1926 presidential
report, Stuart Gibboney asserted that the TJMF's educational activities
were 'non-partisan and purely patriotic' in nature. Gibboney, *Report of
the President* (25 Sept. 1926), 1. Theodore Kuper recalled that around
the same time as the Smith contretemps the Foundation became involved
in a controversy in Charlottesville when the TJMF invited Senator
Simeon Fess of Ohio, chairman of the Republican National Committee,
to speak at Monticello. A delegation from the Charlottesville Chamber
of Commerce confronted Kuper before Fess's speech and objected to
Fess's presence because he was a Republican. Kuper assured the businessmen that the TJMF 'was not a Political Organization – only
Patriotic' and that Fess was qualified to speak as a former history
professor and member of the TJMF's board of governors. According to
Kuper, 'Fess delivered his address, well received. – exercises successful.'
T. F. Kuper's Notes (26 Jan. 1973), ms. in Box: James A. Bear, ed., 'The
History of Monticello and the Thomas Jefferson Memorial Foundation:
Preparatory Notes and Manuscripts', TJF archives. Kuper's thirty-two-
page handwritten notes, drafted sometime between 1968 and 1973, are
a response to the first edition of James A. Bear's unpublished report,
Monticello since 1826. They provide valuable information about the
early days of the TJMF.

17. *Monticello since 1826*, 4–15. Attendance figures from *Celebrating
    Seventy-five Years of Preservation and Education*, 20–1.
18. Peterson, *Jefferson Image*, 384–8. Peterson suggested (385) that educa-
    tion was eclipsed by patriotic efforts during the TJMF's early days.
    Walter Muir Whitehill, 'Foreword', in Hosmer, *Presence of the Past*, 12.
    For Kuper's response to the criticism see: Theodore Fred Kuper to
    Walter Muir Whitehill, 18 Feb. 1971, typescript copy in James A. Bear,
    ed., The History of Monticello and the Thomas Jefferson Memorial
    Foundation: Preparatory Notes and Manuscripts, TJF archives; and
    T. F. Kuper's Notes, 11. Bear quotation: *Monticello since 1826*, 4.
19. See Appendix: Educational Activities Sponsored by Foundation Prior to
    1933 in James A. Bear, The History of Monticello and the Thomas
    Jefferson Memorial Foundation, Preparatory Notes and Manuscript.
20. T. F. Kuper's Notes, 24.
21. T. F. Kuper's Notes, 1.
22. *Monticello since 1826*, 15.
23. *Monticello since 1826*, 24. The restoration of Monticello is one of the
    most important developments in historic presentation in the United
    States during the twentieth century. For a brief overview see William
    L. Beiswanger, 'Musings on Seventy-five Years of Restoration', in
    Celebrating Seventy-five Years of Preservation and Education, 17–19.
    Also see, Hosmer, *The Presence of the Past*; West, *Domesticating
    History*; James M. Lindgren, *Preserving the Old Dominion: Historic*

Preservation and Virginia Traditionalism (Charlottesville: University Press of Virginia, 1993); and Norman Tyler, *Historic Preservation: An Introduction to its History, Principles and Practice* (New York: W. W. Norton, 2000).

24. Peterson, *Jefferson Image*, 384–94. For attendance figures see *Celebrating Seventy-five Years of Preservation and Education*, 21–2.
25. Monticello Staff Handbook (1989), 4, TJF Archives. This statement also appeared in the 1997 Staff Handbook.
26. T. F. Kuper's Notes, 18.
27. It should be noted that the 'Preservation and Education' mission has been sustained by a combination of successful fundraising that would make Stuart Gibboney proud (and envious). Monticello does not receive any state or federal funding. Rather, 'Support for the daily operation of Monticello is derived from ticket, Museum Shop and Catalog sales, annual giving, and income from a modest endowment. Restoration, conservation, acquisitions, capital improvements, and special programs are funded increasingly by gifts and grants.' Lucia C. Stanton, *Facts and Figures: A Quick Reference to Monticello and the Thomas Jefferson Memorial Foundation* (Charlottesville, VA: TJMF, 1987), revised by Mindy Keyes Black (Charlottesville: TJMF, 1997), 10. In recent years the Foundation, under the leadership of its current president, Daniel P. Jordan, has proved extremely adept at private and corporate fundraising. In 2003 the Foundation received more than $7.4 million in gift income. In the spring of 2000 the trustees announced an ambitious fundraising effort, *Jefferson Lives: A Campaign for Monticello in the Twenty-First Century*, with a stated goal of raising $100 million by April 2005, 'to expand Monticello's research, education, and publications programs; to support restoration, preservation, and interpretive projects; and to enhance the experience of Monticello's visitors'. By 30 June 2004 the campaign had raised $100,358,925. See 'Contributions Advance Monticello's Mission', *Monticello Newsletter*, 15:1 (Spring, 2004); 'Campaign Surpasses $100 Million Goal', *Monticello Newsletter*, 15:2 (Winter, 2004).
28. Wayne Mogielnicki, 'Monticello Passes 25 Million Mark in All-Time Attendance', TJF Press Release, 9 April 2004, www.monticello.org/pressroom, 'Monticello Passes 25 Million Plateau', *Monticello Newsletter*, 15:2 (Winter, 2004).
29. In 2002 just under 493,000 people visited Monticello. The figures on recent attendance are from the *Monticello Newsletter*, 14:1 (Spring, 2003) and 15:1 (Spring, 2004).
30. Report to the ad hoc Committee on Interpretation, 22 June 1978, TJF Archives, 11–12.
31. [Terry Tilman], Recollections [1986], TJMF Misc. Unprocessed Papers, TJF Archives; T. F. Kuper's Notes, n.p.; [Terry Tilman], Memoirs of a

Monticello Hostess [n.d.], TJMF Misc. Unprocessed Papers, TJF Archives. Local African American men had served as unofficial guides during the time when the Levys owned Monticello. See Cummings, *National Humiliation*. Between 1923 and 1951 the following men served as guides at Monticello: Willis Henderson, William Page, Benjamin Carr, Robert Sampson, Frank Page, Louie Carr, William Sampson, Monroe Smith, Donald Allen, Grover Draker, Frank Allen and Harry Taylor. Terry Tilman remembered, 'Willis Henderson was the outstanding guide, a photogenic, wise and witty gentleman. Because of his age he was asked, "Uncle, how long have you been here?" His reply always, "since 7 this morning." Guests came by the graveyard to enter – so when asked "Is Mr J. home?" he would reply, "You passed him on your way up." He could convey his opinion of a guest to me by raising his eye brows and wrinkling his nose. He often said in evaluating guests, "You can't tell a book by its cover." I would like to know how many times he posed for pictures.' Tilman, Recollections.

32. Report to the ad hoc Committee on Interpretation, 22 June 1978, 7–8.
33. Quotation, Tilman, Memoirs, n.p. Also see Report to the ad hoc Committee on Interpretation, 22 June 1978, 7.
34. T. F. Kuper's Notes, n.p. These views are echoed in the Report to the ad hoc Committee on Interpretation, 22 June 1978 and (perhaps unsurprisingly) Tilman, Memoirs, and Tilman, Recollections.
35. For an account of the Monticello tour after the hostesses took over see 'Our Man Stanley at Monticello', *New Yorker*, 34 (1958), 23–4; repr. in Peterson, *Visitors to Monticello*, 199–201. There is a syllabus of the tour, providing themes which hostesses could raise in each of the ground-floor rooms as well an account of their furnishings as they relate to Jefferson, in Appendix G of the Report to the ad hoc Committee on Interpretation, 22 June 1978, 52–7. For the Monticello tour c. 1951–78 see James A. Bear Papers, Box 90, 1967–1971: Topical – Hostess tours (script, daily record, 1967–1971), TJF Archives, Series 10; Frederick D. Nicholas and James A. Bear, Jr., *Monticello: A Guidebook* (Charlottesville: Thomas Jefferson Memorial Foundation, 1967) and see Terry Tilman, *Questions I Forgot to Ask My Hostess* (Charlottesville, VA: Holden Printing, 1975).
36. Report to the ad hoc Committee on Interpretation, 22 June 1978, 3.
37. Report to the ad hoc Committee on Interpretation, 22 June 1978, 28–9. For visitor responses to Monticello see James A. Bear Papers, esp. Box 87 (Hostess biographies, complaints, compliments), TJF Archives, Series 10.
38. *Celebrating Seventy-five Years of Preservation and Education*; William M. Kelso, *Archaeology at Monticello* (Charlottesville, VA: Thomas Jefferson Memorial Foundation, Monticello Monographs, 1997).
39. James Oliver Horton and Spencer C. Crew, 'Afro-Americans and

Museums: Towards a Policy of Inclusion', in Warren Leon and Roy Rosenzweig, eds., *History Museums in the United States* (Urbana: University of Illinois Press, 1989), 215–36, quotation, 230–1. Horton and Crew echoed the views of Thomas A. Greenfield, who visited Monticello in 1975:

> Even the docents' language denied the troublesome existence of slaves, euphemistically called servants when a reference was absolutely unavoidable. Greenfield also noted that the site interpreters used the passive voice when referring to Monticello's blacks, focusing away from the majority of the plantation's residents. Docents switched to the active voice, however, when they pictured Jefferson's actions. They might explain that 'Mr. Jefferson designed these doors' but use a passive 'The doors were installed originally in 1809' when referring to the activities of slaves. As surely as Jefferson designed the doors, black slaves built and installed them, yet interpreters' language highlighted the master's actions but buried the slaves' contributions.

Thomas A. Greenfield, 'Race and Passive Voice at Monticello', *Crisis*, 82, (1975), 146–7.

40. Elizabeth [Dowling Taylor] to Guides, 27 July 1992, Re: The interpretation of slavery on our tours. This advice was expanded upon in Elizabeth Dowling Taylor, Important Themes in the Interpretation of Slavery at Monticello, Nov. 1994, revised Oct. 1996; and Jay Boehm, Incorporating Slavery into Your House Tour, May 1997. All of these documents are in the Guides' Handbook, TJF Archives.
41. Lucia C. Stanton, Sally Hemings (1773–1835), Nov. 1989, revised Oct. 1994; Lucia C. Stanton, The Hemings–Jefferson Controversy: A Brief Account, March 1995, revised Nov. 1998, Guides' Handbook, TJF Archives. David Ronka, 'DNA Results Discussed', *The Moose and Elk: The Monticello Guides' Newsletter*, 5:2 (Winter, 1998–9), 2–3. The Hemings controversy is discussed at length in Chapter 6.
42. 'President's Letter', *Monticello Newsletter*, 11:2 (Winter, 2000).
43. Report to the ad hoc Committee on Interpretation, 22 June 1978, 11.
44. Monticello since 1826, 20–1.
45. Report to the ad hoc Committee on Interpretation, 22 June 1978, 4.
46. Peterson, *Jefferson Image*, 388, 387. See 387–94 for a discussion of the undemocratic image fostered by Monticello.
47. Nonetheless the TJF has endeavoured to present Jefferson's intellectual interests to visitors. In 1998 the main themes of the basic Monticello tour were identified as:

> 1. Thomas Jefferson is important to the story of American democracy.

2. Thomas Jefferson valued highly home and family life.
3. Monticello is a metaphor for Jefferson's mind.
4. Thomas Jefferson was a public-spirited universal man.
5. Monticello was a plantation, home to a vital community of enslaved African-Americans.

Elizabeth Dowling Taylor, Interpretive Objectives, Aug. 1998, Guides Handbook, TJF Archives. On the main tour this is done in the entrance hall, where Jefferson's collection of Native American and natural history artifacts is displayed. These items relate to Jefferson's interest in natural history rather than his political philosophy. In January and February 2004 a themed winter tour was offered, 'Feast of Reason: The Enlightenment at Jefferson's Monticello', which interpreted various material objects – such as Native American and natural history artifacts, portraits, scientific instruments and maps – as manifestations of Jefferson's interest in the Enlightenment. 'Tour to Center on the Enlightenment', *Monticello Newsletter*, 14:2 (Winter, 2003).

48. T. F. Kuper's Notes, 'Education-6', 2
49. T. F. Kuper's Notes, 'Education-6', 2; Monticello since 1826, 21–2.
50. The titles in order of publication are: Merrill D. Peterson, ed., *The Political Writings of Thomas Jefferson* (1993); Dumas Malone, *Thomas Jefferson: A Brief Biography* (1993); Lucia Stanton, *Slavery at Monticello* (1996); Douglas L. Wilson, *Jefferson's Books* (1996); William M. Kelso, *Archaeology at Monticello* (1997); Eugene R. Sheridan, *Jefferson and Religion* (1998); Lucia Stanton, *Free Some Day: The African American Families at Monticello* (2001); James P. Ronda, *Jefferson's West: A Journey with Lewis and Clark* (2001); Melvin I. Urofsky, *The Levy Family and Monticello, 1834–1923* (2001); Andrew Burstein, ed., *Letters from the Head and Heart: Writings of Thomas Jefferson* (2002); Silvio Bedini, *Jefferson and Science* (2002); Noble E. Cunningham, Jr., *Jefferson and Monroe: Constant Friendship and Respect* (2003); James E. Lewis, Jr., *The Louisiana Purchase: Jefferson's Noble Bargain?* (2003); Jennings Wagoner, *Jefferson and Education* (2004).
51. 'International Center for Jefferson Studies Marks Anniversary', *Monticello Newsletter*, 15:1 (Spring, 2004). Also see the various editions of the *ICJS Bulletin* available online at www.monticello.org.
52. Peterson, *Jefferson Image*, 446.

CHAPTER 5

JEFFERSON'S EPITAPH

I

Thomas Jefferson died at Monticello on 4 July 1826, the fiftieth anniversary of the adoption of the Declaration of Independence. In the months before his death, Jefferson prepared for the posthumous struggle over his place in history. As we have seen, he filed and organized his papers, which he left to his grandson, Thomas Jefferson Randolph, anticipating their future publication. He also designed his tombstone. He left specific instructions that his grave should be marked by a six-foot obelisk set atop a three foot square cube, of 'coarse stone'. Jefferson composed a simple epitaph that he wanted inscribed on the monument, '& not a word more'. It read:

> Here was buried Thomas Jefferson
> Author of the Declaration of American Independence
> Of the Statute of Virginia for Religious Freedom
> & Father of the University of Virginia

Jefferson explained that he had chosen these three actions from his myriad accomplishments 'because by these, as testimonials that I have lived, I wish most to be remembered'. He sketched the monument and wrote out his instructions and folded the paper with a copy of the epitaph he had composed for his wife, Martha, when she had died forty-four years earlier, in 1782. The instructions were discovered among his papers after his death and the tombstone was erected according to Jefferson's wishes.[1]

Why did Jefferson choose his authorship of the Declaration of Independence and the Virginia Statute for Religious Freedom, as well as his role in founding the University of Virginia, as the actions for which he most wanted to be remembered? He had, after all, served as a congressman, governor of Virginia, American ambassador to France, secretary of state, vice president and president of the United States as well as president of the American Philosophical Society. By eschewing these other accomplishments and activities to focus on the three which appeared on his gravestone, he underscored the importance of those three activities. If, as a two-term president of the United States, Jefferson chose not to mark his presidency on his gravestone, then he signalled to posterity that the accomplishments by which he wanted to be remembered were important indeed.

II
'Author of the Declaration of American Independence'

Thomas Jefferson wrote his autobiography between January and July 1821 (see Chapter 2). The original version of Jefferson's memoir contained a relatively short account of his drafting of the Declaration of Independence. Sometime between 1822 and 1825, probably in 1823, he excised this brief explanation and replaced it with a lengthier twenty-page version of the events in Congress during the summer of 1776. Jefferson asserted that he based this account, which focused on the adoption of the Declaration of Independence and the debates over the Articles of Confederation, on his own contemporaneous records. 'I took notes in my place while these things were going on,' he wrote, 'and at their close wrote them out in form and with correctness.' It is likely that Jefferson compiled his notes in 1776 and annotated and amended them over the years before inserting them into his autobiography.[2]

Thomas Jefferson took particular pride in his role as primary author of the Declaration of Independence, as is evidenced by his retention and amendment of his notes from the summer of 1776. In the years after 1776 he was unusually forthcoming in sharing his recollections and insights into the drafting of the Declaration with friends, associates, strangers and even rivals.[3] Jefferson sought in his autobiography, by recourse to the sources, to assert his primacy as the author of the Declaration at a time when that role was of increasing partisan significance.[4] Beginning in the 1790s Jefferson's authorship of the Declaration assumed partisan importance as Jefferson's Republicans appropriated the document as their own, in contrast to the counter-revolutionary tendencies of Federalists, who, along with other critics, continued to dismiss or diminish Jefferson's role in drafting the Declaration. In his biography of George Washington, John Marshall relegated Jefferson's contribution to the Declaration of Independence to a passive-voice footnote: 'the draft reported by the committee has generally been ascribed to Mr. Jefferson'. In an 1823 Fourth of July oration in Salem, Massachusetts, Federalist Timothy Pickering asserted, allegedly on the authority of John Adams, that Jefferson's contribution to the Declaration had been exaggerated. Pickering's oration, later published as a pamphlet, likely prompted

Jefferson to insert his amended notes into his autobiography. He sought through his autobiography and his epitaph to declare before posterity that he had been the major author of the founding document of the American republic.[5]

There were several versions of the Declaration of Independence: Jefferson's 'original rough draft', presented to Congress on 2 July 1776; the version as amended by Congress and the Committee of Five (Jefferson, John Adams, Benjamin Franklin, Roger Sherman and Robert Livingston) created by Congress to draft the Declaration; and the final version as adopted on 4 July 1776. The Continental Congress debated Jefferson's draft Declaration between 2 and 4 July 1776. Congress made a number of minor stylistic changes as well as deleting nearly 25 percent of Jefferson's original draft. Among the major changes, Congress excised clauses condemning the transatlantic slave trade (and blaming George III for fostering it); criticising the British people, and excoriating the British for the use of 'Scotch & foreign mercenaries' in attempting to suppress the American rebellion.[6]

Jefferson chafed at the changes made to his handiwork by Congress. When he inserted his record of Congress's deliberations into his auto-biography more than forty-five years later, he included the following passage:

> The pusillanimous idea that we had friends in England worth keeping terms with, still haunted the minds of many. For this reason those passages which conveyed censures of the people of England were struck out, lest they should give them some offence. The clause too, reprobating the enslaving the inhabitants of Africa, was struck out in complaisance to South Carolina & Georgia, who had never attempted to restrain the importation of slaves, and who on the contrary wished to continue it. Our Northern brethren also I believe felt a little tender under those censures; for tho' their people have very few slaves themselves yet they had been pretty considerable carriers of them to others.[7]

Although he had no alternative but to accept the changes – which he felt were the result of misguided political and diplomatic calculations – Jefferson always believed that his original draft of the Declaration of Independence was superior to the edited and amended document adopted by Congress. Immediately after the adoption of the amended Declaration Jefferson circulated copies of his original draft to friends and allies.[8] When he inserted his account of events in 1776 in his autobiography he was careful to include his draft 'as originally reported. The parts struck out by Congress shall be distinguished by a black line drawn under them; & those inserted by them shall be placed in the margin or in a concurrent column.'[9] Discerning readers, guided by Jefferson, would be able to read Jefferson's original draft while tracing the alterations – all of them for the worse – made by Congress.

The Declaration of Independence is in some ways the single most revealing case study in Jefferson's efforts to control his posthumous legacy. By inserting into his autobiography his contemporaneous (though edited and amended) notes on the drafting and adoption of the Declaration, as well as his original draft of the document, with the congressional changes, Jefferson answered his critics from beyond the grave. In his view, he demonstrated that he was the primary author of the founding document of the United States and, hence, the most important expositor of the nation's ideals – self-determination, republican government and equality – as outlined in the Declaration's eloquent preamble. This demonstration was a direct rebuke to his Federalist adversaries, such as John Marshall and Timothy Pickering, who had sought to downplay his contributions. By including his original draft of the Declaration Jefferson, the sensitive author, also claimed the last word in his argument with his congressional critics of 1776. He sought to show posterity that *his* version of the Declaration was superior to the one adopted by Congress in 1776. Jefferson again called the attention of posterity to the Declaration of Independence when he composed his epitaph, claiming authorship of the document. His autobiography, published a few years after his death, sought to determine how future generations would treat the Declaration.

For most of the nineteenth century the Declaration of Independence remained at the center of political controversy. Abolitionists and other opponents of slavery embraced the Declaration's assertion of universal equality to attack involuntary servitude. In so doing they appropriated the posthumous memory of Jefferson. Abraham Lincoln eloquently stated their position in 1859:

> All honor to Jefferson – to the man who, in the concrete pressure of a struggle for national independence by a single people, had the coolness, forecast, and capacity to introduce into a merely revolutionary document, an abstract truth, and so to embalm it there, that to-day and all coming days, it shall be a rebuke and a stumbling block to the very harbingers of re-appearing tyranny and oppression.[10]

By contrast, slavery's defenders sought to downplay the significance of the Declaration of Independence's claims in support of human equality, preferring to emphasize Jefferson's advocacy of states' rights in the Kentucky Resolutions when they did not dispute his authority altogether.[11]

The Declaration of Independence, long a subject of political controversy, did not really become an object of scholarly study until the twentieth century. Historians analyzing the document have followed two distinct, but related, lines of inquiry. In so doing they have closely followed the analysis of the Declaration presented by Jefferson. First, scholars have studied the evolution of the document through its various drafts, considering the changes made to Jefferson's draft by the Continental Congress. This textual analysis, originally undertaken by Jefferson himself in his autobiography, began early in the twentieth century with the publication in 1906 of John H. Hazelton's *The Declaration of Independence – Its History* and culminated in Julian P. Boyd's 1945 study, *The Declaration of Independence – The Evolution of the Text as Shown in Facsimiles of Various Drafts by its Author, Thomas Jefferson.* Boyd reproduced all known drafts of the Declaration, thirty-two pages of facsimile reproductions, along with an introductory essay that provided a context and explanation for the evolution of the Declaration from Jefferson's draft to the final version adopted by Congress. Boyd's collection – compiled to accompany an exhibit of the various drafts at the Library of Congress to mark the bicentenary of Jefferson's birth in 1943 – provided readers with definitive reproductions of the each of the Declaration's various drafts. The evidence presented and examined by Boyd allowed scholars to pursue the second main theme in their analysis of the Declaration, the study of its content.[12]

One question in particular has fascinated those who have written about the content of the Declaration of Independence: what are the origins and meaning of the ideological assertions – republican self-government, national self-determination, universal equality – contained in the different versions of the Declaration? Broadly speaking, all of the major studies of the Declaration have focused on this question to some degree. The first major intellectual history of the Declaration of Independence was Carl L. Becker's 1922 book, *The Declaration of Independence: A Study in the History of Political Ideas.* Becker argued that a doctrine of natural rights lay at the heart of the Declaration and the American Revolution more broadly. He traced the various origins and sources of natural rights in Jefferson's thinking, giving particular emphasis to John Locke's *Essay Concerning the Human Understanding* and *Two Treatises of Government.* According to Becker, Jefferson drew on Locke to assert that George III had violated the natural rights of Americans, thereby breaking the contract between the king and his subjects and justifying revolution.[13]

Carl Becker's analysis of the intellectual origins of the Declaration of Independence held sway for more than five decades.[14] Not until the late 1970s was Becker's analysis challenged. In 1978 the American intellectual, scholar and cultural commentator Garry Wills published a remarkable book, *Inventing America: Jefferson's Declaration of Independence,* which offered a dramatic reinterpretation of America's founding document and its primary author.[15] Wills argued that Jefferson's version of the Declaration of Independence is best understood as a product of the Scottish Enlightenment, transmitted to Jefferson, in part, by his tutor at William and Mary, William Small.

Garry Wills was at pains to distinguish between the different versions of the Declaration of Independence. His focus was Jefferson's original Declaration, submitted to Congress on 2 July 1776. He endeavored to recover the intellectual world of Thomas Jefferson in order to delineate the ideas and influences that lay behind Jefferson's Declaration and thus to recover its original meaning and intent. Wills contended that Jefferson's document was a product of the Scottish Enlightenment and that Jefferson's beliefs about the nature of man and society were derived from the writings of Scottish thinkers including David Hume, Adam Smith, Adam Ferguson and, particularly (in ascending order of importance), Lord Kames, Thomas Reid and Francis Hutcheson. According to Wills, Jefferson's Declaration can only be understood properly if it is read as the product of Scottish moral philosophy.

According to Wills, Jefferson's Declaration is not a 'Lockean' document – stressing individualism, property rights, and the contractual nature of society. Rather, Jefferson's Declaration, grounded in Francis Hutcheson's moral sense philosophy, presents the fledgling United States with a communitarian, egalitarian and humane origin at odds with the tradition of acquisitive Lockean individualism. Wills may have recovered Jefferson's alternative vision of America in his reading of Jefferson's Declaration but he knew that that vision did not come to pass. The opportunity was lost. As one reviewer wrote, 'The philosophy that surfaced in the Declaration of Independence was an alternative to individualism, but Wills is not under the illusion that the Scottish Enlightenment is a usable past. That world remains lost, an Atlantis submerged beneath the culture that crystallized around the essays of Emerson, the fiction of Alger, the metaphor of the competitive race.'[16]

From its first appearance *Inventing America* generated a great deal of interest. It appealed on several levels. Jefferson's admirers could find comfort in a portrait of their hero that stressed his egalitarianism. Wills argued at length that Jefferson advocated racial equality because Africans and Europeans, despite their physical differences, were equal when it came to their moral sense. This, according to Wills, was the motivation behind Jefferson's advocacy of emancipation. Wills goes so far as to suggest that Jefferson's proposal for the removal of free blacks from the United States after manumission was not racist.[17] Appearing as it did in the wake of the Civil Rights movement and the publication of Fawn Brodie's best-selling biography of Jefferson which affirmed that Jefferson had a sexual relationship with one of his slaves, *Inventing America* offered a means to reconcile the apparent contradiction between Jefferson as the author of the Declaration of Independence and Jefferson as the owner of more than six hundred African slaves.[18]

Inventing America also caught the spirit of the United States in the wake of the débâcle in Vietnam, the scandal of Watergate and the economic upheaval of the 1970s. For those who felt that America had gone off track, Wills implied that the wrong turn had been taken between 2 and 4 July 1776 when the Continental Congress transformed Jefferson's egalitarian vision of an enlightened society into a Lockean paen to possessive individualism.[19]

More generally, *Inventing America* impressed readers because of the audacity of its argument and Garry Wills's breadth of knowledge. An early reviewer of *Inventing America* suggested that Wills had produced 'a landmark volume for the third century of Declaration studies' which would influence subsequent investigations in the way that Carl Becker's book, *The Declaration of Independence*, had dominated the subject since its appearance in 1922.[20] Wills's argument challenged the received wisdom concerning America's founding document and the mind of its author. This was more than a dry intellectual exercise. In the words of Gordon S. Wood, 'it was the character of America that was at stake'.[21] Many readers were persuaded by Wills's analysis. *Inventing America* received favorable reviews in the *Journal of American History*, the *William and Mary Quarterly*, the *New York Review of Books*, and the *New York Times Book Review*. In 1979 the Organization of American Historians awarded *Inventing America* the Merle Curti Prize as the most distinguished book in American intellectual history.[22]

Unsurprisingly, given the boldness of this thesis, Wills attracted critics as well as admirers. Writing in the *American Historical Review*, Paul Conkin declared, 'I have never struggled with a more perverse book. Its strengths justify all the effort, while its faults insure intense frustration.' Conkin praised Wills for recovering the Scottish influence on Jefferson's thinking while criticizing his rejection of the importance of Locke. In essence, Conkin argued that Wills grossly overstated his case. This was a consistent theme of those who were initially critical of *Inventing America*.[23]

The criticism of *Inventing America* gathered pace in October 1979 when the *William and Mary Quarterly* published a comprehensive examination of the book by Ronald Hamowy. Hamowy accepted Wills's contention that Jefferson was familiar with the Scottish moral philosophers. Indeed, Hamowy asserted, 'All educated Englishmen on both sides of the Atlantic – indeed all educated Europeans – were familiar with their writings.'[24] What Hamowy challenged was Wills's assertion that the Scots moral philosophers were the only influence on Jefferson when he drafted the Declaration. Just as all educated Englishmen would have been aware of the major figures in what historians would come to know as the Scottish Enlightenment, Hamowy argued, so too they would have been aware of the writers of the English whig tradition that Bernard Bailyn had demonstrated was central to the ideology of the American Revolution. Perhaps more significantly, Hamowy demonstrated that the Scottish thinkers were also (unsurprisingly) aware of, and influenced by, the English whigs. Hamowy presents similar extracts from Jefferson's version of the Declaration, Francis Hutcheson's *Short Introduction to Moral Philosophy* (1747) (highlighted by Wills) and Locke's *Second Treatise of Government* (ignored by Wills) to show that the influences on Jefferson that Wills ascribes to Hutcheson may have originated with Locke.[25]

Inventing America has not had the scholarly impact that its admirers hoped for (and its critics feared). In 1992 the University of Virginia hosted a six-day conference intended to commemorate the 250th anniversary of Jefferson's birth. The conference 'sought new perspectives on the Jefferson legacy by measuring Jefferson's life and values against major concerns of the 1990s'.[26] In an essay collection based on the proceedings of the conference, which represented the state of the art with respect to Jefferson scholarship – and included several essays on Jefferson's intellect and ideology – *Inventing America* received only passing mention in an essay by Gordon Wood concerning the evolution of Jefferson's reputation.[27] Fifteen years after the publication of *Inventing America*, it appeared that Ronald Hamowy's conclusion about the book had prevailed: 'Future scholars may feel called upon to consult *Inventing America* when investigating Jefferson's intellectual roots, for completeness' sake if for no other reason.'[28]

Several notable studies of the Declaration of Independence have appeared since the publication of *Inventing America*. While each has noted Wills's thesis, the weight of evidence suggests that Carl Becker's interpretation is still dominant. Locke still rules the roost, though he has to share it with a few other birds – English, Scottish and American. In a novel 1993 study, Jay Fliegelman examined Jefferson's original draft and interpreted the presence of diacritical marks to mean that the document was intended to be read aloud. This interpretation led Fliegelman to argue that Jefferson was influenced by new books on rhetoric and rhetorical theory such as those by James Burgh and Richard Sheridan. According to Fliegelman the Declaration derives its power not only from the words Jefferson wrote but from the rhetorical structure that mediates and alters the meaning of Jefferson's words.[29]

In his 1996 study of Jefferson, *American Sphinx*, Joseph J. Ellis expressed skepticism about Fliegelman's emphasis on the Declaration as a rhetorical document and Garry Wills's emphasis on the Scottish

Enlightenment. With regard to the former, Ellis contended that Jefferson inserted diacritical marks into his draft of the Declaration in case he had to read it aloud to Congress when the drafting committee presented it on 28 June 1776. With regard to Wills, Ellis argued that Jefferson's fundamental claim that revolution is justified if rulers disregard the rights of the governed originated with Locke, while acknowledging that Jefferson may have borrowed his specific language from George Mason's Virginia Declaration of Rights (which, in turn, borrowed language from the English Declaration of Rights of 1689). Ellis accepted that Jefferson believed that all human being had an equal moral sense but dismissed the question of where he acquired this view. 'Whether he developed that belief by reading Hutcheson or any of the other members of the Scottish school or from his own personal observation of human behavior is ultimately unknowable and not terribly important.' Rather than attempt to reconstruct the intellectual genealogy of the Declaration as Becker and Wills did, Ellis argued that the document was a unique reflection of Jefferson's thinking which drew on myriad sources, including Jefferson's own experiences, and a diverse group of writers, including Locke. The resulting document was Jeffersonian more than anything. 'Though indebted to Locke, ' Ellis writes, 'Jefferson's political vision was more radical than liberal, driven as it was by a youthful romanticism unwilling to negotiate its high standards with an imperfect world.'[30]

In 1825 Jefferson wrote of the Declaration of Independence:

> With respect to our rights, and the acts of the British government contra-vening those rights, there was but one opinion on this side of the water. All American whigs thought alike on these subjects. When forced, therefore, to resort to arms for redress, an appeal to the tribunal of the world was deemed proper for our justification. This was the object of the Declaration of Independence. Not to find new principles, or new arguments, never before thought of, not merely to say things which had never been said before; but to place before mankind the common sense of the subject, in terms so plain and firm as to command their assent, and to justify ourselves in the independent stand we are compelled to take.[31]

This is the view taken by Pauline Maier in her 1997 study of the Declaration of Independence, *American Scripture*. Maier argued that the Declaration reflected attitudes that were commonplace in America by the summer of 1776. Rather than ransacking the writers of the whig tradition or the Scottish Enlightenment for the origins of Jefferson's thinking, Maier examined what she terms 'the other Declarations of Independence', the actions, proclamations and statutes adopted by the rebellious colonies by the summer of 1776 that had made them independent by the time Congress had declared them as such. For Maier, Jefferson was not the sole author of the Declaration but a skilled draftsman whose work was improved by Congress and reflected beliefs that were widespread in America at the time. While Jefferson is foremost in most of the previous studies of the Declaration of Independence – including those of Becker, Wills, Fliegelman and Ellis – for Maier the Declaration is a more general expression of American thinking rather than a unique expression of Jefferson's mind. As such the particular intellectual influences and traditions upon which Jefferson may or may not have drawn are not especially important to Maier.[32]

In the twenty years after its publication, *Inventing America* clearly did not have the impact its admirers had anticipated. Garry Wills had propounded an ambitious thesis that called into question the received wisdom regarding the Declaration of Independence. Ronald Hamowy's critique constituted an antithesis to Wills that seemingly won the approval of most students of the subject. Most of the major writings on the Declaration of Independence dismissed *Inventing America* or dealt with it briefly. In the late 1990s, however, a new synthesis emerged as two works on the Declaration embraced, in part, Wills's interpretation. The first of these was Jean M. Yarborough's *American Virtues: Thomas Jefferson on the Character of a Free People*, which appeared in 1998. Yarborough's main concern was the connection between Jefferson's ethics and his political theory. She began her analysis by considering the trilogy of natural rights that Jefferson included in the Declaration: 'life, liberty and the pursuit of happiness'. Most historians, following Carl Becker, have seen these as Lockean in origin, whereas Wills argued they were derived from Hutcheson. In a novel analysis Yarborough argued that Jefferson drew on both traditions – the selfish liberal sources delineated by Locke and the Scottish Enlightenment's concern with benevolence. Crudely put, 'life and liberty' can be attributed to Locke and 'the pursuit of happiness' to the Scots.[33]

In 1998 Allen Jayne's *Jefferson's Declaration of Independence*, argued that the Declaration revealed not only Jefferson's political philosophy but also a theology. The Declaration, argued Jayne, 'attacked two claims of absolute authority – that of any government over its subjects and that of any religion over the minds of men as respects religious and moral truth – by putting the authority of both government and religion in the hands of the individual human beings that make up the populace'. In Jayne's view Jefferson was indebted to Bolingbroke for his concept of 'nature's God' which appears in the Declaration; to Locke for his political theory; and to Lord Kames for his belief that man 'could independently and easily find the moral law of nature by using his moral sense and a minimal amount of reason'.[34] Like Yarborough, Jayne sees Jefferson as drawing on various intellectual traditions, both Locke and the Scots, in drafting the Declaration. Like Becker, Wills and Hamowy, Jayne proves his point by juxtaposing passages from the Declaration and works that he feels influenced Jefferson.

Jefferson wanted his authorship of the Declaration of Independence to be among his best-remembered accomplishments. This is why he highlighted it on his gravestone and inserted extensive information on its adoption in his autobiography. A survey of the modern literature on the subject suggests that he was successful in this effort. Most scholarship on the Declaration has focused on the document's meaning and Jefferson's contribution to it. To take Wills's title, the situation could be summarized as follows. According to Carl Becker, Thomas Jefferson and John Locke invented America. According to Garry Wills, Thomas Jefferson and Francis Hutcheson (with assistance from miscellaneous Scotsmen) invented America. For Jay Fliegelman, America was invented by Jefferson and Richard Sheridan and James Burgh. According to Joseph Ellis, Thomas Jefferson invented America by himself with Locke, the Scots, George Mason and miscellaneous other thinkers providing assistance. For Pauline Maier, Americans, at least those who actively supported the Revolution and had been influenced by Locke and other whigs, invented America with the assistance of Jefferson. Jean Yarborough and Allen Jayne argue that Jefferson, Locke and different Scotsmen invented America. The only constant for all of these scholars is Jefferson.

III
'Author . . . of the Statute of Virginia for Religious Freedom'

Thomas Jefferson left the Continental Congress in September 1776 and returned to Virginia to represent his native county, Albermarle, in the state's House of Delegates. Jefferson served in the legislature from October 1776 until June of 1779, when he was elected governor of Virginia. During this period he served as a member of the legislature's Committee of Revisors, which undertook to rewrite Virginia's laws in light of the independent state's new constitution, an activity made necessary by the Declaration of Independence. Over the course of the decade from 1776 to 1786 the legislature enacted many of the revised laws proposed by the committee, mostly in the 1780s in response to the efforts of Jefferson's friend and ally, James Madison. Among the legislation that Jefferson framed and championed were bills to abolish primogeniture and entail, to reform the state's penal code and to disestablish the Anglican Church. After a lifetime of often quite bitter political controversy, Jefferson recalled his legislative struggles for religious freedom as 'the severest contests in which I have ever been engaged'. They were also struggles of which he was especially proud.[35]

When Jefferson entered the House of Delegates in the autumn of 1776, he was also named to its Committee on Religion. That committee was inundated with petitions from dissenting religious groups – mainly Baptists, Presbyterians and Methodists – who petitioned for relief from taxes to support the Anglican establishment, equality in the exercise of religious belief and the complete disestablishment of the Anglican Church. Jefferson sympathized with the petitioners and on 19 November 1776 he submitted resolutions calling for Anglican disestablishment and the repeal of all laws granting special privileges and support to Anglican clergy and abolition of compulsory tax support for the church. The resolutions died in the committee; 'our opponents carried in the general resolutions of the comm[itt]ee of Nov. 19', wrote Jefferson, 'a declaration that religious assemblies ought to be regulated, and that provision ought to be made for continuing the succession of the clergy, and superintending their conduct'. Failing to disestablish the Church of England, Jefferson did succeed in sponsoring legislation that exempted dissenters from paying taxes to support the church and phased out state contributions to the salaries of Anglican clergymen.[36]

Responding to these modest legislative steps in favor of religious toleration, opponents and proponents of state support for religion continued to petition the legislature for the full restoration of funding to the Anglican Church or for a more complete separation of church and state. The legislature debated 'Whether a general assessment should not be established by law', wrote Jefferson, 'on every one, to the support of the pastor of his choice; or whether all should be left to voluntary contributions' at each of its sessions between 1776 and 1779.[37] In 1777 Jefferson drafted a Bill for Establishing Religious Freedom. After a lengthy preamble in which he advanced the view that religious belief should derive from reason rather than state coercion, Jefferson's bill asserted:

> that no man shall be compelled to frequent or support any religious worship, place, or ministry whatsoever, nor shall be enforced, restrained, molested, or burthened in his body or goods, nor shall otherwise suffer on account of his religious opinions or belief; but that all shall in no wise diminish, enlarge or affect their civil capacities.

Jefferson, fearing the actions of future legislatures yet aware that they could not be bound, concluded, 'the rights hereby asserted are of the natural rights of mankind, and that if any act shall be hereafter passed to repeal the present or to narrow its operation, such an act will be an infringement of natural right'. Jefferson's bill was not presented to the

House of Delegates until 1779, when it was published as a broadside. Initially the bill was tabled. It was not adopted, in amended form, until January 1786, when James Madison ushered it through the legislature in Richmond while Jefferson represented the United States in Paris.[38]

The Statute for Religious Freedom completely severed the ties between church and state in Virginia and guaranteed freedom of conscience throughout the state. Jefferson took great satisfaction in his authorship of the bill, and when it became law he distributed copies, in the form of a short pamphlet, throughout Europe. When his *Notes on the State of Virginia* was published in English in 1787 he had the statute added to the text as an appendix.[39] His pride is apparent in a letter he wrote to James Madison in December 1786:

> The Virginia act for religious freedom has been received with infinite approbation in Europe and propagated with enthusiasm. I do not mean by the governments, but by the individuals which compose them. It has been translated into French and Italian, has been sent to most of the courts of Europe, has been the best evidence of the falsehood of those reports which stated us to be in anarchy. It is inserted in the new Encyclopedie, and is appearing in most of the publications respecting America.

While Jefferson was gratified that the law, the first such act in modern history, had been enacted in Virginia, he believed that the statute had significance far beyond the borders of his native state, or even of the United States.

> In fact it is comfortable to see the standard of reason at length erected, after so many ages during which the human mind has been held in vassalage by kings, priests and nobles; and it is honorable for us to have produced the first legislature who has had the courage to declare that the reason of man may be trusted with the formation of his own opinions.[40]

Jefferson viewed the Virginia Statute for Religious Freedom as a crucial step in the triumph of 'the standard of reason' and the liberation of humanity from the tyranny of clerical superstition.

In Jefferson's mind, political and religious tyranny were closely allied. Historically, state churches – by fostering obedience and ignorance – had assisted unjust rulers in subverting the liberties to which all humanity were entitled as natural rights. The overthrow of religious oppression went hand in hand with the defeat of secular tyranny. In consequence it was necessary to limit the interference of the government in religion. As Jefferson wrote in the *Notes on the State of Virginia*, 'The legitimate powers of government extend to such acts only as are injurious to others. But it does me no injury for my neighbour to say there are twenty gods, or no god. It neither picks my pocket nor breaks my leg.'[41] Conversely, it was also necessary to insure that religious bodies did not exercise undue influence over the state. Jefferson later sought to disconnect church and state in the United States permanently so that they could not collude in the future to endanger liberty. In 1802, while president, Jefferson wrote to the Danbury Baptist Association in Connecticut to explain why he would not continue his predecessors' tradition of proclaiming public fast days:

> Believing with you that religion is a matter which lies solely between man and his God, that he owes account to none other for his faith or his worship, that the legislative powers of government reach actions only, and not opinions, I contemplate with sovereign reverence that act of the whole American people which declared that their legislature should 'make no law respecting an establishment of religion, or prohibiting the free exercise thereof,' thus building a wall of separation between church and state.[42]

Jefferson interpreted the First Amendment to the Constitution as erecting a 'wall of separation between church and state', thereby safeguarding the rights won in the American Revolution. In the Declaration of Independence Jefferson had asserted that all men were equal and had a right to govern themselves. In the Virginia Statute for Religious Freedom he advanced the view that government should not interfere with an individual's right to worship as he or she saw fit.

As Jefferson intended, his efforts to separate church and state in Virginia have commanded considerable attention in the years since his death. As a leading student of the subject, Philip Hamburger, writes: 'Jefferson's words seem to have shaped the nation. Beginning with his draft of the Declaration of Independence, Jefferson's taut phrases have given concentrated and elevated expression to some of the nation's most profound ideals.' Hamburger continues, 'Few of Jefferson's phrases appear to have had more significance for the law and life of the United States than those in which he expressed his hope for separation of church and state.'[43] Unlike the literature on the Declaration of Independence, which has focused on the origins of Jefferson's thinking in drafting that document, students of Jefferson's activities and writings with respect to the separation of church and state have not been as concerned with the sources of his ideas so much as with how those ideas should be interpreted in light of contemporary legal and political disputes. If the students of the Declaration of Independence have looked backward to divine its intellectual lineage, those who consider the 'wall of separation' have attempted to trace the contours of its foundation in order to delineate how high the wall can or should be built in the future.[44]

According to the traditional view of Jefferson and religious freedom – a view propounded by Jefferson's biographers as well as those scholars who have approached Jefferson as students of the history of American religion and politics – Jefferson is *the* architect of separation of church and state in the United States. From the Virginia Statute for Religious Freedom and his interpretation of the First Amendment of the Constitution in his letter to the Danbury Baptists, Jefferson erected the 'wall of separation' that guarantees freedom of conscience to all Americans. This interpretation places Jefferson at the center of the story, casting him in an heroic light, as a forward-looking advocate of toleration and liberty in the face of bigotry, superstition and tyranny.[45]

The traditional Jefferson-centered interpretation of church–state relations received the imprimatur of the Supreme Court in 1947. In the case of *Everson v. the Board of Education of Ewing* the court considered an appeal challenging state-funded transportation for Catholic school students in New Jersey. In a 5–4 decision, the court ruled that New Jersey's funding of busing for parochial school students did not violate the Constitution's prohibition of state involvement in religion because the benefit of the program accrued to the children, not to the religious schools or churches backing the schools. Even so, the majority insisted on reading the First Amendment's Establishment Clause in strict separationist terms. Writing for the majority, Justice Hugo L. Black cited the Bill for Establishing Religious Freedom and then quoted Jefferson's letter to the Danbury Baptists. Justice Black concluded, 'The First Amendment has erected a wall between church and state. That wall must be kept high and impregnable. We could not approve the slightest breach. New Jersey has not breached it here.' Justice Black of Alabama was a life-long admirer of Thomas Jefferson. He cited Jefferson's *Memoirs* as one of the books that shaped his development. His opinion in the *Everson* case put Jefferson's 'wall of separation' metaphor at the center of modern American jurisprudence and politics. In so doing, it reinforced the traditional view of Jefferson as the main mover behind the separation of church and state in America. The *Everson* decision was released just before the appearance of the first volume of Dumas Malone's sympathetic biography of Jefferson – which said of the Virginia Statute for Religious Freedom, 'Its fame was not fortuitous. After more than a century and a half it remains an ineffaceable landmark of human liberty; and men in any land would do well to turn to it at any time that persecution for opinion may raise its ugly head.' Five decades later Joseph J. Ellis wrote, 'the principle that the government has no business interfering with a person's religious beliefs or practices is the one specific Jeffersonian idea that has negotiated the passage from the late eighteenth to the late twentieth century without any significant change in character or coloration'. The standard history of the relationship between Jefferson and the separation of church and state closely follows Jefferson's own interpretation of events. Students of church–state relations have seen Jefferson as he wanted to be seen when he included the Virginia Statute for Religious Freedom in his epitaph. With regard to the question of religious freedom, perhaps more than in any other area, Jefferson has been remarkably successful at shaping his legacy.[46]

On 4 June 1998 the Library of Congress opened an exhibit entitled 'Religion and the Founding of the American Republic' which included Jefferson's original draft letter to the Danbury Baptist Association as one of its major exhibits. The FBI assisted the library, through the use of infrared scanning, to recover portions of the letter that Jefferson had blotted out. The deletions appeared to show that Jefferson was guided by contemporary political concerns as much as ideology when he crafted the 'wall of separation' metaphor. The chief of the library's Manuscript Division, James H. Hutson, presented these findings at a press conference on 1 June 1998. Hutson's findings, which he outlined in detail in a written report included in the packet distributed to the press that day, generated criticism, particularly from Americans United for Separation of Church and State, which issued a 'letter of concern' on 29 July 1998 refuting Hutson's interpretation of the Danbury Baptist letter. In response to the controversy, Hutson prepared a fuller version of his report, with full citations and scholarly apparatus for publication. His report appeared in the *William and Mary Quarterly* in 1999 as part of a collection of articles discussing various aspects of the controversy over Jefferson's letter. In that article Hutson reiterated his original claim that Jefferson was motivated primarily by political concerns – addressing Federalist claims that he was an atheist – and that the 'wall of separation' was never as strong as later advocates of separation claimed. As evidence Hutson demonstrated that Jefferson had attended religious ceremonies in public buildings throughout his life.[47]

Surprisingly, Jefferson's major writings on the subject have, until recently, received little intensive scrutiny. James Hutson's examination of the Danbury Baptist letter represented an effort to contextualize Jefferson's writings on church–state relations. 'It is odd', writes Philip Hamburger, 'that this standard history of separation is so remarkably free of detail.' Unlike the Declaration of Independence, nearly every phrase of which has been subjected to close study, neither the Virginia Statute for Religious Freedom nor the letter to the Danbury Baptists has received anything like that degree of consideration from historians. In recent years that has begun to change as a small group of scholars has undertaken to consider in detail the context and content of Jefferson's views on the separation of church and state in an effort to understand their meaning in Jefferson's time and their relevance in contemporary America. As scholars have undertaken this effort, they have revised the traditional interpretation of Jefferson as the father of religious freedom in the United States.[48]

Perhaps the leading revisionists when it comes to the study of church–state relations are Daniel L. Dreisbach and Philip Hamburger. Dreisbach, a legal historian, spent the better part of two decades studying Jefferson's 'wall of separation' metaphor in its constitutional, political and religious contexts before he published *Thomas Jefferson and the Wall of Separation between Church and State* in 2003. In the book Dreisbach presents a history of the 'wall of separation' metaphor, tracing its origins from Richard Hooker, Roger Williams and James Burgh through to Jefferson. Like James H. Hutson, Dreisbach reads the 1802 letter as an answer to Federalist attacks – especially those made by New England Congregationalists – on Jefferson's supposed irreligion during the election of 1800. Further, he also highlights Jefferson's participation in religious services in the Capitol and other public buildings and routine employment of religious rhetoric in official statements and documents. Dreisbach argues that Jefferson interpreted the First Amendment as prohibiting Congress from establishing religion but not as separating religion from civil government, nor as prohibiting individual states from legislating with respect to religion. According to Dreisbach the 'wall of separation' referred to by Jefferson 'served primarily to separate state and nation in matters pertaining to religion, rather than to separate ecclesiastical and all governmental authorities'. In consequence, the absolute wall of separation alluded to by Justice Black in the *Everson* case has no basis in history.[49]

While Daniel L. Dreisbach focused on the 'wall of separation' in a book that is effectively a history of that metaphor, Philip Hamburger set out to write nothing less than a history of the separation of church and state in the United States over more than two centuries. After describing the traditional, Jefferson-centered interpretation of the history of separation which, Hamburger notes, lacks detail, he considers precisely how separation of church and state became a part of American constitutional law. He does so by addressing two questions: whether separation is the religious liberty guaranteed by the First Amendment; and how religious liberty came to be defined as separation. Hamburger closely interrogates the origins and history of separation. In his analysis of the 'wall of separation', Hamburger, building on the work of Hutson and Dreisbach, argues that Jefferson's understanding of the relationship between church and state was far more complicated than later strict separationists, such as Hugo Black, have claimed. He shows that political considerations were foremost in Jefferson's mind when he wrote to the Danbury Baptists – a letter, Hamburger notes, that had no legal or constitutional standing. In tracing the history of the separation of church and state, Hamburger demonstrates that many of the advocates of separation were motivated, not by a supposed Jeffersonian notion of toleration, but rather by intolerance as they sought to exclude the Catholic Church from the public life of the United States. In tracing the history of the *Everson* case, for example, Hamburger showed that the case was brought by a member of a xenophobic, anti-Catholic group. This group held views with which Hugo Black, a former member of the Ku Klux Klan who harbored anti-Catholic views himself, was sympathetic when he introduced Jefferson's 'wall of separation' into American jurisprudence.[50]

The revisionist historians, such as Dreisbach and Hamburger, have made a valuable contribution to our knowledge of Jefferson's thinking and actions with respect to matters of church and state. Whereas the advocates of the traditional view, holding that Jefferson was the father of separation, have taken his advocacy of strict separation as given, the revisionists have sought to place Jefferson's words in their appropriate context. Unsurprisingly, perhaps, they have recovered a world in which the distinction between religious and political language and actions was blurred. While these findings do not discredit the 'wall of separation' they do suggest that the story is more complex and nuanced than the interpretation advanced by strict separationists. The scholars who seek to analyze the meaning and intent of Jefferson's writings with regard to separation of church and state are engaging in a larger debate over the original meaning of the Constitution. For originalists, constitutional and legal history becomes a form of biblical exegesis, a search for the true meaning of the Constitution that can be implemented by the courts today. Americans United for Separation of Church and State objected so strongly to James Hutson's reading of the Danbury Baptist letter because they feared it could undermine the legal and political standing of the 'wall of separation'. While, strictly speaking, Jefferson's writings are not part of the Constitution, when Justice Black introduced the 'wall of separation' metaphor in the *Everson* decision as an interpretation of the First Amendment, he effectively demanded that they be subjected to the kind of originalist interpretation to which the Constitution has been subject.[51]

Owing to its powerful resonance in American culture, politics and law, historians have been drawn into contemporary political and legal disputes relating to the debate over the separation of church and state (and Jefferson's contribution to it). In some cases these interventions have been deliberate. In 1985 when Supreme Court Justice William Rehnquist repudiated the Danbury Baptist letter (and his predecessor Hugo Black's interpretation of that letter) as bad history, 'all but useless as a guide to sound constitution adjudication', historian Rosemarie Zagarri challenged Rehnquist's interpretation in the pages of the *New Republic*, claiming that the Virginia Statute for Religious Freedom demonstrated that Jefferson and Madison favored a complete separation of church and state. The great

Jefferson scholar Merrill Peterson amplified this view nine years later in a long article that appeared in the *Atlantic Monthly* asserting Jefferson's advocacy of strict separation, recounting its benefits and cautioning against contemporary efforts to undermine the 'wall of separation'.[52]

In most cases historians have not intervened directly into contemporary political debates over separation. Nonetheless, the two major historiographical interpretations of the Virginia Statute for Religious Freedom and the letter to the Danbury Baptists coincide roughly with the political divisions in contemporary America. The traditional interpretation, which sees Jefferson as the father of a strict separation of church and state, correlates with the views of liberals and other advocates of secularism. The revisionist reading of events, which suggests that there was considerable interaction between religion and government (and Jefferson's thinking) during the early republic, appeals to religious conservatives, particularly evangelical Christians, who seek to breach the 'wall of separation' between church and state. From this perspective, it is fortuitous for religious conservatives that the revisionist interpretation has emerged at the same time that the religious right has risen as a formidable power in American politics. Although most historians have not explicitly engaged in this debate, the proponents and opponents of strict separation have drawn on the historiography to bolster their respective cases. For the moment the traditional interpretation continues to hold sway. The emergence of the revisionist interpretation simultaneously with the increased potency of conservative Christians in politics suggests that this may not remain the case. The advocates and opponents of the separation of church and state agree, however, that their debate begins with Thomas Jefferson. This is as Jefferson intended when he included the Virginia Statute for Religious Freedom in his epitaph.[53]

IV
'*& Father of the University of Virginia*'

In the autumn of 1778 Jefferson, as part of his contribution to the work of the Committee of Revisors, drafted a series of bills to reform education in his native state. These included proposals to create a system of state-funded education at the primary and secondary levels; to reform the curriculum, funding and governance of the College of William and Mary (and weaken its links with the Anglican Church); and to create a public library for the state in Richmond. Of these, Jefferson considered the most important to be the Bill for the More General Diffusion of Knowledge. Under its terms Jefferson proposed that each county in Virginia be subdivided into wards or 'hundreds', each of which would contain a primary school. According to Jefferson's plan, 'all the free children, male and female, resident within the respective hundred shall be entitled to receive tuition gratis for a term of three years, and as much longer, at their private expense, as their parents, guardians and friends, shall think proper'. Promising male students could continue their education at one of twenty secondary schools to be created throughout the state. Among these would be a small number of well-qualified poor students who would be provided with their education at state expense. Other students would pay for their tuition at the secondary level. Among the scholarship students the most worthy would be provided with state funding in order to attend the College of William and Mary, the state's pre-eminent institution of higher education.[54]

Jefferson believed that his plan for state-funded education for all free Virginians was necessary to safeguard the achievements of the Revolution. He declared in the education bill's preamble:

> Whereas it appeareth that however certain forms of government are better calculated than others to protect individuals in the free exercise of their natural rights, and are at the same time themselves better guarded against degeneracy, yet experience hath shewn, that even under the best forms, those entrusted with power have, in time, and by slow operations, perverted it into tyranny; and it is believed that the most effectual means of preventing this would be, to illuminate as far as practicable, the minds of the people at large, and more especially to give them knowledge of those facts, which history exhibiteth, that possessed thereby of the experience of other ages and countries, they may be enabled to know ambition under all its shapes, and prompt to exert their natural powers to defeat its purposes.

Widespread education was not only a necessary weapon that allowed the citizens of a republic to guard their liberties; it was also essential if people were to govern themselves properly. Because the Declaration of Independence had placed equality at the center of the revolutionary ideology, the best way to guarantee good government was through education. That is why Jefferson's plan made provision for the education of poor children lacking the means to pay for schooling. He continued:

> And whereas it is generally true that that people will be happiest whose laws are best, and are best administered, and that laws will be wisely formed, and honestly administered, in proportion as those who form and administer them are wise and honest; whence it becomes expedient for promoting the publick happiness that those persons, whom nature hath endowed with genius and virtue, should be rendered by liberal education worthy to receive, and able to guard the sacred deposit of rights and liberties of their fellow citizens, and that they should be called to that

charge without regard to wealth, birth or other accidental condition or circumstance; but the indigence of the greater number disabling them from so educating, at their own expence, those of their children whom nature hath fitly formed and disposed to become useful instruments for the public, it is better that such should be sought for and educated at the common expence of all, than that the happiness of all should be confined to the weak or wicked.

Providing free education for poor students of clear ability (and need) would allow for the cultivation of a natural aristocracy of talent as the best way to insure good government and the survival of liberty in the United States. As Jefferson wrote from France in 1786, 'I think by far the most important bill in our whole code is that for the diffusion of knowledge among the people. No other sure foundation can be devised for the preservation of freedom, and happiness.'[55]

Unfortunately the Virginia House of Delegates did not agree with Jefferson and declined to enact the educational measures included in the revisal of the laws. Jefferson never realized his ambition to create a comprehensive education system in Virginia. Nonetheless, he continued to believe in the importance of education. While he was president, Jefferson supported the creation of the United States Military Academy at West Point. During his retirement years, Jefferson devoted considerable efforts to creating a new university in Virginia. Dissatisfied with the curriculum and religious affiliation of the College of William and Mary, he, along with interested parties inside and outside of the legislature, sought to establish a first-class, state-sponsored, secular university in Virginia. After a prolonged struggle – both to win state funding and to have the university placed in Charlottesville, within sight of Monticello – the legislature agreed to fund the university in 1819. During the years between 1819 and the admission of the university's first students in 1825 Jefferson was involved in virtually every aspect of the new institution's development. He designed the university's campus – 'the academical village' – as well as its curriculum. Further, he helped to recruit professors and served as the university's first rector.[56]

In 1818, during the debate over the location of the university, Jefferson prepared the famous 'Rockfish Gap Report', in which he listed the objectives of university education. It stands as the mission statement for the new university:

To form the statesmen, legislators and judges, on whom public prosperity and individual happiness depend;

To expound the principles and structure of government, the laws which regulate the intercourse of nations, those formed municipally for our own government, and a sound spirit of legislation, which, banishing all arbitrary and unnecessary restraint on individual action, shall leave us free to do whatever does not violate the equal rights of another;

To harmonize and promote the interests of agriculture, manufactures and commerce, and by well informed views of political economy to give free scope to the public industry;

To develop the reasoning faculties of our youth, enlarge their minds, cultivate their morals, and instill into them the precepts of virtue and order;

To enlighten them with mathematical and physical sciences, which advance the arts, and administer to the health, the subsistence, and comforts of human life;

And generally to form them to habits of reflection and correct action, rendering them examples of virtue to others, of happiness within themselves.[57]

Jefferson believed that education should prepare persons to be responsible *citizens* of the new republic. By preparing future leaders for Virginia and the United States, the university would play a key role in advancing and protecting the republican principles enshrined in the Declaration of Independence. To this end, Jefferson and Madison took a particular interest in the appointment of the professor of law – the 'one branch', Jefferson opined, 'in which I think we are the best judges'. They agreed that the holder of the university's chair in law, who would be responsible for teaching government, should be an American well versed in the canonical works of republicanism – including the writings of John Locke and Algernon Sidney, the Declaration of Independence, *The Federalist*, Washington's inaugural and farewell addresses, and the Virginia Resolutions of 1798.[58] Apart from this intervention in the teaching of government, Jefferson believed the university's students and faculty should have academic freedom, and that the institution should recruit professors who were active researchers and specialists in their fields. In keeping with the principles of the Virginia Statute for Religious Freedom, the university would be a secular institution. These characteristics, essential to the republican mission of the university, set it apart from other American institutions of higher education in the early nineteenth century, which were generally characterized by their sectarian religious affiliations and rigid curricula delivered by relatively few professors who tended to be both generalists and ordained ministers.[59]

Scholars have accorded Jefferson's educational initiatives far more respect than Virginia legislators did. During the twentieth century, historians were remarkably consistent in praising Jefferson's educational efforts, especially his role in the establishment of the University of Virginia. The positive interpretation was first articulated early in the century by Philip Alexander Bruce in his five-volume *History of the University of Virginia, 1819–1919,* the thesis of which was summed up in its subtitle: *The Lengthened Shadow of One Man.* A decade later Roy J. Honeywell examined Jefferson's educational efforts and concluded that he was in the forefront of the movement to create a comprehensive, democratic system of publicly funded schools in the United States. This was the view articulated by biographers such as Dumas Malone and Merrill Peterson, as well as by historians of education.[60] In recent years historians have examined the links between Jefferson's thinking in other areas and his educational policies. The most profitable area of investigation has been connections between Jefferson's political ideology and his educational beliefs.[61] Other scholars have examined the Enlightenment origins of Jefferson's architectural designs for the university's 'academical village', the neo-classical rotunda flanked by ten pavilions built in different styles, intended to provide living space and classrooms for students and professors. While recent scholarship has given us a more nuanced understanding of Jefferson's educational activities, the tenor of the scholarship remains positive. When *National Geographic* asked Garry Wills to write a book for a travel series on a favorite locale he visited often, Wills considered writing about Monticello. Upon reflection, Wills decided, 'I found the university at the foot of [Jefferson's] mountain in some ways even more complex, complete and endlessly fascinating than the home perched above it. Over the years, as I have gone back there year by year, the university has become more convincingly a reflection of Jefferson's entire personality, its naïve flaws as well as its towering strengths.' Although Wills mainly wrote about the design and building of the university, his comment aptly characterized the scholarly treatment of Jefferson's efforts to promote education. This is, as Jefferson's epitaph suggests, the way Jefferson wanted to be remembered.[62]

V

Thomas Jefferson was aware that his public activities would be scrutinized, debated and criticized. That, as we have seen, is why he carefully preserved and organized most of his papers and compiled the Anas. His tombstone, by contrast, condensed the hundreds of thousands of pages and millions of words that Jefferson bequeathed to posterity to four simple lines. It would be a signpost directing future generations to remember what he considered his most notable achievements. The Declaration of Independence helped to advance political freedom by asserting humanity's right to self-government and equality. The Statute for Religious Freedom pressed humanity's claim to freedom of conscience. The establishment of the University of Virginia would insure that future generations enjoyed the blessings of enlarged liberty. By limiting his epitaph to these achievements, Jefferson underscored their importance and the connections between them. He demonstrated that he wanted them to be remembered together, and linked to him, in the eyes of posterity.

Andrew Burstein has written that Jefferson 'knew how he wanted to embark on his voyage into historical memory'.[63] As a man who approached the study of the past from the perspective of the Enlightenment, with its emphasis on reason and progress, Jefferson believed that his efforts to expand the boundaries of liberty were the most important achievements of a lifetime of public service. The scholarly treatment of the achievements noted on Jefferson's tombstone has been remarkably sympathetic to Jefferson. While the question of the origins of the ideas expressed in the Declaration of Independence has sparked a significant scholarly debate and the meaning of the 'wall of separation' continues to be a source of political and legal controversy, Jefferson remains central to any examination of these events and their meaning. There have been several contrary voices, of course. Pauline Maier argued that too much credit had been given to Jefferson as the primary author of the Declaration of Independence, and Philip Hamburger suggested that Jefferson has played too prominent a role in the debate over separation of church and state. Even with regard to the relatively uncontroversial subject of Jefferson's educational achievements, Joseph F. Kett demonstrated that Jefferson's ideas, for all their breadth and originality, were often not acted upon. These discordant voices, while significant, underscore the generally positive and Jefferson-centered nature of the scholarship.[64]

Jefferson's tombstone stands today in the family graveyard at Monticello. A replacement, larger than the original monument, which was damaged by Jefferson's admirers (who showed their admiration by prying away pieces of the original monument for souvenirs) was erected in the late nineteenth century. Visitors can read Jefferson's epitaph from outside of the wrought-iron fence that surrounds the graveyard. And yet, despite Jefferson's apparent success in drawing attention to what he considered his major accomplishments, he was not successful in controlling his posthumous reputation. Historians and biographers have not confined themselves to the topics and themes – especially politics and liberty – that Jefferson felt should be at the center of historical inquiry. Like the visitors to Monticello, some historians have taken inspiration from Jefferson's epitaph, but they have been bound by neither the confines of the cemetery nor the limits imposed by Jefferson's epitaph. Like the souvenir hunters who chipped away at Jefferson's gravestone, historians asking new, difficult questions about the meaning of the freedom and equality at the heart of the Declaration of Independence have been chipping away at the image which Jefferson sought to preserve 'in coarse stone'. They have considered the world beyond Jefferson's grave at Monticello, a world inhabited by men and women who did not enjoy the benefits of the Declaration of Independence or the Virginia Statute for Religious Freedom because they were not citizens of Jefferson's republic – men and women whose labor built the beautiful pavilions at the University of Virginia where they could never study. They have also considered the inner life of the master of Monticello, rather than his public life. In so doing they have radically altered our understanding of Jefferson and his time and his reputation in our own time.

NOTES

1. TJ, Epitaph, n.d., TJP. Jefferson's design for his tombstone is reprinted in *TJW*, 706. Also see Sarah N. Randolph, *The Domestic Life of Thomas Jefferson* (New York: Harper, 1871, repr. Charlottesville: University Press of Virginia, 1978), 431. For an analysis of Jefferson's epitaph see Ronald L. Hatzenbuehler, 'Growing Weary in Well-Doing: Thomas Jefferson's Life among the Gentry', *Virginia Magazine of History and Biography*, 101 (1993), 5–36. For Jefferson's death preparations see Andrew Burstein, *Jefferson's Secrets: Death and Desire at Monticello* (New York: Basic Books, 2005), chs. 9–10.
2. Autobiography, *TJW*, 24. The most complete version of the notes, with a helpful introduction that explains the tangled history of their composition, is Notes on the Proceedings in the Continental Congress [7 June to 1 Aug. 1776], *PTJ*, 1:299–329.
3. TJ to James Madison, 1 June 1783, *PTJ*, 6:273–4; Answers to Soulés' Queries, 13–18 Sept. 1786, *PTJ*, 10:380; TJ to the editor of the *Journal de Paris*, 29 Aug. 1787, *PTJ*, 12:61–5; TJ to Samuel Adams Wells, 12 May 1819, *TJW*, 1417–22; TJ to Augustus B. Woodward, 3 April 1825, TJP; Thomas Jefferson to Henry Lee, 8 May 1825, in *TJW*, 1501; TJ to John Vaughn, 16 Sept. 1825, TJP.
4. Robert M.S. McDonald, 'Thomas Jefferson's Changing Reputation as Author of the Declaration of Independence: The First Fifty Years', *Journal of the Early Republic*, 19 (1999), 169–95. McDonald argues that the anonymity of the Declaration's author was originally an advantage as the document purported to represent the views of all Americans. With the appearance of intense political partisanship in the 1790s, Jefferson's authorship of the Declaration became known and celebrated. Also see Philip F. Detwiler, 'The Changing Reputation of the Declaration of Independence: The First Fifty Years', *WMQ*, 19 (1962), 557–74.

5. John Marshall, *The Life of George Washington*, 5 vols. (Philadelphia: C. P. Wayne, 1804–7), 2:377n. Timothy Pickering, *Colonel Pickering's Observations Introductory to Reading the Declaration of Independence* (Salem, MA: William Palfray, 1823). For Jefferson's response to Pickering's oration see TJ to James Madison, 30 Aug. 1823, in James Morton Smith, ed., *The Republic of Letters: The Correspondence between Thomas Jefferson and James Madison, 1776–1826*, 3 vols. (New York: W.W. Norton, 1995), 3:1875–7.

6. For the various versions of the Declaration see Julian P. Boyd, *The Declaration of Independence – The Evolution of the Text as Shown in Facsimiles of Various Drafts by its Author, Thomas Jefferson* (Princeton: Princeton University Press, 1945) and Boyd's editorial note which accompanies the different versions in the Declaration of Independence [11 June to 4 July 1776], *PTJ*, 1:413–33. To trace the changes made by Congress see Notes of Proceedings in the Continental Congress, *PTJ*, 1:318–19.

7. Autobiography, *TJW*, 18; Notes of Proceedings in the Continental Congress, *PTJ*, 1:314–15.

8. See TJ to Richard Henry Lee, 8 July 1776, *PTJ*, 1:455–6; Edmund Pendleton to TJ, 10 Aug. 1776, *PTJ*, 488–91. Julian Boyd (*PTJ*, 1:415) reports that TJ also sent copies of his draft to George Wythe, Philip Mazzei 'and probably John Page'.

9. Autobiography, 18; Notes of Proceedings in the Continental Congress, *PTJ*, 1:315.

10. Abraham Lincoln to H. L. Pierce and others, 6 April 1859, in Don E. Fehrenbacher, ed., *Lincoln: Speeches and Writings, 1832–1865*, 2 vols. (New York: Library of America, 1989), 2:19.

11. Peterson, *Jefferson Image*, 162–9, 201–4. Peterson notes that the Declaration of Independence became more attractive to Southern slaveholders in 1860–1 when they sought to justify secession.

12. John H. Hazelton *The Declaration of Independence – Its History* (New York: Dodd Mead, 1906); Boyd, *The Declaration of Independence*. Hazelton's study was anticipated by Herbert Friedenwald's *The Declaration of Independence: An Interpretation and an Analysis* (New York: MacMillan, 1904). While Hazelton concentrated on a close textual analysis, Friedenwald presented a more general analysis of the drafting and adoption of the Declaration. Boyd reviewed his analysis of the Declaration's drafting in his 1950 'Editorial Note' accompanying Jefferson's draft in *PTJ*, 1:299–308. For the two-part analysis of the Declaration see Peterson, *Jefferson Image*, 304–5.

13. Carl L. Becker, *The Declaration of Independence: A Study in the History of Ideas* (New York: Harcourt Brace, 1922).

14. See for example Dumas Malone's analysis of the Declaration in his biography *Jefferson and His Time*, 1:226–8. Although Bernard Bailyn

argued persuasively in 1967 that the American revolutionaries drew heavily on the English Real Whig tradition for their ideas, including Locke, his analysis did not focus on the Declaration of Independence so much as on the ideas that motivated Americans prior to 1776. Bernard Bailyn, *The Ideological Origins of the American Revolution* (Cambridge, MA: Harvard University Press, 1967; expanded edn., 1992).

15. Garry Wills, *Inventing America: Jefferson's Declaration of Independence* (New York: Doubleday, 1978).
16. Stephen J. Whitfield, 'The Pertinence of Garry Wills', *American Quarterly*, 33 (1981), 232–42, quotation 237.
17. Wills, *Inventing America*, chs. 15, 22.
18. Fawn Brodie, *Thomas Jefferson: An Intimate History* (New York: Norton, 1974).
19. James T. Patterson, *Grand Expectations: The United States, 1945–1974* (New York: Oxford University Press, 1996), chs. 24–5.
20. Robert Ginsberg, 'Review of Garry Wills, *Inventing America: Jefferson's Declaration of Independence*', *Eighteenth-Century Studies*, 12 (1979), 562–6, quotation 566.
21. Gordon S. Wood, 'The Trials and Tribulations of Thomas Jefferson', in Peter S. Onuf, ed., *Jeffersonian Legacies* (Charlottesville: University Press of Virginia, 1993), 395–417, quotation 400.
22. David Brion Davis, *New York Times Book Review*, 2 July 1978, 1, 17; John Howe, 'Review of Garry Wills, *Inventing America: Jefferson's Declaration of Independence*', *WMQ*, 36 (1979), 462–4; Edmund Morgan, *New York Review of Books*, 17 Aug. 1978, 38–40; Rush Welter, 'Review of Garry Wills, *Inventing America: Jefferson's Declaration of Independence*', *Journal of American History*, 66 (1979), 380–1.
23. Paul Conkin, 'Review of Garry Wills, *Inventing America: Jefferson's Declaration of Independence*', *American Historical Review*, 84 (1979), 530–1. For other critical views see Philip F. Detweiler, 'Review of Garry Wills, *Inventing America: Jefferson's Declaration of Independence*', *Journal of Southern History*, 45 (1979), 11–12, and Gilman M. Ostrander, 'New Lost Worlds of Thomas Jefferson', *Reviews in American History*, 7 (1979), 183–8.
24. Ronald Hamowy, 'Jefferson and the Scottish Enlightenment: A Critique of Garry Wills's *Inventing America: Jefferson's Declaration of Independence*', *WMQ*, 36 (1979), 503–23, quotation 506. Hamowy subsequently published *The Scottish Enlightenment and the Theory of Spontaneous Order* (Carbondale, IL: Southern Illinois University Press, 1987) and edited John Trenchard and Thomas Gordon's *Cato's Letters* (Indianapolis: Liberty Fund, 1995).
25. Hamowy, 'Jefferson and the Scottish Enlightenment', 506–8. Hamowy, however, did not accept the view that Jefferson obtained his knowledge of Locke via Hutcheson. On the contrary he argued that there is copious

evidence for Jefferson's familiarity with Locke, especially the *Second Treatise*, which Wills 'minimizes, misinterprets, or disregards'. He then reviewed the evidence for Jefferson's having made reference to the Scottish moral philosophers, especially Hutcheson. He concluded, 'What evidence is adduced that Jefferson had the Scottish philosophers, specifically Hutcheson, in mind when writing the Declaration? There is none. Indeed, Hutcheson, who among the Scots comes closest in his views to those expressed in the Declaration, is not once quoted, cited, referred to, or recommended, in any connection, in any of Jefferson's writings.' Hamowy then proceeded to consider the manner in which Wills, in his view, misread, misinterpreted and misunderstood the Scottish Enlightenment. Hamowy, 'Jefferson and the Scottish Enlightenment', 512, 514.

26. Daniel Jordan, 'Foreword', in Onuf, ed., *Jeffersonian Legacies*, vii.
27. Wood, 'Trials and Tribulations of Thomas Jefferson', 399–400.
28. Hamowy, 'Jefferson and the Scottish Enlightenment', 523.
29. Jay Fliegelman, *Declaring Independence: Jefferson, Natural Language, and the Culture of Performance* (Stanford: Stanford University Press, 1993). Also see Stephen E. Lucas, 'Justifying America: The Declaration of Independence as a Rhetorical Document', in Thomas W. Benson, ed., *American Rhetoric: Context and Criticism* (Carbondale, IL: Southern Illinois University Press, 1989), 67–130.
30. Joseph J. Ellis, *American Sphinx: The Character of Thomas Jefferson* (New York: Alfred A. Knopf, 1997), 63–70, quotations, 68, 69–70.
31. Thomas Jefferson to Henry Lee, 8 May 1825, *TJW*, 1501.
32. Pauline Maier, *American Scripture: Making the Declaration of Independence* (New York: Alfred A. Knopf, 1997).
33. Jean M. Yarborough, *American Virtues: Thomas Jefferson on the Character of a Free People* (Lawrence: University Press of Kansas, 1998).
34. Allen Jayne, *Jefferson's Declaration of Independence: Origins, Philosophy, and Theology* (Lexington, KY: University of Kentucky Press, 1998), quotations 174, 168.
35. Autobiography, *TJW*, 34. For Jefferson's contributions toward rewriting Virginia's laws see Malone, *Jefferson and His Time*, 1:235–85; and the Revisal of the Laws, 1776–1786, *PTJ*, 2:305–665, esp. the 'Editorial Note', 305–24.
36. Autobiography, *TJW*, 35. See also Notes and Proceedings on Discontinuing the Establishment of the Church of England [11 Oct. to 9 Dec. 1776], *PTJ*, 1:525–58.
37. Autobiography, *TJW*, 35.
38. A Bill for Establishing Religious Freedom, *PTJ*, 2:545–53, quotations 544, 545. Jefferson's version of the bill appeared as a broadside, *A BILL for establishing RELIGIOUS FREEDOM, printed for the considera-*

tion of the PEOPLE (Williamsburg, n.p., 1779). For the textual changes made to Jefferson's draft by the House of Delegates see the textual notes in *PTJ*, 2:547–53. For the drafting and adoption of the bill see Thomas E. Buckley, *Church and State in Revolutionary Virginia, 1776–1787* (Charlottesville: University Press of Virginia, 1977); William Lee Miller, *The First Liberty: Religion and the American Republic* (New York: Alfred A. Knopf, 1988), 1–75; Malone, *Jefferson and His Time*, 1:274–80 and Edwin S. Gaustad, *Sworn on the Altar of God: A Religious Biography of Thomas Jefferson* (Grand Rapids: W.B. Eerdmans, 1996), 63–70.

39. Thomas Jefferson, *Notes on the State of Virginia* (London: John Stockdale, 1787), repr. in *TJW*, 123–325. Writing before the adoption of the bill in 1786, he included a lengthy statement on the benefits of freedom of conscience in his *Notes on the State of Virginia*, 283–7.

40. TJ to James Madison, 16 Dec. 1786, *PTJ*, 10:603–4.

41. *Notes on the State of Virginia*, *TJW*, 285.

42. To Messrs. Nehemiah Dodge and Others, a Committee of the Danbury Baptist Association, in the State of Connecticut, 1 Jan. 1802, *TJW*, 510.

43. Philip Hamburger, *Separation of Church and State* (Cambridge, MA: Harvard University Press, 2002), 1.

44. By contrast with the scholars who have considered the origins of the Declaration of Independence, those who have considered the origins of the Virginia Statute for Religious Freedom agree that Locke was an important source for Jefferson's thinking. Most agree that Locke's *Letter Concerning Toleration* (1689) was the critical source of Jefferson's ideas with regard to freedom of conscience but that Jefferson moved beyond Locke, extending legal toleration to Catholics, for example, in drafting the Virginia Statute. See J. G. A. Pocock, 'Religious Freedom and the Desacralization of Politics: From the English Civil Wars to the Virginia Statute', in Merrill D. Peterson and Robert C. Vaughn, eds., *The Virginia Statute for Religious Freedom: Its Evolution and Consequences in American History* (New York: Cambridge University Press, 1988), 43–73; David A. J. Richards, *Toleration and the Constitution* (New York: Oxford University Press, 1986), 111–16; Sanford Kessler, 'Locke's Influence on Jefferson's "Bill for Establishing Religious Freedom'", *Journal of Church and State*, 25 (1983), 231–52; S. Gerald Sandler, 'Lockean Ideas in Thomas Jefferson's Bill for Establishing Religious Freedom', *Journal of the History of Ideas*, 21 (1960), 110–16.

45. For the most prominent of many examples of this interpretation see: Malone, *Jefferson and His Time*, 1:274–80; Merrill D. Peterson, *Jefferson and the New Nation* (New York: Oxford University Press, 1970); Richard B. Bernstein, *Thomas Jefferson* (New York: Oxford University Press, 2003); Gaustad, *Sworn on the Altar of God*; Miller, *The First Liberty*; Buckley, *Church and State in Revolutionary Virginia*; Cushing

Strout, 'Jeffersonian Religious Liberty and American Pluralism', in Peterson and Vaughn, eds., *The Virginia Statute for Religious Freedom*, 201–36; Isaac Kramnick and R. Laurence Moore, *The Godless Constitution: The Case Against Religious Correctness* (New York: W. W. Norton, 1996); Frank Lambert, *The Founding Fathers and the Place of Religion in America* (Princeton: Princeton University Press, 2003). For a brief overview and critique of this 'standard history of separation', see Hamburger, *Separation of Church and State*, 3–6.

46. *Everson v. Board of Education*, 330 U.S. 1 (1947), 18; Malone, *Jefferson and His Time*, 1: 280; Ellis, *American Sphinx*, 356. Also see Edwin S. Gaustad, 'Thomas Jefferson, Religious Freedom, and the Supreme Court', *Church History*, 67 (1998), 682–94; Barbara A. Perry, 'Justice Hugo Black and the "Wall of Separation between Church and State"', *Journal of Church and State*, 31 (1989), 55–72; and Daniel J. Meador, 'Hugo Black and Thomas Jefferson', *Virginia Quarterly Review*, 79 (2003), 459–68. The *Everson* case is discussed in detail in Hamburger, *Separation of Church and State*, 454–78.

47. James Hutson, ' "A Wall of Separation": FBI Helps Restore Jefferson's Obliterated Draft', *Library of Congress Bulletin*, 57 (1998), 136–9, 163; 'Leading Church–State Scholars Refute Library of Congress' Views on Thomas Jefferson and Church–State Separation', American United for Separation of Church and State, 29 July 1998, www.au.org. James H. Hutson et al., 'Thomas Jefferson's Letter to the Danbury Baptists: A Controversy Rejoined', *WMQ*, 56 (1999), 775–824. Most of the participants in the forum were not persuaded by Hutson's argument – that the deleted passages in the letter required a reinterpretation of Jefferson's letter in light of contemporary politics. See the essays by Robert M. O'Neill, Thomas E. Buckley, Edwin S. Gaustad, and Isaac Kramnick and R. Laurence Moore. Daniel L. Dreisbach concurred with Hutson's findings. Also see James H. Hutson, *Religion and the Founding of the American Republic* (Washington, DC: Library of Congress, 1998).

48. Hamburger, *Separation of Church and State*, 4.

49. Daniel L. Dreisbach, *Thomas Jefferson and the Wall of Separation between Church and State* (New York: New York University Press, 2003), 56. Dreisbach rehearsed and developed his analysis of Jefferson's thinking on separation of church and state in a number of articles. See Daniel L. Dreisbach, 'Thomas Jefferson and Bills Number 82–86 of the Laws of Virginia, 1776–1786: New Light on the Jeffersonian Model of the Church–State Relations', *North Carolina Law Review*, 69 (1990), 159–211; Daniel L. Dreisbach, 'A New Perspective on Jefferson's Views on Church–State Relations: The Virginia Statute for Establishing Religious Freedom in its Legislative Context', *American Journal of Legal History*, 35 (1991), 172–204; Daniel L. Dreisbach, ' "Sowing Useful

Truths and Principles": The Danbury Baptists, Thomas Jefferson, and the "Wall of Separation'", *Journal of Church and State*, 39 (1997), 455–501. For religion in the election of 1800 see Robert M. S. McDonald, 'Was There a Religious Revolution of 1800?' in James Horn, Jan Ellen Lewis and Peter S. Onuf, eds., *The Revolution of 1800: Democracy, Race & the New Republic* (Charlottesville: University of Virginia Press, 2002), 173–98.

50. Hamburger, *Separation of Church and State*, esp. chs. 7 and 14.
51. According to Jack N. Rakove, a leading student of the phenomenon, 'The advocates of *originalism* argue that the meaning of the Constitution (or of its individual clauses) was fixed at the moment of its adoption, and that the task of interpretation is accordingly to ascertain that meaning and apply it to the issue at hand'. Jack N. Rakove, *Original Meanings: Politics and Ideas in the Making of the Constitution* (New York: Alfred A. Knopf, 1996), xiii.
52. *Wallace v. Jaffree*, 472 U.S. 38 (1985), 107. Rehnquist wrote a dissenting opinion in this case. Rosemarie Zagarri, 'Founding Intentions: Jefferson & Madison on School Prayer', *New Republic*, 193 (9 Sept. 1985), 10–11; Merrill D. Peterson, 'Jefferson and Religious Freedom', *Atlantic Monthly*, 274 (Dec. 1994), 112–24.
53. For the liberal use of the traditional interpretation see, John Brummett, 'What would Thomas Jefferson Do?', *Times Record* (Fort Smith, Arkansas), 22 Feb. 2005, www.arkansasnews.com; Kimberly Correa-Luna, 'Jefferson Right About Church–State Separation', *Tucson Citizen*, 22 Feb. 2005, www.tucsoncitizen.com; Jane Lampman, 'Bringing the Case Against Judges', *Christian Science Monitor* (Boston), 13 April 2005, www.csmonitor.com. For conservative attacks on separation that draw on the revisionist interpretation and invoke Jefferson's religious beliefs see Michael J. Malbin, *Religion and Politics: The Intentions of the Authors of the First Amendment* (Washington, DC: American Enterprise Institute, 1978); Jerry Falwell, 'The Impending Death of Christmas?', 10 Dec. 2004, www.theconservativevoice.com; Cheri Pierson Yecke, 'The Separation Myth, Notion of a Wall between Church and State is Nowhere to be found in the Constitution', *Star Tribune* (Minneapolis), 17 June 2004; Julia Duin, 'Religion under a Secular Assault', *Washington Times*, 13 April 2005, www.washingtontimes.com; Pat Boone, 'Religion in the Public Square', *Washington Times*, 1 May 2005, www.washingtontimes.com.
54. A Bill for the More General Diffusion of Knowledge, *PTJ*, 2:526–35; A Bill for Amending the Constitution of the College of William and Mary, and Substituting More Certain Revenues for Its Support, *PTJ*, 2:535–43; A Bill for Establishing a Public Library, *PTJ*, 2:544. These were bills 79, 80 and 81 respectively of the proposed Revisal of the Laws submitted by the Committee of Revisors to the House of Delegates on 18 June 1779.

55. A Bill for the More General Diffusion of Knowledge, *PTJ*, 2:526–7; TJ to George Wythe, 13 Aug. 1786, *PTJ*, 10:244. Jefferson elaborated upon his revolutionary-era educational ideas in Query XIV of his *Notes on the State of Virginia*, 272–5. For a concise, yet thorough, overview of the subject see Jennings L. Wagoner, Jr., *Jefferson and Education* (Charlottesville: Thomas Jefferson Foundation, 2004).

56. Robert M. S. McDonald, ed., *Thomas Jefferson's Military Academy: Founding West Point* (Charlottesville: University of Virginia Press, 2004). For Jefferson's role in founding the University of Virginia see Wagoner, *Jefferson and Education*, ch. 8; Malone, *Jefferson and His Time*, 6:365–425; Philip Alexander Bruce, *History of the University of Virginia, 1819–1919: The Lengthened Shadow of One Man*, 5 vols. (New York: Macmillan, 1922), vol. 1.

57. *Report of the Commissioners Appointed to Fix the Site of the University of Virginia* (Richmond: John Warrock, 1818), 5. This report is known as the Rockfish Gap Report from the place where the commissioners met.

58. TJ to James Madison, 1 Feb. 1825, and James Madison to TJ, 8 Feb. 1825, in, *The Republic of Letters*, 3:1923.

59. On the distinctiveness of the University of Virginia, and its correlation with Jefferson's political goals, see Wagoner, *Jefferson and Education*, ch. 10; Harold Hellenbrand, *The Unfinished Revolution: Education and Politics in the Thought of Thomas Jefferson* (Newark: University of Delaware Press, 1990); David P. Peeler, 'Thomas Jefferson's Nursery of Republican Patriots: The University of Virginia', *Journal of Church and State*, 28 (1986), 79–93.

60. Bruce, *History of the University of Virginia*; Roy J. Honeywell, *The Educational Work of Thomas Jefferson* (Cambridge, MA: Harvard University Press, 1931); James B. Conant, *Thomas Jefferson and the Development of American Public Education* (Berkeley: University of California Press, 1962); Robert M. Healey, *Jefferson on Religion in Public Education* (New Haven: Yale University Press, 1962).

61. James Gilreath, ed., *Thomas Jefferson and the Education of a Citizen* (Washington, DC: Library of Congress, 1999); Peeler, 'Thomas Jefferson's Nursery of Republican Patriots'; Harold Hellenbrand, *The Unfinished Revolution*; Lorraine Smith Pangle and Thomas K. Pangle, *The Learning of Liberty: Educational Ideas of the American Founders* (Lawrence: University Press of Kansas, 1993); Peter Nicolaisen, 'Civic Virtue and the Demands of the Individual: Jefferson's Views on Education', *Amerikastudien/ American Studies*, 41 (1996), 67–82; Martin D. M. Carcieri, 'Democracy and Education in the Thought of Jefferson and Madison', *Journal of Law and Education*, 26 (1997), 1–30.

62. Garry Wills, *Mr. Jefferson's University* (Washington, DC: National Geographic, 2002), 1. For other studies of the architecture of the

university see Richard Guy Wilson, ed., *Thomas Jefferson's Academical Village: The Creation of An Architectural Masterpiece* (Charlottesville: Bayly Art Museum of the University of Virginia, 1993); Louis S. Greenbaum, 'Thomas Jefferson, the Paris Hospitals, and the University of Virginia', *Eighteenth-Century Studies*, 26 (1993), 607–26; Frank Edgar Grizzard, 'Documentary History of the Construction of the Buildings of the University of Virginia, 1817–1828', Ph.D. diss., University of Virginia, 1996. http://etext.lib.virginia.edu/jefferson/grizzard.

63. Burstein, *Jefferson's Secrets*, 10.

64. Maier, *American Scripture*; Hamburger, *Separation of Church and State*; Joseph F. Kett, 'Education,' in Merrill D. Peterson, *Thomas Jefferson: A Reference Biography* (New York: Scribners, 1986), 233–52.

CHAPTER 6

SALLY HEMINGS

I

On 12 April 2001, President George W. Bush welcomed several dozen descendants of Thomas Jefferson to the White House to commemorate the 258th birthday of his predecessor. The gathering included persons descended from Jefferson and his wife, Martha Wayles Jefferson, as well as those descended from Jefferson and one of his slaves, Sally Hemings. 'I want to thank all the descendants of Thomas Jefferson who are here,' declared Bush. The president added, surveying the mixed-race gathering, 'No wonder America sees itself in Thomas Jefferson.'[1] In so doing Bush entered into a two-hundred-year-old controversy concerning Jefferson's paternity of Sally Hemings's children. In the autumn of 1802 James Callender, a disgruntled officer-seeker and muckraking journalist with whom Jefferson had dealt in the past, reported in the pages of the *Richmond Recorder* rumors he had heard in the Charlottesville area about Jefferson and Hemings.[2] The original charges were politically motivated, and Jefferson's Federalist opponents repeated and elaborated upon them throughout the remainder of his presidency. Rumors and allegations about the nature of Jefferson's relationship with Hemings persisted after his death. In 1873 an Ohio newspaper published a memoir of Madison Hemings, Sally Hemings's son and a former Monticello slave.[3] Madison Hemings asserted that he was the son of Thomas Jefferson. Despite Madison Hemings's memoir and circumstantial evidence that lent credence to James Callender's reports, most historians and biographers either ignored or dismissed the claim that Thomas Jefferson and Sally Hemings had had a sexual relationship.

By the late 1990s there emerged a new scholarly consensus, which accepted that a sexual relationship between Jefferson and Hemings was probable. This was brought about by two publications. The first was a book by Annette Gordon-Reed, *Thomas Jefferson and Sally Hemings: An American Controversy*, which was published in 1997. Gordon-Reed, a professor of law at New York Law School, presented a devastating indictment of the unfair and biased manner in which previous historians had treated the evidence for a relationship between Jefferson and Hemings. She demonstrated that the evidence for the relationship was much stronger than previous historians had recognized. A year later a second publication, a DNA study in the British journal *Nature*, proved that a male in the Jefferson family was the father of at least one of Sally Hemings's children. These two publications caused historians to re-evaluate the evidence and to conclude that it was likely that Jefferson and Hemings had a sexual relationship.[4] Indeed the relationship was quickly accepted as a new orthodoxy. In January of 2000 the Thomas Jefferson Foundation produced its own study of the question in light of the new research. The report concluded that Jefferson was the father of one, and probably all, of Sally Hemings's six children. Having gone from a subject that historians long ignored or dismissed, to one that they deemed was an unlikely possibility, by the end of the twentieth century the Jefferson–Hemings relationship was widely accepted as likely. The climax of this historical and historiographical shift was the White House ceremony hosted by George W. Bush. When critics declared that the ceremony was 'an embarrassment' and said that Bush had been 'duped' into accepting the relationship, a White House spokeswoman contended that President Bush found the evidence in favor of the relationship to be 'very compelling'.[5]

As the criticism of Bush suggests, the new consensus regarding the Jefferson–Hemings relationship has inspired considerable academic and popular opposition. This chapter has three purposes. First, it examines the longstanding and formerly successful 'defense' against the charge of Jefferson's paternity, and examines and explains the historiographical shift that took place in the late 1990s and resulted in the widespread acceptance of the Jefferson–Hemings relationship. Secondly, it considers the passionate critique of this new orthodoxy. After successfully defending Jefferson from James Callender's charges for nearly two centuries, some of Jefferson's advocates undertook a desperate rearguard action to protect, as they saw it, Jefferson's reputation. Finally, having limned the contours of the recent debate over the Jefferson–Hemings relationship, this chapter will consider its significance for the future study of Jefferson. This chapter does not directly review the evidence for and against the Jefferson–Hemings relationship. This has been done elsewhere – in many of the works discussed below. Rather it seeks to chronicle and explain the most dramatic and controversial change in our understanding and knowledge of Jefferson since the publication of the Anas in 1829.

II

For most of the nineteenth and twentieth centuries white male historians and biographers dominated Jefferson scholarship. During the post-war period, Dumas Malone and Merrill Peterson were the most important Jefferson biographers. Both men, based at Jefferson's University of Virginia, dismissed the Sally Hemings 'legend'. Peterson believed that the story of the Jefferson–Hemings liaison had been fostered by Jefferson's political enemies, embraced in the mid-nineteenth century by abolitionists and perpetuated in the twentieth century by African Americans pursuing a 'pathetic wish for a little pride'. In 1970 Peterson articulated what has been called the 'character defense' to dismiss the story. He wrote, 'The evidence, highly circumstantial, is far from conclusive, however, and unless Jefferson was capable of slipping badly out of character in hidden moments at Monticello, it is difficult to imagine him caught up in a miscegenous relationship.'[6] In other words the relationship between Jefferson and Hemings was impossible because it would have been completely out of character for Jefferson to have had sex with one of his slaves. Although such relationships were commonplace in the slave South, Jefferson was too good to engage in such behavior.

Merrill Peterson did not invent the character defense. Jan Ellen Lewis has persuasively argued that Jefferson's white descendants, particularly his daughter Martha and his grandchildren and great-grandchildren, perpetuated the view that their ancestor was too good to have had a sexual relationship with Sally Hemings. Two of Martha's children – Jefferson's grandchildren – Thomas Jefferson Randolph and Ellen Wayles Coolidge went so far as to identify their cousins Peter and Samuel Carr as the likely fathers of Sally Hemings's children, shifting the focus from their virtuous grandfather by providing morally flawed alternatives.[7] The Carr brothers – Jefferson's nephews – remained the favored candidates as potential fathers for Sally Hemings' children throughout the twentieth century. In a closely argued essay written in 1960, which privileged an account by Monticello overseer Edmund Bacon, Douglass Adair sought to 'prove' that Peter Carr rather than Jefferson was the father of Hemings's children. He refused to accept Madison Hemings's memoir, declaring, 'Such behavior is completely at variance with Jefferson's known character, revealing a hypocrisy, a gross insensitivity and a callous selfishness that he conspicuously lacked, whatever other failings are credited to him.' Adair found it unthinkable that Jefferson 'the great Virginian' could have fathered Sally Hemings's children. The 'character defense' is a tautology: Jefferson was a great and good man therefore he could not have had a relationship with Sally Hemings because he was too good to engage in such behavior.[8]

Dumas Malone, who spent the best part of four decades writing his massive six-volume biography of Jefferson, generally regarded as authoritative, also accepted the character defense as an explanation for the 'miscegenation legend' and suggested that Jefferson tragically bore in silence the human burdens produced by the irresponsible sexual activities of his various relatives that were wrongly attributed to him. For most of the twentieth century the interpretation promoted by Malone and Peterson shaped and reflected the views of academic historians on the Jefferson–Hemings question.[9] The character defense rests on the implied inferiority of Sally Hemings and her children. As Annette Gordon-Reed wrote, after DNA testing confirmed the relationship, 'Traditional Jefferson scholars were simply ill-equipped to see the humanity of blacks as equal to that of Jefferson and his white family.'[10]

The implication of Gordon-Reed's analysis is that the Jefferson scholars of the mid-twentieth century were limited by their race, gender and class from recognizing or accepting Jefferson's relationship with Sally Hemings. Their training and approach to the past would have contributed as well. Many of the men who denied the very idea of a relationship between Jefferson and Hemings were themselves steeped in a neo-whig tradition that Jefferson helped to propagate. Dumas Malone, Merrill Peterson and others were products of the pre-war Progressive or post-war Consensus schools of history, which underscored the importance of the ideas and principles of the Revolution. Their scholarly efforts were tied to a defense of those ideas, particularly the Jeffersonian vision. They wrote the history of the American founding as Jefferson intended it to be written, and were Jefferson's intellectual heirs as well as his scholarly defenders. For them, as for Jefferson, republican principles were the central theme of history, and for these reasons they could not accept the possibility that Jefferson, the great articulator or definer of those principles, had had a sexual relationship with his slave. Even if they did accept the relationship, it is unlikely that they would have deemed it a suitable matter for historical study.

If historians, mainly white, male and often Virginia-based, established an academic consensus that the relationship between Jefferson and Hemings was unlikely, this interpretation was challenged by three writers, all women and each, in different ways, an outsider in the world of Jefferson scholarship. The first of these, Fawn Brodie, was an historian at UCLA. Brodie was an iconoclastic biographer who in the 1940s had written a controversial study of Brigham Young that had led to her expulsion from the Mormon Church. In 1974 Brodie published *Thomas Jefferson: An Intimate History*, the first major Jefferson biography to take the relationship seriously.[11] Brodie argued that Jefferson and Hemings had had a loving relationship that lasted nearly four decades. She speculated about Jefferson's personality and relationships by drawing insights from Freudian analysis in what she described as a work of 'psychohistory'. *Thomas Jefferson: An Intimate History* was a popular success, selling more than 80,000 copies in hardback and 250,000 paperback copies by 1980.[12]

Perhaps because of the popularity of Fawn Brodie's biography, a number of scholars attacked her interpretation and methodology. Foremost among these was Dumas Malone. According to Malone, Brodie 'presents virtually no evidence that was not already known to scholars, and wholly disregards testimony which I regard as more reliable.' Moreover, Malone criticized Brodie's methodology, claiming that her book went 'far beyond the evidence and carries psychological speculation to the point of absurdity; the resulting mishmash of fact and fiction, surmise and conjecture is not history as I understand the term'.[13] Malone was not alone. In his 1977 study, *A Wolf by the Ears: Thomas Jefferson and Slavery*, a book one reviewer suspected was written 'in part out of an irritation with Fawn Brodie', the historian John Chester Miller mocked Brodie's romantic interpretation of the relationship between Hemings and Jefferson. Miller reiterated the character defense of Jefferson and asserted that one or both of the Carrs fathered Sally Hemings's children. In 1981 Virginius Dabney, a Virginia journalist descended from Thomas Jefferson's sister Martha and Dabney Carr, devoted an entire volume, *The Jefferson Scandals: A Rebuttal*, to denying the relationship. Dabney invoked what had become the standard defense – upholding Jefferson's character and implicating one of the Carrs (Samuel, his ancestor) as the likely father of Sally Hemings's children.[14]

One reader who accepted Brodie's view was an African American novelist and sculptor, Barbara Chase-Riboud. In 1979 Chase-Riboud published a novel, *Sally Hemings*, which presented a fictionalized account of the alleged Jefferson–Hemings relationship from Hemings's perspective. While most historians had approached the question from the perspective of Jefferson, and concluded that the relationship was unlikely, Chase-Riboud created a voice for Hemings, about whom little is known, and portrayed her as an emotionally complex and complete person whom Jefferson loved. *Sally Hemings* sold more than a million and a half copies by the early 1980s.[15]

By the early 1990s many members of the public were aware of the controversy concerning the Jefferson-Hemings relationship. Owing to the popular success of the books by Fawn Brodie and Barbara Chase-Riboud, many people accepted the relationship as an historical fact.[16] In the new preface to the 1998 edition of his *Jefferson Image in the American Mind*, Merrill Peterson, who did not believe in the Jefferson–Hemings relationship, conceded, 'No book of the last quarter century has left a more indelible mark on the Jefferson image than Fawn M. Brodie's *Thomas Jefferson: An Intimate History*.'[17] Given the vigorous denial of the relationship by Jefferson's prominent biographers and other scholarly defenders one might ask why their campaign seemingly failed. John C. Miller offered an explanation:

To explain the eager popular acceptance of this new perception of Jefferson requires recognition of the fact that in the post-Watergate, post-Vietnam era there exists a strong compulsion to belittle the great men of the past, not excluding the Founding Fathers of the American Republic, to the stature of contemporary politicians. It is somehow consoling to believe that Jefferson had a slave mistress, that he brought up his own children as slaves and succeeded in concealing the fact from the American people by lies, evasions and subterfuges. Finally, Jefferson's romantic involvement with a 'black' slave woman serves dramatically to refute his often-expressed conviction that whites and blacks could not live together in the United States in amity and concord. By virtue of practicing integration at Monticello, regardless of what he preached, Jefferson becomes in Ms. Brodie's book one of the culture-heroes of the present-day integration movement – and this despite the 'fact' that he raised five of his natural children as slaves.[18]

In other words, sections of the public accepted the Jefferson–Hemings relationship as portrayed by Brodie and Chase-Riboud because it served a convenient contemporary political agenda. It was not that the defenders were in the wrong; indeed, they had truth on their side. Rather, disillusionment with and distrust of the political establishment combined with increased demands for African American civil rights created momentum in favor of accepting the Jefferson – Hemings relationship in the public mind. 'Perhaps an author must contrive a sensation to make the public aware of a contemporary issue. Misrepresentation of historical fact deludes both authors and readers, however, and impoverishes public debates,' lamented Virginius Dabney and Jon Kukla.[19] Miller, Dabney and Kukla, writing in the late 1970s, anticipated the main line of argument that a subsequent generation would employ to deny the Jefferson–Hemings relationship: we have the truth on our side but the facts of the case are politically unacceptable.

Although Jefferson's defenders largely failed to persuade the public to disregard the Jefferson–Hemings relationship as propounded by Fawn Brodie and Barabara Chase-Riboud, they enjoyed greater success among their peers. Academic historians, while more willing to allow for a sexual relationship between Jefferson and Hemings than their predecessors had been, remained skeptical. Joseph J. Ellis declared in 1996, 'Within the scholarly world, especially within the community of Jefferson specialists, there seems to be a clear consensus that the story is almost certainly not true.' Ellis referred to what historians believed about Jefferson's personality, asserting, 'a long-term sexual relationship with one of his slaves was not in character for Jefferson.' In other words Ellis echoed the generation-old view of Merrill Peterson: the relationship was possible but not probable because of Jefferson's character. During the 1990s a split emerged between academic historians and the public at large. Most historians, at least 'the community of Jefferson specialists', rejected the relationship between Jefferson and Hemings while those members of the public who considered the matter tended to accept the relationship as true.[20] Early in the 1990s Nathan Huggins, an expert in African American history, wrote of the Jefferson–Hemings relationship: 'The evidence is circumstantial; we will never get a truth everyone will accept. Custodians of the Jefferson legacy seek to protect his historical reputation and demand substantial and irrefutable evidence.'[21] It seemed that matters would remain fixed – with the public believing in the relationship and scholars doubting it.

It was not until almost a quarter of a century after Fawn Brodie's book appeared (and nearly two centuries since James Callender made his original accusations in the *Richmond Recorder*) that many academic historians came to accept that Thomas Jefferson and Sally Hemings had a sexual relationship. A major turning point in the debate was the appearance of Annette Gordon-Reed's *Thomas Jefferson and Sally Hemings: An American Controversy* in 1997. Like Brodie and Chase-Riboud, Gordon-Reed was an outsider in the traditional world of Jefferson scholarship. She wrote from multiple perspectives: lawyer, woman and African American, and in her introduction she made clear that her profession, gender and race influenced her approach to her subject. She decried the biases and racial assumptions that were reflected in histories she read as a child and student: 'To see my ancestors presented through the prism of others' prejudices was not easy and it has not gotten easier as the years have passed.' Gordon-Reed saw similar bias at work in the treatment of the Jefferson-Hemings story, since the 'character defense' rested on an assumption of Jefferson's superiority to Sally Hemings.

> The underlying theme of most historians' denial of the truth of a liaison between Thomas Jefferson and Sally Hemings is that the whole story is too impossible to believe. This line of argument is troubling. For in order to sustain the claim of impossibility, or even to discuss the matter in those terms, one has to make Thomas Jefferson so high as to have been something more than human and one has to make Sally Hemings so low as to have been something less than human. It is the latter part of the equation that has prompted me to write this book.

Gordon-Reed also approached the Jefferson–Hemings question as a legal scholar, not an historian. She felt that her legal background was important to the project. 'I approach this task', she wrote, 'as a law professor and a lawyer looking at how professionals in other disciplines – historians and to a lesser extent journalists – analyze evidence and the concept of proof.'[22]

Gordon-Reed's analysis, therefore, operated on two levels: as an examination of the evidence concerning the Jefferson-Hemings controversy and as a study of its historiography. Gordon-Reed presented a devastating analysis which showed that most scholars who had considered the issue in any detail – Merrill Peterson, Dumas Malone, Douglass Adair, John C. Miller and Virginius Dabney in particular – had failed to give the evidence from African American sources the same weight as comparable evidence from white sources. She concluded, 'those who are considered Jefferson scholars have never made a serious objective attempt to get to the truth of this matter'.[23] By contrast, she presented a detailed examination of all the extant evidence, comparing the accounts by Madison Hemings and other Monticello slaves with those of Jefferson's white descendants. She also considered the circumstantial evidence – such as Jefferson's treatment of Sally Hemings's children and the pattern of Hemings's conceptions when juxtaposed with that of Jefferson's presence at Monticello. Although Gordon-Reed began by saying that she could not definitely believe the story of the Jefferson–Hemings relationship to be true, she made what was to that date the most convincing case for it to appear in print. That she did so based entirely on evidence that had been available for decades substantiated her view that previous Jefferson scholars had been biased in their treatment of the subject.

Although some reviewers were hostile to what they considered the polemical, iconoclastic tone of *Thomas Jefferson and Sally Hemings*, the book was crucial in shifting the terms of the Jefferson–Hemings debate.[24] When Winthrop D. Jordan, one of the first scholars to treat the story seriously, reviewed *Thomas Jefferson and Sally Hemings*, he noted, 'When I first wrote about this matter, I thought there was possibly a 60 percent likelihood that the essential story was correct as to fact; when I later reviewed Brodie's book, I recall thinking that 65 percent might be closer. Now I would raise the probability to 80 or even 85 percent.'[25] In the wake of Gordon-Reed's publication the scholarly momentum began to shift in favor of the Jefferson–Hemings relationship. That momentum would continue to build in the following year when Gordon-Reed's argument was substantiated by the first new evidence to be introduced into the controversy for over a century: the results of DNA testing.

In November 1998, just as the American public was riveted by the impending impeachment of President Bill Clinton for his involvement in a sex scandal, an article with the headline 'Jefferson Fathered Slave's Last Child' appeared in the scientific journal, *Nature*. The article was based on a study carried out by a team led by Dr. Eugene Foster, a pathologist at the University of Virginia. Foster's team compared nineteen genetic markers on the Y-chromosomes of fourteen subjects: five male-line descendants of Field Jefferson (Thomas Jefferson's paternal uncle); three male-line descendants of John Carr (grandfather of Jefferson's nephews Samuel and Peter Carr); five male-line descendants of Thomas Woodson (a Monticello slave, whose own family tradition held that he was Jefferson's son), and one male line descendant of Eston Hemings (Sally Hemings's last child). The study showed that Thomas Jefferson and Eston Hemings were related. It further proved that there was no genetic link between the Carrs and Hemings, thereby disproving the longstanding Jefferson family claim that either or both of the Carr brothers fathered children by Sally Hemings. Finally, the study demonstrated that there was no genetic link between the Jefferson and Woodson families.[26]

Despite its rather sensational headline, the *Nature* study did not conclusively prove that Thomas Jefferson was the father of Eston Hemings. Rather, it proved that they were related and that *a* male Jefferson was the father of Eston Hemings. However, when read in conjunction with Annette Gordon-Reed's *Thomas Jefferson and Sally Hemings*, the *Nature* study seemed to clinch the argument. Indeed Joseph J. Ellis, who only two years before had declared, 'there seems to be a clear consensus that the story is almost certainly not true', co-wrote an article to accompany the Foster study accepting that Jefferson was the father of Eston Hemings and, by implication, Sally Hemings's other children.[27] Within two years, Annette Gordon-Reed's book and the DNA study had destroyed the arguments made by Jefferson's defenders for nearly two centuries. In 2000, Fraser D. Neiman of Monticello published a statistical study that analysed the correlation between Jefferson's visits to Monticello and Hemings's conceptions. Neiman concluded that there was a 99 percent probability that Jefferson was the father of Sally Hemings's six children.[28] Taken together, *Thomas Jefferson and Sally Hemings*, the DNA study in *Nature*, and Neiman's analysis seemed to offer the 'substantial and irrefutable evidence' that Nathan Huggins had called for.

In the immediate aftermath of the *Nature* study, Daniel P. Jordan, president of the Thomas Jefferson Memorial Foundation, appointed a research committee composed of nine members of the staff at Monticello to evaluate the DNA study in the context of all of the historical and scientific evidence available. The committee met ten times between December 1998 and April 1999. Subcommittees were established to consider the scientific and documentary evidence. The committee prepared a draft report, which included testimony from scientific experts who reviewed the Foster DNA study as well as extensive consideration and samples from the documentary record. The report reached the following conclusions:

    1. Dr. Foster's DNA Study was conducted in a manner that meets the standards of the scientific community, and its scientific results are valid.

2. The DNA study, combined with multiple strands of currently available documentary and statistical evidence, indicates a high probability that Thomas Jefferson fathered Eston Hemings, and that he most likely was the father of all six of Sally Hemings's children appearing in Jefferson's records. Those children are Harriet, who died in infancy; Beverly; an unnamed daughter who died in infancy; Harriet; Madison; and Eston.

3. Many aspects of this likely relationship between Sally Hemings and Thomas Jefferson are, and may remain, unclear, such as the nature of the relationship, the existence and longevity of Sally Hemings's first child, and the identity of Thomas C. Woodson.

4. The implications of the relationship between Sally Hemings and Thomas Jefferson should be explored and used to enrich the understanding and interpretation of Jefferson and the entire Monticello community.[29]

One member of the research committee, White McKenzie Wallenborn, MD, dissented from the main findings of the committee. While he conceded that 'The results of the DNA studies enhance the possibility that Thomas Jefferson was the father of one of Sally Hemings [*sic*] children', he noted that 'the findings do not prove that Thomas Jefferson was the father of Eston. This is a very important difference.' Dr. Wallenborn prepared a minority report that outlined his concerns over how the committee conducted its business. He felt the committee was biased in favor of a conclusion that Jefferson was the father of Hemings's children and treated the evidence accordingly – ironically the same charge, in reverse, that Annette Gordon-Reed had made against previous students of the question.[30] The Thomas Jefferson Memorial Foundation released its final report on the Internet in January 2000. A new consensus had emerged that accepted the Jefferson–Hemings relationship as a fact.

III

The publication of the TJMF report was a decisive moment in the history of the Hemings controversy. That the TJMF, the caretaker of Monticello and on a broader level the keeper of Jefferson's reputation, officially and publicly accepted the relationship epitomized the dramatic shift that had taken place within Jefferson scholarship between 1997 and 2000. It also epitomized the increasingly scholarly approach that the Foundation had brought to the study and presentation of Jefferson since the early 1980s. Acceptance of the Hemings relationship required considerable intellectual courage on the part of the Daniel P. Jordan and his staff. As we have seen, with regard to questions of race the Foundation's record was mixed at best. Nonetheless, at the end of the twentieth century the Foundation forthrightly acknowledged that Thomas Jefferson and Sally Hemings had had a sexual relationship. This development was not welcomed by some of Thomas Jefferson's most fervent admirers and descendants.

For two centuries Jefferson's defenders had, more or less, successfully denied the Jefferson–Hemings relationship. As the twenty-first century began, the tide had turned against Jefferson's partisans. The Jefferson–Hemings relationship was widely reported as a fact by the mainstream media; it had, apparently, been proven by scientific testing; and it was accepted by a majority of the academic community, including the Jefferson scholars based at Monticello and the University of Virginia.[31] Despite, or because of, these setbacks, Jefferson's defenders undertook to fight a desperate rearguard action to 'protect' his reputation from the allegation that he was the father of Sally Hemings's children.

In May 2000 a self-styled 'group of concerned businessmen, historians, genealogists, scientists and patriots formed a corporation called the Thomas Jefferson Heritage Society, Inc. [TJHS]'. According to John H. Works, Jr., the president of the TJHS, the society was created to 'undertake an independent and objective review of all the facts and circumstances surrounding the possible paternity of Sally Hemings' [sic] children by Thomas Jefferson'.[32] In order to achieve its ends the TJHS has, thus far, undertaken two major initiatives. Soon after its founding the society convened what it called a 'blue ribbon commission' of thirteen scholars to examine the evidence relating to the Jefferson–Hemings question – the same evidence that had been considered by the committee established at Monticello the previous year by the TJMF. The commission consisted of thirteen scholars, most of them specialists on early American history who had published on aspects of the intellectual and political history of the Jeffersonian era; none was a specialist in slavery, social or family history, however. The commission was funded by an anonymous $20,000 donation by a benefactor who was not associated with the TJHS. The donor agreed that she 'was funding scholarly research and would have neither influence on the outcome nor advanced knowledge of our conclusions prior to the public release of our report'.[33]

The members of the commission asserted they were given complete freedom to reach their conclusions: 'We were to have complete intellectual freedom to pursue the truth, including authority to establish our own procedures, to add new members, and to carry on our own work independent of the influence of the TJHS or any other group.'[34] The Scholars' Commission concluded:

> The question of whether Thomas Jefferson fathered one or more children by his slave Sally Hemings is an issue about which honorable people can and do disagree. After a careful review of all the evidence, the commission

agrees unanimously that the allegation is by no means proven; and we find it regrettable that public confusion about the 1998 DNA testing and other evidence has misled many people. With the exception of one member . . . our individual conclusions range from serious scepticism about the charge to a conviction that it is almost certainly false.[35]

The members of the TJHS commission specifically focused on the 1998 DNA tests, accepting that the results established that the father of Eston Hemings was one of more than two-dozen Jefferson men. Because the DNA tests had ruled out the Carr brothers – the traditional suspects for those who refuse to accept Jefferson's paternity – the commission identified Thomas Jefferson's brother, Randolph, as the likely father of Eston Hemings.[36]

While there is no reason to question the independence of the Scholars' Commission convened by the Thomas Jefferson Heritage Society, it is clear that the commission's findings found a welcome audience among the members of the TJHS. At the outset of the commission's deliberations John H. Works dismissed the TJMF's earlier report on the issue as 'shallow, shoddy, and biased'. 'Our report', Works anticipated, 'is going to lay it out there and necessarily probably embarrass them.' The Scholars' Commission issued its report on 12 April 2001, the day that George Bush received the Jefferson descendants at the White House, a move likely intended to counter the press coverage accorded to the reception in Washington. The TJHS report received considerable media attention and, in the short term at least, diverted attention from the TJMF's earlier report and the White House ceremony. The press release that accompanied the report was not as objective and balanced in its language as the report itself. Whereas the report stated that reasonable people could disagree over the Hemings matter, the TJHS's press release asserted that 'the [Hemings] story was too juicy for some to pass up, and over the years it has resurfaced to illustrate the evil character of Jefferson, America, or slavery in general'. Apart from the (probably unintended) defense of slavery in this statement, it shows that the work of the TJHS, while cloaked in scholarly objectivity, promotes an explicit political agenda.[37]

The second major initiative of the TJHS was the publication in 2001 of an essay collection, *The Jefferson–Hemings Myth: An American Travesty*. Although the volume resembles a collection of academic essays, it is not. The book has twelve major sections, all but one of which is written by an officer of the TJHS. The contributors distinguished themselves from the scholars who had served on the 'blue ribbon commission', which they described as 'a completely independent and separate group of scholars doing its own research and publication'.[38] The distinction was important because, unlike the Scholars' Commission, which was given academic independence, *The Jefferson–Hemings Myth* is intended to achieve several interrelated objectives and each of its essays serves that end.

First and foremost, the TJHS sought to 'defend' Jefferson against the 'accusation' that he had had a sexual relationship with Sally Hemings. Second, it sought to disprove and discredit the findings of the TJMF, alleging that the Monticello committee ignored contrary evidence and suppressed dissenting opinions in an effort to promote a revisionist portrait of Jefferson as 'a hypocrite, a liar and a fraud'. According to TJHS president John Works, 'In the forefront of this historical revisionist movement is the organization that owns Thomas Jefferson's home, Monticello, the Thomas Jefferson Memorial Foundation (TJMF).'[39] In his introduction to the collection Works explained the connection, as he saw it, between the Jefferson–Hemings controversy and questions of contemporary politics and culture.

> The allegations concerning [Jefferson's] behavior do not merely provide an interesting sidelight on an otherwise great man. They are, in fact, a frontal assault on him and his principles, and have as a stated purpose by many proponents the aim to throw out those principles and replace them with something new but as yet poorly defined. These accusations have not just been leveled against Thomas Jefferson personally, but they have devolved into a denunciation of everything he stood for, and this we cannot allow to take hold.

Works continued:

> Many scholars, including some of those at the TJMF, have adopted the modern 'politically correct' propaganda that those who laid the bricks and plowed the fields were the real builders of this nation, not the man who wrote the Declaration of Independence, doubled the size of the nation with the Louisiana Purchase, and established the University of Virginia. These scholars have begun tearing down the reputation of Jefferson and focusing instead more broadly on the lives and work done by the Negro slaves, and on their contributions to the building of this nation.[40]

For Works and the members of the TJHS, the writing of history is a zero-sum game. They are, perhaps unwittingly, subscribers to a simplified version of Jefferson's whig interpretation: the history of the American Revolution is the story of Jefferson's contribution to human freedom. This is the all-important theme of its history and anything that undermines this view is dangerous. One cannot write the history of Monticello's slaves without endangering the legacy of their owner. To criticize Jefferson – for the TJHS found the thought of Jefferson engaging in sexual relations with an African American woman repugnant – is to criticize America.

In *The Jefferson Image in the American Mind*, Merrill Peterson demonstrated that Jefferson's legacy had long been an object of political controversy. The activities of the TJHS suggest that the Hemings question has embroiled Jefferson in the current culture war over political correctness. As David N. Mayer, one of the members of the Scholars' Commission, wrote:

> Sadly the historical profession today has lost much [*sic*] of the standards by which evidence can be objectively weighed and evaluated in the search for historical truth. History, in effect, has become politicized in America today, as illustrated by the widespread acceptance of the Jefferson–Hemings myth as historical fact.
>
> Taken together, political correctness, multiculturalism, and post-modernism have created an environment in the academic world today in which scholars feel pressured to accept the Jefferson–Hemings myth as historical truth. White male scholars in particular fear that by questioning the myth – they will be called racially 'insensitive' if not racist . . . [A]mong many proponents of the Jefferson paternity claim there has emerged a truly disturbing McCarthy-like inquisition that has cast a pall over Jefferson scholarship today. Questioning the validity of the claim has been equated with the denigration of African Americans and a denial of their rightful place in American history. In this climate of scholarly and public opinion, it requires great personal courage for scholars to question the Jefferson paternity thesis and to point out the dubious historical record on which it rests.[41]

Mayer did not provide examples to illustrate his claim that there is a 'McCarthy-like inquisition' compelling white male scholars to accept the Jefferson–Hemings relationship. Nor did John Works provide any evidence to support his assertion that 'a stated purpose' of advocates of the Jefferson–Hemings relationship is 'to throw out those [Jeffersonian] principles and replace them with something new but as yet poorly defined'. Neither allows for the possibility that Jefferson scholars, whatever their race and gender, have been convinced by the new evidence and scholarship that came to light between 1997 and 2000. Rather, the real issue for them is defending Jefferson and the United States from the advocates of political correctness and multiculturalism. As Works declared, 'Defending Thomas Jefferson, therefore, has come to mean defending what America means, and we feel compelled to rise to that defense.'[42]

Among scholars, this defense has been ineffective. For most of the twentieth century serious Jefferson scholars denied the likelihood of a sexual relationship between Thomas Jefferson and Sally Hemings. That, by 2001, the primary 'defense' of Jefferson was maintained by a fringe group espousing reactionary politics and employing hysterical rhetoric is testimony to how quickly the historiographical consensus regarding the Jefferson-Hemings question shifted in 1997–8.

IV

In reviewing Annette Gordon-Reed's book, Winthrop Jordan wrote, '*Thomas Jefferson and Sally Hemings* offers the most persuasive case that I know for Jefferson's having fathered mulatto children. But that alone seems to me of limited historical significance. Even if exhumation and DNA testing were to be attempted, what would the effort prove?'[43] Jordan identified the key question. Apart from the small number of people who may or may not be entitled to burial at Monticello, what is the broader significance of the Jefferson–Hemings relationship? Does it matter that Thomas Jefferson and Sally Hemings had sexual relations?

At first sight it would seem that the relationship makes little difference – except for those who have invested so much in denying it. After all, the historical and scientific developments of the past decade have merely confirmed what many people had long suspected. This may be so, but the confirmation of the Jefferson–Hemings relationship requires a re-evaluation of Jefferson's public achievements and principles, not in an effort to debunk or undermine them as the TJHS fears, but to better understand them. Peter S. Onuf has demonstrated how this might be done. He has examined Jefferson's longstanding advocacy of colonization for emancipated African Americans as the solution to the problem of slavery in light of the Hemings relationship. Onuf argues that Jefferson advocated colonization because he knew, based on his own experience, that miscegenation was inevitable and would undermine and ultimately endanger America's republican experiment. Jefferson advocated colonization not simply for philosophical or racist reasons. Colonization was necessary because slavery invited sexual license that was at odds with a virtuous republic – as evidenced by Jefferson's own life and home.[44] As Jan Ellen Lewis and others have shown, Jefferson and other theorists saw the family as the fundamental unit in republican society. The family should nurture the values of virtue and citizenship that were necessary to the success of republican government. The Jefferson who retained a lock of his deceased wife's hair for more than forty years and was, apparently, devoted to her memory and to their two surviving children, Martha and Maria, seemed to embody the republican notion of the family as a source of virtue and a haven from a corrupt and dangerous world. However, we now know that

Jefferson not only cherished the memory of his wife and doted upon their daughters and grandchildren, but that he had a much larger family, some of whom he owned as slaves. If slavery is the great moral failure at the heart of the early American republic, we also find it at the heart of Thomas Jefferson's family. This set of facts suggests that while the family was the fundamental unit, political as well as social, in the early republic, at Monticello, at least, the relationship between family and republicanism was complex and needs to be redefined.[45] Though there may be no obvious link between Jefferson's attitudes toward politics and his relationship with Sally Hemings, Onuf's article suggests how historians may re-examine well-known aspects of Jefferson's life and legacy in the light of the Hemings relationship.

At the same time that the TJMF was preparing its report on Thomas Jefferson and Sally Hemings, scholars (some of whom participated in the TJMF deliberations) began to assess the implications and meaning of the new Jeffersonian consensus. The first fruits of this effort – which will likely take many years – appeared in the form of two essay collections published in late 1999 and early 2000. On 5 and 6 March 1999 a group of specialists in early American and African American history met in Charlottesville at a conference entitled 'Sally Hemings and Thomas Jefferson: History, Memory, and Civic Culture'. The proceedings of that meeting were published in late 1999 by the University Press of Virginia as an edited collection with the same title. Soon thereafter, the *William and Mary Quarterly* published a forum containing seven essays entitled 'Thomas Jefferson and Sally Hemings Redux'.[46] These two collections suggest that historians will be exploring several areas in light of the widespread acceptance of the relationship.

In the first place, as Merrill Peterson demonstrated in his *Jefferson Image in the American Mind*, Jefferson's importance has not been confined to his own lifetime. Scholars and commentators will consider the Jefferson–Hemings relationship in light of subsequent American development. If, as Joseph Ellis suggests, the DNA study 'confirms Jefferson's unique status as the dead-white-male who matters most', then the broader cultural meaning of his thirty-eight-year relationship with one of his slaves must be explained, especially in the context of an America which is more ethnically and racially diverse than it had been in Jefferson's time.[47] A second line of research is likely to consider the intersection of race and sex in eighteenth- and early nineteenth-century America. Jefferson and Hemings are important as perhaps the most famous interracial couple in American history. Their relationship will act as a catalyst to further investigations into interracial sexuality and slavery.[48] In this regard, the central question, probably unanswerable, concerns the nature of the relationship between Jefferson and Hemings.

Was it, as Fawn Brodie suggested more than thirty years ago, a loving relationship that spanned the racial and social barriers dividing Jefferson and Hemings? Alternatively, as some commentators have asked, did Thomas Jefferson exploit the power he wielded over Sally Hemings to coerce sex from her – was he guilty of rape? Short of new evidence coming to light it will likely be impossible to answer this question, yet the attempt to do so will go a long way toward determining the future development of Jefferson's reputation.

A third area of research interest will consider the implications of the relationship for our understanding of Jefferson's attitudes toward the women in his life, black and white. Jan Lewis has begun to help us to understand how Jefferson's daughters reacted to the Hemings relationship, and Andrew Burstein has recently written about Jefferson's attitudes regarding suitable reading for young females. Nonetheless, the Hemings relationship calls for fuller consideration of Jefferson's attitudes, relationships and beliefs with regard to women of all races. While race has been a key category of analysis in the re-evaluation of Jefferson over the past forty years, relatively little work has been done on Jefferson and gender. This is likely to be the key area in Jefferson studies in the immediate future.[49]

A fourth area of research will consider how Jefferson's descendants – black and white – remembered and perpetuated their connection with their famous antecedent and how historians have treated and interpreted those memories and sources.[50] Scholars will continue to examine the massive documentary record associated with Jefferson in an effort to learn more about the relationship and its impact on Jefferson, Hemings and Monticello.[51] For example, Lucia Stanton has demonstrated that the DNA testing corroborates many of the accounts of Monticello's slaves while calling into question aspects of those left by Jefferson's white descendants. As Annette Gordon-Reed argued, many historians had previously accepted the accounts of Jefferson's white descendants uncritically while subjecting those of the slaves to excessive scepticism. Stanton suggests that we should give fuller credence to what Monticello's slaves had to say about their owner (and, in some cases, father), while questioning more closely the accounts of his white descendants.[52] Although such a re-evaluation may have little to tell us regarding Jefferson's accomplishments as a statesman, politician and public figure, they have a direct bearing on our understanding of Jefferson's life at Monticello, which has implications for our understanding of his philosophy and character.

Perhaps the most important consequence of the Hemings relationship is that it will require a thorough rereading and reinterpretation of Jefferson sources – both primary and secondary. Though only a small portion of the vast corpus of Jefferson-related primary sources will be affected by the confirmation of the Hemings relationship, the impact on the secondary literature will be much greater. Annette Gordon-Reed was careful to distinguish between scholars' treatment of the Hemings relationship and other aspects of their scholarship. She wrote, 'It is my belief that those who are considered Jefferson scholars have never made a serious and objective attempt to get to the truth of this [the Hemings] matter. This is not a criticism of their work on any other aspect of Thomas Jefferson's life or any other subject about which they have written.'[53] While Gordon-Reed's graciousness towards her fellow scholars is admirable, she may be conceding too much. Because many of Jefferson's scholarly advocates based their rejection of the Hemings relationship on their understanding of Jefferson's character, then it would appear that many biographers have misread and misinterpreted that character. This is not to say that the massive, seemingly encyclopedic, biographies of Dumas Malone and Merrill Peterson are without merit. Both men immersed themselves in and mastered the vast corpus of Jeffersonian primary and secondary sources, without the benefit of as many published documents (let alone searchable digitized versions) as current scholars rely upon as a matter of course. Despite their mastery of the sources, Malone and Peterson failed to recognize one of the central features of Jefferson's life: his relationship with Sally Hemings. On one hand this is understandable in so far as Hemings made relatively little impression on Jefferson's documentary legacy. Nonetheless, Gordon-Reed demonstrated, with access to the same records that Malone and Peterson enjoyed, that one could reach a radically different conclusion regarding the relationship between Jefferson and Hemings.

This misreading of Jefferson's life has significant consequences for how historians have treated Jefferson, and will treat him in the future. For example, in six concise sentences Annette Gordon-Reed summed up the way in which the accepted facts of Jefferson's biography have changed dramatically in light of recent research:

> Thomas Jefferson had thirteen children, six of whom lived to adulthood. Some of his children were white and some of them were black. He had four sons born to him, three of whom lived to adulthood. He had three daughters who lived to adulthood, not two. Jefferson did not live in celibacy for the forty-five years after the death of his wife of ten years, Martha Jefferson. He had a thirty-eight-year apparently monogamous, relationship with Sally Hemings, an enslaved black woman on his plantation, and fathered a child with her when he was sixty-five years old.[54]

These six sentences underscore the level of error in the basic outline of Jefferson's life as reflected in Dumas Malone's six volumes and other biographies. In coming years historians and biographers will need to reinterpret Jefferson's character in light of these newly confirmed facts.

V

Undoubtedly, Thomas Jefferson would be horrified at the notion that historians and members of the public have immersed themselves in and engaged in debate over the most intimate details of his personal life. As we have seen, he conceived of his place in history in terms of his public life and achievements. His autobiography was concerned almost exclusively with his public career, and largely succeeded in drawing a veil over his private life. Although he meticulously preserved his letters and papers for future publication, he destroyed his letters to and from his wife. Similarly, Sally Hemings received only the most cursory mention in Jefferson's papers. This presents future scholars with a daunting challenge indeed. Arguably Merrill Peterson and Dumas Malone 'knew' Jefferson as well as any biographer could, yet they failed to read his character correctly. At the outset of his biography Peterson made the 'mortifying confession' that 'Jefferson remains for me, finally, an impenetrable man.'[55] One might reasonably ask whether, if a scholar of Peterson's ability and acumen was unable to penetrate Jefferson's character, anyone will be able to. This is as Jefferson would have wished it. The common genetic markers discovered by Eugene Foster and his colleagues among the descendants of Thomas Jefferson and Sally Hemings demonstrate that the definitive study of Jefferson has yet to be written.

Perhaps the first serious effort to reinterpret Jefferson's character in light of the new evidence has been undertaken by Andrew Burstein. In 1995 Burstein published an insightful study of Jefferson's character in which he briefly considered the Hemings matter. While acknowledging that with regard to the evidence both for and against Jefferson's paternity of Hemings's children, 'nothing fully satisfies', like his predecessors Burstein sought answers in Jefferson's character. He concluded:

> Knowing what we do about Jefferson's Heart and Head, that the first made him generous and the second ruled his actions, it seems highly unlikely that because light-skinned Sally Hemings bore light-skinned children at Monticello, they necessarily were fathered by Monticello's master. Moreover, Jefferson would have been *uncharacteristically* imprudent to be responsible for giving Sally Hemings the two children that she bore in the years after the charges surfaced, while he remained president.[56]

In light of Annette Gordon-Reed's re-evaluation of the sources as well as the new evidence produced by the studies of Eugene Foster and Fraser

Neiman, Burstein revisited the subject in his 2005 book, *Jefferson's Secrets*.[57]

In *Jefferson's Secrets*, Burstein acknowledged the power of the new evidence and sought to move beyond the question of whether Thomas Jefferson and Sally Hemings had a sexual relationship to consider the nature of their relationship. Burstein wrote, 'To reframe the cultural environment in which Jefferson moved requires new information with regard to Jefferson's feelings about race and sex – it requires unearthing sources that historians (myself included) have missed.' Burstein set out to examine two of the most vexing topics in Jefferson's and our own time – race and sex – in order to determine the significance of Jefferson's relationship with Sally Hemings. His conclusions, like so much written on the topic, are likely to arouse strong differences of opinion.[58]

The issue of race is very much at the center of the debate over Sally Hemings and Thomas Jefferson. Both those who advocate and those who deny the relationship have difficulty reconciling Jefferson's stated racial attitudes with the possibility that he engaged in a sexual relationship with an African American slave. In perhaps the most notorious passage he ever wrote, Jefferson advanced his 'suspicion' in *Notes on the State of Virginia* that Africans were inferior to Europeans intellectually and physically (but not morally). He introduced sexuality into his racial analysis, noting that Africans preferred whites as sexual partners, 'as uniformly as is the preference of the Oranootan for the black women over those of his own species'. According to Jefferson's bizarre interpretation of natural history, just as orangutans allegedly preferred to mate with Africans as a superior and more attractive species, so too Africans preferred Europeans. He asked, 'The circumstance of superior beauty, is thought worthy attention in the propagation of our horses, dogs and other domestic animals; why not in that of man?' According to Jefferson's own words he found Africans unattractive (and by implication, unacceptable) as sexual partners, yet he engaged in a prolonged sexual relationship with one of his slaves. For those who deny the relationship, Jefferson's racial writings seem to provide evidence, albeit problematic – particularly for those mounting a 'character defense' – against the relationship. For those who accept the relationship these writings suggest further evidence for Jefferson's hypocrisy. Jefferson's racism and the Sally Hemings relationship sit quite nicely alongside the Declaration of Independence's assertion of universal equality and Jefferson's ownership of more than six hundred slaves.[59]

In *Jefferson's Secrets*, Andrew Burstein advances another explanation to reconcile Jefferson's racism with his relationship with Sally Hemings. While Jefferson's contemporaries and many subsequent scholars and commentators have emphasized Sally Hemings's African ancestry,

Burstein considers her European antecedents. Sally Hemings was the daughter of Jefferson's father-in-law, John Wayles, and Wayles's slave Betty Hemings. Betty Hemings was of mixed European and African ancestry. This meant that Sally Hemings was the half-sister of Jefferson's late wife, Martha Wayles Skelton Jefferson, *and* that three of her four grandparents were of European descent. 'Did Jefferson imagine Sally Hemings as one-quarter black or three quarters white'? asks Burstein. He demonstrates that Jefferson did not adhere to the 'one drop' rule that pertained in later generations in the South whereby *any* African ancestry rendered a person black in the eyes of the law and society. Rather in an 1814 letter Jefferson provided a mathematical demonstration of the 'cleaning' of blood. Jefferson advanced the view that anyone whose ancestry was no more than three-sixteenths African was white in the eyes of the law – though not necessarily free. Sally Hemings herself was one-quarter African, and her children by Thomas Jefferson were two-sixteenths African and thus, according to Jefferson's calculations and thinking, white. According to Burstein, 'If we take him at his word . . . and accept as fact that black skin repelled him, Sally Hemings was not a register of skin pigmentation but something else. She may have been "dusky" to the satirists who had never seen her, but to Jefferson, who had know her from her early years, she was anything but an anthropological stereotype. Her presence may have caused him to feel his own privilege, but it did not make him think of Africa.'[60]

If, as Jefferson calculated, Sally Hemings was nearly white, Burstein argues that their relationship breached the barrier of class – widely accepted in the eighteenth-century Atlantic world – rather than race. How did Jefferson reconcile such a relationship with his devotion to his two surviving daughters by his deceased wife and to their numerous grandchildren? How did he feel about the six children that Sally Hemings bore him, four of whom lived to adulthood? Burstein sought the answers to these questions in Jefferson's library. He notes that Jefferson owned and read the works of the Swiss physician, Samuel Auguste David Tissot. Tissot wrote on the relationship between sexuality and health. He argued that men of letters, such as Jefferson, should have regular sexual contact with attractive women as a means of finding physical and mental release that would further their intellectual activities. Sally Hemings, according to Burstein, fulfilled this role for Jefferson. Owing to her status as a slave, and their apparently monogamous, nearly four-decades' long relationship, he could have sex with her in a manner that maintained his privacy and protected him from venereal disease. In addition to his familiarity with the writings of Tissot, Jefferson was well versed in the culture and literature of ancient Greece. According to Burstein, Jefferson may have learned from the Greeks that sex with a servant concubine – the word

Madison Hemings used in his memoir to describe his mother – was socially acceptable. Jefferson, while favoring his legitimate children as members of his family, provided for his surviving illegitimate children by Hemings in the classical Greek manner. They were trained in skills and were either freed or allowed to escape.[61]

Jefferson's Secrets seeks to interpret the relationship in light of Jefferson's intellect and to situate it in the context of the eighteenth-century intellectual world in which Jefferson lived. Andrew Burstein is suspicious of anachronistic interpretations that see Sally Hemings as using her sexuality to negotiate and transcend the boundaries of slavery and race with her master. We simply know too little about Sally Hemings to make such claims. Burstein is still more critical of the view, most readily associated with Fawn Brodie, that the length of the Jefferson–Hemings relationship suggests that the pair – clearly unequal – loved each other. 'Without knowing more about Sally Hemings's real personality and the nature of the privacy she and Thomas Jefferson shared, ' wrote Burstein, 'no evidence exists on which to conjure a loving intimacy.' Burstein concludes, 'It is only in the imaginations of modern champions of inter-racial harmony that attribute to Jefferson a progressive ideology and, in turn, the acceptance of Sally Hemings as a putative social equal.'[62] In fact, Burstein argues, the relationship provided Jefferson with a socially and intellectually acceptable means of gratifying his sexual desires. It did not figure in Jefferson's vast written literary legacy. This was not because Jefferson was ashamed of the relationship. On the contrary, according to Burstein, Jefferson's reading of the Enlightenment's vast literature on the body, especially the works of Tissot, as well as his interpretation of the sexual mores of ancient Greece, meant that he did not feel any guilt about his relationship with Sally Hemings, his nearly white concubine.

Andrew Burstein presents a plausible and persuasive analysis of the relationship between Sally Hemings and Thomas Jefferson. Owing to the absence of written records – especially with regard to Hemings – we likely will never know the exact nature of their relationship. *Jefferson's Secrets* is likely to be seen as the first major study in the next phase of an important aspect of Jefferson scholarship. Now that most scholars accept the Jefferson–Hemings relationship as a fact, it will be necessary to re-evaluate Thomas Jefferson's life and character, so Burstein's will not be the last word on the subject. The relationship between Sally Hemings and Thomas Jefferson underscores the degree to which slavery was at the heart of Jefferson's world. Slavery helped to make Jefferson the man, public and private, that he was. Since World War II this, more than any other aspect of his life, has contributed to the decline in his reputation.

NOTES

1. William Branigan, 'Pruning Jefferson's Family Tree', *Washington Post*, 13 April 2001, B03; Randall Mikkelsen, 'Jefferson Kin, Black and White, Meet at White House', *Boston Globe*, 13 April 2001, p. 7.
2. *Richmond Recorder*, 1 Sept. 1802, 20 Oct. 1802. The relevant extracts have been reprinted in Jan Ellen Lewis and Peter S. Onuf, eds., *Sally Hemings and Thomas Jefferson: History, Memory, and Civic Culture* (Charlottesville: University Press of Virginia, 1999), 259–61.
3. 'Life among the Lowly, no. 1', *Pike County Republican* (Ohio), 13 March 1873, repr. in Annette Gordon Reed, *Thomas Jefferson and Sally Hemings: An American Controversy* (Charlottesville: University Press of Virginia, 1997), 245–8.
4. Gordon-Reed, *Thomas Jefferson and Sally Hemings*; E. A. Foster, et al., 'Jefferson Fathered Slave's Last Child', *Nature*, 5 Nov. 1998, 27–8.
5. Branigan, 'Pruning Thomas Jefferson's Family Tree'.
6. Peterson, *Jefferson Image*, 187; Merrill D. Peterson, *Thomas Jefferson and the New Nation* (New York: Oxford University Press, 1970), 707.
7. Jan Ellen Lewis, 'The White Jeffersons', in Lewis and Onuf, *Sally Hemings and Thomas Jefferson*, 127–60. Also see Gordon-Reed, *Thomas Jefferson and Sally Hemings*, 107–8. For the origins of the character defense among Jefferson's white descendants see Sarah N. Randolph, *The Domestic Life of Thomas Jefferson* (New York: Harper, 1871; repr. Charlottesville: University Press of Virginia, 1978); Edwin Morris Betts and James Adam Bear, eds., *The Family Letters of Thomas Jefferson* (Charlottesville: University Press of Virginia, 1966).
8. Douglass Adair, 'The Jefferson Scandals', in Trevor Colbourn, ed., *Fame and the Founding Fathers: Essays by Douglass Adair* (New York: W.W. Norton, 1974; repr. Indianapolis: Liberty Fund, 1998), 227–73, quotation 259–60.
9. Malone, *Jefferson and His Time*, 4:494–8.
10. Annette Gordon-Reed, ' "Memories of a Few Negroes": Rescuing America's Future at Monticello', Lewis and Onuf, eds., *Sally Hemings and Thomas Jefferson*, 236–52, quotation 237.
11. Winthrop Jordan was one of the first academic historians to take seriously the allegation that Jefferson and Hemings had a sexual relationship. Although he remained undecided, Jordan gave serious consideration to the possibility and its significance for Jefferson and American society. See Winthrop Jordan, *White Over Black: American Attitudes toward the Negro, 1550–1812* (Chapel Hill: University of North Carolina Press, 1968), 461–9.
12. Fawn Brodie, *Thomas Jefferson: An Intimate History* (New York: Norton, 1974). Circulation figures from Peter Nicolaisen, 'Thomas Jefferson, Sally Hemings, and the Question of Race: An Ongoing

Debate', *Journal of American Studies*, 37 (2003), 99–118, 101. Also see
Fawn Brodie, 'The Great Jefferson Taboo', *American Heritage*, 22 (June
1972), 49–57, 97–100; Fawn Brodie, 'Jefferson Biographers and the
Psychology of Canonization', *Journal of Interdisciplinary History*, 2
(1971), 161; Fawn Brodie, 'The Political Hero in America', *Virginia
Quarterly Review*, 46 (1970), 57–60; Fawn Brodie, 'Thomas Jefferson's
Unknown Grandchildren: A Study in Historical Silences', *American
Heritage*, 27 (Oct. 1976), 28–33, 94–9; Newell G. Bringhurst, *Fawn
McKay Brodie: A Biographer's Life* (Norman: University of Oklahoma
Press, 1999); and Newell G. Bringhurst, 'Fawn Brodie's *Thomas Jef-
ferson*: The Making of a Popular and Controversial Biography', *Pacific
Historical Review*, 62 (1993), 433–54.
13. Virginius Dabney and Jon Kukla, 'The Monticello Scandals: History
and Fiction', *Virginia Calvalcade*, 29 (Autumn, 1979), 52–61, quota-
tion 56. For criticism of Brodie's interpretation and methodology see
Dumas Malone, 'Mr. Jefferson's Private Life', American Antiquarian
Society, *Proceedings*, 84 (1974), 65–72; Dumas Malone, 'Jefferson's
Private Life', *New York Times*, 10 May 1974; Dumas Malone and
Stephen H. Hochman, 'A Note on Evidence: The Personal History of
Madison Hemings', *Journal of Southern History*, 41 (1975), 523–8;
Holman Hamilton, 'Review of *Thomas Jefferson: An Intimate History*,
by Fawn Brodie', *Journal of Southern History*, 41 (1975), 107–9; Bruce
Muzlish, 'Review of *Thomas Jefferson: An Intimate History*, by Fawn
Brodie', *Journal of American History*, 61 (1975), 1090–1; Benjamin F.
Wright, 'Review of *Thomas Jefferson: An Intimate History*, by Fawn
Brodie', *Social Science Quarterly*, 56 (1975), 157; *New York Times
Book Review*, 5 May 1974; Garry Wills, 'Uncle Thomas's Cabin', *New
York Review of Books*, 21 (18 April 1974), 26–8; Edwin M. Yoder, 'An
Unshaken Hero', *National Review*, 26 (10 May 1974), 542.
14. John Chester Miller, *The Wolf by the Ears: Thomas Jefferson and
Slavery* (New York: The Free Press, 1977), 165 n.; Robert Dawidoff,
'The Fox in the Henhouse: Jefferson and Slavery', *Reviews in American
History*, 6 (1978), 503–11, quotation 509; Virginius Dabney, *The
Jefferson Scandals: A Rebuttal* (New York: Dodd Mead, 1981).
15. Barbara Chase-Riboud, *Sally Hemings* (New York: St. Martin's, 1979;
repr. 1994 and 1999). Chase-Riboud wrote a sequel to *Sally Hemings*
called *The President's Daughter*. Another popular fictional account
which accepted the Jefferson–Hemings relationship was Gore Vidal's
Burr (1974).
16. For an excellent discussion of the twentieth-century historiography of
the Hemings question down to the early 1990s see Scot A. French and
Edward L. Ayers, 'The Strange Career of Thomas Jefferson: Race and
Slavery in American Memory', in Peter S. Onuf, ed., *Jeffersonian
Legacies* (Charlottesville: University Press of Virginia, 1993), 418–56.

17. Peterson, *The Jefferson Image*, ix.
18. Miller, *Wolf by the Ears*, 172n.
19. Dabney and Kukla, 'The Monticello Scandals', 61.
20. Joseph J. Ellis, *American Sphinx: The Character of Thomas Jefferson* (New York: Random House, 1996), 365, 260. Another major study of Jefferson's character that appeared in the mid-1990s, Andrew Burstein's *The Inner Jefferson: Portrait of a Grieving Optimist* (Charlottesville: University Press of Virginia, 1995), also cast doubt on the Hemings-Jefferson relationship (see below). In their introduction to *Sally Hemings and Thomas Jefferson*, Jan Lewis and Peter Onuf suggested that a consensus was emerging among historians prior to the publication of the results of the *Nature* DNA study. They argue that a curious paradox developed under which many historians accepted the relationship but failed to write about it because they deemed it unimportant, while those, especially Jefferson biographers, who denied the relationship felt it was important and thus dominated the published record with their denials.
21. Nathan I. Huggins, *Revelations: American History, American Myth*, ed. Brenda Huggins (New York: Oxford University Press, 1995), 277.
22. Gordon-Reed, *Thomas Jefferson and Sally Hemings*, xiii, xiv, xv.
23. Gordon-Reed, *Thomas Jefferson and Sally Hemings*, 224.
24. See, for example, Robert A. Rutland, 'Review of *American Sphinx: The Character of Thomas Jefferson* by Joseph J. Ellis and *Thomas Jefferson and Sally Hemings: An American Controversy* by Annette Gordon-Reed', *Journal of American History*, 84 (1997), 1051–2.
25. Winthrop D. Jordan, 'Review of *Thomas Jefferson and Sally Hemings: An American Controversy* by Annette Gordon-Reed', in *WMQ*, 55 (1998), 316–18, quotation 317.
26. Eugene Foster et al., 'Jefferson Fathered Slave's Last Child', *Nature*, 396 (5 Nov. 1998), 27–8.
27. Eric S. Lander and Joseph J. Ellis, 'Founding Father', *Nature*, 396 (5 Nov. 1998), 13–14. Also see Joseph J. Ellis, 'Jefferson: Post-DNA', *WMQ*, 57 (2000), 125–38.
28. Fraser D. Neiman, 'Coincidence or Causal Connection? The Relationship between Thomas Jefferson's Visits to Monticello and Sally Hemings's Conceptions', *WMQ*, 57 (2000), 198–211.
29. Report of the Research Committee on Thomas Jefferson and Sally Hemings, Thomas Jefferson Memorial Foundation, January 2000, 10. The report is available at www.monticello.org.
30. Dr White McKenzie Wallenborn, Thomas Jefferson Foundation, DNA Study Committee, Minority Report, 12 April 1999. Dr. Wallenborn's minority report was added to the Monticello website in March 2000, three months after the majority report was released to the public. Although the tone of his minority report is fairly balanced, Dr Wallenborn is much more outspoken in his criticism of the research committee

and its methods in White McKenzie Wallenborn, MD, 'A Committee
Insider's Viewpoint', Eyler Robert Coates, Sr., ed., *The Jefferson–
Hemings Myth: An American Travesty* (Charlottesville: Thomas Jeffer-
son Heritage Society, 2001), 55–68. Dr. Daniel P. Jordan, the president
of the Thomas Jefferson Foundation, asked Lucia C. Stanton, the
Shannon Research Historian at Monticello, to prepare a response to
Wallenborn's criticisms. Her Response to the Minority Report was
submitted in April 2000 and added to the Monticello website in
May. The relevant documents can be found at www.monticello.org.

31. For an analysis of media coverage of the DNA study see Nicolaisen,
'Thomas Jefferson, Sally Hemings, and the Question of Race', 103–10.

32. John H. Works, 'Foreword', in Coates, *Jefferson–Hemings Myth*, 8.

33. See Thomas Jefferson Heritage Society, Report of the Scholars' Commission on the Jefferson–Hemings Matter, 12 April 2001, 6, 2. This
report is available at www.tjheritage.org. The members of the Scholars'
Commission were Lance Banning of the University of Kentucky (political history and history of ideas); James Ceaser of the University of
Virginia (political science); Robert H. Ferrell of Indiana University
(diplomatic history); Charles R. Kesler of Claremont McKenna College
(political science, history of ideas); Alf J. Mapp, Jr., of Old Dominion
University (Jefferson biographer and Virginia historian); Harvey C.
Mansfield, Jr., of Harvard University (political science, political theory,
government, and history of ideas); David N. Mayer of Capital University (constitutional history, history of ideas); Forrest McDonald of
the University of Alabama (constitutional history, political history,
history of ideas); Paul Rahe of the University of Tulsa (history of ideas
and classical history); Thomas Traut of the University of North Carolina
(biology and medicine); Robert F. Turner of the University of Virginia
Law School (law, diplomacy, government); Walter E. Williams (eco-
nomics and journalism); and Jean Yarborough of Bowdoin College
(history of ideas, political history, political science, government).

34. Report of the Scholars Commission on the Jefferson-Hemings Matter, 6.

35. Report of the Scholars Commission on the Jefferson-Hemings Matter, 2.

36. Report of the Scholars Commission on the Jefferson-Hemings Matter,
26–30.

37. Edward Hock, 'Foundations Conflict Over Names, Hemmings (sic)
Situation', *The Cavalier Daily* (University of Virginia), July 7, 2000;
'Senior Scholars Vote 12–1 Following Year-Long Probe that Thomas
Jefferson Probably Did *Not* Father any of the Children of Sally
Hemings', Press Release, TJHS, April 12, 2001. For press coverage
of the TJHS report see William Branigan, 'Pruning Jefferson's Family
Tree', *Washington Post*, April 13, 2001, page B03; Michael Kilian,
'Panel Rebuts Jefferson-Hemings Theory', *Chicago Tribune*, April 13,
2001; John J. Miller and Ramesh Ponnuru, 'The Jefferson-Hemings

Affair: If You Thought it Happened, Think Again', *National Review Online*, April 12, 2001, www.nationalreview.com. But see also Alexander O. Boulton, 'Review Essay: The Monticello Mystery: Case Continued', *WMQ*, 58 (Oct. 2001), 1039–46. This vigorous review essay challenges many components of the TJHS approach to this question.

38. Coates, *Jefferson-Hemings Myth*, 200.
39. Works, 'Foreword', 9. Also see Wallenborn, 'A Committee Insider's Viewpoint'.
40. Works, 'Foreword', 12.
41. David N. Mayer, 'The Thomas Jefferson – Sally Hemings Myth and the Politicization of American History', John M. Ashbrook Center for Public Affairs, Ashland University, www.ashbrook.org. This paper is avalable through a link at the TJHS website, www.tjheritage.org.
42. Works, 'Foreword', 12. The defense of Jefferson may be about something less than the defense of America's Jeffersonian principles from the proponents of political correctness. Jefferson's descendants are entitled to burial in the Monticello cemetery. An organization of descendants called the Monticello Association (which is not affiliated with the Thomas Jefferson Foundation) controls the half-acre burial site and, despite the evidence produced since 1997, has resisted calls that the Hemingses and their descendants be allowed into the Monticello graveyard. In April 2002 the Association issued its own report into the matter suggesting that a separate cemetery be created at Monticello, out of the land owned by the TJF, for the descendants of all of Monticello's slaves and artisans. The Association met in Charottesville in early May 2002 to vote on the proposal. The TJHS's John H. Works, a former president of the Monticello Association, criticized the proposal – not because it smacked of Jim Crow-era segregation, but because he feared that the lines between the two cemeteries 'would blur' over time and lead to 'a graveyard of Jefferson's descendants, real and imagined'. On 5 May 2002 the Monticello Association voted by a margin of 74 to 6 to deny the descendants of Sally Hemings the right to join the Association and to be buried at the Monticello graveyard. They also voted against creating a separate burial site for Monticello's slaves. 'Jefferson's Heirs Plan Cemetery for Slave's Kin at Monticello', *New York Times*, 21 April 2002; Leef Smith, 'Monticello's Theories of Relativity', *Washington Post*, 4 May 2002, p. B1; Leef Smith, 'Jefferson Group Bars Kin of Slave', *Washington Post*, 6 May 2002, B1. John H. Works had been concerned about the implications of the DNA testing for the membership of the Monticello Association. On 23 December 1999 he wrote a lengthy letter to the membership of the association to oppose the admission of the Hemings descendants to the Monticello Association. He argued that there was no legal, scientific or historical basis for their

admission to the group. 'John H. Works to the Monticello Association, December 23, 1999', www.monticello-assoc.org/jhw-letter.htm.

43. Jordan, 'Review of *Thomas Jefferson and Sally Hemings*', WMQ, 55 (1998), 318.

44. Peter S. Onuf, 'Every Generation is an "Independent Nation": Colonization, Miscegenation, and the Fate of Jefferson's Children', WMQ, 57 (2000), 153–70.

45. Jan Ellen Lewis, *Pursuit of Happiness: Family and Values in Jefferson's Virginia* (New York: Cambridge University Press, 1983); Jan Ellen Lewis, ' "The Blessings of Domestic Society": Thomas Jefferson's Family and the Transformation of American Politics', in Onuf, ed., *Jeffersonian Legacies*, 109–46. Also see Ruth Bloch, 'The Gendered Meanings of Virtue in Revolutionary America', *Signs*, 13 (1987), 27–58; Linda K. Kerber, 'The Republican Mother: Women and the Enlightenment – An American Perspective', *American Quarterly*, 28 (1976), 187–205; Jan Ellen Lewis, 'The Republican Wife: Virtue and Seduction in the Early Republic', WMQ, 47 (1987), 689–721; and Rosemarie Zagarri, 'Morals, Manners, and the Republican Mother', *American Quarterly*, 44 (1992), 192–215. In 'The White Jeffersons', Jan E. Lewis has begun the effort to re-evaluate and redefine Jefferson's family in light of the Hemings relationship. She considers the history of the Hemings story from the perspective of Jefferson's white descendants and traces the lies he told them about Sally Hemings and the means by which they perpetuated those lies to defend Jefferson and themselves.

46. Lewis and Onuf, *Sally Hemings and Thomas Jefferson*, and Jan Lewis et al., 'Forum: Thomas Jefferson and Sally Hemings Redux', WMQ, 57 (2000), 121–210.

47. Ellis, 'Jefferson: Post-DNA', 136. Also see the essays by Clarence Walker, Werner Sollors, Lucia Stanton, Dianne Swann-Wright and Jack N. Rakove in *Sally Hemings and Thomas Jefferson*.

48. Here the *Sally Hemings and Thomas Jefferson* collection is especially strong. See the essays by Gordon S. Wood, Winthrop D. Jordan and Philip D. Morgan.

49. Lewis, 'The White Jeffersons', 'Blessings of Domestic Society', *Pursuit of Happiness*; Andrew Burstein, *Jefferson's Secrets: Death and Desire at Monticello* (New York: Basic Books, 2005), ch. 4.

50. See the essays by Joshua D. Rothman, Rhys Isaac and Jan Ellen Lewis in *Sally Hemings and Thomas Jefferson*.

51. The *William and Mary Quarterly* forum devotes considerable attention to this area. See Ellis, 'Jefferson: Post-DNA'; Lucia Stanton, 'The Other End of the Telescope: Jefferson Through the Eyes of His Slaves', WMQ, 57 (2000), 139–52; Andrew Burstein, 'Jefferson's Rationalizations', WMQ, 57 (2000), 183–97; and Neiman, 'Coincidence or Causal Connection?'

52. Lucia Stanton, 'The Other End of the Telescope: Jefferson through the Eyes of his Slaves', *WMQ*, 57 (2000), 139–52.

53. Gordon-Reed, *Thomas Jefferson and Sally Hemings*, 224.

54. Gordon-Reed, 'Memories of a Few Negroes', 252.

55. Peterson, *Thomas Jefferson and the New Nation*, viii.

56. Burstein, *The Inner Jefferson*, 230, 231. Emphasis added.

57. Andrew Burstein, *Jefferson's Secrets*, esp. ch. 5–6.

58. Burstein, *Jefferson's Secrets*, 117. Burstein discusses the evidence that came to light since he published *The Inner Jefferson* on 114–17.

59. *TJW*, 265.

60. TJ to Francis Gray, 4 March 1815, TJP; Burstein, *Jefferson's Secrets*, 145–9, quotations 149.

61. Burstein, *Jefferson's Secrets*, ch. 6, esp. 153–66, 182–3.

62. Burstein, *Jefferson's Secrets*, 185.

CHAPTER 7

SLAVERY

I

In 2003 several teachers at the Thomas Jefferson Elementary School in Berkeley, California, wrote to the parent-teacher association to propose changing the name of the school. The teachers appealed to the parents because, 'For some of our staff, it has become increasingly uncomfortable to work at a site whose name honors a slaveholder.' After a lengthy consultation, the students, staff and parents at the school submitted a petition to the Berkeley school board requesting that the school be renamed Sequoia, after California's giant redwood tree. For proponents of the name change, Jefferson's association with slavery outweighed his various achievements. 'Thomas Jefferson is revered as the primary author of one of the world's most respected and beloved documents,' read the petition. 'Jefferson is also a man who held as many as 150 African and African-American men, women and children in bondage, denying them the very rights which he asserted for all in the Declaration of Independence.' The petition continued, 'A school name which fails to acknowledge or respect the depth and importance of their people's collective sorrow is personally offensive . . . It is time to consider a name which unites us as a community.'

The staff and students at the school strongly favored the name change. 'It's an awkward position to ask African-American children and African-American teachers to celebrate a historical figure who was a slave owner,' said teacher Marguerite Talley-Hughes. For Talley-Hughes, Jefferson's ownership of slaves made it difficult to teach children the moral lessons that Jefferson felt should be at the heart of education. 'Many people realize that Thomas Jefferson was a slaveholder,' said Talley-Hughes; 'that is a kind of a dilemma when you call someone a hero, a dilemma when you're trying to teach children right from wrong.' Parents were more evenly divided, voting 67 to 61 in favor of the name change. Some felt that Jefferson's association with slavery would make it easier to teach children values. As Mark Piccillo, a parent at the school, said, 'There's kind of an evolution in goodness and badness in children K–12. Jefferson is kind of the perfect foil – he represents everything that's good in this country and he's got sides that represent our dark underbelly.' After a contentious debate, on 22 June 2005 the school board voted 3–2 to retain the Jefferson name.[1]

The relatively minor controversy over the name of the primary school in Berkeley reflects a larger cultural and historiographical debate over Jefferson's relationship with slavery. Jefferson was aware of the danger that slavery posed to his posthumous reputation. In his writings, particularly his autobiography, the *Notes on the State of Virginia* and some of his correspondence (particularly with foreigners) he sought to present himself as an opponent of slavery trapped by an inherited dilemma. For a long time – even in recent years – this interpretation found favor among historians and biographers. Beginning in the 1960s historians began to interrogate Jefferson's record on slavery more closely. The post-war Civil Rights movement gave particular energy to the academic study of slavery. This, in turn, led to intense scrutiny of Jefferson's actions as a slave master and his apparent inaction with regard to slavery as a statesman. Slavery has cast a dark shadow that has obscured Jefferson's record as a revolutionary republican. For some historians, like the proponents of the school name change, Jefferson's relationship with slavery casts a pall over his other activities; calling into question his achievements, many of which were made possible either directly or indirectly by slavery. Others, like those who favored retaining the school's name, seek to place Jefferson's slaveholding in its historical context not necessarily to defend Jefferson's actions but to explain them. The result is the most contentious and morally challenging aspect of Jefferson scholarship.

II

Thomas Jefferson was aware that he would be judged by posterity over his relationship with slavery. In anticipation of this posthumous judgment Jefferson sought to present himself in his writings as an opponent of chattel slavery trapped by a system that he had inherited and could do little to change. Jefferson expressed this view in several of his prominent writings. In his original draft of the Declaration of Independence, he inserted a clause condemning the Atlantic slave trade and blaming George III for his support of it.

> He has waged cruel war against human nature itself, violating it's most sacred rights of life & liberty in the persons of a distant people who never offended him, captivating & carrying them into slavery in another hemisphere, or to incur miserable death in their transportation thither. [T]his

piratical warfare, the opprobrium of *infidel* powers, is the warfare of the
CHRISTIAN king of Great Britain.

When Congress excised the clause prior to adopting the Declaration,
Jefferson circulated copies of his original draft to friends. He insured that
his draft would find a larger audience by including it in his autobiography, to be published after his death.[2]

A decade later, when Jefferson's *Notes on the State of Virginia* was
privately published in France in 1785, it contained criticisms of slavery.
According to Jefferson, slavery turned masters into despots and degraded
the enslaved. He concluded his examination: 'I tremble for my country
when I reflect that God is just: that his justice cannot sleep for ever: that
considering numbers, nature and natural means only, a revolution of the
wheel of fortune, an exchange of situation, is among the possible events:
that it may become probable by supernatural interference!' In the *Notes*
Jefferson outlined a plan for gradual emancipation. Although John
Adams praised the passages on slavery as 'worth Diamonds. They will
have more effect than Volumes written by mere Philosophers', Jefferson
was reluctant for his comments on slavery to appear in print. In June
1785 he wrote to the Marquis de Chastellux, with whom he had shared
the private printing of the *Notes*, 'The strictures on slavery and on the
constitution of Virginia . . . are the parts which I do not wish to have
made public, at least till I know whether their publication would do more
harm or good. It is possible that in my own country these strictures might
produce an irritation which would indispose the people towards the two
great objects I have in view, that is the emancipation of their slaves, and
the settlement of their constitution on a firmer and more permanent
basis.' When a French publisher obtained the private edition of the *Notes
on the State of Virginia* and brought out a poorly translated pirate
edition, Jefferson was compelled to publish the whole treatise, including
his criticisms of slavery, in 1787.[3]

The *Notes on Virginia* epitomized Jefferson's approach to slavery.
Although Jefferson condemned slavery, he did so cautiously. His attack
on the slave trade in the original draft of the Declaration of Independence
was not widely known during his lifetime – the clause was struck from the
version of the Declaration most familiar to his contemporaries and
Jefferson was not widely identified as the primary author of the Declaration until the late 1790s. While he welcomed the encomiums of men such
as Adams and Chastellux, he did not intend that the strictures on slavery
in the *Notes on the State of Virginia* should be widely circulated. He
attacked slavery, but also sought to avoid controversy. He was more
concerned that future generations rather than his contemporaries should
consider him to be an opponent of slavery. In consequence he saved his

strongest criticisms of slavery for his autobiography, which would not appear in print until after his death.

In his autobiography Jefferson presented himself as a consistent and longstanding foe of slavery. He did so deliberately, and with an eye on his place in history. Joseph J. Ellis wrote of Jefferson's efforts, 'He regarded it as absolutely imperative for the historical record, as well as his own place in the American pantheon, that his moral revulsion against slavery be made clear to posterity, along with his sincere conviction that it was incompatible with the principles on which the republic was founded.'[4] To achieve this end Jefferson claimed that when he entered the House of Burgesses in 1769 he proposed a plan to abolish slavery that was rejected. He then included his draft of the Declaration of Independence, complete with its clause condemning the slave trade, noting that it was struck from the text in deference to South Carolina and Georgia, states that continued to import slaves, and 'our Northern brethren' who continued to transport and sell them. In his discussion of his contributions to the revisal of Virginia's laws Jefferson mentioned a plan for gradual emancipation that was never introduced.

> The bill on the subject of slaves was a mere digest of the existing laws respecting them, without any intimation of a plan for future & general emancipation. It was thought better that this should be kept back, and attempted only by way of amendment whenever the bill should be brought on. The principles of the amendment however were agreed on, that is to say, the freedom of all born after a certain day, and deportation at a proper age. But it was found that the public mind would not yet bear the proposition, nor will it bear it even at this day.

Jefferson claimed that he had been the author of a bill for gradual emancipation in Virginia – similar to those adopted across the north during the revolutionary era – but that public opinion prevented him from bringing it before the legislature. This was the plan he included in the *Notes on the State of Virginia*. More than forty years later, writing his autobiography in the wake of the Missouri crisis, he warned, 'Yet the day is not distant when [the public] must bear and adopt it, or worse will follow. Nothing is more certainly written in the book of fate than that these people are to be free.'[5]

While carefully presenting himself as an opponent of slavery, Jefferson made no secret of his racial views. The *Notes on the State of Virginia* contain not only his attack on slavery but a lengthy discourse in which Jefferson advances evidence for his 'suspicion' of African inferiority, intellectual and physical, which precluded the creation of a racially integrated society in America after emancipation.[6] Although slavery was unjust, according to Jefferson, slaves and their descendants could not remain in the United States when emancipation finally came at some unspecified date in the future. Near the end of his life, Jefferson reiterated the point in his autobiography:

> Nor is it less certain that the two races, equally free, cannot live in the same government. Nature, habit, opinion has drawn indelible lines of distinction between them. It is still in our power to direct the process of emancipation and deportation peaceably and in such slow degree as the evil will wear off insensibly, and their place be pari passu filled up by free white laborers. If on the contrary it is left to force itself on, human nature must shudder at the prospect held up.[7]

In Jefferson's mind emancipation *must* be accompanied by the removal of slaves from the country.

Jefferson cast himself as an opponent of slavery in his correspondence as well as his other writings. He wrote perhaps his most famous letter on the subject to a young Albermarle neighbor, Edward Coles, in 1814. Coles proposed to free his own slaves (he eventually took them to Illinois Territory in order to emancipate them) and wrote to request Jefferson's support for the project. Jefferson replied to Coles on 25 August. He began by stating that his opposition to slavery was longstanding and well known, and recounted his effort when a young member of the Virginia assembly to legalize manumission. He expressed regret that slavery had not been abolished during the revolutionary era and stated the hope that it would be achieved peacefully at some time in the future. Having established his anti-slavery position, Jefferson revealed his antipathy towards the slaves themselves, claiming that African Americans were 'as incapable as children of taking care of themselves' and arguing that freeing them would lead to racial mixing that would degrade white Americans. Reluctantly, Jefferson refused to give Coles his consent, arguing that if the younger man freed his slaves he would be doing them a disservice, as the former bondsmen and bondswomen would be unable to provide for themselves. Rather, he urged Coles to remain in Virginia and 'become the missionary of this doctrine truly christian; insinuate & inculcate it softly but steadily, through the medium of writing and conversation; associate others in your labours, and when the phalanx is formed, bring on and press the proposition perseveringly until its accomplishment'.[8]

Thomas Jefferson carefully cultivated an image of himself as a foe of slavery in his writings. When he advised Edward Coles to eschew direct action against slavery in favor of writing and speaking in support of gradual emancipation at some unspecified date in the distant future, he aptly summarized how he conceived of his own actions over the previous decades. Jefferson sought to present himself as a longstanding opponent of slavery. He opposed slavery because of its moral impact on both slaves and masters yet, fearing the consequences of emancipation (fears derived from his clear and publicly expressed racism), he argued in favor of caution in taking action against the institution. As such, he saw himself as caught in a dilemma. He knew slavery was wrong but felt it was not possible to take decisive action against it because doing so would have dangerous consequences. Ever adept at turning a phrase, in 1820 Jefferson wrote of the predicament in which he and his fellow slaveholders found themselves: 'we have the wolf by the ear, and we can neither hold him, nor safely let him go. Justice is on one scale, and self-preservation on the other.'[9] The metaphor is memorable. It invites sympathy for the man holding the wolf and understanding of his unwillingness to let it go. Indeed, for many years historians were sympathetic to this dilemma as presented by Jefferson.

III

Ironically, the sectional crisis caused by slavery, which in his later years Jefferson feared might destroy the republic that he had helped to create, did much to promote Jefferson's carefully created self-image as an opponent of slavery. During the nineteenth century abolitionists embraced and perpetuated the view that Jefferson was a foe of slavery. Drawing on the anti-slavery passages in the *Notes on the State of Virginia* as well as selections from the 1829 four-volume edition of Jefferson's writings, which included the autobiography, slavery's opponents invoked Jefferson's posthumous authority to give legitimacy to their cause. As one abolitionist confidently declared, 'Were I to write a history of American slavery, I should be constrained in all honesty and truth, to say, that Mr. Jefferson was entitled to the credit of first publicly expressing anti-slavery sentiments in this country; that he was the prime mover of the anti-slavery movement.' Some abolitionists, as well as those who sought to restrict the expansion of slavery, were troubled by the racist opinions Jefferson expressed in the *Notes on Virginia* because they were embraced by pro-slavery ideologues. Nonetheless, the opponents of slavery (many of whom shared Jefferson's racism) believed there was much to gain in associating the author of the Declaration of Independence with their cause.[10]

Jefferson's carefully constructed image as an opponent of slavery endured well into the twentieth century. It was cast in stone when President Franklin D. Roosevelt, an admirer of Jefferson, dedicated the Jefferson Memorial in 1943. In addition to a 10,000 pound bronze statue of Jefferson, the memorial contains four panels engraved with words selected from Jefferson's writings. One of the panels deals with slavery. It reads:

> God who gave us life gave us liberty. Can the liberties of a nation be secure when we have removed a conviction that these liberties are a gift of God? Indeed I tremble for my country when I reflect that God is just, that his justice cannot sleep forever. Commerce between master and slave is despotism. Nothing is more certainly written in the book of fate than that these people are to be free.

While the inscriptions on the other panels are largely taken from individual documents – letters, the Declaration of Independence and the Virginia Statute for Religious Freedom – the inscription pertaining to slavery is a *mélange* of quotations from various sources. The first sentence comes from the *Summary View of the Rights of British America*. The second and third come from separate passages in the *Notes on the State of Virginia* and the fourth comes from the autobiography. The next sentences from the autobiography, advocating the deportation of African Americans, were omitted. It seems that the members of the Jefferson Memorial Commission, who consulted President Roosevelt on the selection of texts for the engravings, sought to present Jefferson as a clear opponent of slavery. In order to do so, they followed the trail left by Jefferson in his writings on the subject, selecting and blending passages to show Jefferson in the most favorable light.[11]

Although Jefferson's twentieth-century scholarly admirers were not constrained by limits of space, nor did they have Franklin Roosevelt looking over their shoulders, many of them followed the Memorial Commission's practice of judiciously selecting from Jefferson's writings in order to portray the Virginian in a sympathetic light as an opponent of slavery. In a popular collection of Jefferson's writings first published in 1944, Adrienne Koch and William Peden edited Jefferson's 1814 letter to Edward Coles in such a way as to suggest that Jefferson favored Coles's emancipation plans.[12] When, in 1948, Dumas Malone published the first volume of *Jefferson and His Time*, he presented Jefferson as a man who 'strongly favored emancipation'. According to Malone, 'Jefferson's opposition to slavery was primarily on moral grounds; and he combined compassion for the victims with an even deeper concern for the character of the masters and the dignity of human nature.' In his third volume, published at the height of the Civil Rights movement in 1962, Malone explained that it would have been impossible for Jefferson to free his own slaves during the 1790s: 'To have emancipated the whole body of his slaves, depriving himself thereby of his entire labor force and a large part of his property while turning them loose in an inhospitable world, would have been neither practicable nor kind.' Malone did not address slavery at length until his sixth and final volume, published in 1981. As he completed his life's work Malone reiterated his view that Jefferson was committed to emancipation. In a charitable interpretation of Jefferson's response to Edward Coles's plan to leave Virginia and free his slaves, Malone speculated that Jefferson would have supported Coles's plan but was unable to do so because of his age and his attachment to his family and Virginia.[13]

Other biographers have followed Malone in presenting Jefferson as he wanted to be portrayed with regard to slavery. In his 1970 biography, Merrill D. Peterson depicted Jefferson as a dedicated emancipator, asserting, 'All of Jefferson's values and goals dictated the extermination of slavery. This was as self-evident as the principles of 1776 themselves.' Elsewhere Peterson wrote, 'Basically his position was a moral one, founded in the immutable principles of human liberty. No abolitionist of later time ever cried out more prophetically against slavery.' Peterson acknowledged, however, that there were constraints on Jefferson's anti-slavery views. Writing of the failed effort to secure gradual emancipation as a part of the revision of Virginia's laws after independence, Peterson conceded, 'While [Jefferson] continued to favor the plan of gradual emancipation, first published in the *Notes on Virginia* in 1785, neither he nor any other prominent Virginian was ever willing to risk friends, position, and influence to fight for it.' In his 1987 biography Noble Cunningham wrote that Jefferson 'never wavered in his conviction that slavery was an evil that must be extinguished.'[14]

Jefferson's more sympathetic biographers, while admiring his opposition to slavery, have been troubled by their subject's racism. Writing in the 1940s, Dumas Malone sought to qualify Jefferson's racial judgments. 'His comments on race', wrote Malone, 'were those of a scientific mind, softened by humanitarianism. Or to put it more precisely, they represented the tentative judgment of a kindly and scientifically minded man who deplored the absence of sufficient data and adequate criteria.' When Merrill Peterson addressed the subject in the wake of the Civil Rights movement, he wrote of Jefferson's belief in African inferiority as 'honest, disinterested, and no doubt true to his personal observation and knowledge. Jefferson's opinion was also a product of frivolous and tortuous reasoning, of preconception, prejudice, ignorance, contradiction, and a bewildering confusion of principles.' Noble Cunningham was more concise. He declared, 'ahead of his time in his stand on emancipation, Jefferson was much the product of his age in his views on race'. It is notable that Malone, writing in the 1940s, was more sympathetic to Jefferson than Peterson or Cunningham, who were unable to reconcile

Jefferson's 'suspicion' that Africans were inferior to whites to contemporary values of racial equality during the periods in which they wrote. Jefferson's biographers have sought, at best, to explain his views as tentative conclusions which reflected commonplace opinions in eighteenth-century Virginia.[15]

In November 1992, Douglas L. Wilson, soon to be appointed the first director of Monticello's International Center for Jefferson Studies, published a lengthy defense of Jefferson, 'Thomas Jefferson and the Character Issue', in the *Atlantic Monthly*. Wilson began his defense by asserting that many of Jefferson's critics were guilty of presentism, 'applying contemporary or otherwise inappropriate standards to the past'. As a result of presentism, those who write about Jefferson ask, 'How could the man who wrote that "All men are created equal" own slaves?' more than any other question. The question itself, Wilson claimed, is unfair and distorts the past. It presupposes a judgment that Jefferson was guilty of hypocrisy because he owned slaves. Wilson suggested reframing the question in a manner to take account of historical circumstances: 'How did a man who was born into a slave holding society, whose family and admired friends owned slaves, who inherited a fortune that was dependent on slaves and slave labor, decide at an early age that slavery was morally wrong and forcefully declare that it ought to be abolished?' Wilson then considered Jefferson's failure to manumit all but a few of his slaves. He argued that conditions for free African Americans in early national Virginia – prior to the adoption of a law in 1806 requiring that emancipated slaves leave the state – were such that 'emancipated slaves would enjoy little, if any, real freedom and would, unless they could pass as white, be more likely to come to grief in a hostile environment'. Wilson rounded out his analysis by considering Jefferson's racial views. While he did not defend Jefferson's racism *per se*, Wilson argued that Jefferson's racial opinions had to be placed in their appropriate context. To this end he asserted that Jefferson's writings on race should be read with two important qualifications: Jefferson offered his views as a hypothesis, not as a firm conclusion, and he did not use his racial views to justify slavery. He advocated gradual emancipation despite his suspicion that blacks were inferior to whites.[16]

For much of the twentieth century Jefferson's carefully constructed self-image as a determined opponent of slavery who was limited by larger forces – intolerance, debt and bad timing – from taking concrete action against involuntary servitude found favor among his major biographers. The biographers accepted Jefferson's putative abolitionism while seeking to explain his racism. They presented this anti-slavery Jefferson before increasingly sceptical fellow scholars as well as a doubtful public at large. As we shall see presently, the anti-slavery Jefferson came under increasing criticism beginning in the early 1960s. An increasingly critical, revisionist interpretation of Jefferson's relationship with slavery gathered strength over the next generation. The revisionist interpretation proved so potent that it has endangered the anti-slavery image that Jefferson and his biographers had carefully constructed. 'Thomas Jefferson and the Character Issue' constitutes the last and most fluent expression of the sympathetic interpretation of Jefferson's relationship with slavery first articulated by Jefferson himself in 1776 when he distributed copies of his original draft of the Declaration of Independence. For more than 150 years the view that Jefferson was a reluctant slaveholder and an ardent supporter of emancipation – a view Jefferson explicitly promoted in his writings – predominated. However, the question of how the man who wrote the Declaration of Independence could own slaves has persisted. Indeed, Douglas Wilson concedes that it has been 'the question most persistently asked of those who write about Thomas Jefferson, and by all indications it the thing that contemporary Americans find most vexing about him'. In a 1993 review of Jefferson scholarship Peter S. Onuf wrote, 'The most heated current controversy centers on Jefferson's slaveholding.'[17] Historians have sought to interpret, explain and in some cases apologize for Jefferson's dependence on slavery and his unwillingness to take concrete steps to abolish it. Confronted by the ethical issues raised by slavery, and contemporary struggles for civil rights and racial justice, historians over the past two generations have found Jefferson wanting. Despite the best efforts of scholars from Dumas Malone to Douglas L. Wilson (guided by the dead hand of Jefferson), no single issue has contributed as much to the decline of Jefferson's reputation since World War II as the slavery question.

IV

In October 1992, just before Douglas Wilson's defense of Jefferson's character appeared in the *Atlantic Monthly*, a six-day conference was held at the University of Virginia marking the beginning of the university's year-long celebration of its founder's 250th birthday. The conference 'sought new perspectives on the Jefferson legacy by measuring Jefferson's life and values against the major concerns of the 1990s'. Among the speakers was Professor Paul Finkelman of Virginia Polytechnic Institute and State University. Finkelman presented a detailed and damning examination of Jefferson's relationship with slavery. He argued that Jefferson was never dedicated to ending slavery, despite his statements to the contrary. Rather, 'his lack of any serious commitment to emancipation reflects his upbringing, class origins, and lifelong status as a wealthy landowner, slaveowner, and southern aristocrat'. Finkelman asserted that Jefferson's undeserved anti-slavery reputation is largely derived from the deleted clause in the Declaration of Independence condemning the slave trade. He reviewed Jefferson's career and determined that rather than opposing slavery from anything but a rhetorical standpoint, Jefferson took steps to promote the expansion of slavery and that, while perhaps not a terrible master, he bought and sold his own slaves, pursued and punished runaways, and made no serious attempt to manumit his slaves (with the exception of a few members of the Hemings family) as George Washington had. For Finkelman, Jefferson was not a conflicted opponent of slavery trapped by a system he could not change. On the contrary, Finkelman concluded, 'The history of Jefferson's relationship to slavery is grim and unpleasant. His words are those of a liberty-loving man of the Enlightenment. His deeds are those of a self-indulgent and negrophobic Virginia planter.' Taking the conference's brief to measure Jefferson against the concerns of the 1990s, Paul Finkelman found little in Jefferson's life and values to admire.[18]

Although neither Douglas L. Wilson nor Paul Finkelman addressed the other's work in their near-simultaneous examinations of Jefferson and slavery, each seemed to epitomize the historiographical tradition against which the other directed his criticism. Wilson explicitly defended Jefferson against charges such as those of Finkelman and posited that Jefferson was opposed to slavery and did what he could, within the limited range of options available to him, to undermine it. This might be termed the emancipationist interpretation. Finkelman dismissed defenses such as Wilson's and concentrated on the record of Jefferson's actions rather than his words. He found that Jefferson did not measure up to the standards set by his contemporaries, some of whom took much more substantive actions, such as manumitting their own slaves, than Jefferson contemplated. Two years after he delivered his paper (which was published in 1993), Finkelman published a follow-up article that directly addressed the charge of presentism made by Wilson. In an article in the *Virginia Magazine of History and Biography*, Finkelman reviewed the analyses of Jefferson's defenders, including Wilson. He accused *them* of presentism, concluding:

> Because they know that slavery is wrong, they have tried to shape Jefferson into their image of properly liberal opponent of slavery. They wish to make a lifelong slave owner, a man who sold numerous slaves to support his extravagant life-style, into a proto-abolitionist so that Jefferson will fit into their presentist conception of what Jefferson believed and felt . . . They are forced to ignore contrary evidence and thus paint a false picture of Jefferson or to explain away his views and actions in ways that undermine their otherwise credible accounts of his life.

Paul Finkelman made a very strong case against Jefferson's credentials as an opponent of slavery. In attacking Jefferson's modern defenders, he is actually assaulting the anti-slavery image that Jefferson himself carefully constructed and intended to place before posterity.[19]

Finkelman's revisionist interpretation, which emphasizes Jefferson's multiple connections to and support for slavery, is a direct challenge to the interpretation of Dumas Malone, Douglas L. Wilson and other emancipationist historians. Finkelman's critical view has a substantial pedigree – though not as lengthy as the emancipationist tradition that can be traced back to Jefferson himself. As a consequence of the movement for increased civil rights for African Americans that began after World War II, scholars started to re-examine the history of slavery in the United States. By the 1960s race and slavery emerged as dominant themes in American historiography and historians began to review Jefferson's record with respect to slavery. Many were less willing than their predecessors (and some of their contemporaries) to accept Jefferson's version of events.

The first major work to question Jefferson's relationship to slavery was Robert McColley's 1964 study *Slavery and Jeffersonian Virginia*. McColley forthrightly acknowledged that he was influenced by the times in which he wrote. For much of the twentieth century, he argued, Jefferson had benefited at the hands of Progressive historians who saw him as the leader of agrarian democracy in opposition to Alexander Hamilton's advocacy of industrial capitalism. McColley's research, which originated as a Ph.D. dissertation at Berkeley in the early 1960s, reflected that era's disputes over civil rights and racial justice.

> Inevitably, the historian who today rethinks the problems of early America must shed the preoccupations of the progressive era and replace them with his own. Jefferson and his contemporaries may have set down great maxims of liberty, they may have struck courageously against special and undeserved privileges, but they also accepted, as the *Notes on Virginia* demonstrate, doctrines of racism. Coupled to simple economic interest, these have kept the American Negro in a subordinate position throughout our national history.[20]

This is not presentism of the type that Douglas Wilson and Paul Finkelman laid at the feet of their adversaries. Rather, McColley concisely explained how the issues of racial and economic equality that came to the fore during the 1950s and 1960s caused him to ask different questions of the past from his predecessors, who had other concerns. When Jefferson's record and achievements were interrogated with race and slavery in the foreground, rather than as unfortunate background details, it is not surprising that his reputation suffered. Indeed, since racial equality has remained an ongoing concern in modern American life, this has been reflected in the historical literature. Despite the persistence of scholars and biographers who advocate the emancipationist interpretation, the revisionists, beginning with McColley, have dominated the debate over the past two generations.

Robert McColley set out to examine 'the powerful and varied influences of slavery on the life, thought, and politics of Jeffersonian Virginians'. In so doing he challenged the traditional view of slavery during the early national era as a failing institution on its way to extinction before it was saved by the invention of the cotton gin and the opening of the Old Southwest to plantation agriculture. McColley noted that there was a forty-year period between the adoption of the Declaration of Independence and the end of the War of 1812, before cotton agriculture took off. Despite a lengthy opportunity and the supposed weakness of slavery during this period, white Virginians took negligible steps against slavery. '[T]he antislavery pronouncements of Virginia's statesmen', wrote McColley, 'were so rarely accompanied by any positive efforts against slavery as to cast doubt on their sincerity, and when initiative against slavery was proposed by others, they normally resisted it.' Of course the foremost of those Virginia statesmen was Jefferson. McColley portrayed Jefferson as a man who refused to act on his youthful anti-slavery sentiments, yet who continually spoke of his opposition to slavery, especially in the company of 'liberal intellectuals abroad', while doing little at home. McColley observed that Jefferson generally received favorable treatment from historians. For example, he noted that Jefferson was generally regarded as responsible for the exclusion of slavery in the Northwest yet as president he guaranteed Spanish and French slavery in Louisiana: 'Jefferson's reputation has indeed been fortunate, when one considers that he has been recognized universally as the father of exclusion in the Old Northwest, but has never been labelled as the father of slavery in Louisiana.' For McColley, Jefferson was typical of his class, race and region, which is to say that his opposition to slavery was largely rhetorical and rarely resulted in concrete action.[21]

Although Thomas Jefferson's racial attitudes were central to McColley's criticism of Jefferson, they were not a major theme of his book, which was an institutional study of slavery in early national Virginia. Several years after *Slavery and Jeffersonian Virginia* was published, a landmark study of racial attitudes in early America appeared in which Jefferson's racial thinking figured prominently. Winthrop D. Jordan's *White Over Black: American Attitudes toward the Negro, 1550–1815* was first published in 1968, the year of Martin Luther King's assassination and of widespread racial violence and rioting in the United States.

Like McColley, Jordan recognized the contemporary resonance of his work. Although Jordan pointed out that *White Over Black* was not 'about the current, continuing crisis in race relations in America' he recognized that his book might provide the 'value of studying current attitudes toward Negroes by taking, as they say, "the historical approach." What the historian contributes, ' Jordan continued, 'inevitably, is a sense and appreciation of the important effect – perhaps even the great weight – of prior upon ensuing experience.' Against a contemporary climate of racial discord, Jordan examined the history of European and European American attitudes toward Africans and African Americans from the age of Elizabeth to that of Jefferson.[22]

For Jordan, Jefferson embodied many of his book's themes and he devoted a lengthy chapter of his study to Jefferson's racial attitudes. 'With one man only', wrote Jordan, 'is there opportunity to glimpse the interactions among deep emotions, intellectual constructs, long-accumulated traditions concerning the Negro, and the social problem of slavery in a free society.' Jordan, who focused on the intellectual and emotional consequences of Jefferson's thinking, portrayed Jefferson as torn between his opposition to slavery and his racism: 'Thomas Jefferson combined, publicly and painfully, a heartfelt hostility to slavery and a deep conviction, inconsistently expressed, that Negroes were inferior to white men.' According to Jordan, Jefferson refused to accept environmental explanations for the apparent inferiority of slaves, and this presented him with a 'monumental' intellectual problem. If African American slaves were innately inferior, then 'the Creator might have in fact created men unequal; and he could not say this without giving his assertion exactly the same logical force as his famous statement to the contrary'. Jordan concluded that Jefferson articulated 'the most intense, extensive, and extreme formulation of anti-Negro "thought" offered by any American in the thirty years after the Revolution'. According to Jordan, Jefferson's virulent racism, grounded in his emotions as well as his intellect, was tempered by his political philosophy. 'Yet', concludes Jordan, 'Thomas Jefferson left to Americans something else which may in the long run have been of greater importance – his prejudice for freedom and his larger equalitarian faith.'[23]

In some respects Winthrop Jordan was more sympathetic to Jefferson than Robert McColley or subsequent critics such as Paul Finkelman. He accepted that Jefferson *was* sincere in his professed abhorrence of slavery. Nonetheless, Jordan's detailed examination of Jefferson's racial thinking exposed the least appealing aspects of Jefferson's character and intellect. In contrast to the tentative scientific judgments of a mind tempered by humanitarianism, as portrayed by Dumas Malone twenty years previously, Jordan presented Jefferson as an emotionally confused, intellectually contradictory racist. Although sympathetic, to a point, it was hardy a flattering picture.

In his study, Winthrop Jordan focused almost exclusively on slavery as an intellectual and emotional problem for Jefferson. He did not explore Jefferson's day-to-day involvement with slavery and the consequences of that association for Jefferson's public career. These are tasks that William Cohen undertook in a landmark article published in the *Journal of American History* in 1969. Cohen reviewed Jefferson's record both as a slave owner and as a statesman confronted by the problem of slavery. He sought to challenge the traditional view of Jefferson as a would-be emancipationist trapped by an unjust inherited system which he sought to ameliorate by acting as a benevolent master. Cohen saw a contrast in Jefferson's actions before and after 1784. Between 1774 and 1784 Jefferson was most active on the anti-slavery front, seeking to ban the Atlantic slave trade and prohibit slavery from the western territories of the United States. These efforts, both of which failed, should not be overemphasized, however. After 1784 Jefferson's anti-slavery efforts diminished. Cohen succinctly stated what has come to be the main criticism of Jefferson by revisionists: 'On the whole, however, there was a significant gap between his thought and action with regard to the abolition question.' Influenced by Winthrop Jordan's work and his own reading of the *Notes on Virginia*, Cohen advances the view that the gap between Jefferson's beliefs and actions stemmed from his racism:

> Jefferson's views on slavery and race suggest that his libertarian sentiments were more than counterbalanced by his conviction that Negroes were members of a race so alien and inferior that there was no hope that whites and blacks could co-exist side by side on terms of equality. Jefferson's libertarian views, however, had virtually no impact upon his actions after 1784, and his belief in the inferiority of the slaves was completely congruent with his behavior as both a planter and a politician.

According to Cohen, while Jefferson believed himself to be a benevolent master (and he was not, in fact, especially harsh according to the prevailing standards of the day), he bought and sold slaves, meted out punishments and sought to recapture runaways. As a statesman he took steps – promoting the spread of slavery in the Southwest, insuring its survival in Louisiana and isolating the Haitian Republic (established by slaves who successfully rebelled against their masters) – that were decidedly pro-slavery. Cohen's article, anticipating Paul Finkelman's analysis by a generation, is probably the most important contribution to the revisionist interpretation of Jefferson's relationship with slavery. It was the first study that sought to examine Jefferson's engagement with slavery on multiple levels: as intellectual, slaveholder and statesman. In so doing, Cohen revealed the degree to which Jefferson's thoughts and actions – private and public – complemented each other. Cohen's Jefferson was not especially conflicted or ambivalent about unfree labor. He was committed to promoting and protecting slavery.[24]

The pioneering work of Robert McColley, Winthrop Jordan and William Cohen on Jefferson, race and slavery during the 1960s laid out the basic tenets of the revisionist interpretation: Jefferson's actions against slavery were not as significant as his words; Jefferson's opposition to slavery, such as it was, was more pronounced early in his career than later; Jefferson took a number of steps which were explicitly pro-slavery; and Jefferson's failure to take more substantial action against slavery was a direct result, in part, of his racism. The revisionist interpretation was summarized in John Chester Miller's *The Wolf by the Ears: Thomas Jefferson and Slavery*, published in 1977. *The Wolf by the Ears* is a curious, somewhat contradictory work. Miller began with the emancipationist premise that Jefferson 'was resolved to destroy' slavery, yet presented a thorough summary of 'such aspects of Jefferson's personality, conduct, and ideas which impinge upon the subject of slavery' that comprehensively disproved his opening assertion. In the wake of Fawn Brodie's 1974 biography, Miller included a lengthy discussion of the Sally Hemings controversy in which he denied that there was a sexual relationship between Hemings and Jefferson (see Chapter 6). Miller seemed so intent on undermining Brodie's claims that he conceded Jefferson's other failings with respect to slavery. Although he did not interrogate Jefferson's racism or his intellectual beliefs about slavery to the same degree as his predecessors, Miller presented a useful, popular summary of the revisionist interpretation as it stood in the mid-1970s.[25] While many Jefferson scholars – especially biographers – continued to adhere to the older emancipationist interpretation, the new view was favorably received by students of race and slavery.[26]

By 1980 the main contours of the emancipationist and revisionist interpretations, later rehearsed by Douglas L. Wilson and Paul Finkelman, were in place. The former closely reflected the image that Jefferson himself carefully constructed for posterity (although Jefferson's racism presents the emancipationists with difficulties). The revisionists have found much to write about in the yawning chasm that seems to exist between Jefferson's words and his actions. In recent years a number of publications have provided more detail for the revisionists' portrait of Jefferson as a friend of slavery. For example, in 1995 Tim Matthewson published a lengthy article in the *Journal of Southern History* examining Jefferson's policies toward Haiti during his presidency. According to Matthewson, Jefferson was opposed to slavery and originally favored assisting the Haitian rebels in their struggle against France. However, his fear of slave rebellion in the United States – particularly in the wake of Gabriel's Rebellion in Virginia in 1800 – and an unwillingness either to challenge the political power of southern planters or to endanger the strategic interests of the United States caused him to adopt policies aimed at suppressing the Haitian Republic.[27]

Matthewson argued that Jefferson supported French efforts to reacquire St. Domingue (as Haiti was formerly known) in order to secure French support for the American acquisition of West Florida. West Florida and other territory in the Old Southwest were the focus of Roger G. Kennedy's 2003 book, *Mr. Jefferson's Lost Cause*. Kennedy argued that the acquisition of this territory by the United States was an environmental and human disaster. Anglo-American settlers, especially large planters, displaced Native Americans in order to obtain their land and to replace them with enslaved Africans who were forced to cultivate cotton. Cotton cultivation in turn depleted the soil and degraded the environment.

Kennedy contended that there were competing visions of land-use in the newly acquired lands of the South. He argued that Native Americans and southern yeoman farmers – who were interested in managing the land and raising food – advocated more sensible and environmentally friendly patterns of land-use than the great planters of the South whose views and practices prevailed in the region. It is in such contingency that Kennedy's title (and his thesis) may be found. Jefferson's 'lost cause', according to Kennedy, was his failure to use his influence to create a yeoman republic in the South rather than an hierarchical society where wealth depended on slavery. Jefferson's 'tragedy', writes Kennedy,

lay in his unwillingness to make full use of his talent for persuasion to tip the balance when, on a series of occasions, choices were made to permit, and sometimes to encourage, the spread of slavery. Had he exerted himself, the Southern land might have become a seed-bed for family farmers. Instead, time after time, he recoiled from opposing the pursuit of a way of life dominated by great plantations and a reliance upon both slavery and world markets.

Jefferson, according to Kennedy, had an opportunity to promote yeoman agriculture in the newly acquired territory but failed to do so in order to benefit the slaveholding class of large planters of which he was a prominent member.[28]

According to Roger Kennedy, Thomas Jefferson was beholden to the southern planting class and thus defended slavery at crucial moments in his public life. In *'Negro President'* Garry Wills explained why this was so. Wills argued that Jefferson was a direct beneficiary of the 'federal ratio' or 'three-fifths clause' of the Constitution, according to the terms of which slaves would count as three-fifths of the free population when apportioning taxes and representation. Since votes in the electoral college are apportioned according to representation, this compromise (when the Constitution was drafted northerners had not wanted slaves counted at all, and southerners favored that they be valued at 100 percent) meant that holding slaves gave southerners an advantage in Congress and the electoral college. Southern whites derived greater political power based on their slaves, who, of course, were denied all political rights. Owing to this advantage, Wills argued, Jefferson was able to win the election of 1800. It also meant, according to Wills, that any increase in slave territory would increase the political power of the Jeffersonian Republicans. In consequence, whenever slavery and westward expansion arose as issues during his presidency, Jefferson favored slavery. 'This had less to do', writes Wills, 'with theories about slavery than with the concrete advantage the three-fifths clause gave to any added slave territory.' This interpretation of Jefferson's support for slavery is more plausible than Roger Kennedy's assertion that Jefferson might have opposed slavery but was found wanting at crucial moments. Wills's Jefferson knew exactly where his political interests lay and acted accordingly.[29]

The debate between the emancipationists and revisionists regarding Jefferson's relationship with slavery has been imbued with moral judgments. Indeed, a critical approach to Jefferson's relationship with slavery invites such judgments. As Peter Onuf writes, 'The slavery problem, for Revolutionaries generally and Jefferson in particular, has especially complicated our understanding of the Revolutionary transformation and brought moral questions to the fore.' Paul Finkelman, as perhaps Jefferson's most prominent and persuasive scholarly critic on the slavery question, has been explicit in his condemnation of Jefferson's actions as a slaveholder – and his inaction as a statesman. This interpretation might be termed 'moral revisionism' because it seeks to overturn the previously dominant emancipationist interpretation in explicitly ethical terms. Ironically, Finkelman's moralistic and judgmental approach to the past is remarkably similar to Jefferson's (see Chapter 1). Finkelman, a legal scholar as well as an historian, adopts an adversarial approach to the past that is very similar to Jefferson's. Like Jefferson, Finkelman finds in the past, moral lessons that inform the present. As with Jefferson, this encourages Finkelman to approach history as an ethical zero-sum game. It is a game that Jefferson and, by implication, those scholars who have defended his record on slavery, lose. Since the 1970s, however, some scholars have sought a middle way between the moral judgments of the emancipationists and the revisionists. In so doing they have opened new perspectives on Jefferson and, more importantly, his slaves.[30]

V

As is the way in historiography, it was not long after the advent of the revisionist interpretation in the 1960s before some historians sought to revise the revisionists. The first important challenge to the revisionist interpretation came from William W. Freehling. In a 1972 article entitled 'The Founding Fathers and Slavery' published in the *American Historical Review*, Freehling noted the potency of the revisionist interpretation but suggested that it had gone too far. 'The new charge that the Founding Fathers did next to nothing about bondage is as misleading as the older notion that they almost did everything, ' wrote Freehling. 'The abolitionist process proceeded slowly but inexorably from 1776 to 1860: slowly in part because of what Jefferson and his contemporaries did not do, inexorably in part because of what they did.' Freehling enumerated the steps the revolutionary generation took that restricted, and in the long run crippled, slavery. These included the gradual abolition of slavery across the North, which rendered it the South's 'peculiar institution'; excluding slavery from the Northwest Territory; abolishing the Atlantic slave trade; and adopting laws allowing for individual manumission in the South. Slavery was not the primary concern of the Founding Fathers, according to Freehling. While they disliked slavery they were more concerned with creating a durable republic and maintaining peaceful (and unequal) race relations than eliminating unfree labor. Thus, Freehling writes, 'whenever dangers to the Union, property, or racial order seemed to them acute the Founding Fathers did little . . . But whenever abolition dangers seemed to them manageable Jefferson and his contemporaries moved effectively, circumscribing and crippling the institution and thereby gutting its long-range capacity to endure.' This analysis is persuasive if one takes a long-range view of abolition. It is kind to Jefferson, who, while central to Freehling's analysis, is grouped with 'his contemporaries' in taking the steps that eventually doomed slavery. Thus Jefferson seemingly benefits from the actions of his peers – such as abolition in the North, or individual manumissions – in which he was not involved. Nonetheless, as a corrective to the more critical view of Jefferson, especially as portrayed by William Cohen, Freehling's analysis suggested an alternative interpretation.[31]

Several years after Freehling's article appeared, Edmund S. Morgan's book *American Slavery, American Freedom* made one of the most important contributions to Jefferson historiography (as well as the literature on American slavery). While Morgan's book was about the

evolution of slavery in colonial and revolutionary Virginia generally and
dealt with Jefferson only briefly, his treatment of Jefferson suggested a
radically different way of interpreting his relationship with slavery.
Morgan challenged both the emancipationists and the revisionists. Rather
than portray Jefferson as a would-be abolitionist unwillingly holding a
wolf by the ears, or as a hypocrite who professed to abhor slavery while
actively strengthening the institution, Morgan closely interrogated the
relationship between slavery and republicanism for Jefferson, Virginia
and, by implication, the early American republic. Morgan's Jefferson
'was the greatest champion of liberty this country has ever had'. Yet
Jefferson, as was well established by more than a decade's scholarship
prior to the appearance of Morgan's book, owned hundreds of slaves,
held racist views and took steps to strengthen slavery in America. In a
subtle, perceptive and persuasive argument, Morgan posited the view that
Virginia's planters, especially Jefferson, became staunch republicans
because of their slaveholding, not despite it.

> Aristocrats could more safely preach equality in a slave society than in a
> free one. Slaves did not become levelling mobs because their owners would
> see to it that they had no chance to. The apostrophes to equality were not
> addressed to them. And because Virginia's labor force was composed
> mainly of slaves, who had been isolated by race and removed from the
> political equation, the remaining free laborers and tenant farmers were too
> few in number to constitute a serious threat to the superiority of the men
> who assured them of their equality.

According to Morgan, Jefferson and his peers were not especially
troubled by slavery because slavery was integral to their understanding
of a properly ordered society and only by denying liberty to African
Americans were they able to extend liberty and equality to poorer whites.
During the American Revolution the lexicographer Samuel Johnson
famously asked, 'How is it we hear the loudest yelps for liberty among
the drivers of Negroes?' After two centuries Edmund Morgan provided
the most cogent answer to Johnson's query.[32]
    The scholars who have sought to challenge the revisionist interpreta-
tion have not been seeking to revive or defend the emancipationist
Jefferson so much as to place his actions (and inaction) and attitudes
in a broader context; we might even bestow the somewhat awkward title
of 'contextualizers' on this third group of historians. Among these is
Joseph J. Ellis, a student of Edmund Morgan. In his 1996 study of
Jefferson's character, *American Sphinx*, Ellis conceded that slavery exposed a 'moral chasm between what [Jefferson] knew to be right and
what he could not do without'. While recognizing this ethical gap, Ellis

had little sympathy with the judgments of some of Jefferson's revisionist critics. '[L]atter-day moral judgments are notoriously easy to render from the comfortable perch that hindsight always provides, ' sniffs Ellis. Rather than judge Jefferson, he argued that our understanding of Jefferson's relationship to slavery would be 'enhanced if we do two things: First try to relate Jefferson's position on slavery as a social problem with his own predicament as an owner of slaves and, second, recognize the shift that occurs in his thinking somewhere between 1783 and 1794, a shift toward passivity and procrastination'. He advanced the view that, prior to 1784, Jefferson 'was a member of the vanguard that insisted on the incompatibility of slavery with the principles on which the American republic was founded'. As evidence, Ellis cited Jefferson's rhetorical denunciation of slavery and his early advocacy of an end to the slave trade, the prohibition of slavery from the western territories, and the adoption of a fixed date for gradual emancipation – all of which, if adopted, would have ended slavery in the United States.[33]

Sometime in the 1780s, according to Ellis, Jefferson's attitude toward slavery began to change. '[H]is abiding posture', writes Ellis, 'was that the current configuration of political forces blocked any meaningful reform at present, so that all one could realistically do was wait for the future to prepare public opinion for the inevitable.' Ellis explained the change in Jefferson's attitude as resulting from several factors. First, Jefferson was stung by the hostility of his fellow slave owners in Virginia to his criticisms of slavery in the *Notes on Virginia*. Second, he could never come up with a realistic answer to the question of what to do with the former slaves after emancipation. Finally, Jefferson's personal circumstances – notably his own growing personal debt – meant that he increasingly depended on his slaves to maintain his way of life. 'The net result of all of these influences', Ellis concludes, 'was a somewhat tortured position on slavery that combined unequivocal condemnation of the institution in the abstract with blatant procrastination whenever specific emancipation schemes were suggested.'[34]

How did Jefferson live with his 'tortured position' on slavery, a position that he held, if Ellis is correct, over the course of five decades? Ellis suggests that Jefferson 'possessed the psychological dexterity to overrule awkward perceptions, including the day-by-day realities of slave life'. Further, he shielded himself from the worst aspects of slavery: Monticello's slave quarters along Mulberry Row housed his immediate servants, who were given preferential treatment, and the quarters themselves were obscured from the view of Jefferson's home. Finally, Jefferson embraced the role of patriarchal plantation master who devoted paternal care to his 'family' of slaves by means of (relatively) benign treatment. For Ellis, Jefferson willingly ignored the harshest aspects of slavery while doing what he could to treat his slaves as well as possible. While this may not satisfy posterity, in Ellis's view Jefferson sought through evasion and beneficence to reconcile himself to a moral problem which he lacked the will and ability to solve.[35]

In contrast to Ellis, who saw Jefferson's position on slavery as inconsistent and incoherent, thus necessitating evasion and 'psychological dexterity', Ari Helo and Peter Onuf sought to historicize Jefferson's moral thinking on slavery in a 2003 article that appeared in the *William and Mary Quarterly*. They neither defend nor condemn Jefferson's position on slavery, but rather demonstrate that Jefferson's thinking provided him with a coherent view of his world and slavery's place in it. For Helo and Onuf, who found the origins of Jefferson's moral assumptions about the nature of man and society among the thinkers of the Scottish common sense school, Jefferson's opposition to slavery was limited by public opinion. His understanding of republican society began with the premise that political and moral enlightenment must proceed from the body of citizens and could not be imposed from without by a vanguard elite. Thus, although he was personally opposed to slavery, Jefferson could not move beyond popular will in attacking unfree labor. To do so would not have much effect on slavery but it would undermine the main achievements of the American Revolution. 'The civic community should be expanded, the radical democratic reformer urged,' they write, 'but never beyond the limits of contemporary public opinion. In the case of slaves, the community's progress toward achieving universal and equal benevolence was fundamentally circumscribed by the deeply rooted racist suspicions of white society.'

Although he opposed slavery and favored gradual emancipation (and expatriation of the former slaves), Jefferson could and would not compel others to share his views. The only way to change the moral assumptions of white Virginians about slavery was through education. Thus Jefferson's support for the establishment of the University of Virginia during his retirement was not a distraction from the problem of slavery but a contribution to its long-term solution. Similarly, when Jefferson enjoined Edward Coles – with whose personal morality Jefferson agreed – not to leave Virginia to emancipate his slaves, it was because Coles could help shift public opinion against slavery. For Helo and Onuf, Jefferson was not as troubled by slavery as other commentators, such as Joseph Ellis, would have us believe, or as we would like him to be.[36]

Andrew Burstein is another contextualizer who has sought to find a middle way between the emancipationists' admiration and the revisionists' criticism. In his 2005 study of Jefferson's retirement, Burstein portrayed Jefferson as finding refuge from the ethical dilemma posed by slavery in benevolent paternalism. With respect to the tendency among critics and admirers to praise or excoriate Jefferson, Burstein asks, 'must we judge Thomas Jefferson entirely on whether he was, ultimately, as munificent as the most susceptible, most compassionate southerner? Must he be all racist or all liberator?' The problems posed by Jefferson's relationship with slavery are complex and do not lend themselves to such easy judgments. For example, Burstein observed, the *Notes on Virginia* were controversial in the 1780s because of their criticism of slavery, not because of their pseudoscientific racism. Since the 1960s, by contrast, historians have often dismissed the strictures against slavery as insincere while highlighting and criticizing the passages on racial differences. Despite such changing ethical concerns (and unlike Joseph Ellis), Burstein allows that modern historians should make moral judgments regarding Jefferson's relationship with slavery:

> It is entirely appropriate for us to weigh the moral burden we ought to put on Jefferson for having embraced the role of master. We do not like his attitude and no one can defend slavery, but that does not mean that we should automatically affirm that the intelligence and wherewithal to create a just biracial or multiracial society existed in, say, 1809, when Jefferson retired to private life, and that he could have formulated such a society as efficiently as he went about conceiving his university. Though select individuals did emancipate their slaves, no one in a position of power was articulating a large-scale plan for a healthy post-emancipation society. That is why Jefferson's myopic choice – to accommodate mild, benevolent slavery or to work for mass deportation and colonization – continued to strike him as the most 'practicable' plan.

In rendering judgments on the past, therefore, historians must exercise caution and be aware of the context in which Jefferson lived. This task is complicated as we bring our own ethical and moral concerns (and limitations) to the past. Burstein writes of Jefferson, 'We magnify his limits as a political actor by forcing his racism to define him. We would probably contextualize his racism better if racial injustice did not still manifest itself in our lifetime.'[37]

The historians seeking to contextualize Jefferson's relationship with slavery have broadened our understanding in two different directions. Some, such as Edmund Morgan, Joseph J. Ellis, Ari Helo, Peter Onuf and Andrew Burstein, have revisited Jefferson's life and some of his most familiar writings and reinterpreted them with special sensitivity to time and place. In so doing they have given us a more subtle understanding of Jefferson's complex, and often problematic, relationship with slavery. The effort to contextualize Jefferson and slavery has encouraged other scholars to go in a completely different direction. There are two perspectives on Jefferson's relationship with slavery: that of Jefferson and that of his slaves. The former has been exhaustively studied over the course of two centuries – although the recent work of Andrew Burstein demonstrates that there are still new insights to be found. The study of Jefferson's slaves, by contrast, has only just begun. To take Jefferson's famous phrase, since the 1980s scholars have increasingly looked at the problem of the 'wolf by the ear' from the perspective of the wolf rather than the man holding its ear. What they have found, of course, is that Jefferson did not hold a wolf which threatened to destroy him, but approximately 600 hundred human beings – as many as 200 at any one time – in bondage. Because a famous man, and a meticulous record-keeper, owned them, it has been possible to recreate the lives of some of Jefferson's slaves. Their story gives us fresh insights into their owner and a fuller picture of plantation life in early national Virginia.

The leading student of Monticello slave life is Lucia Stanton of the Thomas Jefferson Foundation. In a series of articles and books published during the 1990s, Stanton recreated the lives of Monticello's slaves. Several themes emerge from her research: Jefferson tried within the limits imposed by slavery to be a humane master; nonetheless those limits, cultural, economic, social and political, were significant and Jefferson's slaves suffered as a result; Monticello's slaves struggled valiantly to forge independent lives and to establish families within the constraints imposed on them by slavery. Stanton's most valuable contribution to the literature derives from her focus on slavery from the perspective of Monticello's slaves rather than their master. From the perspective of Mulberry Row – the slave dwellings and shops at the summit of Monticello near the main house – it was Jefferson who depended on his slaves. Stanton concludes, 'The African Americans of Monticello had a quite different view of who was the supporter and who the burden. Their accounts perpetuated the understanding that Thomas Jefferson could not do what he did alone. He needed their skills and ingenuity in order to preserve life and property and, by extrapolation, to pursue his scientific enquiries and his public purposes.'[38]

Stanton based her analysis on a variety of sources: Jefferson's extensive plantation records, four reminiscences by former Monticello slaves, oral histories of the descendants of Monticello's slaves and archaeological evidence. Beginning in the 1980s the Thomas Jefferson Foundation made the study of slave life at Monticello a priority (see Chapter 4). As a result archaeological investigations of Mulberry Row were undertaken. The excavations, under the direction of William M. Kelso, the head archaeologist at the Foundation, revealed much about slave life at Monticello. These findings, Kelso cautioned, were limited in that most of Jefferson's slaves lived in more modest quarters below the mountaintop or on

Jefferson's more scattered land holdings. With this important qualification in mind, Kelso's findings suggest some tentative conclusions with regard to the lives of those house servants and skilled artisans who lived on Mulberry Row – and about Thomas Jefferson's actions as a slave master.

Kelso's findings suggest that the slaves who lived along Mulberry Row may have enjoyed a more varied diet than was typical of slaves in the late eighteenth and early nineteenth centuries. Moreover, there was an improvement in the quality and design of slave quarters after Jefferson returned from France in 1789. It is problematic to extrapolate too much from this evidence. Nonetheless, if read in conjunction with Joseph Ellis's argument regarding Jefferson's evolving position on slavery, Kelso's findings might suggest that, having given up on emancipation sometime in the 1780s, Jefferson sought to improve the material lives and living conditions of the slaves on Mulberry Row as a means of reconciling himself to his (self-conceived) role as a benign patriarch. Kelso's excavations indicate that the slaves' lot on the mountaintop was not enviable (except, perhaps, to field hands further down the mountain). There is evidence of poor sanitary conditions along Mulberry Row. Further, artifacts recovered from the shallow cellars dug by the slaves for storage reveal evidence of pilfering among Jefferson's bondsmen and women – a common tactic employed by slaves to resist their masters and to improve their living conditions. Taken together, the work of Lucia Stanton and William M. Kelso provides crucial information about the context of slavery at Monticello.[39]

VI

The tripartite division within the literature on Jefferson and slavery mirrors Hegel's historical dialectic. The emancipationist interpretation, the original thesis on the subject, first advanced by Jefferson himself, predominated for many years, and still finds adherents among some of Jefferson's admirers. The revisionist challenge to the emancipationists, the antithesis, began in the 1960s and gathered strength over the subsequent four decades. The contextualist view synthesizes elements from both traditions. It accepts the sincerity, at least early in his life, of Jefferson's professed opposition to slavery but seeks to explain the circumstances that prevented him from acting on his beliefs. Drawing on the revisionist tradition, it acknowledges Jefferson's failure to take substantive action against slavery, but seeks to provide an explanation for it. The challenge for the contextualizers is to specify the context in which they place Jefferson and his slaves. Some are interested in the moral and ideological dimension to Jefferson's thinking on slavery. Others focus on the economic, political and material contexts of his slaveholding. Still others consider the world made by Jefferson's slaves.

In 1943 Franklin Roosevelt dedicated the Jefferson Memorial as a monument to the principles for which the United States was fighting during World War II. Among these, suitably edited as we have seen, was opposition to slavery. Six decades later the staff, students and parents at the Jefferson Elementary School in Berkeley, California, voted to change the name of their school because of Jefferson's life-long association with slavery. These two actions epitomize the range of efforts to come to terms with Jefferson and slavery over the past two centuries. Many – like Roosevelt – have followed the path carefully plotted by Jefferson and concluded that he was a flawed opponent of slavery. Others – like the staff, students and parents at Jefferson Elementary – have concluded that slavery taints Jefferson's legacy to such an extent as to invalidate his other achievements. This view has become more commonplace since World War II, among scholars and the public at large, as equal rights and racial justice emerged as central issues in American public life. The result has been a steady decline in Jefferson's reputation. Despite the best efforts of Jefferson's defenders, such as Douglas L. Wilson, the more critical view – epitomized by Paul Finkelman's work – is predominant at the time of writing. The differences between the two are fundamentally imbued with moral questions. This explains the intensity that characterizes the debate over Jefferson and slavery. For Jefferson's defenders, his overall contribution to expanding the boundaries of human freedom outweighs the significance of slavery in his life. The emancipationists are halfway relativists, choosing to emphasize what they admire in Jefferson's legacy – transcendent self-evident principles of universal equality – while dismissing contemporary criticism of his less savory views as 'presentist'. For revisionists, Jefferson's ownership of slaves and his failure to take substantive action against slavery comprehensively undermine his historical legacy. They are consistent in their anachronism when they apply contemporary ethical standards to condemn Jefferson's relationship with slavery.

The contextual interpretation offers the best way ahead for the study of Jefferson and slavery – though the recent work of Garry Wills and Roger G. Kennedy demonstrates that the revisionists still have much to say. Edmund Morgan, Joseph J. Ellis, Lucia Stanton and William M. Kelso have all shown that we can acquire new and important insights into the lives of Jefferson *and* his slaves that deepen our knowledge and understanding. Ari Helo and Peter Onuf have shown that we can make sense of Jefferson's views on slavery by grounding them in Enlightenment thought. To contextualize slavery is not to excuse it: Andrew Burstein has demonstrated that we can place Jefferson's engagement with slavery in its appropriate context without divesting ourselves of ethical judgments – often informed by contemporary concerns. The contextualizers seek to explain rather than to defend or condemn Jefferson. Richard B. Bernstein's recent one-volume biography of Jefferson augurs well for the future of the contextualist interpretation. This work, likely to be the standard short life of Jefferson for the foreseeable future, describes Jefferson's 'deep ambivalence about slavery', noting his opposition to slavery as well as the constraints placed on his anti-slavery by his racism and political considerations.[40]

Jefferson wrote his 'wolf by the ear' letter during the Missouri crisis to former congressman John Holmes of Massachusetts. He was despondent that the American republic had almost foundered on the rock of slavery. He likened the crisis to 'a fire bell in the night' that sounded 'the knell of the Union'. Jefferson feared that slavery would still cause a sectional schism that would destroy the United States:

> I regret that I am now to die in the belief, that the useless sacrifice of themselves by the generation of 1776, to acquire self-government and happiness to their country, is to be thrown away by the unwise and unworthy passions of their sons, and that my only consolation is to be, that I live not to weep over it. If they would but dispassionately weigh the blessings they will throw away, against an abstract principle more likely to be effected by union than by scission, they would pause before they would perpetrate this act of suicide on themselves, and of treason against the hopes of the world.[41]

If slavery shattered the American union it would undo the achievements of the American Revolution, setting back the advance of human liberty initiated in 1776. For Jefferson, slavery was an unfortunate and regrettable distraction from his life's work of advancing republican government in the United States and beyond. He hoped that his posthumous efforts to portray himself as an opponent of slavery would answer future critics and allow scholars to concentrate on what was really important. As the next chapter shows, Jefferson dedicated most of his efforts in public life to protecting the fragile American republic in a dangerous world. It is one of the supreme ironies of a life abounding in ironies that Jefferson's republic was threatened from within by an unjust institution on which Jefferson depended throughout his life.

NOTES

1. J. Douglas Allen-Taylor, 'School Board Postpones Jefferson Name Change', *Berkeley Daily*, 10 June 2005, www.berkeleydaily.org; Eric Kurhi, 'Jefferson School Seeks New Namesake', *Contra Costa Times*

(Walnut Creek, CA), 11 March 2005; Cindy Peng, 'School Mulls Moral Dilemma in Deciding Whether to Change Name', *Daily Californian* (Berkeley), 5 May 2005, www.dailycal.org; Mengly Taing, 'After Emotional Debate, Board Keeps "Jefferson"', *Daily Californian* (Berkeley), 23 June 2005, www.dailycal.org.

2. *PTJ*, 1:426, emphasis in original. For the distribution of Jefferson's draft see TJ to Richard Henry Lee, 8 July 1776, *PTJ*, 1:455–6; Edmund Pendleton to TJ, 10 Aug. 1776, *PTJ*, 1: 488–91. Julian Boyd, *PTJ*, 1:415, reports that TJ also sent copies of his draft to George Wythe, Philip Mazzei, 'and probably John Page'. This clause appears in Jefferson's autobiography, *TJW*, 22. For an analysis of this passage see Ari Helo and Peter Onuf, 'Jefferson, Morality, and the Problem of Slavery', *WMQ*, 60 (2003), 583–614.

3. *Notes on the State of Virginia*, *TJW*, 289, also see 264; John Adams to TJ, 22 May, 1785, *PTJ*, 8:160; TJ to Chastellux, 7 June 1785, *PTJ*, 8:184.

4. Joseph J. Ellis, *American Sphinx: The Character of Thomas Jefferson* (New York: Random House, 1996; Vintage, 1998), 315.

5. Autobiography, *TJW*, 43–4.

6. *Notes on the State of Virginia*, *TJW*, 264–70.

7. Autobiography, *TJW*, 44.

8. TJ to Edward Coles, 25 Aug. 1814, *TJW*, 1343–6. Also see TJ to John Holmes, 22 April 1820, TJ to Jared Sparks, 4 Feb. 1824, and TJ to James Heaton, 20 May, 1826, in *TJW*, 1433–5, 1484–7, 1516.

9. TJ to John Holmes, 22 April 1820, *TJP*.

10. Peterson, *Jefferson Image*, 164–209, quotation 171.

11. 'Thomas Jefferson Memorial, Statue Chamber Inscriptions', National Park Service, www.nps.gov/thje/memorial/inscript.htm; Conor Cruise O'Brien, *The Long Affair: Thomas Jefferson and the French Revolution, 1785–1800* (Chicago: University of Chicago Press, 1996), 306; Pauline Maier, *American Scripture: Making the Declaration of Independence* (New York: Knopf, 1997), 209–11.

12. Adrienne Koch and William Peden, eds., *Life and Selected Writings of Thomas Jefferson* (New York: Modern Library, 1944), 641–2. This edition, still in print, was for many years the most popular single-volume collection of Jefferson's writings. It has been supplanted by Merrill D. Peterson's one-volume collection published by the Library of America in 1984. Peterson's edition publishes the Coles letter in full, 1343–6. For the editing of the letter by Koch and Peden see Paul Finkelman, 'Jefferson and Slavery: "Treason Against the Hopes of the World"', in Peter S. Onuf, ed., *Jeffersonian Legacies* (Charlottesville: University Press of Virginia, 1993), 181–221, n.136.

13. Malone, *Jefferson and His Time*, 1:264, 266; 3:208; 6:316–27.

14. Merrill D. Peterson, *Thomas Jefferson and the New Nation* (New York:

Oxford University Press, 1970), 998, 260, 153; Noble E. Cunningham, Jr., *In Pursuit of Reason: The Life of Thomas Jefferson* (Baton Rouge: Louisiana State University Press, 1987), 63. These views are echoed in Willard Sterne Randall's popular, but less reliable, biography, *Thomas Jefferson: A Life* (New York: Henry Holt, 1993), 300–3, 590–2.

15. Malone, *Jefferson and His Time*, 1:267; Peterson, *Thomas Jefferson and the New Nation*, 262; Cunningham, *In Pursuit of Reason*, 62.

16. Douglas L. Wilson, 'Jefferson and the Character Issue', *Atlantic Monthly*, 270:5 (Nov. 1992), 57–74. This article is available at www.theatlantic.com.

17. Peter S. Onuf, 'The Scholars' Jefferson', *WMQ*, 50 (1993), 671–99, quotation 674.

18. Daniel P. Jordan, 'Foreword', in Peter S. Onuf, ed., *Jeffersonian Legacies*, vii; Finkelman, 'Jefferson and Slavery', 186, 210.

19. Paul Finkelman, 'Jefferson and Antislavery: The Myth Goes On', *Virginia Magazine of History and Biography*, 102 (1994), 193–228, quotation 201. Later versions of this essay as well as 'Jefferson and Slavery' appeared in Paul Finkelman, *Slavery and the Founders: Race and Liberty in the Age of Jefferson* (Armonk, NY: M.E. Sharpe, 1996; 2nd edn, 2001).

20. Robert McColley, *Slavery and Jeffersonian Virginia* (Urbana: University of Illinois Press, 1964), 5.

21. McColley, *Slavery and Jeffersonian Virginia*, 1, 124, 125. Jefferson's role in the drafting of the Northwest Ordinance is discussed more fully in Chapter 8. With regard to Jefferson's role in drafting the ordinances of 1784 and 1787 and the prohibition of slavery in the Northwest see Robert F. Berkhofer, Jr., 'Jefferson, the Ordinance of 1784, and the Origins of the American Territorial System', *WMQ*, 29 (1972), 231–62, esp. 247–8.

22. Winthrop D. Jordan, *White Over Black: American Attitudes toward the Negro, 1550–1812* (Chapel Hill: University of North Carolina Press, 1968), viii, ix.

23. Jordan, *White Over Black*, xii, 453, 481. For a subsequent study that considered Jefferson's racism in the context of Enlightenment thought see John P. Diggins, 'Slavery, Race, and Equality: Jefferson and the Pathos of Enlightenment', *American Quarterly*, 28 (1976), 206–28.

24. William Cohen, 'Thomas Jefferson and the Problem of Slavery', *Journal of American History*, 56 (1969), 503–26, quotations 512, 514.

25. John Chester Miller, *The Wolf by the Ears: Thomas Jefferson and Slavery* (New York: Free Press, 1977, repr. Charlottesville: University of Virginia Press and the Thomas Jefferson Memorial Foundation, 1991), xi, 1. For a perceptive analysis of *The Wolf by the Ears* see Robert Dawidoff, 'The Fox in the Henhouse: Jefferson and Slavery', *Reviews in American History*, 6 (1978), 503–11.

26. For example, see David Brion Davis, *The Problem of Slavery in the Age of Revolution* (Ithaca, NY: Cornell University Press, 1975), 166–84; and Diggins, 'Slavery, Race, and Equality'.

27. Tim Matthewson, 'Jefferson and Haiti', *Journal of Southern History*, 61 (1995), 209–48.

28. Roger G. Kennedy, *Mr. Jefferson's Lost Cause: Land, Farmers, Slavery, and the Louisiana Purchase* (New York: Oxford University Press, 2003), 29.

29. Garry Wills, *'Negro President:' Jefferson and the Slave Power* (Boston: Houghton Mifflin, 2003), 9. My analysis of Kennedy and Wills closely follows my essay, 'Founders Chic', *History*, 89 (2005), 411–19.

30. Peter S. Onuf, 'The Scholars' Jefferson', 675. It should be noted that the emancipationists also use moral language to defend Jefferson. Jefferson's defenders assert his fundamental goodness despite his multiple ties to slavery while the revisionists condemn him because of them.

31. William W. Freehling, 'The Founding Fathers and Slavery', *American Historical Review*, 77 (1972), 81–93, quotations 82, 84. Nearly two decades later Freehling was more critical of Jefferson, whom he portrayed as favoring the conditional termination of slavery, yet he never felt the conditions for abolition were right. William W. Freehling, *The Road to Disunion: Secessionists at Bay, 1776–1854* (New York: Oxford University Press, 1990), 121–31.

32. Edmund S. Morgan, *American Slavery, American Freedom: The Ordeal of Colonial Virginia* (New York: W.W. Norton, 1975) ch. 18, quotations 376, 380; Donald J. Greene, ed., *Samuel Johnson: Political Writings* (New Haven: Yale University Press, 1977), 454. Also see Jack P. Greene, *All Men are Created Equal: Some Reflection on the Character of the American Revolution* (Oxford: Clarendon Press, 1976), repr. in Jack P. Greene, *Imperatives, Behaviors & Identities: Essays in Early American Cultural History* (Charlottesville: University Press of Virginia, 1992), 236–67.

33. Ellis, *American Sphinx*, 171, 176, 394 n.47, 172.

34. Ellis, *American Sphinx*, 173, 175. The best study of the impact of debt on Jefferson's life, including his relationship with slavery, is Herbert Sloan's excellent study, *Principle and Interest: Thomas Jefferson and the Problem of Debt* (New York: Oxford University Press, 1995; Charlottesville: University Press of Virginia, 2001). The debt issue exemplifies the difference between Ellis's approach and that of revisionists such as Paul Finkelman. Where Ellis simply states that Jefferson was 'aware how much his own financial well-being depended upon the monetary value and labor of his slaves' (174–5), he takes no notice of the role played by Jefferson's lifestyle in fostering such dependence. Finkelman, by contrast, identifies a direct connection between Jefferson's extravagant spending – debt is not a neutral factor imposed on Jefferson from

without – and his slaveholding: 'Jefferson could not maintain his extravagant life style without his slaves and, to judge from his lifelong behavior, his grand style was far more important than the natural rights of his slaves.' Finkelman, 'Jefferson and Slavery', 183.

35. Ellis, *American Sphinx*, 177.

36. Helo and Onuf, 'Jefferson, Morality, and the Problem of Slavery', quotation 601–2. Also see Peter S. Onuf, ' "To Declare them a Free and Independant People": Race, Slavery and National Identity in Jefferson's Thought', *Journal of the Early Republic*, 18 (1998), 1–46, revised and repr. in Peter S. Onuf, *Jefferson's Empire: The Language of American Nationhood* (Charlottesville: University Press of Virginia, 2000), 147–88. In those earlier works, which set the stage for 'Jefferson, Morality, and the Problem of Slavery', Onuf argued that Jefferson saw Americans and Africans as distinct nations. The latter were a 'captive nation' of the former and the only way the injustice of slavery could be remedied was through emancipation and expatriation.

37. Andrew Burstein, *Jefferson's Secrets: Death and Desire at Monticello* (New York: Basic Books, 2005), 124, 132, 133.

38. Lucia Stanton, 'The Other End of the Telescope: Jefferson through the Eyes of his Slaves', *WMQ*, 57 (2000), 139–52, quotation 152. Also see Lucia Stanton, ' "Those who Labor for My Happiness": Thomas Jefferson and His Slaves', in Onuf, ed., *Jeffersonian Legacies*, 147–80; Lucia Stanton, *Slavery at Monticello* (Charlottesville: Thomas Jefferson Memorial Foundation, 1996); and Lucia Stanton, *Free Some Day: The African American Families of Monticello* (Charlottesville: Thomas Jefferson Memorial Foundation, 2000).

39. William M. Kelso, 'The Archaeology of Slave Life at Thomas Jefferson's Monticello: "A Wolf by the Ears" ', *Journal of New World Archaeology*, 6 (1986), 5–20; William M. Kelso, 'Mulberry Row: Slave Life at Thomas Jefferson's Monticello', *Archaeology*, 39 (1986), 28–35; William M. Kelso, *Archaeology at Monticello: Artifacts of Everyday Life in the Plantation Community* (Charlottesville: Thomas Jefferson Memorial Foundation, 1997), ch. 3.

40. R. B. Bernstein, *Thomas Jefferson* (New York: Oxford University Press, 2003), 39–41.

41. TJ to John Holmes, 22 April 1820, *TJW*, 1434. For an analysis of this letter and Jefferson's response to the Missouri crisis see Onuf, *Jefferson's Empire*, ch. 4.

CHAPTER 8

AMERICA AND THE WORLD

I

In April 1809, one month into his retirement, Jefferson wrote to his friend and successor in the White House, James Madison, concerning the international situation. Despite wartime restrictions on American trade imposed by the major European belligerents, Britain and France, Jefferson was fairly sanguine about the state of affairs. He felt that the United States was in an especially strong position vis-à-vis Napoleon. Believing that the French emperor depended on American trade, Jefferson wrote:

> He ought the more to conciliate our good will, as we can be such an obstacle to the new career opening on him in the Spanish colonies. That he would give us the Floridas to withhold intercourse with the residue of those colonies cannot be doubted. But that is no price, because they are ours in the first moment of the first war, and until a war, they are of no particular necessity to us. But, altho' with difficulty, he will consent to our receiving Cuba into our union to prevent our aid to Mexico and other provinces. That would be a price, and I would immediately erect a column on the Southernmost limit of Cuba and inscribe on it a Ne plus ultra as to us in that direction. We should then have only to include the North in our confederacy, which would be of course in the first war, and should have such an empire for liberty as she has never surveyed since the creation: and I am persuaded no constitution was ever before so well calculated as ours for extensive empire and self government.[1]

The passage is notable for several reasons. It shows that Jefferson, far from being a 'half-way pacifist', accepted war as a legitimate means for the United States to expand its borders and defend its interests. Further, rather than speak in generalities, Jefferson demonstrated that he believed that East and West Florida, Cuba and Canada should be added to the United States, alongside the recently acquired Louisiana Territory. Further, he advanced the view that the Constitution ensured that republican principles and geographic expansion could go hand in hand.[2]

During his presidency, Jefferson was called upon to exercise power to promote and defend American interests in two major areas: the southwestern frontier and at sea. In the southern and western borderlands Jefferson pursued a policy of geographic expansion that brought the United States into conflict with the French, Spanish, Native Americans and British. At sea he sought to defend American commerce from interference by the French and British. These efforts met with mixed results. This chapter examines the efforts by scholars to understand and interpret Jefferson's presidential statecraft. It begins by considering Jefferson's thinking with regard to overseas commerce and westward expansion. It then examines the greatest achievement of Jefferson's presidency, the Louisiana Purchase, before concluding with an assessment of his most significant failure, his effort to protect American commerce by means of economic coercion through the Embargo of 1807–9. Unlike other aspects of Jefferson historiography where it is possible to discern general trends, the literature of Jefferson's statecraft is more diffuse and does not lend itself to easy generalization. There is wide disagreement among scholars about the success of Jefferson's foreign policy and the nature, extent and significance of his 'empire for liberty'.

II

Jefferson had long been an advocate of western expansion. In 1784 and 1785 he drafted two ordinances – one a plan of government for western territory and the other a mechanism for the survey and sale of western land – that established a system for orderly settlement of the West and the admission of new states from the national domain. The ordinances – largely, but not completely, subsumed by the Land Ordinance of 1785 and the Northwest Ordinance of 1787 – with their provisions that western territory should be divided into new states which would enjoy parity with older original states when admitted to the union, were testimony to Jefferson's belief that the future of the republic lay in western expansion and settlement.[3]

Over the past several decades, historians have sought to explain the intellectual origins of Jefferson's 'empire for liberty'. Writing in the late 1940s, Julian P. Boyd argued that Jefferson believed that there was a close correlation between the attachment of Americans to both their land and their individual liberties. In other words, there was a connection between republican government and western expansion.[4] Dumas Malone developed this theme. For Malone, Jefferson was a pragmatist who believed that American settlers would inevitably move west, displacing Native Americans and undermining the authority of the Spanish and French in the South and West (as well as the British in the North). Jefferson welcomed this development. He once wrote that he had a 'peculiar confidence in the men from the western side of the mountains'. According to Malone, this confidence guided Jefferson's thinking about western expansion. Settlers would spread republican government throughout North America and Jefferson saw it as his role to assist the process. 'No one more than he', wrote Malone, 'deserves to be described as the architect of orderly expansion, and at every stage he upheld the interests of the actual settlers, seeking to facilitate their acquisition of land and to prevent the exploitation of the vast interior by privileged land companies. He sought to bind the West to the East by extending to it the full benefits of political union and the right of self-government.' For Malone, Jefferson welcomed western expansion but his actions and thinking were essentially reactive to events on the ground in the South and the West. He sought to insure that inevitable western expansion was systematic, orderly and peaceful.[5]

Writing several years after Malone, Alexander DeConde, a specialist in the history of early American foreign relations, saw more sinister motives at work in Jefferson's thoughts and actions. DeConde, who published a study of the Louisiana Purchase in 1976, argued that Jefferson's acquisition of Louisiana was the result of 'pious imperialism' and 'conscious expansionism of an imperial creed promoting action'. Inheriting this creed from the British, Jefferson and the American people 'systematically reduced, absorbed, or annihilated tribal, or other native peoples' as they pushed west. While Dumas Malone viewed western settlement as a force unto itself that Jefferson sought to control and ameliorate, DeConde held it be an ominous process that its proponents, including Jefferson, cloaked in platitudes.[6]

Alexander DeConde's otherwise admirable study of the Lousiana Purchase is marred by ahistorical assumptions about Jeffersonian imperialism. DeConde, writing in the immediate aftermath of Watergate and Vietnam, was skeptical about the motives of Jefferson and the other leaders of the revolutionary generation. They, he wrote, 'unabashedly thought of themselves as expansionists and proudly tried to justify their implicit ideology with pious assertions of hazy continental destiny'. Driven by this expansionist creed, Jefferson employed military pressure, threats of war, diplomacy and public opinion to extract the Louisiana Territory from France and to displace its indigenous peoples. DeConde questioned neither the use of the term 'empire' by Jefferson and his contemporaries, nor its relationship with the concept of liberty. In DeConde's analysis, the 'empire for liberty' is nothing more than a convenient trope employed to obscure what was, fundamentally, an immoral and racist land grab. Since Alexander DeConde's *This Affair of Louisiana* appeared in 1976 intellectual historians, most notably Drew

R. McCoy and Peter S. Onuf, have closely interrogated what the 'empire for liberty' meant to Jefferson.[7]

In 1980 McCoy published *The Elusive Republic*, a seminal study of Jefferson's thinking on political economy. McCoy persuasively demonstrated that the agrarian philosophy espoused by Jefferson and Madison was predicated on a belief that republics, like all states, experienced a life cycle not unlike that of individuals. Jefferson and Madison contended that maintaining itself as an agrarian republic would keep the United States youthful, vigorous and healthy. As McCoy portrayed the choice facing the leaders of the fledgling United States, they could opt either for intensive development concentrated on manufacturing in the cities and towns of the eastern seaboard, or for extensive agricultural production spread throughout the United States, especially in the South and West. To pursue a program of intensive manufacturing along the lines which Alexander Hamilton had advocated, while it might increase the prosperity of a few, would lead to an increase in luxury and corruption, which would eventually undermine America's republican institutions. Manufacturing, Jefferson had observed during his travels in Europe during the 1780s, depended on a large class of propertyless laborers who were normally mired in poverty and ignorance. Such men and women were not fit material with which to build a lasting republic. On the contrary, Jefferson believed that the American republic should be based on commercial agriculture if liberty was to flourish. He was optimistic that so long as the majority of American citizens held their own property, then the republic would have a stable foundation. The American experiment in republicanism would succeed – politically and economically – providing the majority of its citizens tilled the land and exported their surpluses. Some small-scale manufacturing would be necessary – Jefferson himself sought to make nails commercially at Monticello – to service the agricultural economy, but Americans should purchase most of their manufactured goods from Europe. In *The Elusive Republic*, McCoy explicated the close connection between western expansion and transatlantic commerce in Jefferson's thinking. Jefferson held that the American republic would flourish as long as it was based on agriculture rather than manufacturing. He did not intend Americans to be subsistence farmers eking out a living from the land. Rather they should sell their surplus produce at a profit and purchase manufactured goods from Europe. For the United States – and its globally important experiment with republican government – to flourish it required access to land for its farmers and overseas markets for their surpluses.[8]

McCoy demonstrated the correlation between Jefferson's understanding of political economy and the need for the United States to expand in the West and to promote transatlantic commerce. In so doing he added a new degree of complexity to the study of Jeffersonian expansionism. *The Elusive Republic* is not concerned with questions of whether Jefferson's actions were positive, as portrayed by Dumas Malone, or deleterious, as suggested by Alexander DeConde's analysis. Rather, McCoy sought to recover the thinking behind the actions of Jefferson and his peers. This is the intention of Peter S. Onuf as well. Where Drew McCoy concerned himself with Jeffersonian political economy, Onuf has concentrated – in a series of books and essays over the course of the past two decades – mainly on Jeffersonian expansionism as it relates to questions of American nationality and constitutionalism. Like Drew McCoy, Onuf has sought neither to defend nor to condemn but to explain Jefferson.[9]

Onuf's most important work on western expansion is *Jefferson's Empire*, published in 2000. Onuf begins with the premise that Jefferson's imperial vision was also republican. He does not see a conflict between imperialism and republicanism for Jefferson. Rather, he seeks to explain the relationship between 'empire' and 'republic' in Jefferson's thinking. He does not assume that their meaning is the same in 1800 and 2000. Written prior to the attacks on 11 September 2001, and thus uncontaminated by the current debate over America's place in the world, *Jefferson's Empire* seeks to explain and historicize the relationship between two major themes in Jefferson's thinking: 'empire' and 'nation'.[10]

According to Onuf, Jefferson believed that the United States must create a new imperial model if its republic was to survive. Unlike the European empires of the eighteenth and early nineteenth centuries that were characterized by far-flung geographic holdings serving a metropolitan center where power and wealth coalesced, Jefferson wanted the United States to pursue geographic expansion without a metropolitan center. Onuf writes:

> For Jeffersonians the American Revolution was the prototype for the spontaneous popular mobilization that made a strong central government unnecessary and dangerous. Within the community of sentiment and interest that defined the new republican empire, a self-governing people would mobilize men and resources much more effectively than any despotic regime. Banishing metropolitan power from the New World, Jefferson imagined a great nation, a dynamic and expansive union of free peoples.

In the American empire political and economic power would be diffused across a vast territory, thus forestalling dangerous concentrations of power in a metropolitan center that would ultimately endanger the republic.[11]

It was crucial to Jefferson's imperial vision that new territories enter the union on an equal basis with the older states. Jefferson's belief in individual liberty was closely linked to the dispersal of political power in the individual 'state-republics' that constituted the federal union. For Jefferson, the American empire would be comprised of numerous equal state-republics, each its own locus of power within the federal union. Because political power would be concentrated locally, individual rights would be guaranteed yet the states as a whole would be strong enough to 'assert their collective claims against the other sovereignties of the world and simultaneously reconcile their conflicting claims without risking a dangerous concentration of power in Congress'. According to Onuf, 'From the beginning of his political life, Jefferson recognized the central importance of the autonomy, integrity, and equality of republics as corporate entities – as well as of the republican institutions that alone could guarantee the equal rights of self-governing individuals within the new states.'[12]

Onuf finds the origins of Jefferson's understanding of American national identity in his conception of an American empire of state-republics. Americans would not be too parochial, despite the importance of their individual states. They would be bound by the common political and constitutional principles of the unique American empire. Subscription to these values would be the test of American identity. It was a test that Jefferson's Federalist adversaries, who sought to concentrate power in a strong Federal government, would fail. Jeffersonianism and American identity became one and the same.[13]

Federalists were not the only ones who were excluded from Jefferson's conception of American nationhood, according to Onuf. So too were Native Americans and African American slaves. The former were excluded because they were, in cultural and historical terms, not at the same level of development as European Americans. Indians were not inherently inferior to whites but their apparent lack of cultural development meant that they could not be easily incorporated into the American empire. Since the very success of America's republican experiment, an achievement with global historical consequences in Jefferson's thinking, depended on the success of its western empire, Native Americans must, regrettably but inevitably, be displaced, swept aside by history. African American slaves, Onuf argues, presented a different problem in Jefferson's thinking. Jefferson saw Africans and European Americans as distinct nations. The former had been unjustly captured and enslaved by the latter; as such they could never be incorporated into the nation of their captors. Rather, the only solution to the problem posed by African slavery was emancipation and expatriation.[14]

It was a commonplace belief in the eighteenth century, derived from Montesquieu, that republics must be small. By the early nineteenth century, as demonstrated by Drew McCoy and Peter Onuf, Jefferson had articulated a coherent vision for a geographically extensive American empire. Taken together, McCoy and Onuf delineate the economic, political, constitutional and theoretical bases for Jefferson's conception of an American empire in the West. Rather than dismiss Jefferson's 'empire for liberty' as a contradiction in terms, or a rhetorical device intended to hide baser motives, they show that Jefferson believed that the American republic could thrive only through western expansion. Jefferson may have been driven by a coherent intellectual vision of American development; when he became president he learned how difficult making that vision come to pass might be.

III

While Drew McCoy and Peter Onuf have persuasively outlined Jefferson's conception of America's place in the world, there is little agreement among historians as to how he sought to achieve his geopolitical objectives during his two presidential terms. There is a wide range of opinions among diplomatic historians regarding Jefferson's methods and achievements when it came to exercising power. In 1957 Lawrence S. Kaplan argued that, although he employed radical rhetoric in discussing international relations, Jefferson was most successful when he acted in a more traditional manner, respecting the conventional European balance of power. For Kaplan, Jefferson's statecraft was less radical than his rhetoric. Scholars of almost all facets of Jefferson's life have frequently made this criticism, as we have seen. Kaplan, however, suggested that the cautious diplomacy that he felt characterized Jefferson's approach to foreign affairs was successful in advancing Jefferson's goal of westward expansion.[15]

Another early American diplomatic historian, Bradford Perkins, in a series of books and articles published between the mid-1950s and the 1990s, presented a much more critical view of Jefferson's diplomacy. Like Kaplan, Perkins saw a disjunction between Jefferson's aspirations and his actions. 'As president, ' Perkins writes, 'Jefferson strangely combined idealism, even utopianism, with cynical craft.' Unlike Kaplan, Perkins saw nothing of value in Jefferson's statecraft. According to Perkins, Jefferson and Madison badly mishandled American foreign policy during the first decade of the nineteenth century, until they blundered into a near-disastrous war with Britain. In his volume in the *Cambridge History of American Foreign Relations* Perkins writes: 'Their inept diplomacy produced national disgrace and then a war with England, which, but for good fortune, might well have destroyed the union. Both deservedly left the White House with tarnished reputations.' Perkins, a World War II combat veteran, was especially critical of Jefferson and Madison for miscalculating and leading the United States into what he considered an unnecessary military conflict.[16]

In contrast to Perkins, who saw Jefferson as helping the United States blunder into the War of 1812, in part because he threatened to use force irresponsibly, Reginald C. Stuart presented a close examination of Jefferson's attitudes toward the use of force in his 1978 book, *The Half-Way Pacifist*. Stuart persuasively demonstrated that Jefferson, who had opposed funding a large military establishment, particularly a substantial salt-water navy, was not a pacifist as he was sometimes portrayed by his Federalist opponents and by some subsequent historians. According to Stuart, Jefferson approached foreign relations from the perspective of an Enlightenment ruler and he viewed war as one of several instruments to be employed in achieving diplomatic ends. According to this view, war should be used as a last resort and in a limited way. The object of war for Jefferson, according to Stuart, was not to destroy one's enemies but to make them realize their errors. In such a conception, war should be employed when all else fails, to enforce reason. Like other students of Jefferson's foreign policy, Stuart finds a gap between Jefferson's thoughts and his actions. He seemed more willing to use force, or threaten to do so, against the French and Spanish over Louisiana and the Floridas, and he occasionally threatened hostile Native Americans with annihilation far beyond the 'limited' force characteristic of Enlightenment theories of international relations. Stuart's title is unfortunate, because as he himself demonstrated, Jefferson was anything but a 'half-way pacifist'. Nonetheless, his book showed that Jefferson produced a coherent understanding of the use of force and, consequently, a more subtle understanding of how he might achieve his foreign policy ends than previous authors such as Kaplan or Perkins had allowed.[17]

While Reginald Stuart saw Jefferson's foreign policy as a reflection of Enlightenment theories about war and the use of force, subsequent students of the subject have taken exception to this view. In 1990 political scientists Robert W. Tucker and David C. Hendrickson published *Empire of Liberty: The Statecraft of Thomas Jefferson*, probably the most important study of the theory and means of Jefferson's foreign policy. Tucker and Hendrickson argued that Jefferson's approach to international relations rejected traditional eighteenth-century theories of balance of power and *raison d'état* in favor of a new, revolutionary diplomacy for a revolutionary republic.

The United States, [Jefferson] believed, was the bearer of a new diplomacy, founded on the confidence of a free and virtuous people, that would secure ends based on the natural and universal rights of man, by means that escaped war and its corruptions. This new diplomacy broke radically, Jefferson thought, from the practices and principles of the old European tradition of reason of state, with its settled belief in the primacy of foreign over domestic policy. That the security and even aggrandizement of the state ought to have priority over domestic welfare, and that the actions of the state ought to be judged according to a different moral calculus than the conduct of individuals, were ideas that Jefferson found utterly anti-thetical to human progress and enlightenment.

In a republic, Jefferson believed, foreign policy should meet the needs and demands of its citizens. Tucker and Hendrickson argued that he sought both territorial expansion and access to markets for American produce, but he sought to achieve these ambitious objectives without recourse to the methods of European statecraft – diplomatic negotiation and warfare. Rather, he sought to pursue American interests as a matter of right and his foreign policy was imbued with a counter-productive moralistic and righteous tone which has plagued the foreign relations of the United States ever since.[18]

Empire of Liberty showed Jefferson to be a rather weak moralist whose Anglophobia blinded him to the threat posed by Napoleon. Tucker and Hendrickson argued, contrary to Lawrence Kaplan's interpretation, that Jefferson eschewed the traditional balance of power in favor of asserting a moral claim that the maritime interests of the United States as a neutral trader must be respected by both France and Britain. Since Jefferson was unwilling and unable to enforce this claim, a claim premised on the assumption that American interests were of greater importance than the defeat of Napoleon, his foreign policy was largely ineffective. American interests would have been better served, according to Tucker and Hendrickson had Jefferson sought to reach an accommodation with Britain on maritime issues – if he had been less concerned about neutral rights and more concerned with the old balance of power. Read in conjunction with Bradford Perkins's detailed examination of Jefferson's diplomatic failures, *Empire of Liberty* presents a strong basis for comprehending Jefferson's limitations in the realm of international relations.

The main area of disagreement for students of Jefferson's foreign policy seems to be the nature and source of his failure. For Lawrence Kaplan, Jefferson was radical in his use of rhetoric but traditional in his approach. Bradford Perkins, Robert Tucker and David Hendrickson argued that Jefferson was radical, and mistaken, in his foreign policy methods as well as his rhetoric, and this led him to make serious errors that harmed the interests of the United States.

A few diplomatic historians have praised Jefferson. In 1955, Mary P. Adams argued that Jefferson took appropriate and active steps – military and diplomatic – after Spain retroceded Louisiana to France in 1800. Forty years later Tim Matthewson argued that Jefferson employed vigorous diplomacy in the effort to win support from France for the American acquisition of Louisiana and West Florida. In 1993, the eminent diplomatic historian Walter LaFeber argued that Jefferson ably managed his foreign policy, which was responsive to domestic, political and economic concerns.

> The dynamics of Jefferson's foreign policy ran as follows: his early belief in the virtues of, and need for, agrarian expansionism helped lead to a series of conflicts in the international arena that forced him to devise a set of stronger central governmental policies to protect both agrarian and, increasingly, more broadly defined national interests. These governmental policies included military action and a dominant presidency. The implementation of Jeffersonian foreign policies helps explain contradictions and paradoxes that turn out more apparent than real.

For LaFeber, Jefferson was consistent in the ends he sought – the extension and protection of the United States as an agrarian republic. What changed were the means he employed, with mixed results, to secure those ends, ranging from diplomacy, to the use of force, to economic coercion.[19]

LaFeber felt that Robert Tucker and David Hendrickson misread the political realities that Jefferson confronted when he formulated his foreign policy. He took them to task for alleging that Jefferson erred when he rejected European-style *raison d'état* as a guiding principle of his diplomacy.

> To argue, as scholars recently have, that Jefferson (rather naively in these authors' views), sought to break the European tradition of reason of state, with its assumption that foreign policy has a dominant role over domestic policy, misses the central point of the Virginian's approach to both domestic and foreign affairs: given the nature of his agrarian republic, and given the proper working of the federal system in the necessarily large territorial sphere, Jefferson could rightly assume that foreign and domestic policies were two sides of the same national interest. Europeans posited a distinction because their governments were not sufficiently responsible to the welfare of their own people. The American presidency was responsible – or, more accurately, in Jeffersonian hands could be made responsible.[20]

In a republic, unlike a monarchy or an empire, the head of state must be responsible to popular will when formulating and implementing its foreign policy. Jefferson recognized this and shaped his foreign policy accordingly. Given Jefferson's importance in establishing the American republic, some blame could be laid at Jefferson's feet for the new republican diplomacy. Nonetheless, LaFeber implied, it was not as though Jefferson had any alternative but to reject the old diplomacy for the new.

Jefferson's major biographers have generally been more sympathetic in their treatment of his foreign policy than most diplomatic historians. Dumas Malone, for example, anticipated Walter LaFeber's position when he argued that Jefferson did as well as he could to promote and protect the interests of the fledgling American republic despite its relative weakness in a world of warring great powers.[21] Jefferson's critics, emphasizing his failures and inconsistencies, have not always appreciated the impotence of the United States during the first decade of the nineteenth century. Given the relative military, diplomatic and economic limitations faced by the United States, as well as its geographic isolation, it is debatable whether a foreign policy more robust and intellectually consistent than Jefferson's would have been effective. The scholarly critics and defenders of Jefferson's foreign policy have focused on his greatest diplomatic success – the Louisiana Purchase of 1803; and his most significant failure – the unsuccessful attempt to convince Britain and France to respect American maritime rights through economic coercion during the Embargo of 1807–9. In order to assess Jefferson's statecraft, it is important to examine these actions more fully.

IV

In October 1800 Spain ceded Louisiana, including the port of New Orleans, to France in exchange for an enhancement of Spanish interests in Italy. Napoleon acquired Louisiana as a prelude to reviving the French empire in North America and the Caribbean. In January 1802 he sent a 30,000–man army to Saint-Domingue to suppress Toussaint Louverture's slave revolt against French rule. In reserve, Napoleon held a second army to be sent to Louisiana after the conquest of Saint-Domingue. According to Napoleon's plan, Saint-Domingue would be re-established as a major source of wealth for France and it would be supplied by Louisiana. Further, the French presence in Louisiana would serve to check American and British ambitions in North America. In Washington, Thomas Jefferson viewed the French acquisition of Louisiana with concern. American settlers depended on access to the Mississippi and New Orleans in order to market their produce. Whoever controlled New Orleans would control the economic well being and political future of the trans-Appalachian west.

In 1801 Jefferson instructed Robert Livingston, the American ambassador in Paris, to open discussions with the French government over

American access to the Mississippi – including a possible purchase of New Orleans. The situation became acute in October 1802 when Spanish officials at New Orleans (Spain had not yet formally returned Louisiana to France) denied Americans access to the port. Jefferson dispatched James Monroe as an extraordinary envoy to assist Livingston in his negotiations with the French. Soon thereafter Napoleon's ambitions in the New World diminished. The expeditionary force in Saint-Domingue failed to recapture the colony and renewed warfare between Britain and France was imminent. Aware that the Americans were willing to purchase New Orleans, Napoleon instructed Talleyrand, his foreign minister, to offer them the whole of Louisiana. On 12 April 1803, several days after Monroe arrived in Paris, Livingston agreed to purchase not just New Orleans but the whole Louisiana Territory, approximately 828,000 square miles, extending from the Mississippi to the Rocky Mountains, for 80 million francs, approximately $15 million. The empire for liberty had doubled in size.

In the late nineteenth century Henry Adams portrayed Jefferson as a passive observer who did not deserve much credit for the acquisition of Louisiana. He acquiesced when Napoleon presented the opportunity to his representatives, shedding his previous strict construction of the Constitution. These criticisms, Jefferson's passivity and constitutional inconsistency, were first made by Adams's Federalist forebears, and have persisted among historians ever since. Bradford Perkins saw the Louisiana Purchase as Jefferson's sole success in foreign policy. Yet, according to Perkins, Jefferson deserved little credit for this success, which was a consequence of luck rather than of adroit diplomacy. 'Events outpaced Jefferson', writes Perkins, 'and while passing, bestowed unearned, even unsought laurels upon him.'[22]

Some of Jefferson's critics have argued that he took a more active role in the Louisiana Purchase, if only so that they can indict him for his actions. As we have seen, Alexander DeConde believed that the Louisiana Purchase was a manifestation of an inherent imperialist and expansionist creed in the United States. DeConde argued that Jefferson fully subscribed to this creed, and actively sought to acquire Louisiana, mainly through 'repeated truculence' in his dealings with the French. That Jefferson was able to obtain 828,000 square miles from Napoleon through churlishness is a remarkable achievement. What DeConde sees as truculence – Jefferson used hints of war and a possible alliance with Britain to coerce the French to reach an accommodation over New Orleans – could be interpreted as skillful negotiating from a relatively weak position.[23]

Robert Tucker and David Hendrickson were willing to acknowledge that Jefferson's diplomacy over the Mississippi crisis had been successful.

They felt, however, that Jefferson had benefited more from good luck and the military successes of Saint-Domingue's rebellious former slaves than his own half-hearted threats of war and a possible American alliance with Britain. In contrast to Reginald Stuart they argued that Jefferson was unwilling to seriously consider the use of force and that this weakened his statecraft. Although he was successful in obtaining Louisiana, Tucker and Hendrickson argued that Jefferson learned the wrong lessons from the negotiations.

> Louisiana had shown that there was no need to arm and to make sacrifices when vital interests are at stake. Instead, it was sufficient to hold up the prospect of alliances that would probably never be made and to threaten wars that one had no intention of waging. Another lesson was the wisdom of conducting negotiations in which one asks for much while offering little. In the affair of Louisiana there had been few quid pro quos in the American diplomatic armory. The conviction that there was no need to accept the principle of reciprocity in negotiations was related to still another lesson of Louisiana: that the United States held a position of central importance in the scales of European diplomacy. By virtue of our trade alone, American support of or hostility to one or the other of the great European powers was likely to prove decisive in any conflict between them.[24]

Buoyed by his success in obtaining Louisiana and drawing the wrong lessons from the experience, Tucker and Hendrickson contended, Jefferson sought to apply those lessons in his unsuccessful efforts to obtain the Floridas and to use commercial pressure to press for the rights of the United States as a neutral trader during the Napoleonic wars. While Tucker and Hendrickson make a strong case for the subsequent failure of Jeffersonian diplomacy, the fact remains that the American negotiators in Paris succeeded beyond their hopes (and their instructions). With regard to Louisiana Jefferson's diplomacy was successful, or at least, if one subscribes to Henry Adams's interpretation, appeared to be successful.

The defenders of Jefferson's foreign policy have, unsurprisingly, focused on his success in obtaining Louisiana. Dumas Malone contended that Jefferson's administration demonstrated flexibility in its approach to the negotiations. According to Malone, Jefferson sought to maintain the peace in the Mississippi valley but had been willing to use force if necessary to protect American interests. 'The administration', he writes, 'was alert and skillful, and except in minor details, one wonders how its procedure could have been improved upon.'[25] This view was echoed by Walter LaFeber, who argues that Jefferson and his secretary of state, James Madison, were not merely the lucky recipients of Europe's distresses when Louisiana fell into their hands in the spring of 1803. Jefferson had used his presidential powers, especially his prerogatives as commander-in-chief under the Constitution, along with shrewd diplomacy to acquire New Orleans and, beyond it, an area that he and Madison had assumed would someday become another, if distant, part of an American agrarian system. The settlers' demands for access to the most important outlet for their trade had led to crises in both the American West and relations with Europe; those crises in turn had required mobilizing troops, surreptitiously aiding African-American rebels (aid that Jefferson did not allow without much thought given the presence of African-American slaves in his own country), and suddenly accepting without any explicit constitutional authority an incredible 828,000 square miles of landed empire.

Jefferson's proponents argue that by exploiting the limited range of options available to him – threatening war and an alliance with Britain, providing covert aid to the rebels in Saint-Domingue – Jefferson created the circumstances that facilitated reaching an agreement over the sale of Louisiana.[26]

If the critics of Jefferson's foreign policy must contend with his apparent success, his admirers must reconcile themselves to the fact that his achievement may be more limited than it appears. Jefferson was thousands of miles away from the negotiations when the agreement to purchase Louisiana was completed. More importantly, Napoleon's decision to sell Louisiana – the crucial development in the story – had more to do with his failure to reconquer Saint-Domingue and his need for money to wage war again in Europe than any pressure brought to bear by the American administration. While many, perhaps most, of the key factors in the transaction were beyond Jefferson's control, he did what he could to assure a favorable outcome in the negotiations for the United States. When presented with an opportunity to obtain Louisiana, perhaps owing to good fortune rather than wise policy, he seized the chance. If Jefferson's critics see him as weak and lucky, his scholarly advocates believe that he adroitly exploited the opportunity which fortune (and Napoleon) placed before him.

Historians and publishers, undoubtedly with a popular market in mind, marked the 2003 bicentennial of the Louisiana Purchase with numerous books on the subject.[27] Most tended toward a favorable portrayal of Jefferson. Thomas Fleming's brief account, for example, is celebratory. Fleming argues that the failure of Napoleon's efforts in Saint-Domingue was the catalyst for the sale. He argues that the Federalists were willing to go to war in 1802 after the Spanish closed New Orleans to Americans but that Jefferson and the Republicans were somewhat feeble in response to this threat. Nonetheless, Fleming credits Jefferson with seizing the opportunity presented to him by Napoleon. In so doing Jefferson transformed the United States. Fleming concludes on a grandiose and nationalistic note, 'For the immediate future, by doubling the size of the United States, the purchase transformed it from a minor to a major world power. The emboldened Americans soon absorbed West and East Florida from enfeebled Spain, and fought mighty England to a bloody stalemate in the War of 1812.' For Fleming, the Louisiana Purchase was a crucial step in the rise of the United States to global power. Since Jefferson was, ultimately, responsible for the transaction, he deserves credit for helping to transform America's relationship with the rest of the world and, by implication, the acquisition of Floridas and the 'success' of the United States in the War of 1812.[28]

While most scholars are not quite as triumphalist as Fleming when considering the Louisiana Purchase, it seems that a positive view of Jefferson's handling of the Mississippi crisis and the negotiations over Louisiana between 1801 and 1803 has prevailed. Despite the criticisms of some diplomatic historians, the Louisiana Purchase is one subject on which most historians seem willing to give Jefferson the benefit of the doubt. As Bernard W. Sheehan recently noted, when confronted by the Mississippi crisis Jefferson and Madison 'proposed a reasonable solution: the purchase of New Orleans and the Gulf Coast'. Further, Sheehan continues, 'What should be said for the American president and secretary of state, and what virtually every historian does say, is when the opportunity became clear they acted wisely and swiftly. They allowed neither the letter of the Constitution nor money to cloud their perception of the grand prospect for the American future in the lands beyond the Mississippi.'[29]

Despite the generally favorable view of Jefferson's handling of the Mississippi crisis, the history of his involvement with the West, particularly the Louisiana Territory, has done little to reverse the long-term decline in his reputation. This is because historians have not paid as much attention to the diplomacy of the Louisiana Purchase as they have to its consequences for the *mélange* of peoples – French, Spanish, Creole, African and Native American – who inhabited the newly acquired territory. In general these studies have not reflected well upon Jefferson. Indeed, they have contributed to the more critical view of him that has prevailed over the past forty years.

One of the early studies of the immediate consequences of post-purchase Louisiana was George Dargo's 1975 book, *Jefferson's Louisiana: Politics and the Clash of Legal Traditions*. Dargo concentrated on the legal history of lower Louisiana from 1803 to 1808, focusing on the uneasy and uneven transition from civil law inherited from the Spanish and French to Anglo-American common law when the United States governed the territory. Dargo depicted an imperious Jefferson who imposed territorial government and sought to interfere with court decisions in a highhanded manner in defiance of local interests and sensibilities.[30] The transition from French to American rule is the major concern of Peter J. Kastor's 2004 study *The Nation's Crucible*. Kastor deals with the acquisition of the Louisiana Territory in relatively few pages, before focusing on how the United States absorbed and incorporated the various peoples of Louisiana – Europeans, Creoles, free and enslaved Africans, Native Americans and Anglo-American settlers – into the new republic's polity.[31]

Kastor is interested not only in the geographic expansion of the United States but in its demographic expansion. The Louisiana Purchase marked the first time that the United States acquired territory occupied by substantial numbers of peoples and institutions that it was obliged, by treaty, to respect and accommodate. Prior expansion, into the Old Northwest for example, had been as a result of (nominal) military conquest and the occupants were Native Americans who, by their armed resistance, justified (in American eyes) their subsequent displacement. In 1803 the Louisiana Territory was an unstable place, riven by political and racial unrest, uncertain borders and international intrigue. By 1820, according to Kastor, Louisiana was a much more stable place, integrated politically with the United States. This was the result of negotiation and resistance on the part of its myriad residents over the meaning of fundamental concepts such as citizenship, rights and obligations.

The Nation's Crucible is not concerned with Thomas Jefferson *per se*. Rather, Kastor considers how Jefferson's policies for the expansion of the United States – geographic and demographic – worked on the ground. To simplify a very complex story, citizenship for white Louisianans – Europeans, Creoles and Anglo-American migrants – came at the expense of the territory's non-white residents, especially the free African population that had enjoyed a degree of autonomy under French and Spanish rule unique in North America. Where Peter Onuf argues that citizenship in 'Jefferson's empire' could not be extended to Native Americans and African Americans in Jefferson's thinking, Peter Kastor shows how such exclusion played out in Louisiana. As such, *The Nation's Crucible* contributes to the more critical view of Jefferson with regard to questions of race discussed in chapter 7.

Perhaps the most important question raised by Jefferson's interest in the West, particularly the acquisition of Louisiana, concerns the impact of Jefferson's expansionism on Native Americans. This issue, more than any other, explains why, despite the apparent success of his statecraft, the acquisition of Louisiana has contributed to the decline of Jefferson's reputation. The Louisiana Purchase hastened the displacement of Native Americans for which Jefferson has, justly, been criticized. It is yet another irony that the apparent success of Jefferson's diplomacy has contributed to the decline of his reputation – although the ironies that abound in the history of Jefferson's reputation pale in comparison with the tragedy suffered by Native Americans in Jeffersonian America.

In the *Notes on the State of Virginia* Jefferson wrote of Indians with sympathy and admiration (in contrast to his comments on the supposed inferiority of Africans). Throughout his adult life he demonstrated an interest in Native American culture, collecting Indian artifacts – which he displayed at Monticello – and compiling vocabularies of Native American languages. One of his objectives in dispatching the Lewis and Clark expedition to explore the trans-Mississippi west in 1803 was for the explorers to collect ethnographic information on the native peoples of the West.[32] Jefferson's interest in Native American culture won him positive treatment at the hands of biographers and historians. In 1948 Dumas Malone wrote of Jefferson's encounter with a Cherokee delegation during his college days at William and Mary:

> Years afterward, as governor and President he was to receive visits from Indians, to address them as a Father, and to smoke with them the pipe of peace. He was to observe this race as a philosopher and to inquire its languages; as a responsible statesman he was to grapple with the problem of depredations and massacres on the frontier. But he was not soon, if ever, to escape from these early emotions. At this time, unquestionably, he was moved not by fear but by curiosity and compassion.[33]

In subsequent years historians would take a much more critical look at Jefferson's attitudes and actions toward Native Americans.

The literature on Jefferson's relationship with Native Americans parallels that on his position with regard to slavery. Generally sympathetic views in the immediate post-war era were supplanted by more unfavorable interpretations after the Civil Rights movement placed racial justice at the center of American public discourse. In a 1961 article examining government Indian policy during the early republic, Reginald Horsman offered a critique of Jefferson. Horsman wrote that Jefferson 'was convinced that the United States should take every opportunity to persuade the Indians to abandon their old modes of life'. Jefferson subscribed to the view that Native Americans' social and cultural development was determined by their environment. If properly educated and prepared, he believed, Indians could be assimilated into Anglo-American society. While assimilation might save Native Americans, Horsman suggested that Jefferson's 'motives were not entirely altruistic'.

Assimilation would facilitate the American acquisition of Indian lands. Horsman concluded, 'With the ambivalence that is so characteristic of Jefferson, he was able to combine an apparent genuine interest in the welfare of the Indian with a voracious appetite for Indian land. In his public utterances Jefferson viewed the harsh realities of American–Indian relations through a roseate mist.' Horsman's article represented the beginning of the reconsideration of Jefferson's attitudes and actions toward Native Americans.[34]

The revision of Jefferson's relationship with Native Americans continued with the appearance in 1973 of Bernard W. Sheehan's *Seeds of Extinction: Jeffersonian Philanthropy and the American Indian*. Sheehan presented a close examination of Jefferson's racial attitudes, particularly his belief in environmentalism, before considering their policy implications. Sheehan argued that by promoting assimilation, 'Jeffersonian philanthropists' ultimately facilitated the displacement of Native Americans from the eastern United States. When assimilationist policies – educating Indians to adopt Anglo-American cultural practices, farming techniques and Christianity – did not bear fruit quickly enough, pressure on government lands from settlers in the South and West proved difficult to resist. After obtaining Louisiana, Jefferson saw the removal of the eastern tribes to the West as a solution to the 'Indian problem.' Removal and resettlement would allow Indians sufficient time to assimilate Anglo-American values and practices so that they could, eventually, integrate into American society. According to Sheehan, removal was the only alternative to extinction, 'although the policy did not conceive of it as a fundamental change in the philanthropic plan. The goal was still incorporation, but now the civilizing program would be carried on for a longer period of time in a different location.' While Sheehan contended that the Jeffersonians did not intend to harm Indians, the consequences of their policies were disastrous for Native Americans.[35]

Although *Seeds of Extinction* presents the fullest picture of Jeffersonian attitudes toward Native Americans it is, somewhat surprisingly, uncritical of Jefferson. In the first place, Sheehan used such a capacious definition of 'Jeffersonian philanthropists', which included 'every administration from Washington to John Quincy Adams and a variety of private philanthropic organizations', that Jefferson himself gets somewhat lost in his analysis. Second, while sensitive to the deleterious impact of United States Indian policy during the early nineteenth century, Sheehan was eager to take his Jeffersonian philanthropists at their word and contended that they sought to help Indians. 'They confused the means required', he writes, 'with a mere manifestation of goodwill.' Reginald Horsman had been more willing to ascribe mixed motives to Jefferson. Despite softening his criticism somewhat, Sheehan made a direct connection between Jefferson, the purchase of Louisiana and the displacement of Native Americans in the East. As Jon Kukla ruefully writes, 'America's barely visible first steps along the Trail of Tears were taken in the White House as Thomas Jefferson pondered the implications of the Louisiana Purchase.'[36]

Despite its limitations, and because of its strengths, particularly as an intellectual history of Jeffersonian attitudes toward Native Americans, *Seeds of Extinction* remained the most important work on its subject for the better part of a generation.[37] In 1999 Anthony F. C. Wallace published *Jefferson and the Indians: The Tragic Fate of the First Americans*. Wallace, an anthropologist who specializes in the study of Native Americans, presented a comprehensive survey of 'Jefferson's attitudes, beliefs, and behavior toward the Indians'. Unlike Bernard Sheehan, Wallace found Jefferson's actions to be 'hypocritical, arbitrary, duplicitous, even harsh'. He continues:

> Certainly some of the unintended consequences of his policies of civilization, removal, and protection of frontier populations against Indian retaliation for encroachments and atrocities were catastrophic for the Indians. Thomas Jefferson played a major role in one of the great tragedies of recent world history, a tragedy which he so eloquently mourned: the dispossession and decimation of the First Americans.[38]

Wallace's persuasive analysis, richly detailed and multi layered, does not allow for the 'curiosity and compassion' of Dumas Malone's Jefferson nor for the well-intended if misguided Jefferson of Bernard Sheehan.

Anthony F. C. Wallace's *Jefferson and the Indians* demonstrates why, even if one is willing to give Jefferson the benefit of the doubt regarding the effectiveness of his diplomacy, the Louisiana Purchase has not given a boost to Jefferson's flagging reputation. Jon Kukla's gracefully written study, *A Wilderness So Immense*, is the most thorough treatment of the Louisiana Purchase since Alexander DeConde's *This Affair of Louisiana*. Where DeConde's monograph, written in the aftermath of Vietnam and Watergate, reflects the cynicism and distrust of government that were persvasive in the 1970s, Kukla's study reflects the concerns of multicultural America at the dawn of the twenty-first century. Kukla concludes his study:

> If a candid reconsideration of the Louisiana Purchase helps us see diversity rather than dichotomy in the history we share with one another and with the world, perhaps we Americans can begin to look at the Louisiana Purchase as a tributary in a long and slow and often tragic story of eventual inclusion. And perhaps the most fascinating part of the story of the Louisiana Purchase – the destiny of America – remains farther downstream.[39]

Kukla sees the origins of multicultural America in the ethnic diversity of early national Louisiana. As Kukla concedes, one must take a very long view to see America's diverse destiny downstream. Given such a perspective, and the price paid – especially by African Americans and Native Americans in its aftermath – it is problematic to credit Jefferson with the more beneficial long-term consequences of the purchase.

V

If the Louisiana Purchase represented Jefferson's greatest success in foreign policy, the Embargo of 1807–9 was his most disappointing failure. When Britain and France resumed their war in 1803, they sought to impose restrictions on US trade through blockades and ship seizures. Each wanted the United States, as a neutral carrier, to trade with their own country and colonies while denying American trade to their enemy. British-American relations were especially strained during these years. As the pre-eminent naval power, Britain was better able to interfere with American trade than France. Further, the British navy, desperate for manpower during the war, stopped American ships to search for deserters. During these searches British press gangs forced thousands of sailors from American vessels – both British and American – to join the Royal Navy. On 22 June 1807 HMS *Leopard* fired on the US frigate *Chesapeake* off the Virginia coast, killing three and wounding eighteen. The captain of the *Leopard* demanded the surrender of four alleged deserters among *Chesapeake*'s crew.

In the wake of the *Chesapeake–Leopard* affair, there was a clamor for war against Britain in the United States. Jefferson resisted this call, believing that the British could be brought to heel through economic coercion. In December 1807, at Jefferson's behest, Congress adopted the Embargo Act, which prohibited Americans from trading abroad until the rights of the United States as a neutral carrier were respected. Eventually the Embargo was extended to inland waters in an effort to prohibit trade between Americans and British Canada and Spanish Florida. In order to enforce the Embargo the government adopted further legislation that gave unprecedented police powers to federal customs agents and the military to interfere with trade. The Embargo failed to achieve its aim of coercing France and Britain into lifting their restrictions on American trade, and it was repealed in March 1809 after Jefferson left the White House.

Historians agree that the Embargo was a failure. Jefferson's most sympathetic student, Dumas Malone, described the policy as the lesser of two evils, preferable to war but ineffective. More critical writers such as Bradford Perkins, Robert Tucker and David Hendrickson have been less sympathetic. Perkins felt that the Embargo was one in a series of blunders committed by Jefferson that contributed to the deterioration of British–American relations. Tucker and Hendrickson hold the view that the Embargo was an error arising from Jefferson's misreading of the international scene. He should, they argued, have reached an accommodation with Britain over trade in order to forestall the Napoleonic threat.[40]

Those who have studied the Embargo most closely are no more favorable in their judgments. In a 1979 study, Burton Spivak argued that Jefferson conceived of the Embargo in different ways over the life of the policy. He suggested that Jefferson initially viewed the Embargo as a measure to prepare for war; he sought to insure that American vessels had returned home prior to the commencement of hostilities. Over time, as the Embargo went on, Spivak averred, Jefferson came to see it as a means of securing redress of American grievances while at the same time weaning the United States off its economic and cultural dependence on Britain. Nearly fifteen years later, Doron Ben-Atar, in a still more critical study, argued that Jefferson's commercial and foreign policies were misguided, ineffective and harmful to American interests. Ben-Atar contended that Jefferson fundamentally misunderstood the value of commerce as a foreign-policy tool. Like Tucker and Hendrickson, Ben-Atar believed that the economic and international interests of the United States would have been better served through reaching an accommodation with Britain rather than an inadequate attempt at economic coercion.[41]

VI

By the end of the 1990s Jefferson's reputation as an international states-man was uncertain. While many scholars welcomed the outcome of the negotiations that led to the Louisiana Purchase, there was little agreement as to whether Jefferson deserved credit for that achievement or had simply been lucky. The luster of the purchase faded somewhat when considered alongside its consequences for Native Americans. The failure of the Embargo during his second term reinforced the view that Jefferson had been lucky rather than adroit during the earlier negotiations. In the aftermath of the 11 September 2001 attacks Jefferson has been portrayed, rather bizarrely, as an aggressive war president for his actions during Tripolitan conflict of 1801–5. This is a subject to which previous specialists on Jefferson's foreign policy had devoted relatively little attention. It is ironic indeed that the 'half-way pacifist' who has been excoriated by historians for using economic coercion to avoid war with Britain is now being praised for his leadership during America's first armed conflict with the Islamic world. Such are the vagaries of historical reputation, as Jefferson appreciated.[42]

On 14 February 1815 Jefferson wrote a lengthy letter to the Marquis de Lafayette in which he reflected on the War of 1812. As the war wound down (Jefferson was unaware of the peace of Ghent), Jefferson considered the state of international relations. He reflected that the French Revolution had gone too far, exceeding the capacity of the French people to govern themselves and enjoy the benefits of liberty, which in turn led to the 'bloody tyranny of Robespierre, and the equally unprincipled and maniac tyranny of Bonaparte'. The rise of Napoleon, coupled with the British desire to stop the spread of republicanism, had led to war in Europe and, eventually, America. Of the war, Jefferson said that, after initial setbacks, the Americans had acquitted themselves well on land and at sea. With France having been defeated, Jefferson feared that Britain would concentrate its efforts on destroying republicanism in the United States. He wrote of the British:

> Their fears of republican France being now done away, they are directed to republican America, and they are playing the same game for disorganization, which they played in your country. The Marats, and Dantons and Robespierres of Massachusetts are in the same pay, under the same orders, and making the same efforts to anarchise us, that their prototypes in France did there.

Jefferson saw the forces of counter-revolution at work at home and abroad. He was confident that the United States had come out of the war much stronger than it had entered it. 'The cement of this Union', he wrote, 'is in the heart-blood of every American.'[43]

Two years later Jefferson wrote a further letter to Lafayette in which he amplified some of his earlier thoughts on the war. Although the conflict had left Americans in debt, Jefferson was sanguine about its long-term effects. He believed the war had finally destroyed the forces of anti-republican counter-revolution in the United States as New England's Federalists had been fatally undermined by their association with treason and disunion during the conflict. Americans were united as never before under the republican banner, according to Jefferson. 'The evanition of party dissensions has harmonized intercourse, and sweetened society beyond imagination,' he wrote. 'The war then has done us all this good, and the further one of assuring the world, that although attached to peace from a sense of its blessings, we will meet war when it is made necessary.' Jefferson's letter is testimony to his conception of the world. The most important contest on earth was that between the forces of republicanism and counter-revolution – liberty and tyranny. The opponents of liberty could be found at home or abroad. These – whether they be British soldiers or New England Federalists – must be confronted and defeated, by force if necessary. These assumptions underlay Jefferson's statecraft.[44]

Experience had taught Jefferson that the road to a global republican triumph was not always smooth or straight. In his own country he lamented the displacement of Native Americans as an unfortunate prerequisite for the necessary expansion of the republic. He continued his letter to Lafayette by bemoaning the situation in Spanish America where, in the aftermath of the Napoleonic wars, a series of colonial wars of independence had broken out. Having seen the French Revolution lead, not (in the first instance at least) to the expansion of liberty, but to the tyranny of Napoleon, Jefferson feared that Spain's American colonists might follow the same path, owing to centuries of poor government and interference from the Catholic church. 'Ignorance and bigotry,' he wrote, 'like other insanities, are incapable of self-government. They will fall under military despotism, and become the murderous tools of their respective Bonapartes; and whether this will be for their greater happiness, the rule of one only has taught you to judge.' Jefferson advocated that the colonies should reach an accord with Spain, guaranteed by France, Russia, Holland and the United States (*not* counter-revolutionary Britain), under the terms of which Spain would retain nominal control over the colonies until improvements in education and religious liberty prepared their people for complete independence. His years in power had taught Jefferson that war might be necessary to defend republicanism but sometimes cooperation with great powers, including tsarist Russia, might be necessary to advance the cause of liberty. While the means he employed to achieve his end may have varied Jefferson was consistent in the objective he sought in the international arena: the spread of republican liberty.[45]

NOTES

1. TJ to James Madison, 27 April 1809 in James Morton Smith, ed., *The Republic of Letters: The Correspondence between Thomas Jefferson and James Madison, 1776–1826*, 3 vols. (New York: Norton, 1995), 3:1586.

2. Reginald C. Stuart, *The Half-Way Pacifist: Thomas Jefferson's View of War* (Toronto: University of Toronto Press, 1978). Stuart's analysis is more subtle than its title suggests. See below.

3. Plan for Government of the Western Territory [3 Feb.-23 April 1784], *PTJ*, 6: 581–617. Also see Peter S. Onuf, *Statehood and Union: A History of the Northwest Ordinance* (Bloomington, IN: Indiana University Press, 1987), esp. 46–56; and Peter S. Onuf, 'The Expanding Union', in David Thomas Konig, ed., *Devising Liberty: Preserving and*

Creating Freedom in the New American Republic (Stanford: Stanford University Press, 1995), 50–80.

4. Julian P. Boyd, 'Thomas Jefferson's "Empire of Liberty' ", *Virginia Quarterly Review*, 24 (1948), 538–54.

5. TJ to J. P. G. Muhlenberg, 31 Jan. 1781, *PTJ*, 4:487; Dumas Malone, *Jefferson and his Time*, 4:241.

6. Alexander DeConde, *This Affair of Louisiana* (New York: Scribners, 1976), ix, x, 243.

7. DeConde, *This Affair of Louisiana*, 245.

8. Drew R. McCoy, *The Elusive Republic: Political Economy in Jeffersonian America* (Chapel Hill: University of North Carolina Press, 1980). Also see Francis D. Cogliano, *Revolutionary America: A Political History, 1763–1815* (London: Routledge, 2000), 142–3, 162–3.

9. Onuf has written widely on constitutional questions and western expansion during the founding era. His major works on the subject are: *Statehood and Union*; 'The Expanding Union'; 'Thomas Jefferson, Missouri and the "Empire for Liberty' ", in James P. Ronda, ed., *Thomas Jefferson and the Changing West* (Albuquerque: University of New Mexico Press, 1997), 111–53; and *Jefferson's Empire: The Language of American Nationhood* (Charlottesville: University Press of Virginia, 2000).

10. Recent American military intervention in central Asia and the Middle East has prompted interest in and debate over the nature of American imperialism. The protagonists in this debate assume either that the United States, as a republic founded in a colonial struggle for independence, is an anti-imperial nation and that it has departed from its republican traditions in seeking neo-imperial global domination; or, echoing Alexander DeConde, that it has always acted as an aggressive and acquisitive imperial state, while obscuring its actions in anti-imperial, republican rhetoric. Much of this literature either takes 'empire' as a given, or draws on classical history – particularly the transition of ancient Rome from a republic to an empire – or nineteenth-century European examples to explain current developments. The Roman example may be germane when considering the current global role of the United States as it uses military and commercial power to advance its interests, but it is not especially helpful when considering American foreign policy in the age of Jefferson. For example, see Andrew J. Bacevich, *American Empire: The Realities and Consequences of U.S. Diplomacy* (Cambridge, MA: Harvard University Press, 2002); Chalmers Johnson, *The Sorrows of Empire: Militarism, Secrecy, and the End of the Republic* (New York: Metropolitan Books, 2004); Michael Scheuer, *Imperial Hubris* (Washington, DC: Potomac Books, 2004); Niall Ferguson, *Colossus: The Price of America's Empire* (New York: Penguin, 2004); Robert W. Merry, *Sands of Empire: Missionary Zeal,*

American Foreign Policy and the Hazards of Global Ambition (New York: Simon and Schuster, 2005).

11. Onuf, *Jefferson's Empire*, 54.

12. Onuf, *Jefferson's Empire*, 41, 123. Onuf argues that Jefferson's conception of the United States as a federal republic of autonomous republics was crucial to his understanding of the Constitution. This theme is developed by David C. Hendrickson, who sees the Constitution as a diplomatic treaty binding together thirteen rival states. David C. Hendrickson, *Peace Pact: The Lost World of the American Founding* (Lawrence: University Press of Kansas, 2003).

13. Onuf, *Jefferson's Empire*, 85.

14. Onuf, *Jefferson's Empire*, chs. 1, 5.

15. Lawrence S. Kaplan, 'Jefferson, the Napoleonic Wars and the Balance of Power', WMQ, 14 (1957), 196–217. Also see Lawrence S. Kaplan, 'Foreign Affairs', in Merrill D. Peterson, ed., *Thomas Jefferson: A Reference Biography* (New York: Scribners, 1986), 311–30.

16. Bradford Perkins, *The First Rapprochement: England and the United States, 1795–1805* (Berkeley: University of California Press, 1955); Bradford Perkins, 'George Canning, Great Britain, and the United States, 1807–1809', *American Historical Review*, 63 (1957), 1–22; Bradford Perkins, *Prologue to War: England and the United States, 1805–1812* (Berkeley: University of California Press, 1961); Bradford Perkins, *The Creation of a Republican Empire, 1776–1865*, vol. 1 of the *Cambridge History of American Foreign Relations* (Cambridge: Cambridge University Press, 1993), quotations 112, 111. For a brief memoir of his wartime experience see Bradford Perkins, 'Impressions of Wartime', *Journal of American History*, 77 (1990), 563–8. Perkins denied that his wartime experiences had any impact on his scholarship, 567–8.

17. Stuart, *The Half-Way Pacifist*.

18. Robert W. Tucker and David C. Hendrickson, *Empire of Liberty: The Statecraft of Thomas Jefferson* (New York: Oxford University Press, 1990), quotation ix. For a thoughtful essay on *Empire of Liberty* see Eric L. McKitrick, 'Did Jefferson Blunder?', *New York Review of Books*, 37:19, 6 Dec. 1990, available at www.nybooks.com.

19. Mary P. Adams, 'Jefferson's Reaction to the Treaty of San Ildefonso', *Journal of Southern History*, 21 (1955), 173–88; Tim Matthewson, 'Jefferson and Haiti', *Journal of Southern History*, 61 (1995), 209–48; Walter LaFeber, 'Jefferson and American Foreign Policy', in Peter S. Onuf, ed., *Jeffersonian Legacies* (Charlottesville: University Press of Virginia, 1993), 370–91, quotation 371.

20. LaFeber, 'Jefferson and American Foreign Policy', 377–8.

21. Malone, *Jefferson and His Time*, vol. 4, chs. 14–19; vol. 5, chs. 3–5, 22–8. Also see Merrill D. Peterson, *Thomas Jefferson and the New Nation* (New York: Oxford University Press, 1970), chs. 9–10; and

Noble Cunningham, *In Pursuit of Reason: The Life of Thomas Jefferson* (Baton Rouge: Louisiana State University Press, 1987), chs. 18–19.

22. Henry Adams, *History of the United States of America during the Administrations of Thomas Jefferson*, 9 vols. (New York: Charles Scribners, 1889–91; repr. New York: Library of America, 1986), vol. 1 chs. 13–17; Perkins, *Creation of a Republican Empire*, 117.

23. DeConde, *This Affair of Louisiana*, 116.

24. Tucker and Hendrickson, *Empire of Liberty*, 145–6.

25. Malone, *Jefferson and His Time*, 4:286. Also see Peterson, *Thomas Jefferson and the New Nation*, 745–62 for another sympathetic interpretation.

26. Malone, *Jefferson and His Time*, 4:286; LaFeber, 'Jefferson and American Foreign Policy', 380. Also see Peterson, *Thomas Jefferson and the New Nation*, 745–62.

27. Jon Kukla, *A Wilderness So Immense: The Louisiana Purchase and the Destiny of America* (New York: Alfred A. Knopf, 2003); Thomas Fleming, *The Louisiana Purchase* (Hoboken, NJ: John Wiley and Sons, 2003); James E. Lewis, Jr., *The Louisiana Purchase: Jefferson's Noble Bargain?* (Charlottesville: Thomas Jefferson Foundation, 2003); and Charles A. Cerami, *Jefferson's Great Gamble: The Remarkable Story of Jefferson, Napoleon and the Men behind the Louisiana Purchase* (Naperville, IL: Sourcebooks, 2003).

28. Fleming, *The Louisiana Purchase*, 182.

29. Bernard W. Sheehan, 'Jefferson's "Empire for Liberty"', *Indiana Magazine of History*, 100 (2004), www.historycooperative.org/journals/imh/100.4/sheehan.htm. Also see R. B. Bernstein, *Thomas Jefferson* (New York: Oxford University Press, 2003), 141–3.

30. George Dargo, *Jefferson's Louisiana: Politics and the Clash of Legal Traditions* (Cambridge, MA: Harvard University Press, 1975). Also see Reginald Horsman, 'Law and Empire in Louisiana', *Reviews in American History*, 3 (1975), 448–51. Dargo anticipated Alexander DeConde, arguing that the United States acted as an imperial power in acquiring Louisiana (25).

31. Peter J. Kastor, *The Nation's Crucible: The Louisiana Purchase and the Creation of America* (New Haven: Yale University Press, 2004).

32. Jefferson wrote about Native Americans in 'Query VI' of the *Notes on the State of Virginia*. He also inserted an appendix in the *Notes* which included Chief Logan's oration on the massacre of his family at the beginning of Dunmore's War in 1774. He gave this as evidence of the power and quality of Native American oratory. Logan's speech, and its inclusion in the *Notes*, was a source of later controversy. This and Jefferson's ethnographic activities are discussed in Anthony F. C. Wallace, *Jefferson and the Indians: The Tragic Fate of the First Americans* (Cambridge, MA: Harvard University Press, 1999). Also see Roger

Kennedy, 'Jefferson and the Indians', *Winterthur Portfolio*, 27 (1992), 105–21.

33. Malone, *Jefferson and His Time*, 1:61.

34. Reginald Horsman, 'American Indian Policy in the Old Northwest, 1783–1812', *WMQ*, 18 (1961), 35–53, quotations 48, 47. Horsman expanded his analysis in a monograph, *Expansion and American Indian Policy, 1783–1812* (East Lansing: Michigan State University Press, 1967).

35. Bernard Sheehan, *Seeds of Extinction: Jeffersonian Philanthropy and the American Indian* (Chapel Hill: University of North Carolina Press, 1973), 243. Also see Bernard W. Sheehan, 'Paradise and the Noble Savage in Jeffersonian Thought', *WMQ*, 26 (1969), 327–59; and James Axtell, 'Indians, Moralists and Historians', *Reviews in American History*, 2 (1974), 33–8.

36. Sheehan, *Seeds of Extinction*, 123; Kukla, *A Wilderness So Immense*, 303.

37. In the years since *Seeds of Extinction* appeared, historians have fleshed out the details of the Indian policies whose origins Sheehan had delineated. In 1981 Donald Jackson explored Jefferson's dealings with the Sac and Fox Indians and showed that Jefferson sought to use the Louisiana Purchase lands to relocate eastern tribes. Anthony F. C. Wallace argued in 1997 that Jefferson, while possibly sincere in his efforts to 'civilize' Native Americans, made obtaining their lands his top priority. Donald Jackson, *Thomas Jefferson and the Stony Mountains: Exploring the West from Monticello* (Urbana: University of Illinois Press, 1981); Anthony F. C. Wallace, ' "The Obtaining Lands": Thomas Jefferson and Native Americans', in Ronda, ed., *Thomas Jefferson and the Changing West*, 25–42.

38. Anthony F. C. Wallace, *Jefferson and the Indians*, viii.

39. Kukla, *A Wilderness So Immense*, 340.

40. Malone, *Jefferson and His Time*, 5, ch. 26; Perkins, *Prologue to War*, ch. 5; Tucker and Hendrickson, *Empire of Liberty*, chs. 21–3.

41. Burton Spivak, *Jefferson's English Crisis: Commerce, Embargo and the Republican Revolution* (Charlottesville: University Press of Virginia, 1979); Doron S. Ben-Atar, *The Origins of Jeffersonian Commercial Policy and Diplomacy* (New York: St. Martin's, 1993). Most students of the subject agree that the Embargo was ineffective because it did not affect the British economy to the degree that Jefferson had hoped. Jeffrey Frankel provided a dissenting view, arguing that the Embargo harmed the British economy more than that of the United States. For Frankel the Embargo failed for political, not economic, reasons. This was the view taken by Jefferson, who insisted that the Embargo would have worked had it not been repealed. Jeffrey A. Frankel, 'The 1807–1809 Embargo against Great Britain', *Journal of Economic History*, 42 (1982), 291–308.

42. See A. B. C. Whipple, *To the Shores of Tripoli: The Birth of the U.S. Navy and Marines* (Annapolis: Naval Institute, 2001); Joseph Wheelan, *Jefferson's War: America's First War on Terror, 1801–1805* (New York: Carroll and Graf, 2003); Frank Lambert, *The Barbary Wars: American Independence in the Atlantic World* (New York: Hill and Wang, 2005); and Richard Zacks, *The Pirate Coast: Thomas Jefferson, the First Marines, and the Secret Mission of 1805* (New York: Hyperion, 2005). Whipple's account appeared just before September 11th. The other titles were written in the aftermath of the attacks. They each show Jefferson as willing to use force as an instrument to advance American interests.

43. TJ to Lafayette, 14 Feb. 1815, *TJW*, 1360–6, quotations 1361, 1364.

44. TJ to Lafayette, 14 May 1817, *TJW*, 1407–9, quotation 1408.

45. TJ to Lafayette, 14 May 1817, *TJW*, 1408–9. For US relations with Latin America and Spain during the period see James E. Lewis, Jr., *The American Union and the Problem of Neighborhood, 1783–1829: The United States and the Collapse of Spanish Empire* (Chapel Hill: University of North Carolina Press, 1998).

CONCLUSION:
JEFFERSON SURVIVES

On 17 February 1826, Thomas Jefferson, who was then eighty-two years old and in declining health, wrote a letter to his old friend and political ally James Madison. He wrote at length about securing funding, qualified faculty and books for the new University of Virginia. He expressed particular concern that he and Madison should be 'rigorously attentive' to political principles when appointing the university's law professor. Jefferson felt that legal education in the United States was dominated by conservative counter-revolutionaries imbued with 'toryism', as he termed it. The new lawyers, complained Jefferson, 'no longer know what whigism or republicanism means'. By hiring the right law professor, Jefferson believed, the University of Virginia might initiate a revival of republican principles. 'It is in our seminary', he wrote, 'that the vestal flame is to be kept alive; it is thence it is to spread anew over our own and the sister States. If we are true and vigilant in our trust, within a dozen or twenty years a majority of our legislature will be from one school, and many disciples will have carried its doctrines home with them to their several States, and will have leavened thus the whole mass.' Jefferson then complained about the crippling debts that threatened his legacy and his scheme for a lottery of his lands to solve the problem and save his home, Monticello. He concluded his letter to his old friend with a reflection on their life's work:

> It has also been a great solace to me, to believe that you are engaged in vindicating to posterity the course we have pursued for preserving to them, in all their purity, the blessings of self-government, which we have assisted too in acquiring for them. If ever the earth has beheld a system of administration conducted with a single and steadfast eye to the general interest and happiness of those committed to it, one which, protected by truth, can never know reproach, it is that to which our lives have been devoted.

Jefferson closed his letter with the plea that his friend 'Take care of me when dead.'[1]

Jefferson's letter to Madison reflected his concerns in the last months of his life. It reflects on the past and the role played by him and Madison in establishing republican government in the United States. The letter looks forward, with apprehension, to the future political development of the United States. Jefferson conceived of the University of Virginia as a means to safeguard the future health of the American republic by preserving and transmitting to posterity the ideals for which he and Madison had fought throughout their lives. Nonetheless he worried that future generations might misinterpret or misunderstand his own achievements, hence his plea to his younger friend to safeguard his reputation. In his concern over his posthumous reputation Jefferson was not simply motivated by vanity. He believed that his reputation and the success of the nation's experiment with republican government were intimately linked. Madison, who out-lived Jefferson by a decade, heeded his friend's admonition for the remainder of his life.[2]

Thomas Jefferson died at Monticello shortly before one o'clock in the afternoon on 4 July 1826, the fiftieth anniversary of the adoption of the Declaration of Independence. At almost the same time in Quincy, Massachusetts, Jefferson's friend and sometime political rival John Adams is reported by his relatives to have said his last words, 'Thomas Jefferson survives . . .' Five hours later Adams died. The near-simulta-neous deaths of the two revolutionary giants on the fiftieth anniversary of their greatest achievement has been seen as providential intervention in the life of the American republic – God's blessing on the United States on its jubilee. We may understand this story to be poignant testimony to the close links between the two revolutionaries as they lay dying hundreds of miles apart. We can also read Adams's last words ironically, given that Jefferson had just died when Adams supposedly uttered, 'Thomas Jef-ferson survives'. Whether Adams actually said those words as he lay dying, the members of his family understood the power of Jefferson's image. The Adams family understood that Jefferson survived in the hearts and minds of his countrymen after his life ended on a Virginia mountain in a way that their forebear did not.[3]

John Adams's words still ring true. Almost two centuries after his death Thomas Jefferson still survives. He survives in the various monuments erected to honor his achievements. He survives in the hundreds of counties, towns, schools and streets named in his memory. He survives in his home, Monticello, maintained as a museum dedicated to preserving his memory, visited annually by hundreds of thousands of people. He survives in his 'academical village', the University of Virginia. Jefferson survives in the many thousands of books and articles on him, the number of which increases inexorably. Most importantly, Thomas Jefferson survives in his words. His most famous words, the preamble to the Declaration of Independence, have become the American creed and are so well known and so readily identified both with Jefferson and the United

States, that in these words Jefferson and America seem to become one. Jefferson survives in his other words as well: his assertions of religious freedom and African inferiority, his wonderful exchanges with Adams and Madison, his thousands of letters, state papers and memoranda. Jefferson's words are available in manuscript and print and on the Internet. They are available in edited form in various one-volume collections. They are available in the massive Princeton edition of *The Papers of Thomas Jefferson*. When completed, sometime in the course of the next two decades, *The Papers of Thomas Jefferson* will constitute one of the most complete records of an individual life ever assembled. Thomas Jefferson's life, at least as he wanted it remembered, was very much a life of the mind. In so far as *The Papers of Thomas Jefferson* presents 'every known copy of every Jefferson document' for scholars and readers, Jefferson survives in its volumes.

While Jefferson may survive, he failed in his battle with posterity. To be sure, he is remembered – sometimes memorialized, sometimes excoriated – but he is not remembered as he intended that he should be. Jefferson saw the American Revolution and its aftermath as part of a global republican movement for liberty. He recognized that the triumph of republicanism – the end of history, the republican millennium – would not be achieved in his lifetime. He felt that the writing of the history of his life and times would play a crucial part in the struggle to advance human freedom. Jefferson understood that primary sources were the essence of history and so he preserved his papers for posterity. Historians, as interpreters of primary sources, had a vital role to play in spreading republicanism. In order to guide future historians Jefferson compiled a didactic rough draft of the history of post-revolutionary America, in the documents remembered as his autobiography and the Anas. Directed by Jefferson, drawing on his copious writings, future historians should write the history of the Revolution and its aftermath as Jefferson intended – as the story of the struggle between Jefferson and his supporters to defend liberty against the domestic and foreign forces of counter-revolution. By and large, historians have not done this.

As a conscientious record-keeper and a student of Enlightenment historiography, Jefferson preserved nearly all of his personal and public papers (with the notable exception of his correspondence with his wife). While the autobiography and Anas give a clear view of how Jefferson understood his place in history, his papers provide insights far beyond the narrow political concerns that Jefferson believed were suitable for historians to write about. Herein lies the paradox at the heart of Jefferson studies. While we know more about Jefferson than ever before owing in large part to his own documentary bequest now appearing in print, we move further and further from Jefferson's conception of his place in history. Jefferson knew how he wanted to be remembered, he expressed it cogently on his gravestone: as a proponent of natural rights, equality and freedom of conscience, who sought to guarantee these benefits to future generations through education. Unfortunately for Jefferson's legacy – and fortunately for historians – he bequeathed tens of thousands of pages and millions of words to posterity as well as his elegant tombstone. Modern historians have exploited the wealth of Jefferson's papers to explore many different aspects of his life and world. While much attention has been paid to Jefferson's place in the political history of revolutionary America, historians have not generally adhered to Jefferson's whiggish view that the history of the early republic can best be understood as the story of Jefferson's struggle to preserve and promote liberty in the face of the would-be tyranny of the Federalists and the British.

For a brief period, from roughly 1940 until 1960, Jefferson's historical image was, more or less, as he would have wished. The image of Jefferson as Apostle of Freedom eloquently expressed by Franklin Roosevelt at the dedication of the Jefferson Memorial in 1943 coincided with Jefferson's conception of himself and his place in history. These were years when western liberal democracies, particularly the United States, were confronted first by fascism during World War II and then by communism during the Cold War. When Roosevelt dedicated the Jefferson Memorial the nation was fighting for the very principles that Jefferson had stood for. When those ideals were threatened they seemed most relevant. Franklin Roosevelt and later historians like Dumas Malone and Merrill Peterson reflected Jefferson's historical consciousness so well because they believed, along with Jefferson, that the principles he espoused were timeless and universal. Jefferson was at once the embodiment of American principles and had articulated those principles in such a way as to convey their worldwide applicability.

This Jeffersonian moment passed by the early 1960s as Americans became concerned with the limitations of their society during the Civil Rights movement and disillusioned with their government abroad and at home in the wake of Vietnam and Watergate. Historians no longer followed Jefferson in asserting what America had to teach the world. On the contrary, they focused inwardly on the failings of their own society. They rewrote the history of the United States, focusing not only on its flawed leaders but on previously marginalized and neglected social groups. In so doing they have transformed and enriched our understanding of the American past. They have also called into question the achievements and significance of America's leaders, not least Thomas Jefferson. Jefferson continued to attract the attention of scholars, general readers and the public at large, but the scholarly focus, particularly as it concentrated on questions of race and slavery, became more critical. In recent decades Jefferson came, for many people, to epitomize not America's promise but its limitations.

In November 1992 Douglas L. Wilson published his defense of Jefferson, 'Thomas Jefferson and the Character Issue', in the *Atlantic Monthly*. In this he accused Jefferson's recent critics of presentism. Owing to their anachronistic and ahistorical reading of the past, Wilson argued, Jefferson's critics, especially where race is concerned, had misinterpreted the historical record and misunderstood and misrepresented Jefferson, thereby diminishing his achievements.[4] Four years after Wilson's article appeared in *Atlantic*, one of Jefferson's harshest critics, Conor Cruise O'Brien, an Irish historian, diplomat and politician, published a scathing portrait of Jefferson in the same magazine. Surveying Jefferson's views on race and politics, O'Brien condemned him as a racist who advocated violent terrorism in opposition to the federal government. O'Brien saw Jefferson as the inspiration for the militia movement of the mid-1990s including Timothy McVeigh, the Oklahoma City bomber, and concluded that the 'liberal-Jeffersonian tradition' was untenable in the modern United States. 'I believe,' he wrote,

> that in the next century, as blacks and Hispanics and Asians acquire increasing influence in American society, the Jeffersonian liberal tradition, which is already intellectually untenable, will become socially and politically untenable as well. I also believe that the American civil religion . . . will have to be reformed in a manner that will downgrade and eventually exclude Thomas Jefferson. Finally I believe that Jefferson will nonetheless continue to be a power in America in the area where the mystical side of Jefferson really belongs: among radical, violent, anti-federal libertarian fanatics.

O'Brien prophesied that there would be no room for Jefferson in the multiracial America of the twenty-first century and that while some of Jefferson's ideas – those expressed in the Declaration of Independence but not those relating to the French Revolution – would continue to resonate in modern America, Jefferson himself would be expelled from the American pantheon.[5]

The *Atlantic* articles of Wilson and O'Brien epitomize the two main schools of thought on Jefferson in the mid-1990s. Wilson and Jefferson's other defenders recognized their subject's limitations but sought to contextualize and explain them while retaining what they see as his more valuable contributions to American history and culture. By contrast, Jefferson's critics (and O'Brien is among the more vituperative and uncompromising of these) feel that his failures – especially his racism and his relationship with slavery – outweigh his accomplishments. Both sides want to pick and choose. Jefferson's defenders take what they admire and explain or ignore whatever is distasteful. His critics, by contrast, ignore the admirable and emphasize Jefferson's flaws. Both groups have a stake in Jefferson. The iconoclast is as obsessed with the icon as the believer who comes to worship before it. This is certainly true with respect to Jefferson. Conor Cruise O'Brien devoted an entire book to demonstrating why Jefferson (but not all of his ideas) should be expelled from a mythic American pantheon. Jefferson's defenders and attackers cling to the uniqueness of Jefferson, presenting him as either uniquely good or uniquely bad. In so doing they lose sight of Jefferson's conception of the past and his own role in history. In consequence they misinterpret or misunderstanod a vital aspect of Jefferson's legacy.

If Jefferson's defenders and attackers stress his uniqueness, they also, somewhat contradictorily, emphasize his representativeness. For them Jefferson may be singularly good or bad, but he also represents America. Many echo James Parton, one of Jefferson's first biographers, who wrote in 1872, 'If Jefferson was wrong, America is wrong. If America is right, Jefferson was right.' As a result Jefferson's virtues become America's virtues and his flaws are America's flaws. Jefferson's admirers and critics have taken Jefferson to represent America. The result is a personalized version of American exceptionalism – 'the notion', in Michael Kammen's words, 'that the United States has had a unique destiny and history, or more modestly, a history with highly distinctive features or an unusual trajectory' – that when applied to Jefferson further distorts his legacy. It is too much to expect Jefferson's legacy to bear the burden imposed by America's history.[6]

More significantly, the identification of Jefferson with the United States distorts Jefferson's understanding of the global historical nature of his life's work. Jefferson was a Virginian first and foremost and he took great pride in America and the achievements of the United States. Nonetheless, he believed that the spread of liberty was, and must be, an international movement. In 1821 he wrote in his autobiography:

> As yet we are but in the first chapter of it's history. The appeal to the rights of man, which had been made in the U.S. was taken up by France, first of the European nations. From her the spirit has spread over those of the South. The tyrants of the North have allied indeed against it, but it is irresistible. Their opposition will only multiply it's millions of human victims; their own satellites will catch it, and the condition of man thro' the civilized world will be finally greatly ameliorated. This is a wonderful instance of great events from small causes. So inscrutable is the arrangement of causes & consequences in this world that a two-penny duty on tea, unjustly imposed in a sequestered part of it, changes the conditions of all it's inhabitants.[7]

For Jefferson the rise of republicanism began with the American Revolution, continued with the French, and would gather strength in other parts of Europe as well as Latin America and beyond. The reason he placed such emphasis on, and hope in his, interpretation of the republic's history was because he believed it would contribute to the advance of global republicanism. On his tombstone Jefferson identified himself as the author of the 'Declaration of *American* Independence' (emphasis added). We can read this as a statement of national pride. It can also be read as a statement that Jefferson expected other such declarations to emanate from other nations as they joined the family of republics in a peaceful and free future. Since his death Jefferson has been America's mirror. For his critics he reflects the nation's limits and for his admirers he reflects its achievements. Over the past fifty years both groups have pointed the mirror inward. In so doing they have missed the international outlook at the heart of Jefferson's beliefs.

Few now subscribe to the whig interpretation of history embraced by Thomas Jefferson. Jefferson believed that if the correct version of history was written and promulgated, a history that emphasized the importance of protecting liberty in the face of tyranny, it would hasten the global triumph of republicanism – an event of world-historical significance. Although Jefferson felt that he had played an important role in this movement, his reputation was not greater than the republican movement to which he had devoted his life. Rather, he believed that his reputation was closely linked to his interpretation of America's revolutionary history. If he fared well at the hands of historians, then his interpretation of the revolution was likely to prevail. The modern historiography, focused more and more tightly on Jefferson and whether or not his life and achievements were good or bad – unrelated to the broader history of republicanism and its international context – loses sight of the purpose of history for Jefferson.

Thomas Jefferson made many contributions to the history of the revolutionary and early national America. One of his most original offerings was that citizens of a republic need to understand the past if they are to make history themselves. One can only be a functioning citizen of a republic if one has a proper appreciation of the past. That lesson remains as true today as it did during Jefferson's lifetime. Historians have lost sight of this aspect of Jefferson's thinking and the citizens of the republic that Jefferson helped found have largely ignored its history, at least as Jefferson wanted them to understand it. Rather than bring on the end of history by realizing a republican millennium, Jefferson's heirs have chosen to disregard the lessons of their history. The iconic Thomas Jefferson – admired and vilified by turns – survives. Unfortunately, the Jefferson who stressed the importance of the past as he made and then became part of history has not survived. As a result Jefferson's legacy has been distorted, obscured and misunderstood.

NOTES

1. TJ to James Madison, 17 Feb. 1826, Peterson, ed., *TJW*, 1512–15.
2. Madison assisted in the first publication of Jefferson's papers, and promoted a positive image of Jefferson to historians. For Madison's efforts on Jefferson's posthumous behalf see Adrienne Koch, *Jefferson and Madison: The Great Collaboration* (New York: Alfred A. Knopf, 1950), 283–90.
3. The claim that these were Adams's dying words has been called into question, and the story is likely apocryphal. John Quincy Adams reported that his father had said 'Thomas Jefferson survives' at around one o'clock on the 4th, but that 'the last word was indistinctly and imperfectly uttered. He spoke no more.' Charles Francis Adams, ed., *The Memoirs of John Quincy Adams*, 12 vols. (Philadelphia: Lippincott, 1874–77), 7:133. Adams's last words – and the contemporary significance of the simultaneous deaths of Adams and Jefferson – are treated in Andrew Burstein, *America's Jubilee: How a Generation Remembered Fifty Years of Independence* (New York: Knopf, 2001), ch. 11.
4. Douglas L. Wilson, 'Thomas Jefferson and the Character Issue', *Atlantic Monthly*, 270:5 (Nov. 1992), 57–74. This article is available at www.theatlantic.com. Wilson's article is discussed more fully in Chapter 7.
5. Conor Cruise O'Brien, 'Thomas Jefferson: Radical and Racist', *Atlantic Monthly*, 278:4 (Oct. 1996), 53–74. O'Brien developed these ideas in a book, *The Long Affair: Thomas Jefferson and the French Revolution, 1785–1800* (Chicago: University of Chicago Press, 1996). The article that appeared in *Atlantic Monthly* closely follows the epilogue to *The Long Affair*. Douglas L. Wilson wrote a response to O'Brien's criticism which appeared on *Atlantic*'s website in October 1996, 'Counterpoints: Jefferson Scholar Douglas L. Wilson responds to Conor Cruise O'Brien'. Also see Benjamin Schwartz, 'What Jefferson Helps to Explain', *Atlantic Monthly*, 279:3 (March 1997), 60–72. All of these articles are available at www.theatlantic.com.
6. James Parton as quoted in Peterson, *The Jefferson Image*, 234. Michael Kammen, 'The Problem of American Exceptionalism: A Reconsideration', *American Quarterly*, 45 (1993), 1–43, quotation 6. There is a huge literature on American exceptionalism. For recent examples and reviews of the literature see Ian Tyrrell, 'American Exceptionalism in an Age of International History', *American Historical Review*, 96 (1991), 1031–55; Byron E. Shafer, ed., *Is America Different?: A New Look at American Exceptionalism* (New York: Oxford University Press, 1991); Jack P. Greene, *The Intellectual Construction of America: Exceptionalism and Identity from 1492 to 1800* (Chapel Hill: University of North Carolina Press, 1993); David K. Adams and Cornelius A. van Minnen,

Reflections on American Exceptionalism (Keele: Keele University Press, 1994); George M. Frederickson, 'From Exceptionalism to Variability: Recent Developments in Cross-National Comparative History', *Journal of American History*, 82 (1995), 587–604; Seymour Martin Lipset, *American Exceptionalism: A Double-Edged Sword* (New York: Norton, 1996); H. V. Nelles et al., 'Review Essays: American Exceptionalism', *American Historical Review*, 102 (1997), 748–74.
7. Autobiography, *TJW*, 97.

INDEX